Contesting Religion

Contesting Religion

The Media Dynamics of Cultural Conflicts in Scandinavia

Edited by
Knut Lundby

DE GRUYTER

ISBN 978-3-11-050171-1
e-ISBN (PDF) 978-3-11-050206-0
e-ISBN (EPUB) 978-3-11-049891-2

This work is licensed under the Creative Commons Attribution-NonCommercial-No-Derivatives 4.0 License. For details go to https://creativecommons.org/licenses/by-nc-nd/4.0/.

Library of Congress Cataloging-in-Publication Data
Names: Lundby, Knut, author.
Title: Contesting religion : the media dynamics of cultural conflicts in Scandinavia / edited by Knut Lundby.
Description: Berlin ; Boston : Walter de Gruyter GmbH, [2018] | Includes bibliographical references and index.
Identifiers: LCCN 2018017843 (print) | LCCN 2018021832 (ebook) | ISBN 783110502060 (electronic Portable Document Format (pdf) | ISBN 9783110501711 (alk. paper) | ISBN 9783110498912 (e-book epub : alk. paper) | ISBN 9783110502060 (e-book pdf : alk. paper)
Subjects: LCSH: Mass media in religion--Scandinavia. | Religions--Relations. | Church controversies Scandinavia. | Religious disputations--Scandinavia.
Classification: LCC BL863 (ebook) | LCC BL863 .C66 2018 (print) | DDC 200.948--dc23
LC record available at https://lccn.loc.gov/2018017843

Bibliographic information published by the Deutsche Nationalbibliothek
The Deutsche Nationalbibliothek lists this publication in the Deutsche Nationalbibliografie; detailed bibliographic data are available on the Internet at http://dnb.dnb.de.

© 2018 Knut Lundby, published by Walter de Gruyter GmbH, Berlin/Boston
The book is published with open access at www.degruyter.com.
Cover Image. "Blasphemy," by Øyvind Westgård. Used with Permission.
Printing and binding: CPI books GmbH, Leck

www.degruyter.com

Preface

The research behind this book was undertaken within a programme on 'The Cultural Conditions Underlying Social Change' at the Research Council of Norway.[1] This 'SAMKUL' programme understands culture as being 'the sphere within which various groups and individuals think, communicate and act'. Culture, then, is to be analysed 'as a way of thinking and patterns of communication' in *'the interaction between people and their surroundings'*, as expressed in the programme description. This book digs into the interaction over contested public religion in settings where the cultural conflicts are partly shaped by media dynamics. The book is an outcome of the SAMKUL project 'Engaging with Conflicts in Mediatized Religious Environments. A Comparative Scandinavian Study', which has been abbreviated as CoMRel – Co for Conflict, M for Media and Rel for Religion.[2]

Most of the chapters in this book are written by CoMRel researchers, coming from the University of Copenhagen in Denmark, Uppsala University in Sweden and, in Norway, from the University of Agder[3], the MF Norwegian School of Theology, Religion and Society, as well as the University of Oslo, which coordinated the project. In the section on local civic settings, we include contributions from another Research Council of Norway-funded project, namely, 'Cultural Conflict 2.0: The Dynamics of Religion, Media and Locality in North European Cities' (CC2).

The book took shape as a collaborative enterprise during a productive week in a former monastery at Metochi on the island of Lesbos, Greece, now a study centre for the University of Agder. We formulated the outline together, and later reworked it in a collective collaboration, and this is reflected in the Introduction and realized in the chapters that follow.

Knut Lundby
Editor and project leader
Oslo, 9th March, 2018

---

[1] www.forskningsradet.no/samkul
[2] http://www.hf.uio.no/imk/english/research/projects/comrel/
[3] David Herbert is also working at Kingston University, London.

Table of Contents

List of Tables —— XI

List of Figures —— XIII

Acknowledgements —— 1

Knut Lundby
Introduction: Religion and Media in Cultural Conflicts —— 3

Part I: Contexts

Knut Lundby, Pål Repstad
Chapter 1 Scandinavia: Traits, Trends and Tensions —— 13

Mia Lövheim, Haakon H. Jernsletten, David Herbert, Knut Lundby, Stig Hjarvard
Chapter 2 Attitudes: Tendencies and Variations —— 33

Stig Hjarvard, Knut Lundby
Chapter 3 Understanding Media Dynamics —— 51

Mia Lövheim, Liv Ingeborg Lied
Chapter 4 Approaching Contested Religion —— 65

Part II: Controversies

Public Service Media

Knut Lundby, Stig Hjarvard, Mia Lövheim, Mona Abdel-Fadil
Chapter 5 Perspectives: Cross-Pressures on Public Service Media —— 83

Mona Abdel-Fadil
Chapter 6 Nationalizing Christianity and Hijacking Religion on Facebook —— 97

Stig Hjarvard, Mattias Pape Rosenfeldt
Chapter 7 Planning Public Debate: Beyond Entrenched Controversies About Islam —— 117

Mia Lövheim, Linnea Jensdotter
Chapter 8 Contradicting Ideals: Islam on Swedish Public Service Radio —— 135

Local Civic Settings

David Herbert
Chapter 9 Perspectives: Theorizing Mediatized Civic Settings and Cultural Conflict —— 155

Pål Repstad
Chapter 10 Moral Involvement or Religious Scepticism? Local Christian Publications on Asylum Seekers —— 171

Louise Lund Liebmann
Chapter 11 Media, Muslims and Minority Tactics: Compelling Dialogues in Norway —— 187

Janna Hansen, David Herbert
Chapter 12 Life in the Spotlight: Danish Muslims, Dual Identities, and Living with a Hostile Media —— 205

Upper Secondary Schools

Audun Toft, Maximilian Broberg
Chapter 13 Perspectives: Mediatized Religious Education —— 225

Liv Ingeborg Lied, Audun Toft
Chapter 14 'Let me Entertain You': Media Dynamics in Public Schools —— 243

Audun Toft
Chapter 15 Inescapable News Coverage: Media Influence on Lessons About Islam —— 259

Part III: Crosscurrents

Mona Abdel-Fadil, Louise Lund Liebmann
Chapter 16 Gender, Diversity and Mediatized Conflicts of Religion: Lessons from Scandinavian Case Studies —— 281

Knut Lundby
Chapter 17 Interaction Dynamics in the Mediatization of Religion Thesis —— 299

Lynn Schofield Clark, Marie Gillespie
Chapter 18 Globalization and the Mediatization of Religion: From Scandinavia to the World —— 315

Birgit Meyer
Afterword: Media Dynamics of Religious Diversity —— 333

Haakon H. Jernsletten
Appendix: Regression Analyses to Chapter 2 —— 339

Author Bios —— 343

Index —— 347

List of Tables

Table 2.1   Should people in the following groups be allowed to wear a cross or hijab to express their religious faith? Percentage of respondents answering yes. From CoMRel survey, April 2015.
Table 2.2   Percentage of the respondents who fully or partially agree with statements on what the media ought to do in relation to their coverage of religion. From CoMRel survey, April 2015.
Table 3.1   The influences of media dynamics in mediatized conflicts.
Table 3.2   In which contexts have you discussed news on religious extremism in the last 12 months? Percentages. From CoMRel survey, April 2015.
Table 4.1   Contexts for the encounter with, or information about, questions related to religion and belief. Percentages. From CoMRel survey, April 2015.
Table 5.1   Should proclamation programmes in DR/NRK/SVT refer to several religions or only to Christianity? Percentages. From CoMRel survey, April 2015.
Table 7.1   The distribution of Minority Actors' Voices (MAV) in debates about *Rebellion from the Ghetto* in the press and broadcast radio.
Table 7.2   The distribution of Minority Actors' Voices (MAV) in debates about *Rebellion from the Ghetto* on three Facebook sites.

In Appendix:
Table A.1   Variables included in the regression analyses.
Table A.2   Critique and tolerance of religion.
Table A.3   Participation in discussions of news on religious extremism.

List of Figures

Figure 1.1   "Scandinavia," by Hayden120, under a Creative Commons Attribution Share-Alike 3.0 license (CC BY-SA 3.0, https://creativecommons.org/licenses/by-sa/3.0), via Wikimedia Commons.

Figure 1.2   "Inglehart-Welzel's Cultural Map, based on WVS_6, 2015," by the World Values Survey. Presenting the data in R. Inglehart, C. Haerpfer, A. Moreno, C. Welzel, K. Kizilova, J. Diez-Medrano, M. Lagos, P. Norris, E. Ponarin and B. Puranen et al. (eds.). 2014. World Values Survey: Round Six - Country-Pooled Datafile Version: http://www.worldvaluessurvey.org/WVSDocumentationWV6.jsp. Madrid: JD Systems Institute. Used with permission.

Figure 2.1   Religious self-identification in Scandinavia. Percentages. From CoMRel survey, April 2015.

Figure 2.2   Political orientation in Scandinavia (GAL–TAN scale). Percentages. From CoMRel survey, April 2015.

Figure 2.3   Looking at the world, religion leads to conflict rather than to peace. Percentages. From CoMRel survey, April 2015.

Figure 2.4   Do you consider Islam a threat to Danish/Norwegian/Swedish culture? Percentages. From CoMRel survey, April 2015.

Figure 2.5   Agreement with the statement 'hostile attitudes towards foreigners should be accepted' among people considering Islam a threat to national culture. Percentages. From CoMRel survey, April 2015.

Figure 2.6   Influence of selected variables on discussions of news on religious extremism: Substantive effects. Based on CoMRel survey, April 2015.

Figure 5.1   Public Service Media should only cover Islam/Judaism/Christianity in an unbiased and objective way. Percentages. From CoMRel survey, April 2015.

Figure 7.1   New voices in Danish television. Saja, 'Sami', Muna, and Moe from the Danish television documentary series *Rebellion from the Ghetto*; produced by Plus Pictures and broadcast on DR2 in 2015. Photo: Plus Pictures / Photographer: Simon Dixgaard. Used with permission.

Acknowledgements

The Research Council of Norway funded the main project, the findings of which are reported in this book (CoMRel, Grant no. 236920) as well as the other contributing project (CC2, Grant no. 231344), both mentioned in the Preface. The SAMKUL board and Tor Lunde Larsen and his colleagues at the Research Council of Norway have been supportive all the way. The participating university institutions, listed in the Preface, have also contributed time and basic funding to this research. Further, the project – and the book – has benefitted from cooperation with the Impact of Religion Programme and the Teaching Religion in Late Modern Sweden (TRILS) Project at the Uppsala Religion and Society Research Centre, Uppsala University.

The research team has been fortunate to draw upon critique and constructive encouragement during project seminars from the three international advisors, Lynn Schofield Clark, Marie Gillespie, and Birgit Meyer. They also all contribute to the present volume with perspectives at a distance on its Scandinavian locus.

The University of Agder provided good conditions for the project seminar at their study centre on Lesbos, as did Schæffergården in Copenhagen for a concluding workshop.

Haakon H. Jernsletten gave invaluable support with the statistical analyses of the material from the project survey, which brought him in as a co-author of Chapter 2.

Manuscripts penned by non-native speakers of English were for the most part language edited by Maria Way in London. Her great support for the book project and scholarly knowledge of our research field was an asset. Additional language edit services were provided by the University of Agder and the University of Copenhagen for a few of the chapters.

The research assistants, Emili Knutson and Jessica Yarin Robinson, proofread and ensured style consistency for the book as a whole. A special thanks to Jessica Yarin Robinson for her editorial suggestions, that proved helpful in finalising the manuscripts. We also wish to thank the anonymous reviewers for their constructive feedback which helped improve our book.

We are grateful to De Gruyter, and in particular, Sophie Wagenhofer, Aaron Sanborn-Overby and Nancy Christ and their respective teams, for following up the book project with enthusiasm and efficiency.

Knut Lundby
Introduction: Religion and Media in Cultural Conflicts

Abstract: The overall question that is raised in this book is: how do the media influence public engagement with contested issues about religion? Here is an introduction to the media dynamics and the key concepts on religion and cultural conflicts, as well as to the Scandinavian context of the study, and this is to be expanded upon in the following chapters. The approaches to be applied in the case studies of this research are briefly presented before summarizing the three sections of the book comprising its 18 chapters.

Keywords: religion, media dynamics, cultural conflicts, Scandinavia

Religion has become a matter of intensified public concern, as well as a vehicle for diverging opinions in public discussions. These controversies pre-eminently play out across mass media and social media. How do the various media influence public engagement with contested issues about religion? This is the overarching question to which we aim to find answers in this book. The idea is to examine how religion in public spaces becomes thematized and is enacted through media, and is then further articulated in social interaction – either face-to-face or in continued exchange in the various forms of media, including social media. In this way, the media are primarily objects of conflict, but are also possible resources with which to manage tensions.

Public Cultural Conflicts

The chapters in this book focus on *cultural* conflicts in which religion is regarded as playing a key role. The cultural aspects of such conflicts include the interactions, interpretations, and identifications with religion. Culture and cultural conflicts play out in the social patterns, activities, and attitudes that include individual media use, as well as political and religious engagement. The book addresses how their conflictual interactions with, interpretations of, and identifications with religion play into public arenas. We are not studying the nature of private beliefs, scepticism, and religious practices as such, but we observe how individual beliefs and practices may imply controversy when they are enacted in public spaces, or even as performed conflict. Our approach to the study of contested religion is laid out in Chapter 4.

That conflicts are 'public' means that they are brought into 'a visible and open forum of some kind in which the population participates' in order that common 'understandings, identities, values and interests' are contested (Livingstone 2005, 9). Such a 'visible and open forum' is a public arena. We explore the public aspects of contested religion in selected public arenas. We do not enter the debates on the 'public sphere' (Gripsrud et al. 2010) from a theoretical perspective. Rather, we examine concrete public settings in which people engage with media material on religion. We have selected public service media, local contexts for civic participation, and classrooms in public schools as the environments for case studies.

Several terms characterize the contestation of religion in such arenas. *Conflict* denotes open antagonism between stakeholders that may change the balance of power between them. *Tensions* refers to implicit or latent antagonisms, in contrast to open conflict. A *controversy* is primarily a dispute over the role of religion in culture. However, the use of these terms may not be fully uniform throughout the book. We aim to capture the various ways that religion is being contested under the pressure of contemporary media dynamics.

We are concerned with the conflicts and tensions that are amplified, framed, and co-structured by various media and are played out in public arenas (Hjarvard, Mortensen, and Eskjær 2015). The media shape and share cultural conflicts about religion, demanding responses which involve negotiations of values, beliefs, and policies. We study media representations of religion, but primarily from the perspective of the interactions and interpretations that these generate in various settings.

The media feed into, and influence, activities in most public arenas (see Chapter 3) – and the media themselves become public spaces. Various media, be they news media or entertainment media, mass media or social media, become sites for explicit or implicit contestation over religion (see Chapter 4). The media offer resources for people's engagement with contentious public aspects of religion in different public arenas.

The Scandinavian Setting

The processes above are challenges in most modern, diverse societies. We study these contestations as they play out in the Scandinavian countries, Denmark, Norway, and Sweden, seeking to understand how the media shape public engagement with controversies about religion. Although the empirical material in the book is drawn from Scandinavia, the findings and reflections should be relevant to other parts of the world. Scandinavia offers an analytical prism through which to understand how intersecting social, political, and cultural circumstances can exacerbate, or alleviate, conflicts over religion in various media settings.

The particular Scandinavian setting is introduced in Chapter 1. The strong traditions of welfare and solidarity in these three Scandinavian societies are being challenged by globalization and neoliberal policies. There are increased tensions over ethno-religious diversity and there is heightened controversy over religion and secularity. Religion, and especially Islam, has become a contentious subject in political and public discussions, discussions in which right-wing populist parties play an active role, including the politicizing of the Christian heritage. Since Islam has a fairly recent presence in the Scandinavian religious landscape, which has been shaped by 500 years of Lutheran Christianity, the risk is to overemphasize its role. Muslims are, however, only small minorities in each country, and even within these small populations there is great religious diversity. Citizens with Muslim backgrounds vary in their adherence to religion as much as other nationals do. Practicing Muslims may attend mosques and register with Islamic communities, while the secular, 'cultural Muslims' and atheists among those who emigrate from Muslim countries avoid organized religion.

While controversy around Islam is the most visible aspect, there are also other highly contested issues on religion. Atheist and secularist organizations challenge the previous church hegemony and morality. Scandinavia demonstrates challenges that occur as a result of the growing diversity in societies that are built on a model of religious, cultural, and social homogeneity. The controversies indicate that these formerly rather homogenous societies are trying to adapt their symbols, institutions, and public services to a more diverse cultural and religious situation. These tensions easily become intensified in a globalized and mediatized world.

Mediatization

Mediatization is the process in modern societies through which the extensive role of the various media transforms the patterns of social interaction and the workings of social institutions (Hepp 2013; Hjarvard 2013; Lundby 2014). This also applies to communication on religion. Understanding these dynamics is necessary in order to grasp the cultural conflicts over religion. These dynamics are explored in greater detail in Chapter 3, but will be discussed briefly here.

The study of 'mediatization' differs from the study of 'mediation'. The study of mediation concerns the ways in which the use of particular media in communication practices may influence the form and content of the message and its reception, for instance, the way in which a news story may frame Islam and influence the audience's interpretation. The study of 'mediatization' usually focuses on two aspects: The *historical changes* brought about in different fields or institutional contexts of a society following the growing presence of various media in society, and the *mediatized conditions* for social interaction following these historical changes. An example of mediatization is the diminishing authority of religious institutions, given the conditions for communication that are set by the manifold nature of media (Hjarvard, 2018). Conceptually speaking, 'mediation' and 'mediatization' denote different processes, but these processes are interconnected.

Media are not just disseminators of messages. They have become integral parts of the communication and interaction in all of the fields of contemporary culture (Couldry and Hepp 2017). Mediatization theory 'tries to capture long-term interrelation processes between media change on the one hand and social and cultural change on the other' (Hepp, Hjarvard, and Lundby 2010, 223). With our focus on cultural conflicts, it is particularly important to pay attention to the dynamics of mediatized conflicts (Eskjær, Hjarvard, and Mortensen 2015; Cottle 2006) (see Chapter 3).

In contemporary societies, religion, as a social and cultural process, has become increasingly interconnected with mediatization processes (Lövheim 2014). The chapters in this book therefore approach religion as a contested and mediatized social phenomenon. Following Hjarvard (2012) we distinguish between various forms of mediatized religion, namely, 'religious' media that are controlled by religious organizations; journalism on religion, as represented by the secular press, and 'banal religion', or the bricolage of religious symbols and elements in popular cultural media (Hjarvard 2012; Lövheim and Axner 2015). A discussion about the usefulness and possible development of these forms of mediatized religion is introduced in Chapter 4.

'The media' are constantly changing, with the continuous launches of technologies with new affordances and new constellations in the media industries, and this encourages new user patterns. The studies presented in this book focus on media producers, but primarily on the roles that media users play through their interpretations and interactions with the representations that they approach – and in the ways in which these user patterns work back into the formation of religion. Mediatization of religion implies that public practices and expressions of religion are transformed through their interplay with various media. We study mediatization processes during conflicts over religion in discussions over public service broadcasts (see Chapters 5–8), in dialogue and discussions in multicultural local civic settings (Chapters 9–12), and in classroom teaching on religion and ethics (Chapters 13–15). The case studies are complemented by a cross-national, comparative survey which is presented in Chapter 2. Concluding notes on mediatization in general, and on the mediatization of religion, in particular, following the case studies, are to be found in the third part of the book.

Approaches

The book is written by a team of researchers with backgrounds in religious studies, sociology of religion, media and communication studies and media sociology, anthropology, and political science. There is thus an interdisciplinary perspective behind the work. We have applied a variety of methods, primarily case study approaches with qualitative methods, for instance, interviews and observation. Online ethnography is applied in the studies of social media practices. The attitude patterns reported in Chapter 2 are based on statistical analyses of representative national surveys, with the regression analysis being documented in the Appendix.

The cases studied in each part of the book (see below) are selected for comparative analyses across the three Scandinavian countries. The comparisons are conceptually driven, with cases taken from comparable contexts. They illustrate how religion is contested within the media dynamics in the particular settings under study. Not all of the three countries are included in each setting. Still, we claim that the studies offer insight into how the various media influence public engagement with contested issues about religion.

Content of the Book

The first part of the book, on *Contexts*, opens with a chapter on the characteristics of Scandinavia, touching upon its history, cultural foundations, and political and media systems. Chapter 2 outlines the tendencies and variations in attitudes among Scandinavians as well as the role of religion in public settings, and this is based on national surveys that we commissioned. After the survey findings two more theoretical chapters follow. Chapter 3 considers the media dynamics that are at work in contesting religion, while Chapter 4 presents the approach that we apply in analysing religion as a contested phenomenon.

Part two introduces the actual *Controversies* in the series of case studies. This is the most extensive part of the book. Here, we try to answer three questions, each to be studied in one specific setting. First, how do *public service media* provide space for, or control, the visibility of the actors, perspectives, and issues that are related to conflicts around religion in the public realm? (Chapter 5). This question is researched with one selected case study from each of the Scandinavian countries and with emphasis on different outlets within the public service cross-media platforms. Chapter 6 examines the Facebook group that was set up in protest when a Norwegian national broadcaster stopped a news anchor from wearing a cross pendant. Chapter 7 considers the careful framing by producers of *Rebellion from the Ghetto*, a Danish TV documentary, and the reactions to it in both online and offline debates. Chapter 8 looks at the conflicting ideals in the coverage of Islam in a weekly radio programme on Swedish public service radio.

Second, we move to questions on how contested, mediatized religion is handled in *local civic settings* in Denmark and Norway. Chapter 9 provides initial perspectives, theorizes mediatization, and considers cultural conflicts in such contexts. This is followed by a study of the ways in which local Christian publications react to national policies on asylum seekers (Chapter 10). Next is a study of how newly arrived Muslims enter interreligious dialogue initiatives as part of their tactics to counter mass media portrayals of their minority group and to perform 'belonging to the Norwegian nation' (Chapter 11). This section ends with a piece on the ways in which metropolitan Muslim converts handle negative media frames, trying to construct dual identities (Chapter 12).

The third question is: how do teachers and pupils in *classroom situations in public schools* engage with the conflicts around religion that are thematized and made visible in mediatized representations? Following perspectives on mediatized religious education in upper secondary schools in Norway and Sweden (Chapter 13), this section of the book presents a case study of teachers' efforts to curb boredom in classes on religion and ethics through entertainment (Chapter 14), and a report and reflection on media influence on religious education classes on Islam (Chapter 15).

The final part of the book, *Crosscurrents*, first comments on gender, diversity, and the mediatized conflicts of religion across the case studies in the book (Chapter 16), and this is followed by a discussion of the interaction dynamics in the cases as they contribute to the theory on the mediatization of religion (Chapter 17). This concluding part of the book closes with two entries that are written by distinguished international scholars who have been following this research at a distance. Lynn Schofield Clark, a media and communication scholar from the USA, and Marie Gillespie, a sociologist from the UK, put the findings in the previous chapters into a global context, in Chapter 18, 'From Scandinavia to the World', before Birgit Meyer, a German anthropologist and scholar of religion who is based in the Netherlands, provides an afterword.

Through these chapters various intersecting aspects of the processes of negotiating controversies about religion in Scandinavian mediatized public settings are illuminated. By analysing media use and social interaction through public service media, in schools, local civic settings, and on online platforms, this book contributes to a more nuanced understanding of the ways in which media shape and amplify cultural conflicts about religion, and how public interactions in response to these processes incite negotiations relating to values, beliefs, and policies in societies that are undergoing crucial social and cultural transformations.

Bibliography

Cottle, Simon. 2006. *Mediatized Conflict*. Maidenhead: Open University Press.
Couldry, Nick, and Andreas Hepp. 2017. *The Mediated Construction of Reality*. Cambridge: Polity.
Eskjær, Mikkel Fugl, Stig Hjarvard, and Mette Mortensen, eds. 2015. *The Dynamics of Mediatized Conflicts*. New York: Peter Lang.
Gripsrud, Jostein, Hallvard Moe, Anders Molander, and Graham Murdock, eds. 2010. *The Idea of the Public Sphere. A Reader*. Lanham, Maryland: Rowman & Littlefield Publishers.
Hepp, Andreas. 2013. *Cultures of Mediatization*. Cambridge: Polity.
Hepp, Andreas, Stig Hjarvard, and Knut Lundby. 2010. "Mediatization – Empirical Perspectives: An Introduction to a Special Issue." *Communications: The European Journal of Communication Research* 35 (3): 223–228.
Hjarvard, Stig. 2012. "Three Forms of Mediatized Religion: Changing the Public Face of Religion." In *Mediatization and Religion: Nordic Perspectives*, edited by Stig Hjarvard and Mia Lövheim, 21–44. Gothenburg: Nordicom.
Hjarvard, Stig. 2013. *The Mediatization of Culture and Society*. London: Routledge.
Hjarvard, Stig. 2018. "The Logics of the Media and the Mediatized Conditions of Social Interaction." In *Media Logic(s) Revisited. Modelling the Interplay between Media Institutions, Media Technology and Societal Change*, edited by Caja Thimm, Mario Anastasiadis, and Jessica Einspänner-Pflock, 63–84. Basingtoke: Palgrave Macmillan.
Hjarvard, Stig, Mette Mortensen, and Mikkel Fugl Eskjær. 2015. "Introduction: Three Dynamics of Mediatized Conflicts." In *The Dynamics of Mediatized Conflicts*, edited by Mikkel Fugl Eskjær, Stig Hjarvard, and Mette Mortensen, 1–27. New York: Peter Lang.
Livingstone, Sonia. 2005. "Introduction." In *Audiences and Publics: When Cultural Engagement Matters for the Public Sphere*, edited by Sonia Livingstone, 9–16. Bristol: Intellect.
Lundby, Knut, ed. 2014. *Mediatization of Communication*. Vol. 21 of *Handbooks of Communication Science*. Berlin: De Gruyter Mouton.
Lövheim, Mia. 2014. "Mediatization and Religion." In *Mediatization of Communication*, edited by Knut Lundby, 547–570. Berlin: De Gruyter Mouton.
Lövheim, Mia, and Marta Axner. 2015. "Mediatised Religion and Public Spheres: Current Approaches and New Questions." In *Religion, Media, and Social Change*, edited by Kennet Granholm, Marcus Moberg, and Sofia Sjö, 38–53. London: Routledge.

Part I: **Contexts**

Knut Lundby, Pål Repstad
Chapter 1
Scandinavia: Traits, Trends and Tensions

Abstract: The Scandinavian welfare societies depend on strong states to provide public services and to redistribute income. Scandinavians enjoy comprehensive welfare systems that offer citizens social security within open economies. Scandinavia combines international market capitalism with government regulation. The political–economic crisis in Europe influences Scandinavia as well, with pressure from globalization and immigration, and new political divisions that are articulated by right-wing populism.
The Scandinavian countries are built on egalitarian values and practices and the level of trust between people is high. However, the countries are finding that these egalitarian values also have unintended, problematic consequences, especially as these once relatively homogenous societies experience growing diversity. Today, there are peculiar contrasts in the Scandinavian cultural–religious landscape, between old churches with large majorities of the population as members, and levels of secularity in Scandinavian societies that position the region as the most secular corner of the world.

Keywords: Scandinavia, welfare state, welfare society, homogeneity, equality

The Scandinavian countries, Denmark, Norway, and Sweden, are known as welfare societies that are based on cultural homogeneity and the ideals of social equality. Scandinavia, with its surveyable population of 21 million (2017), is small in scale, but it scores high on several indices of social and economic performance.[1] There is a widespread self-understanding of liberal open-mindedness, and secularity is often taken for granted. Equality between the sexes is a core value. Conflicts are usually handled in negotiations within a neo-corporatist system between strong states and collective institutions, or in open public debate (Engelstad et al. 2017b; Hilson 2008). These conflict-solving mechanisms extend to the media system. The Scandinavian countries are on top in world press freedom rankings[2] and have strong public service media (Syvertsen et al. 2014).

---

[1] Most prominent in the UNDP Human Development Reports, see http://hdr.undp.org/en/2016-report
[2] For example, the 2017 index from *Reporters Without Borders*, https://rsf.org/en/ranking_table (Accessed 12 June 2017).

OpenAccess. © 2018, Knut Lundby, Pål Repstad. [CC BY-NC-ND] This work is licensed under the Creative Commons Attribution-Non Commerical-NoDerivs 4.0 License. https://doi.org/10.1515/9783110502060-006

Within this seemingly harmonious framework cultural tensions are evolving. The political–economic crisis in Europe also influences the Scandinavian countries. The above Scandinavian characteristics are under pressure from globalization and immigration, with new political divisions being articulated by right-wing populism. Public tensions over radical Islamism and immigration from Muslim countries ignite discussions about Islam as a threat, although the Muslim population makes up small minorities in the Scandinavian countries. Global influences contribute to contested religion in Scandinavia. Growing diversity in the religious field, as well as in the media landscape, forms part of the conflicts that are arising. This is the core issue in the present book, to be researched throughout the following chapters. The tensions and conflicts are often framed as being cultural, but they may instead be social, economic, and political.

This chapter tries to map how these tensions are spelled out in the domains of religion and media in Scandinavia, as well as in the relations between media and religion. We do not go deep into analysing the issues, as we also need space for giving some basic, but relevant information about social and cultural frameworks in Scandinavia. The main aim of the chapter is to work as a background for the specific case studies to come, and we provide many references to the analyses in the following chapters.

1.1 Scandinavia and the Nordic Region

There is a distinction between Scandinavia and the Nordic region. Scandinavia is part of the Nordic region, which also encompasses Finland and Iceland, as well as Greenland and some smaller islands. There is geographical, cultural, and political proximity between Scandinavia and the wider Nordic sphere. All five Nordic countries are built on egalitarian values and practices. But all five countries experience unintended challenging consequences as these once relatively homogenous societies become more cultural-religious diverse.

Immigration implies a demographic challenge that is causing cultural tensions. Sweden has been the most open to immigration. Of the three countries, Sweden has the biggest population but this amounts to no more than 10 million people. The two other countries are smaller – and more restrictive on immigration. Denmark has the highest population density, with more people (5.8 million) than the more spacious Norway (5.3 million).[3]

---

3 Source: National statistical bureaus as per mid-2017.

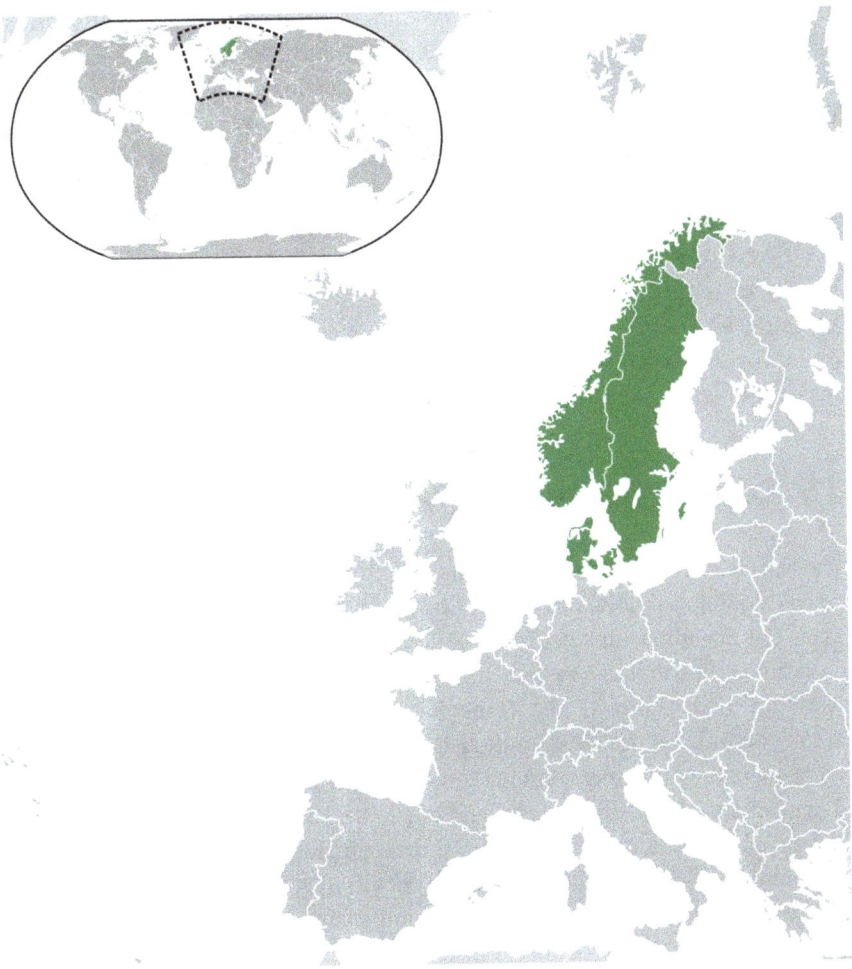

Figure 1.1 Scandinavia is geographically positioned 'on the top' of Europe.

Despite different histories, and even previous internal armed conflicts, the Scandinavian countries are closely knit together (Kouri and Olesen 2016). They are all parliamentarian democracies and formally monarchies. The Scandinavian languages are close and usually people understand each other's writing and speech, although immigrant languages and the use of English are on the rise. The three countries have many cultural traditions in common and thus have easily shared stories. This is slowly changing, with the growing ethnic and religious diversity and the fragmentation of the media landscape.

The Scandinavian countries have chosen different paths in international economic and political cooperation. Denmark and Sweden are members of the EU, while Norway is not, although it is integrated into the European economic market. Denmark and Norway are members of NATO, while Sweden is neutral. The three countries, however, work together in Nordic institutions, with Finland and Iceland included, and have long shared passport-free movements across their borders.

Taken together, the three Scandinavian countries have no more than approximately one-fourth of Germany's population, or about the same number of inhabitants as the US state of Florida. The small scale has been a favourable condition for the development of the Scandinavian welfare system. Changes, like recent immigration, are creating tensions.

1.2 Welfare States in Transition

The Nordic welfare *societies,* built after World War II, depend on strong *states* to provide public services and to redistribute income. In return for relatively high taxes the Scandinavians get free public education through the university level, a national health care system mostly for free, guaranteed paid leave from work for both mothers and fathers of infants, and subsidized child care, among other benefits. The Scandinavian *neo-corporatist states* are characterized by 'a seemingly unlikely combination of a basic liberal orientation with a high degree of state intervention … upheld due to the long term development of democratic institutions, in tandem with a growing inclusion of groups excluded from the public sphere and fields of power' (Engelstad 2017, 265). Peasants', workers' and women's organizations are among the social movements that have made their way into institutionalized negotiations and helped shape the modern state (Aakvaag 2017). Even if some movements in a neo-liberal direction have taken place in recent decades in the Scandinavian countries, they still fit better than most countries into the Social Democratic type in Esping-Andersen's typology of welfare capitalist regimes, and more so than into the two other types, Liberal and Conservative. The main reasons for this are that many welfare benefits are still universal and are not subject to means testing, and, secondly, that many welfare benefits are distributed to people in their capacity as citizens, and are not only reserved for occupationally active people (Esping-Andersen 1990).

Scandinavians, then, enjoy comprehensive welfare state systems that offer the citizens social security within open economies. They combine international market capitalism with government regulations and coordinated negotiations between strong employer's associations and strong unions. Gender equality and women's participation in work are underlined as key values. This way of organizing society has been termed the Nordic or Scandinavian model (Barth, Moene, and Willumsen 2015; Hilson 2008).

The economic base has primarily been industry in Sweden, agriculture in Denmark, and fish and oil in Norway. All three countries experience pressures for change in open, globalized economies. Wage differences have been relatively small, but gaps in income have expanded somewhat over the last 30 years, in Sweden more than in Denmark and Norway, and the gap is even wider in wealth than in income.[4] This implies a growing potential for social tensions, which counter the Scandinavian ideology of equality and small social differences.

1.3 Lutheran Background in Strong States – Deconstructed

The Scandinavian states have since the 1500s been legitimized through state churches: These majority Evangelical Lutheran churches have their roots in the Protestant Reformation five hundred years ago. As the religious landscape slowly became more diverse, particularly since the 1970s (Furseth et al. 2018), tensions have grown over the privileged position of the majority church. Sweden dissolved its state church in 2000. Norway cut the confessional link to the Lutheran religion in the Constitution in 2012, and took further steps to split church and state five years later. Denmark still has a state church, a liberal 'folk church'. In all three countries, state recognition is extended to other registered faith communities and worldview organizations. All three countries give financial support to the majority church as well as to other registered communities, through different national arrangements (Kühle et al. 2018). Such economic funding still seems to have broad political support. However, some politicians argue that violation of human rights should make it possible to withdraw such funding schemes, and voices arguing for secular arrangements across institutional sectors are becoming more vocal. A few politicians, both left-wing and right-wing, even ask why the state should automatically sponsor religious organizations, as long as other voluntary cultural work is not automatically supported. Still, the imprint of the long Christian tradition on the fabric of society is there, e.g. almost every holy day in the Christian calendar is a national holiday in Scandinavia.

---

4 *Perspektivmeldingen 2017,* [Economic perspectives 2017], The Norwegian Government, Meld. St. 29 (2016–2017), 135–137; and OECD Statistics, "Income Distribution and Poverty," accessed 31 March 2017, http://stats.oecd.org/index.aspx?queryid=66670

1.4 Homogeneity, Equality, Similarity, and Trust

The Scandinavian countries, with their relatively sparse populations, have often been considered to be relatively homogeneous. The populations have limited the potential for diverse institutions, and the minorities have been small in number and politically weak. It is true that the three countries, until recently, have had – some would say still have – a dominating national majority church that is relatively closely intertwined with the state. There are also publicly owned public service broadcasting corporations (see Chapter 5), that dominate but which are in competition with commercial radio and TV channels. The Scandinavian school system is also relevant here. Almost all young Danes, Norwegians, and Swedes are pupils in schools that are part of the public sector at both primary and secondary levels. There are openings for commercial schools and schools that are owned by religious and other voluntary organizations, but the number of pupils in such schools is low, and the state has some supervision and control also in these schools, as they are partly financed by public means. Hence, despite some local variations, almost the whole population has received a common socialization within a framework that is set by the state.

Some other characteristics are often presented together with homogeneity: The Scandinavian countries are dominated by egalitarian values and practices, and the level of trust between people is high.[5] Surveys from around 2010 put Denmark on top, Norway second, and Sweden as number six among countries in the world, in terms of responses to the question of trust in other people. The population in Scandinavia is also more state-friendly and has a higher trust in the government than most countries (Listhaug and Ringdal 2008; Bjørnskov and Bergh 2011).

These characteristics are often praised by Nordic researchers (Barth et al. 2014), and by others as well (Wilkinson and Pickett 2010). Small economic differences tend to prevent social conflicts and the development of mutual stereotypes, it is argued. Relatively small differences also make it easier for people to trust each other, and the presence of trust facilitates efficiency, as the number of control mechanisms can be reduced.

However, sometimes egalitarian values have unintended problematic consequences. The Norwegian anthropologist Marianne Gullestad (2002, 46) cites Alexis de Tocqueville, who pointed out in his study of *Democracy in America*

---

5 For Denmark and Norway, data from European Values Study, Wave 4, conducted 2008–2010. For Sweden and most other countries from the World Values Survey, data from Wave 6, conducted 2010–2014.

from 1840 that the idea of equality seems to require similarity, that people have to feel they are more or less the same to be of equal value (Tocqueville 2008 [1840]). Gullestad finds this tendency to be particularly strong in Scandinavia, where equality is conceived of as sameness. This has consequences for the relationship to migration and integration by 'others', she holds.

Many Scandinavians require sameness from newcomers in order to be regarded as equal (Gullestad 2002). This may partly be an explanation when people feel threatened by immigrants, however, this tendency could be countered by deliberate policies and personal experiences with newcomers from other cultures. At the time of writing, Gullestad (2002) observed a growing 'ethnification' of the national identity, with the renewed importance of Lutheran Christianity in contrast to Islam. By 2017, the perceived challenge from Islam is related to national culture as such, and not particularly to a Christian tradition. Gullestad's analysis of equality and similarity is interesting, but so general that it is difficult to confront with specific empirical data. A point that weakens Gullestad's hypothesis about the connection between egalitarianism and a demand for sameness is an impression that the citizens and elite groups who are mostly in favour of equality are also those that are most positive to immigration.[6]

The image of Scandinavian countries as unusually homogeneous countries can be contested. Up North in Norway and Sweden, the Sami have been suppressed by the national governments. The Sami were recognized by the United Nations as an indigenous people, giving them rights to keep their languages, reindeer husbandry, and traditions. Today, they are recognized in their respective countries and have separate parliaments, but with limited scope for making their own decisions. There are still tensions, particularly over the use of land resources (Berg-Nordlie, Saglie, and Sullivan 2015).

Furthermore, we can also find tensions within the majority cultures in Scandinavian countries. The Norwegian sociologist Stein Rokkan is famous for having developed a typology of important cleavages in European politics. His typology is inspired by Norwegian political history, but is relevant also in other countries, not least in Denmark and Sweden. In addition to the socio-economic dimension, from left to right, and focusing on socio-economic inequality and the balance between market and state regulation, he identified two other important dimensions that influence voting behaviour, and politics in general. Firstly, he described a moral–religious dimension, often focusing on support for religion, sexual ethics, family politics, and issues concerning life and death (abortion and the possibility of legalizing euthanasia). Secondly, he identified a territorial dimension, also

---

[6] See Gulbrandsen et al. (2002) for a study of Norwegian elite groups.

called a centre–periphery dimension, comprising issues like centralization versus decentralization, but also cultural issues, like the prestige of rural dialects in the public sphere (Rokkan and Lipset 1967). All these dimensions and cleavages can be found in the three Scandinavian countries, creating social and political tensions. Even in small Denmark, there are cultural, including religious, differences between Copenhagen and the Thy region in Northern Jutland.

1.5 Growing Diversity, Religious Complexity, and New Secularity

In all the Scandinavian countries, from the 19th century until today, there has been a gradually growing diversity in the field of worldviews, first within a Christian framework, then including secular worldviews, and, finally, also including religious traditions other than Christianity.

Today, there are peculiar contrasts in the Scandinavian cultural–religious landscape. On the one hand, the Scandinavian countries have strong collective cultural–religious traditions, with majority churches encompassing between two-thirds and three-quarters of the population. On the other hand, it may hardly be considered religious at all. According to the World Values Study and Inglehart–Welzel's cultural map, the three Scandinavian countries are positioned at the most secular corner of the world. Scandinavians score highest on the combination of Self-Expression Values and Secular–Rational Values (see Figure 1.2). The Swedes have been in this secular cultural values corner for two decades, while Danes and Norwegians had moved there by 2015.[7]

In Norway, in particular, there is a strong, organized non-religious humanist strand. This encompasses 2 percent of the population (2016). However, the growth in the number of those outside any organized and registered religious or life stance community is more remarkable, in Scandinavia as in many other Western countries. In Denmark, the rise was from 9 percent in 1988 to 19 percent in 2014, and in Norway from 3 to 13 percent (Furseth et al. 2018). Figures for Sweden are not available, but they are probably higher than in the other two countries. However, staying out of organized communities do not necessarily imply that people are not concerned with religious or spiritual issues.

---

[7] World Values Survey, Institute for Futures Studies, accessed 23 Aug 2017, http://www.iffs.se/en/world-values-survey/. Strictly speaking, the Inglehart–Welzel cultural map is based mainly on questions about values, but indirectly the map also tells quite a lot about religion.

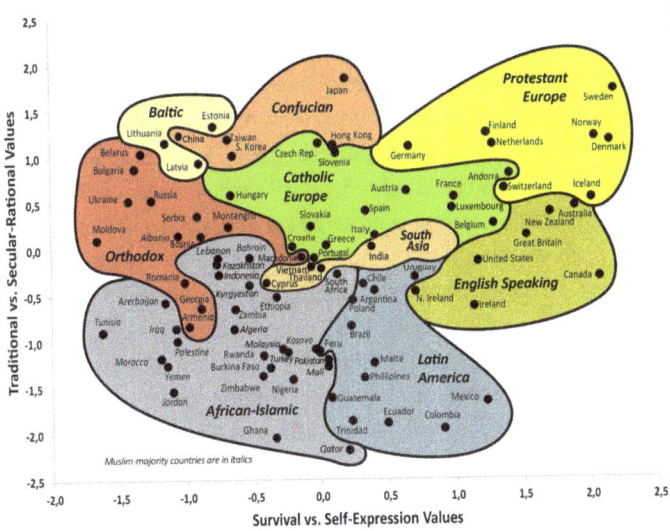

Figure 1.2 Inglehart–Welzel's cultural map (2015) based on the World Values Survey.

There has been a decline in the membership of the majority churches, with the steepest declines in Sweden. While 9 out of 10 Scandinavians were members in 1988, this was down to 7 of 10 Swedes and 3 of 4 Danes and Norwegians in 2014. These are still high shares of the population. However, there has been a decline in participation in the rites of passage among members, as well as an erosion of beliefs and religious self-identification (see Chapter 2).

The relative membership decline of the majority churches is partly due to changing religious practices and beliefs among the native-born population, and partly due to immigration. Many of those coming from other countries bring other religions with them. For example, Polish migrant workers have expanded the number of Catholics, and immigrants from Muslim countries have resulted in a visible Islamic presence. In 2014, Christian communities outside the majority Lutheran churches had a share of 6–7 percent of the populations in Norway and Sweden, but no more than 2 percent in Denmark. Members in registered faith communities from other religions, taken together, made up no more than 3 percent of the Norwegian population in 2014, and in Denmark and Sweden it is even fewer (Furseth et al. 2018).

Islam is the fastest growing among these religions, although the numbers are not easy to trace; there are Muslims who are outside the registered mosques. In any case, non-Muslim Scandinavians perceive the share of Muslims to be much higher than it actually is, according to surveys in 2016. Danes guessed that 15 percent of the population in the country were Muslims, while the actual estimate at that time was 4.1 percent. In Norway, the guess among people was 12 percent, while the actual estimate was 3.7 percent. The Swedes thought the country was 17 percent Muslim, while the figure was 4.6 percent.[8]

With this greater diversity comes a religious complexity, Inger Furseth (2018) suggests. She argues that religious complexity in the Nordic countries 'consists of seemingly contradictory trends, such as a growing secularization in the Nordic populations, trends of both differentiation and de-differentiation of religion at the state level, a growing presence of religion as a topic at the political level, a greater visibility of religion in the media, and a de-privatization of religion at the level of civil society' (ibid, 16). This religious complexity is bringing the Scandinavian countries, with their historically fairly homogenous cultural and religious traditions, more on a par with other Western European societies. There is a growing secularity, higher visibility of religion in public debate, and new expressions of public religion by immigrants. This growing diversity and complexity easily invites tensions and conflicts over religion and religiously infused political issues.

1.6 Globalization, Immigration Policies, and Populist Pressure

As the Scandinavian countries have gradually become more multicultural and multi-religious, social inequality has acquired a new dimension. Social inequality now not only refers to economic inequality, but also to inequality based on ethnicity and immigrant background. The ongoing immigration create tensions in the Scandinavian welfare states (Brochmann and Hagelund 2012). 'The welfare state puts forward important premises for the kind of integration policy that is possible to develop ... while at the same time welfare policy has important consequences for immigrants' everyday lives' in Scandinavia (Brochmann and Hagelund 2012, 1). Tensions over immigration have been increasing recently all over Europe, including Scandinavia. This must be understood against the background of the economic crises in Europe from 2009 onwards, and the increasing number of refugees from conflict areas outside Europe for a period in 2015. Rog-

---

8 Line Fransson, "Ny undersøkelse: Vi tror det er langt flere muslimer enn det egentlig er. I Norge – og resten av verden," [New report: We think there are more Muslims than is the case], *Dagbladet*, 20 Dec 2016, http://www.dagbladet.no/nyheter/vi-tror-det-er-langt-flere-muslimer-enn-det-egentlig-er-i-norge-og-resten-av-verden/66547941.

ers Brubaker (2017) has given a description of the rise of right-wing populist movements in several European countries. These movements, he claims, have partly shifted from nationalism to 'civilizationalism', driven by a perceived civilizational threat from Islam. The movements combine an identitarian 'Christianism' (with a relatively low level of religiosity) and a more secular, and ostensibly liberal, defence of gender equality, freedom of speech, and increasingly also gay rights – all with polemical edges against Islam. This description has some relevance also to Scandinavia. Denmark, Norway, and Sweden have chosen different policies on immigration and the integration of immigrants, with Sweden being the most generous and inviting to newcomers. Denmark approved a generous immigration law in 1983, but following the 9/11 attack in 2001, and the Danish Muhammad cartoon crisis in 2005–2006, the Danish political take on immigration hardened (Lindroth 2016, 82–100).

In Sweden, an anti-immigration party entered parliament in 2010. In Norway, the terror caused by the right-wing Norwegian Anders Behring Breivik, in 2011, was aimed at liberal immigration policies, particularly against Islam. In Denmark, the new centre–left government that was elected in 2011 softened the harsh policies on immigration of the previous governments (Brochmann and Hagelund 2012, ix–x). However, the more liberal policies did not last. In particular, following the many refugees and asylum seekers, in autumn 2015, restrictions on immigration were imposed in all three countries.[9] At the outset, many Scandinavians countered the strict immigration policies of their governments in accordance with their high levels of social trust, which is defined as a shared belief that strangers will not harm or deceive you. Tensions have been sharper since, due to public conflicts over Muslim immigration.

It is difficult to trace comparative figures among the Scandinavian countries. By the beginning of 2016, 16.3 percent of all those living in Norway were immigrants or were Norwegian-born with immigrant parents.[10] In Sweden, the figures are higher. In 2012, the foreign-born counted for 15 percent of the population; in addition, 5 percent were the descendants of immigrants. About half of all immigrants in Scandinavia at that point were from Asia, Africa, and Latin America (Pettersen and Østby 2013). During the refugee and asylum crisis of autumn 2015, Sweden took in a much larger share of asylum seekers (162,000) than Den-

---

9 A presentation of recent Norwegian refugee policy is given in Chapter 10.
10 Statistics Norway, "Key figures for the population," accessed 30 August 2017. https://www.ssb.no/en/befolkning/nokkeltall/population.

mark (21,000) and Norway (31,000).[11] However, the number of people that were arriving created tensions in all three countries.

Established political parties in Scandinavia are experiencing emerging tensions with right-wing populist parties, primarily over issues of immigration from Muslim countries. The meaning of 'populism' differs and it can only be fully understood in the political and cultural context of the various countries (Herkman 2016). In Denmark, Dansk Folkeparti (The Danish People's Party) is a strong force in national politics, receiving one-fifth of the votes in the 2015 election. In Sweden, the established parties have avoided cooperation with the immigration critical Sverigedemokraterna (The Swedish Democrats). By 2017, this front was loosening up, as other parties have had to listen to the growing unrest over immigration. In Norway, Fremskrittspartiet (The Progress Party), in 2018, is part of the government, with the minister for justice and immigration in their portfolio.

1.7 The Public Sphere in the Nordic Model

Religion and media are two of the institutional fields where freedom of expression is particularly important for deliberation and democracy in modern societies (Engelstad et al. 2017b, 2). Public religion (see Chapter 4) and public media (see Chapters 3 and 5) are both part of the public sphere. Besides media and religion, Engelstad et al. (2017b) point out that arts and culture, research and higher education, and voluntary organizations are areas of the public sphere in Scandinavia. The socio-economic base influences cultural expressions, but the public sphere is, at the same time, 'an essential precondition for the shape of the socio-political configuration' (Engelstad et al. 2017b, 2). As we have noted, the Scandinavian countries distinguish themselves from the liberal models of the UK and US, but also from most countries in continental Europe (Esping-Andersen 1990).

The Scandinavian or Nordic public sphere is considered to be part of the ideal model of an extended 'Nordic model' that has its normative preconditions in democratic culture, egalitarianism, and social inclusion (Engelstad, Larsen, and Rogstad 2017). Despite the commonalities with other modern, in particular European, societies, the particularities of the Scandinavian and Nordic welfare societies give the Scandinavian and Nordic public spheres specific characteris-

---

11 Eurostat, "Asylum and first-time asylum applicants by citizenship, age and sex: Annual aggregated data (rounded)," accessed 31 March, 2017. http://appsso.eurostat.ec.europa.eu/nui/show.do?dataset=migr_asyappctza&lang=en.

tics. The specificities are partly due to the neo-corporatist character of the Nordic countries, with state intervention, support, and subsidies in all areas of the public sphere – including the area of religion (Furseth 2017, 222) and of media (Syvertsen et al. 2014). In Scandinavia, churches and mosques, newspapers and public broadcasting, political parties and NGOs alike, receive state funding in order to stimulate the public sphere; with a deep respect for the freedom of expression and the freedom of religion.

Freedom of expression has been enshrined in the law in all of the Scandinavian countries for more than 150 years, with Sweden's 1766 freedom of expression law being the first in the world. With an amendment to the Constitution in 2004, the Norwegian government even obtained the responsibility to establish an infrastructure for 'an open and enlightened public discourse' (§100). However, the freedom of expression is not without exceptions. Hate speech, threats, harassment, discrimination, defamation, the invasion of privacy, libel and slander, are not accepted. National and security interests also impose restrictions. However, freedom of expression is a strongly held value in Scandinavia (Kierulf and Rønning 2009; Rønning 2013).

Defence of this freedom ended in violent conflicts in the Middle East when Muhammad cartoons from Denmark were displayed, which became a transnational media event (Eide, Kunelius, and Phillips 2008). Freedom of expression becomes a fragile human right when statements could be immediately distributed into other contexts with digital mediation (Carlsson 2016). Religiously framed threats by radical Islamists were defended in Norwegian court on the basis of freedom of expression.[12] Norwegian media use the freedom of expression to criticize religion, Islam, and Muslim groups. At the same time, researchers document that Norwegian journalists and editors are becoming more careful with *what* and *how* to publish, in order to avoid attracting reactions from radical Islamists (Elgvin and Rogstad 2017).

Researchers (Midtbøen, Steen-Johnsen, and Thorbjørnsrud 2017) have used the term 'boundary struggles' to describe the contestations of free speech in the public sphere in Scandinavia. The focus on discursive patterns in the public sphere, following the tradition from Habermas, which is discussed within institutional settings by Engelstad et al. (2017a), need to be complemented with a perspective on the boundary work going on in the public sphere, Bernard Enjolras (2017) argues. The public sphere is a social space where cognitive and sym-

---

12 Ubaydullah Hussain was, in 2015, found guilty of threats against journalists, but the courts accepted his support for Islamist terror attacks in public statements. However, on 4 April 2017, he was sentenced to nine years in prison for terror recruitment to IS. The verdict was confirmed in higher court on 18 January 2018.

bolic struggles over recognition take place, he holds. This implies struggles over the symbolic boundaries to who belongs and who doesn't. This view of the public sphere 'as a social space where cultural struggles are fought, where the moral order is shaped, maintained, and contested' (Enjolras 2017, 304), fits with the perspective in this book on how religion is contested in various settings. With public religion, social interactions, identifications, and interpretations must be observed. Still, the institutional frame matters. In our case, the frame set by the media system is of prime interest.

1.8 'Media Welfare States' in Global Connectivity

The Scandinavian welfare states should also be considered 'media welfare states' that stand on four pillars: First, the media are regarded as part of the communication services that offer public goods and therefore should have extensive cross-subsidies, as well as obligations for universality. Second, editorial freedom is secured through self-governance by the media professional associations and, partly, by law. Third, in their cultural policies, the government's responsibility encompasses a 'media manifold' (Couldry and Hepp 2017, 56) that aims to secure diversity and quality. Fourth, solutions to economic and cultural challenges are sought in consensus through cooperation between the main stakeholders: the state, the media and communication industries, and the public (Syvertsen et al. 2014, 17).

This media system is regarded as a cornerstone of Scandinavian democracy, and the standards of the news media are of particular importance. Availability of a diversity of news sources to all citizens, equality and pluralism in media ownership and formats, and the critical assessment of how the news media perform their watchdog task, are criteria that are applied in the Media Democracy Monitor (Donk and Trappel 2011). Sweden comes out as a 'mixed media model under market pressures' (von Krogh and Nord 2011), which is an apt characteristic of the news media system in Denmark and Norway also.

The states support and guard this democratic Scandinavian media system through laws, public funding and subsidies, and by an active media policy and state support for the telecom industries and digitalization. The Scandinavian countries are thus prominent examples of the 'democratic corporatist model' that was laid out by Daniel Hallin and Paolo Mancini in their classic comparison of media systems (2004). Stig Hjarvard disagrees with them that Scandinavia will drift towards a liberal model, similar to that known in the UK and North America. He argues that mediatization (see Chapter 3) implies a further mutual adaptation between media and politics (Hjarvard 2013, 46–47). Hallin and Mancini recently (2016) admitted that the hypothesis of a convergence towards a liberal model has to be abandoned. This is confirmed by Sigurd Allern and Mark Blach-Ørsten's study on Scandinavian news media as political institutions: The ongoing commercialism has produced no more than a revision of the democratic corporatist model. Scandinavia still has large state-owned public service media corporations (see Chapter 5). In Scandinavia, 'a significant involvement of the state in the media sector has and continues to coexist with strong protection for press freedom and a deeply held respect for journalistic autonomy' (Allern and Blach-Ørsten 2011, 101).

Despite the corporatist and consensual frame, tensions over media policies in the Scandinavian media welfare states intensify as competition from networked media and the global connectivity of corporations (van Dijck 2013) change the economic and communicative foundations of the 'legacy' mass media (Svensson and Edström 2016).

Scandinavians are highly connected, thanks to advanced technological networks that include almost everyone. In Norway, 97 percent of the population had Internet access in 2015, in Denmark 92 percent, and in Sweden 91 percent, compared to an EU average of 83 percent.[13] Nearly all Scandinavians with access are daily Internet users.[14] The social media are popular.[15]

Although the national media policies have left the legacy media in Scandinavia in relatively strong positions, the ongoing transformations relating to further digitalization of the media industries do shake the Scandinavian media landscape. Much of the reading, listening, and viewing will move to digital services. Newspapers were, in 2015, read daily by 72 percent of all Norwegians, with a larger share online than in print. The reading shares were somewhat lower in Denmark and Sweden, and the pace of change from print to online news differed. While reading print papers dominated in Sweden, a small majority of Danes preferred online news. Online radio and television consumption is not specified in the comparative statistics. In total, 75 percent of the Danes listened to radio daily in 2015, against 69 percent among the Swedes and 59 percent in Norway. Eighty-one percent of the Swedes, in total, watched television daily in

---

[13] Nordicom, "Mediestatistik," [Media statistics], accessed 30 June 2017. http://nordicom.gu.se/sv/mediefakta/mediestatistik.
[14] Norway 89 percent, Denmark 87 percent, Sweden 82 percent in 2015, against an EU average of 67 percent. Source: Nordicom, ibid.
[15] In Norway, 73 percent of 16–74 year olds reported using social media in 2015, in Denmark 65 percent, and in Sweden 62 percent, against an EU average of 50 percent. Source: Nordicom, ibid.

2015, compared to 70 percent of the Danes and 67 percent of the Norwegians.[16] These figures imply that legacy mass media achieve high audience numbers in Scandinavia, whether in traditional forms or in online services.

The human 'connectedness' among Scandinavians thus extends to 'connectivity', where information about social media users is absorbed into corporate systems behind the platforms which they use to communicate, like Facebook. 'Connectivity' is the 'advanced strategy of algorithmically connecting users to content, users to users, platforms to users, users to advertisers, and platforms to platforms' (van Dijck and Poell 2013, 9). Through the media dynamics (see Chapter 3) in this 'culture of connectivity' (van Dijck 2013), the small-scale Scandinavian populations communicate among themselves and, at the same time, are integrated into large-scale globalization.

1.9 Concluding Note

It is difficult to sum up briefly what characterizes Scandinavia, especially if we want to grasp the nuances and contemporary changes. We have described a comparatively happy, harmonious, peaceful, safe, and egalitarian corner of the world. We have also shown that Scandinavia is becoming increasingly intertwined in European and global processes: right-wing populism, radical Islamism, immigration, and a general economic crisis in Europe. Just one warning: It would be too simplistic to see Scandinavia as a kind of Paradise Island, now threatened from outside. We have tried to nuance and modify the picture, pointing at internal dynamics, diversity, and tensions within the region, often in interaction with global tendencies.

On a more specific level, religion is a contested public issue in the changing Scandinavian media welfare states. Chapter 2 outlines patterns of Scandinavian attitudes on the matter, Chapter 3 takes on the media dynamics, and Chapter 4 introduces the understanding of religion for the case studies to follow.

Bibliography

Aakvaag, Gunnar C. 2017. "Institutional Change in Norway: The Importance of the Public Sphere." In *Institutional Change in the Public Sphere: Views on the Nordic Model*, edited

---

[16] For Denmark 16–89 years old, for Norway and Sweden 9–79 years. The statistics for Denmark are built differently than those for Norway and Sweden. Source: Nordicom, ibid.

by Fredrik Engelstad, Håkon Larsen, Jon Rogstad, and Kari Steen-Johnsen, 71–96. Warsaw/Berlin: De Gruyter Open. DOI: 10.1515/9783110546330-005

Allern, Sigurd, and Mark Blach-Ørsten. 2011. "The News Media as a Political Institution." *Journalism Studies* 12 (1): 92–105. DOI: 10.1080/1461670X.2010.511958.

Barth, Erling, Karl O. Moene, and Fredrik Willumsen. 2015. "The Scandinavian Model: An Interpretation." *Journal of Public Economics* 127 (1): 17–29. DOI: 10.1016/j.jpubeco.2015.05.006.

Berg-Nordlie, Mikkel, Jo Saglie, and Ann Sullivan, eds. 2015. *Indigenous Politics: Institutions, Representation, Mobilisation.* Colchester: ECPR Press.

Bjørnskov, Christian, and Andreas Bergh. 2011. "Historical Trust Levels Predict the Current Size of the Welfare State." *Kyklos* 64 (1): 1–19.

Brochmann, Grete, and Anniken Hagelund. 2012. *Immigration Policy and the Scandinavian Welfare State, 1945–2010.* Basingtoke: Palgrave Macmillan.

Brubaker, Rogers. 2017. "Between Nationalism and Civilizationism: The European Populist Movement in Comparative Perspective." *Ethnic and Racial Studies*, online first. DOI: 10.1080/01419870.2017.1294700.

Carlsson, Ulla, ed. 2016. *Freedom of Expression and Media in Transition. Studies and Reflections in the Digital Age.* Gothenburg: Nordicom.

Couldry, Nick, and Andreas Hepp. 2017. *The Mediated Construction of Reality.* Cambridge: Polity.

Donk, André, and Josef Trappel. 2011. "Indicators and Definitions." In *The Media for Democracy Monitor. A Cross National Study of Leading News Media*, edited by Josef Trappel, Hannu Nieminen, and Lars Nord, 29–50. Gothenburg: Nordicom.

Eide, Elisabeth, Risto Kunelius, and Angela Phillips, eds. 2008. *Transnational Media Events: The Mohammed Cartoons and the Imagined Clash of Civilizations.* Gothenburg: Nordicom.

Elgvin, Olav, and Jon Rogstad. 2017. "Religious Threats and Institutional Change in Norwegian Mass Media." In *Institutional Change in the Public Sphere: Views on the Nordic Model*, edited by Fredrik Engelstad, Håkon Larsen, Jon Rogstad, and Kari Steen-Johnsen, 161–178. Warsaw/Berlin: De Gruyter Open. DOI: 10.1515/9783110546330-009.

Engelstad, Fredrik. 2017. "Afterword: A Viable Model of the Public Sphere?" In *Institutional Change in the Public Sphere: Views on the Nordic Model*, edited by Fredrik Engelstad, Håkon Larsen, Jon Rogstad, and Kari Steen-Johnsen, 265–268. Warsaw/Berlin: De Gruyter Open. DOI: 10.1515/9783110546330-014.

Engelstad, Fredrik, Håkon Larsen, and Jon Rogstad. 2017. "The Public Sphere in the Nordic Model." In *Institutional Change in the Public Sphere: Views on the Nordic Model*, edited by Fredrik Engelstad, Håkon Larsen, Jon Rogstad, and Kari Steen-Johnsen. Warsaw/Berlin: De Gruyter Open. DOI: 10.1515/9783110546330-004.

Engelstad, Fredrik, Håkon Larsen, Jon Rogstad, and Kari Steen-Johnsen, eds. 2017a. *Institutional Change in the Public Sphere: Views on the Nordic Model.* Warsaw/Berlin: De Gruyter Open. DOI: 10.1515/9783110546330.

Engelstad, Fredrik, Håkon Larsen, Jon Rogstad, and Kari Steen-Johnsen, eds. 2017b. "Introduction: The Public Sphere in Change: Institutional Perspectives on Neo-corporatist Society." In *Institutional Change in the Public Sphere: Views on the Nordic Model*, edited by Fredrik Engelstad, Håkon Larsen, Jon Rogstad, and Kari Steen-Johnsen, 1–21. Warsaw/Berlin: De Gruyter Open. DOI: 10.1515/9783110546330-002.

Enjolras, Bernard. 2017. "Boundary Work in the Public Sphere." In *Boundary Struggles: Contestations of Free Speech in the Public Sphere*, edited by Arnfinn Midtbøen, Kari Steen-Johnsen, and Kjersti Thorbjørnsrud, 291–320. Oslo: Cappelen Damm Akademisk (open access). https://press.nordicopenaccess.no/index.php/noasp/catalog/book/16

Esping-Andersen, Gøsta. 1990. *Three Worlds of Welfare Capitalism*. Princeton: Princeton University Press.

Furseth, Inger. 2017. "The Return of Religion in the Public Sphere? The Public Role of Nordic Faith Communities." In *Institutional Change in the Public Sphere: Views on the Nordic Model*, edited by Fredrik Engelstad, Håkon Larsen, Jon Rogstad, and Kari Steen-Johnsen, 221–240. Warsaw/Berlin: De Gruyter Open. DOI: 10.1515/9783110546330-012.

Furseth, Inger. 2018. "Introduction." In *Religious Complexity in the Public Sphere: Comparing Nordic Countries*, edited by Inger Furseth. Basingstoke: Palgrave Macmillan.

Furseth, Inger, Lars Ahlin, Kimmo Ketola, Annette Leis-Peters, and Bjarni Randver Sigurvinsson. 2018. "Changing Religious Landscapes in the Nordic Countries." In *Religious Complexity in the Public Sphere: Comparing Nordic Countries*, edited by Inger Furseth. Basingstoke: Palgrave Macmillan.

Gulbrandsen, Trygve, Fredrik Engelstad, Trond Beldo Klausen, Hege Skjeie, Mari Teigen, and Øyvind Østerud. 2002. *Norske makteliter*. [Norwegian power elites]. Oslo: Gyldendal.

Gullestad, Marianne. 2002. "Invisible Fences: Egalitarianism, Nationalism and Racism." *Journal of the Royal Anthropological Institute* 8 (1): 45–63. DOI: 10.1111/1467-9655.00098.

Hallin, Daniel C., and Paolo Mancini. 2004. *Comparing Media Systems: Three Models of Media and Politics*. Cambridge: Cambridge University Press.

Hallin, Daniel C., and Paolo Mancini. 2016. "Ten Years After Comparing Media Systems: What Have We Learned?" *Political Communication* 34 (2): 155–171. DOI: 10.1080/10584609.2016.1233158.

Herkman, Juha. 2016. "Construction of Populism: Meanings Given to Populism in the Nordic Press." *Nordicom Review* 37 (Special Issue): 147–161. DOI: 10.1515/nor-2016-0029.

Hilson, Mary. 2008. *The Nordic Model: Scandinavia since 1945*. London: Reaktion Books.

Hjarvard, Stig. 2013. *The Mediatization of Culture and Society*. London: Routledge.

Kierulf, Anine, and Helge Rønning, eds. 2009. *Freedom of Speech Abridged? Cultural, Legal and Philosophical Challenges*. Göthenburg: Nordicom.

Kouri, E. I., and Jens E. Olesen, eds. 2016. *Scandinavia 1520–1870*. Vol. 2 of *The Cambridge History of Scandinavia*. Cambridge: Cambridge University Press.

Kühle, Lene, Ulla Schmidt, Brian Arly Jacobsen, and Per Petterson. 2018. "Religion and State: Complexity in Change." In *Religious Complexity in the Public Sphere: Comparing Nordic Countries*, edited by Inger Furseth, 81–135. Basingstoke: Palgrave Macmillan.

Lindroth, Bengt. 2016. *Väljarnas hämd: Populism och nationalism i Norden* [The revenge of the voters: Populism and nationalism in the Nordic countries]. Stockholm: Carlssons Bokförlag.

Listhaug, Ola, and Kristen Ringdal. 2008. "Trust in Political Institutions." In *Nordic Social Attitudes in a European Perspective*, edited by Hekki Ervasti, Torben Fridberg, Mikael Hjerm, and Kristen Ringdal, 131–151. Cheltenham, UK: Edward Elgar Publishing.

Midtbøen, Arnfinn, Kari Steen-Johnsen, and Kjersti Thorbjørnsrud, eds. 2017. *Boundary Struggles: Contestations of Free Speech in the Public Sphere*. Oslo: Cappelen Damm Akademisk (open access). https://press.nordicopenaccess.no/index.php/noasp/catalog/book/16

Pettersen, Silje Vatne, and Lars Østby. 2013. "Scandinavian Comparative Statistics on Integration: Immigrants in Norway, Sweden and Denmark." *Samfunnsspeilet* 2013 (5): 76–83.

Rokkan, Stein, and Seymour M. Lipset. 1967. *Party Systems and Voter Alignments*. New York: Free Press.

Rønning, Helge. 2013. "Freedom of Expression is Not a Given Right." In *Freedom of Expression Revisited*, edited by Ulla Carlsson, 13–25. Gothenburg: Nordicom.

Svensson, Eva-Maria, and Maria Edström. 2016. "Market-Driven Challenges to Freedom of Expression and the Interaction Between the State, the Market, and the Media." *Nordicom Review* 37 (2): 1–16. doi: 10.1515/nor-2016–0013.

Syvertsen, Trine, Gunn Enli, Ole J. Mjøs, and Hallvard Moe. 2014. *The Media Welfare State: Nordic Media in the Digital Era*. Ann Arbor: The University of Michigan Press.

Tocqueville, Alexis de. 2008 [1840]. *Democracy in America, Volume 2*. New York: Quill Pen Classics.

van Dijck, José. 2013. *The Culture of Connectivity: A Critical History of Social Media*. Oxford: Oxford University Press.

van Dijck, José, and Thomas Poell. 2013. "Understanding Social Media Logic." *Media and Communication* 1 (1): 2–14. DOI: 10.12924/mac2013.01010002.

von Krogh, Torbjörn, and Lars Nord. 2011. "Sweden: A Mixed Media Model under Market Pressures." In *The Media for Democracy Monitor. A Cross National Study of Leading News Media*, edited by Josef Trappel, Hannu Nieminen, and Lars Nord, 203–234. Gothenburg: Nordicom.

Wilkinson, Richard, and Kate Pickett. 2010. *The Spirit Level: Why Equality is Better for Everyone*. London: Penguin.

Mia Lövheim, Haakon H. Jernsletten, David Herbert, Knut
Lundby, Stig Hjarvard
Chapter 2
Attitudes: Tendencies and Variations

Abstract: This chapter presents an overview of religiosity and attitudes to religious diversity in media and other public spaces based on a cross-Scandinavian survey conducted in 2015. Although Scandinavians in general have a weak personal connection to religion, Christianity still holds a privileged position as an expression of cultural identity. Scandinavians express support for equal rights to practice religion, but also doubtfulness towards public expressions of religion. More than one-fourth of respondents discuss news about religion and religious extremism regularly. There is a widespread sentiment that Islam is a threat to the national culture, even though most respondents state that they oppose an open expression of hostile attitudes towards foreigners. Political orientation and gender are salient aspects that shape diverging opinions regarding tolerance or scepticism towards the public visibility of religious diversity. Furthermore, Danes and Norwegians are more critical of public expressions of Islam than Swedes.

Keywords: survey, religiosity, political orientation, gender, Islam, religious extremism

2.1 Introduction

Social and political transformations in each society, and on a global scale, are challenging the formerly largely homogeneous culture and self-understanding of the Scandinavian countries. These changes shape attitudes to increasing religious diversity in the populations and the higher visibility of religion, in particular, of Islam, in the public debates that are discussed in Chapter 1. Since changes in values were first measured in the 1980s the World Values Survey Institute[1] has described Scandinavia as the place in which late-modern secular–rational and self-expression values are ranked highest in the world. Given this

---

[1] World Values Survey, Institute for Futures Studies, accessed 23 Aug 2017, http://www.iffs.se/en/world-values-survey/

OpenAccess. © 2018, Mia Lövheim, Haakon H. Jernsletten, David Herbert, Knut Lundby, Stig Hjarvard.
This work is licensed under the Creative Commons Attribution-Non Commerical-NoDerivs 4.0 License. https://doi.org/10.1515/9783110502060-007

background, how are Scandinavians responding to the new diversity of religious expression in public spaces, and to the role of the media in this situation?

In order to provide a context for the following case studies of controversies over religion in various media settings, this chapter presents an overview of religiosity and attitudes to expressions of religious diversity in the media and in other public spaces. This overview is based on a cross-national, comparative survey. The first part of the chapter will present the common tendencies in the survey. In the second part, the differences between and within the populations in Scandinavian countries will be discussed with regard to how social factors, such as age, gender, religiosity, and political opinion, influence views on religion. Finally, we will briefly discuss how the survey findings compare to the findings on religiosity and with attitudes to cultural diversity found in the European Social Survey (ESS).

2.2 A Cross-National Comparative Survey

A survey with population representative samples in Denmark, Norway, and Sweden was undertaken by the project behind this book (see the Preface) in April 2015.[2] There were about 1,000 respondents aged 16 years and above in each country[3]. The media coverage at that time was focused on the dangers experienced by refugees crossing the Mediterranean, and on the terror attacks in Paris and Copenhagen in January and February of the same year. The survey was thus conducted a few months before the peak number of refugees arrived in the Scandinavian countries in the autumn of 2015.

Data were collected through web panels. Such surveys cover the adult population with access to the Internet which, in Scandinavia, is almost everyone (see Chapter 1, section 1.8). The survey is thus sampled to be representative at the country level, but it does not permit meaningful statistical inferences about minority groups in the population.[4] All of the data have been weighted by gender, age, and geographical region.[5]

---

[2] The questions were formulated by CoMRel researchers in cooperation with TNS Gallup in Norway (now Kantar TNS) and were translated into Danish and Swedish. The responses were collected by TNS Gallup in Norway and Denmark, and by TNS Sifo in Sweden, in the period 16–21 April 2015 (Lundby and Jortveit 2015).
[3] 1099 from Norway, 1006 from Denmark and 999 from Sweden. See table 2.2.
[4] This is due to the low number of minority respondents, including ethnic minorities (i.e. respondents that answered that they or their parents were born outside Scandinavia) and small minority religious groups.

2.3 Scandinavian Religiosity: Believing and Belonging

Our study confirms the World Values Survey findings that Scandinavians, in general, have a weak personal connection to religion. As Figure 2.1 shows, fewer than 10 percent of the respondents have a strong religious self-identification.[6] The survey also shows that less than 10 percent report that they visit a religious building to attend a service or prayer meeting each month or more frequently. At least one-third of the respondents in each country do not identify themselves as religious. Religious identification is weaker among Swedes and stronger among the Norwegians and Danes.

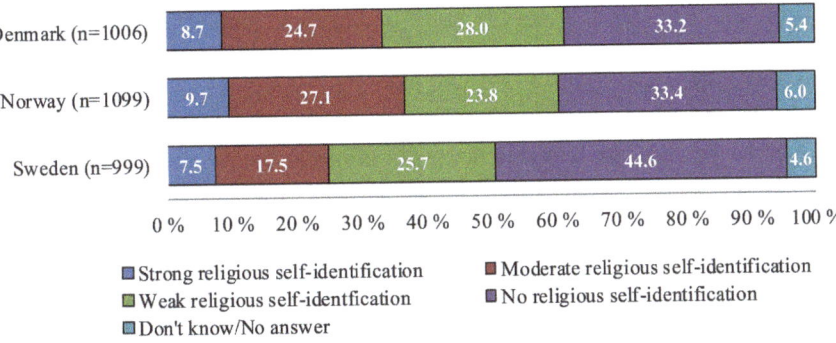

Figure 2.1 Religious self-identification in Scandinavia. Percentages. From CoMRel survey, April 2015.

Despite the low levels of religious self-identification, a majority of the respondents in the survey state that they primarily feel affiliated to Christianity as part of their culture or national identity. As pointed out in Chapter 1, the religious landscape of Scandinavian societies has historically been dominated by

---

5 It was not weighted by education, which may imply some over-representation of higher education.

6 A variable showing the degrees of religious self-identification among the respondents was constructed based on the two following items in the survey: 'To what extent do you regard yourself as religious,' and 'To what extent do you regard yourself to be a believer.' Those who identified themselves with these terms fully or to some extent are considered to have a 'strong or moderate' religious self-identification. Those who did not, or to a small extent, regard themselves as 'religious' or 'believers' have a 'weaker or no' religious self-identification (see further Lundby et al. 2017)

Lutheran majority churches with strong connections to the state. The majority of the populations are still members of these churches. As suggested by Grace Davie, the normal stance in terms of religion in the Nordic countries can be characterized as 'to belong without believing' (Davie 2005, 135). Religion, in the form of Christianity, thus seems to retain significance as a form of cultural belonging for Scandinavians, even though a minority of them identify as 'believers'.

2.4 Political Orientation

The Scandinavian societies have historically been characterized by a relatively stable party structure that is organized primarily around an economic left–right dimension. In recent decades the growth of new political parties, such as environmentalist and right-wing populist parties, have challenged the traditional structure and introduced new political cleavages in which cultural values represent a key dimension (Lövheim et al. 2018; Flanagan and Lee 2003).

In the survey, political orientation is analysed by combining data on the respondents' political party preferences with information from the Chapel Hill Expert Survey on party positions, in terms of views on democratic freedoms and rights (Bakker et al. 2015). Based on this information, we have placed the survey answers in one of three categories: 'libertarian/post-materialist', 'centre', and 'traditional/authoritarian'.[7] The distribution of political orientation in the three Scandinavian countries is shown in Figure 2.2.

As the figure shows, in Norway and Sweden nearly 12 percent of the respondents can be categorized as having a traditional/authoritarian political orientation, on the basis of their political party preferences. In Denmark, political parties with a traditional/authoritarian orientation have greater support among the respondents, with 19 percent of the surveyed population. The tendency to polar-

---

[7] Examples of 'libertarian/post-materialist' parties include *Enhedslisten* and the *Liberal Alliance* in Denmark, *Venstre* in Norway, and *Vänsterpartiet* and *Miljöpartiet de Gröna* in Sweden. Examples of 'traditional/authoritarian' parties include the *Dansk Folkeparti* in Denmark, *Kristelig Folkeparti*, and *Fremskrittspartiet* in Norway, as well as *Sverigedemokraterna* in Sweden. Parties that occupy the 'centre' include *Socialdemokratiet* and *Venstre* in Denmark, *Arbeiderpartiet* and *Høyre* in Norway, and *Socialdemokraterna* and *Moderaterna* in Sweden. A respondent is classified as being 'libertarian/post-materialist' if his or her preferred party scores between 0 and 3 on the GAL–TAN scale, 'centre' if the party scores between 3.01 and 6.99, and 'traditional/authoritarian' if the party scores between 7 and 10. 'Other' includes respondents who said they would not vote, or who would vote for a party that was not included in the survey.

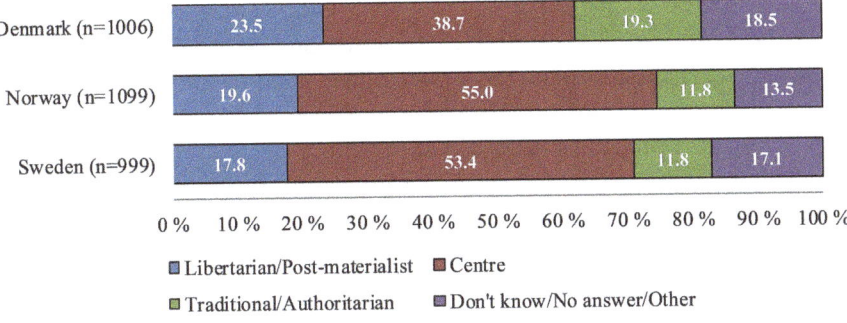

Figure 2.2 Political orientation in Scandinavia (GAL–TAN scale). Percentages. From CoMRel survey, April 2015.

ization between libertarian/post-materialist and traditional/authoritarian orientations is also somewhat stronger in Denmark than in the two other countries.

2.5 Attitudes to Religious Diversity

A particular feature of the Scandinavian society and culture is the strong emphasis on individual self-expression, combined with equal treatment of all citizens, administered by a strong welfare state (Trägårdh 2011). As discussed in Chapter 1, a tendency to link equality with similarity is particularly strong in Scandinavia (Gullestad 2002, 46). How, then, do the Scandinavians respond to increased heterogeneity of religious beliefs and practices in society?

More than 70 percent of respondents in the survey agree that all religions should be respected, and more than half of Norwegians and Danes, and almost two-thirds of the Swedes, strongly or partially agree that all religious groups should be entitled to the same rights in society. On a general level, freedom of religious expression thus seems to be supported in Scandinavian societies. However, when asked about tolerance for particular expressions of religion in public spaces, opinions differ depending on the religion. Around 80 percent of respondents from all Scandinavian countries agree that a cross, church tower, or other Christian symbol may be visible on buildings in public space. Seventy-five percent also agree that signs showing the location of a mosque should be visible. But, when asked about minarets being visible in public space, support drop to about 60 percent of respondents in Sweden and Norway, and 56 percent in Denmark.

That the tendency to support publicly visible expressions of religious faith is conditioned by the particular religion in question is also evident in responses to questions about the display of religious symbols in particular social contexts. Table 2.1 shows stronger support for pupils in school to express their religious faith through wearing a cross rather than a hijab in all the Scandinavian countries. This tendency is also found amongst teachers in high school, hospital staff, news presenters, and police officers, although the strength of support differs depending on the professional group. While a majority of respondents accept that teachers should be free to express their religious faith by wearing a cross, less than half support police officers publicly expressing their faith in this manner.

Table 2.1 Should people in the following groups be allowed to wear a cross or hijab to express their religious faith? Percentage of respondents answering yes. From CoMRel survey, April 2015.

	Denmark		Norway		Sweden	
	Cross	*Hijab*	*Cross*	*Hijab*	*Cross*	*Hijab*
Pupils in school	73%	52%	77%	54%	75%	57%
Teachers in high school	68%	47%	61%	38%	66%	48%
News presenters	56%	36%	55%	32%	57%	40%
Police	46%	27%	39%	16%	49%	31%
Hospital staff	61%	40%	52%	31%	59%	40%
N	1006		1099		999	

Note: 'Do not know' and 'Do not want to answer' excluded from the tabulations.

The survey also asked respondents if they agreed that religious leaders have a stronger right than others to express their views on cultural, moral, and ethical issues in public. Seventy percent or more of the respondents disagree with this statement for Muslim leaders, but also more than 60 percent oppose Christian leaders doing so.

These findings suggest that Scandinavians, on an abstract, general level, support a plurality of expression of religion in society, but that they are more doubtful towards the expressions of Islam than Christianity. This tendency seems stronger when public manifestations of religion are connected to state authority, such as in the case of police officers or other state officials wearing the hijab. Furthermore, the majority of respondents do not think religious leaders should enjoy any privileged position on such matters.

2.6 Media Coverage of Religion

The Scandinavian media model described in Chapter 1 implies that the media are regarded by citizens as part of the communication services that offer public goods, and that therefore they are expected to handle different religions and world-views in an equal manner. A majority of Scandinavians still use conventional mass media, such as newspapers, radio, and television, on a daily basis. What, then, are their opinions about the ways in which media should engage with both religion in general, and with controversial aspects of religious issues in particular?

As can be seen from table 2.2 below our survey shows that, on the one hand, Scandinavians do not think that the media should increase the coverage of religious topics or of the major religions: Judaism, Christianity, and Islam (see further Chapter 5). On the other hand, the majority want the media to be more critical in their coverage of religion.

Table 2.2 Percentage of the respondents who fully or partially agree with statements on what the media ought to do in relation to their coverage of religion. From CoMRel survey, April 2015.

The media ought to…	Denmark	Norway	Sweden
… give more attention to religious topics	26%	32%	24%
… give space to conflicts about religion	72%	85%	75%
… be critical of problematic aspects of religion	76%	81%	71%
… cover religion in satirical ways	65%	68%	64%
… invite dialogue when there are tensions over religion	72%	81%	76%
N	1006	1099	999

Note: 'Don't know' and 'Do not want to answer' included in the tabulations.

Furthermore, the table shows that a large majority in all three countries support the notion that the media should engage with problematic aspects of religion, for instance by giving space to coverage of conflicts, and by being critical and satirical about religion, but also by inviting dialogue when tensions over religious issues occur.

2.7 Religion and Culture in Conflict

The survey findings reveal the contested nature of public expressions of religion, in particular of Islam, among Scandinavians today. As shown in Figure 2.3, a majority of the respondents agree with the statement that religion leads to conflict rather than to peace.

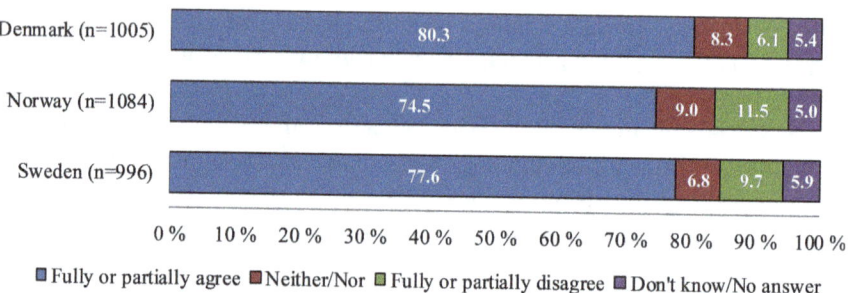

Figure 2.3 Looking at the world, religion leads to conflict rather than to peace. Percentages. From CoMRel survey, April 2015.

This question referred to religion in general. Against the background of emerging political tensions over issues of immigration from Muslim countries and integration policies, a survey question explicitly asked whether Christianity, Judaism, and Islam are perceived as threats to national culture. The responses concerning Islam are shown in Figure 2.4.

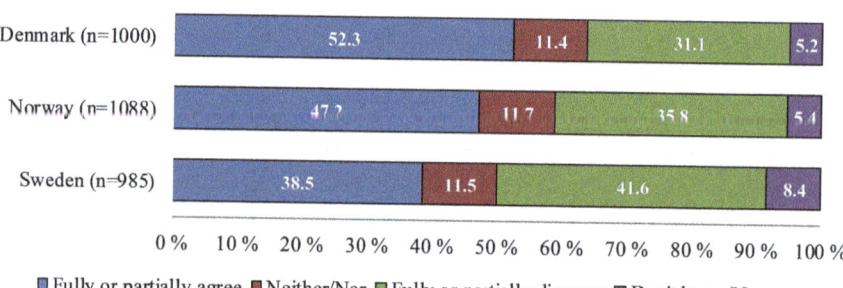

Figure 2.4 Do you consider Islam a threat to Danish/Norwegian/Swedish culture? Percentages. From CoMRel survey, April 2015.

As the figure shows, there are differences between the Scandinavian countries. About half of the Danes (52 percent) fully or partially agree that Islam is a threat to their culture. Among Norwegians, almost half (47 percent) agreed with the statement, while 38 percent of Swedish respondents see Islam as a threat to national culture. The differences regarding the other world religions is remarkable: only around 11 percent of all Scandinavians agreed that Judaism is a threat to their culture, and 6 to 8 percent that Christianity represents a threat.

The survey was taken a few months before the escalation of the war in Syria and the increasing number of refugees going to Scandinavia in the autumn of 2015. These events may subsequently have made the perception of Islam as a threat even more pronounced. Furthermore, the question did not include any specification of 'culture'. We thus do not know how individual respondents interpreted the term, or to what extent these attitudes are related to other opinions or actions. Finally, even though the results show a widespread negative sentiment towards Islam in all three countries, the population is divided over the issue. A third of Scandinavians disagree to some extent with the postulation that Islam poses a threat to national culture.

Following the escalation of media reports on Islamist terror and the general swing towards populism and nationalism in public discourse, one might expect a similar pattern of scepticism towards immigrants in general. The survey shows that between 13 and 18 percent of the respondents agree that hostile attitudes towards foreigners should be accepted in society. While a majority, then, of Scandinavians seem to oppose xenophobic attitudes, the countries differ also on this issue. Sixty percent of Danes, 67 percent of the Norwegians, and 73 percent of the Swedes answered that hostile attitudes to foreigners should not be tolerated. Figure 2.5 shows the need for a closer look at the relationship between the responses of those individuals who perceived Islam to be a threat to national culture and those who accept hostile attitudes against foreigners.

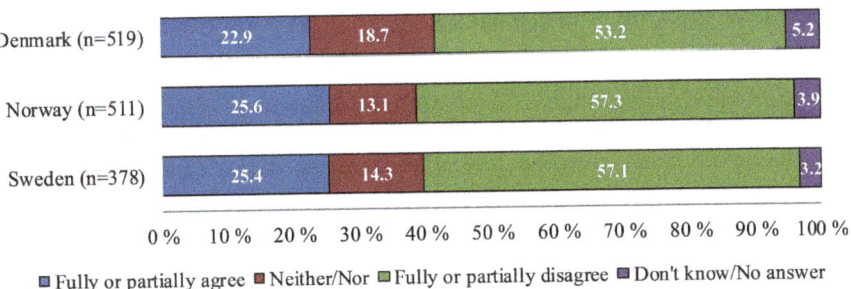

Figure 2.5 Agreement with the statement 'hostile attitudes towards foreigners should be accepted' among people considering Islam a threat to national culture. Percentages. From CoMRel survey, April 2015.

In all three countries, as Figure 2.5 shows, a majority of those who consider Islam a threat to national culture do *not* tolerate hostile attitudes against foreigners, while about a fourth of them tolerate such attitudes. If we look at the whole population in the Scandinavian countries, those who tolerate hostile attitudes against foreigners *and* are sceptical of Islam make up 10–12 percent of the population. This finding also raises the question of whether some of the respondents might interpret tolerance of hostile attitudes towards foreigners as part of an argument supporting freedom of expression, rather than a critique of other ethnic or religious groups *per se*. These findings underline the importance of further analysis of the relationship between attitudes that concern freedom of expression, freedom of religion, and tolerance of religious diversity. The present study did, however, not provide data to conduct this kind of analysis.

2.8 Patterns of Similarity and Difference

The general tendencies in the survey's findings, presented above, strengthen the image that, against the backdrop of high levels of secular–rational values among Scandinavian populations, religious diversity in the public sphere in Scandinavia is a topic on which opinions diverge, and which gives rise to tensions over cultural identity and common values (as suggested in Chapter 1). The similarities and differences between Danes, Norwegians, and Swedes in the survey show the need for a further discussion about how various factors of historical experiences and social stratification in Scandinavian societies play into the general tendencies. The World Values Survey shows that secular–rational values and self-expression values are more frequent among the younger generations, while traditional values and strong religiosity are more common among the older generations. High levels of self-expression values are also connected to the tolerance of foreigners and gender equality. This makes it relevant to ask how the main tendencies in the attitudes towards religion that are found in the survey differ with regard to age and religious self-identification, as well as gender.

In this last part of the chapter, we present an analysis of differences between the countries reported in the previous sections. The purpose of this analysis is to test and validate whether central findings from the descriptive analysis hold when we control for the effects of key independent variables, such as age, gender, political opinion, and religiosity. We focus on differences that are related to a number of issues from the survey's findings which concern attitudes to expressions of religious diversity in public spaces and to controversial issues regarding religion, such as religious extremism and intolerance.

2.9 Critique and Tolerance of Religion

We conducted regression analyses of five dependent variables. The variables in the regression analysis concern two groups of questions. The first set of questions are those that have been discussed on a general level in the previous sections, that is, questions concerning attitudes to Islam as a threat to national culture, tolerance for hostile attitudes against foreigners, and satire of religion as an expression of a critique against religion in public settings. For these variables we conducted multinomial regression analyses. Here, we focus on the general findings from the regression models. For detailed results and information on the variables included in the analysis, please see table A.2 in the Appendix.

The general finding of a widespread concern about Islam as a threat to national culture is qualified by our analysis. Of the different social factors included in the analysis, political orientation is associated with the strongest effect in terms of differences in attitudes. Individuals with a traditional/authoritarian orientation seem more inclined to agree with the statement, particularly if compared to those with a libertarian/post-materialist orientation, but also, to a certain extent, if compared to individuals holding a centrist position. Besides political orientation, there are statistically significant effects of gender and age. Men are more inclined to agree with the statement that Islam represents a threat than are women, and the older generations are also more inclined to agree than the younger ones. Finally, Danes and Norwegians are significantly more inclined than Swedes to regard Islam as a threat. The effect of religious self-identification is not statistically significant.

This pattern is, to a large extent, replicated with regard to responses to the statement about whether xenophobic attitudes should be tolerated. Individuals with a traditional/authoritarian political orientation are more likely to agree that such attitudes should be tolerated, while those identified as libertarian/post-materialist are more likely to disagree. The effect of gender is also statistically significant, with men being more likely to agree with the statement than are women. Again, Swedes are significantly more likely to disagree with the statement about tolerating xenophobic attitudes than are the Danes and Norwegians. Stronger religious self-identification and higher age are also associated with a higher likelihood of agreeing with the statement. However, these effects are far weaker than the effects of political orientation and gender.

The same patterns that show up in attitudes to Islam and to xenophobic statements also seem to be relevant to questions concerning tolerance of satire of religion in public discussions. The effects of gender and political orientation are particularly strong, with men, and individuals with a traditional/authoritarian political orientation, more inclined to agree that such expressions should be allowed in society. The effects of age, religious self-identification, and country are also statistically significant, but the associations are not as strong as are those of gender and political orientation.

2.10 Discussing News on Religion and Religious Extremism in the Media

As the core of this study concerns contestations of public expressions of religion in the media, the second set of questions referred to discussions of news about religious extremism in the media. The survey included a question about the frequency of discussing news coverage of religion and religious extremism. More than one-fourth of the respondents answered that they discuss news on religious extremism daily or weekly. The survey also shows that such discussions primarily take place in settings like the home, and with friends. These findings will be further discussed in Chapter 3. For the analysis in this chapter, we focus on how factors such as age, gender, political orientation, and religiosity affect the probability of discussion of religious extremism. For these variables, we conducted binomial logistic regression analyses. See Table A.3 in the Appendix for detailed results.

The previous sections show that concerns about increased religious diversity and how such concerns should be expressed in public discussions differ, in particular between respondents of different political orientation and gender, but also with a person's age, religiosity and country. Are there similar differences among the quarter of the respondents that discuss news on religious extremism daily or weekly?

The results show, firstly, that respondents with a high or moderate level of religious identification seem more inclined to discuss news about religious extremism with others. Turning to political orientation we see that individuals with traditional/authoritarian and liberal/post-materialist preferences are more likely to discuss news on religious extremism with others compared to individuals voting for centre parties. Gender also has a strong effect with regard to likelihood of discussing news on religious extremism with others and on the contexts where these discussions take place. Men seem more inclined than women to discuss news on religious extremism, and to discuss these issues in the workplace and on social media. Women prefer to discuss such issues in the family or among friends. Men also report higher participation in public debate on religion, for example by participating in debate in print and online

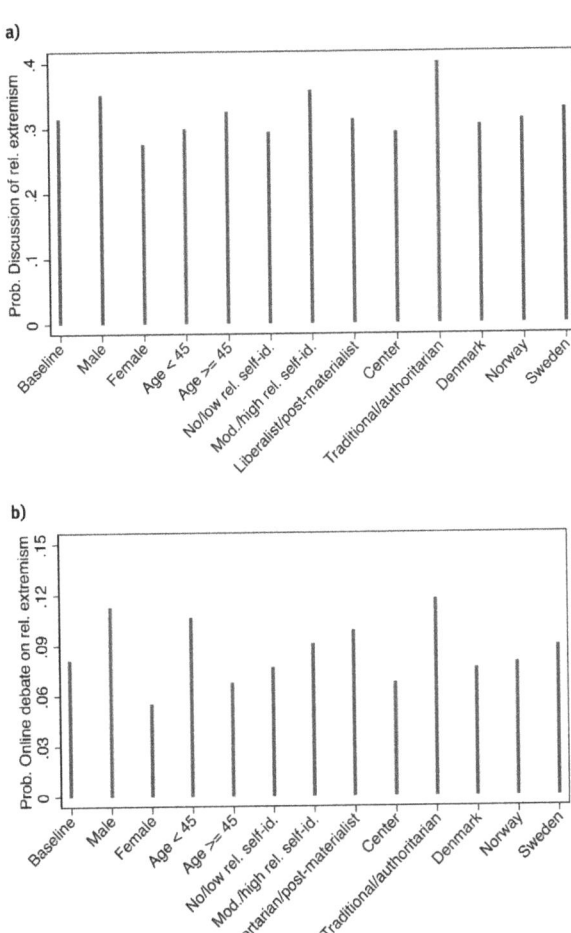

Figure 2.6 Influence of selected variables on discussions of news on religious extremism: Substantive effects. Based on the CoMRel survey, April 2015.

Notes: Baseline in the two graphs (a and b) refers to the predicted probability of participating in (a) a discussion of news on religious extremism and (b) an online debate on religious extremism when all independent variables are held at their mean values. The remaining pillars in each graph show how the probability of participating varies when we alter the value on each variable from 0 to 1 while holding the remaining independent variables constant at their mean values.

media. Men seem in general more critical of expressions of religion in public, especially Islam, and support critical coverage of Islam and Judaism in the media more than women do. Women appear to be more supportive of the statement that all religions should be respected. Finally, age has a strong effect when it comes to discussions of news on religious extremism online. Individuals younger than 45 are more inclined to discuss religion and religious extremism online than older generations.

2.11 Scandinavian Attitudes in European Comparison

The survey findings show that although Scandinavians in general have a weak personal connection to religion, Christianity still holds a privileged position as an expression of cultural identity. Scandinavians express support for equal rights to practice religion in general, but are doubtful towards public expressions of religion that grows when these are connected to public institutions and officials, and explicitly references Islam. A majority in all three countries equate religion with conflict and support media engagement in criticism of religion, but also wish that media would initiate dialogue about tensions over religious issues. More than a quarter of respondents discuss news about religion and religious extremism regularly. There is a widespread sentiment that Islam is a threat to national culture, even though most respondents state that they oppose the open expression of hostile attitudes towards foreigners.

Our analysis of differences related to various social factors indicates that political orientation and gender are salient factors in shaping diverging opinions towards toleration or scepticism of the public expression of religious diversity, and of how such opinions may be expressed in society. There are also differences across countries, where Danes and Norwegians seem more critical of public expressions of Islam than Swedes. These differences mirror to some extent historical and political differences between Scandinavian countries and social groups as discussed in Chapter 1, such as the prominence of right-wing political parties criticizing Islam in public debate.

To what extent do the general tendencies and differences emerging in our survey represent a particular Scandinavian pattern, or are Scandinavians rather becoming more like other European countries in attitudes to religious diversity? We compared the patterns emerging in our survey and similar questions asked in the 2014 European Social Survey (ESS)[8] in Denmark, Norway, Sweden, with four other Western European countries – Germany, the Netherlands, France, and the UK. The comparison confirms that the Scandinavian countries have the relatively

---

[8] The questions and variables used in the ESS 2014 study can be found at ESS online analysis module: http://nesstar.ess.nsd.uib.no/webview/ (Accessed 4 Aug, 2017).

fewest people who consider themselves very religious. Also, gender differences, especially in attitudes to ethnic and religious diversity, are rather more marked in Scandinavian countries than in the other countries. In Scandinavia as well as in the other countries chosen for comparison women score slightly higher than men on most measures of liberal/post-materialist values.

Individual Scandinavian countries have some outlier results in the ESS relevant to attitudes to mediatized conflicts involving religion. Sweden stands out (in 2014), for welcoming attitudes to Muslim migrants compared to a European average.[9] Norwegians rate their contact with people from other ethnic or racial groups less favourably than the European average.[10] Finally, Danish respondents give the most negative evaluation of laws against ethnic discrimination in the workplace, with 12 percent judging these 'extremely bad for the country', which is more than twice as high as anywhere else in Europe.

These differences between the Scandinavian countries belies the idea that Scandinavia represents a homogeneous cultural entity. Looking at the particular set of values asked about in the ESS 2014, individual Scandinavian countries are closer to other European countries than to each other on some items. Sweden is for example on several issues closer to Germany than to Denmark, which often comes out closer to the UK. This suggests that a variety of social and political factors are needed to explain attitudes to religious and cultural diversity. The differences between the countries should be related to different experiences of migration and institutional multiculturalism (Vertovec and Wessendorf 2010), combined with differences in the media representation of Islam and Muslims; certainly, recent studies point to a more negative media frame in Denmark than in Sweden (ECRI 2012; Lundby et al. 2018; see also Chapter 12), which may in turn reflect different recent histories. For example, experiences of crises such as the Muhammad cartoon affair have made the Danish debate about immigration and Islam somewhat more polarized than in other Scandinavian countries.

The CoMRel survey indicates that, within the group of respondents frequently discussing religion and religious extremism in the media, men are more inclined to engage in such discussions in public settings while women prefer private settings like family and friends. The ESS data support that women in Scandinavia seem to be more tolerant to religious diversity than men. Previous research points to the importance of exposure to other religious faiths, through

---

9 The ESS shows 37.6 percent of Swedes agreed with the statement 'allow many to come and live here' compared to a European average of 11 percent.
10 In Norway, 48 percent rate their contact at 7–10 on a scale from 1 'extremely bad' to 10 'extremely good' compared to a European average of 57 percent.

personal encounters and in communities, for tolerance of religious diversity (Smith 2007, 351). The ESS includes questions about frequency and quality of contact with people of other cultures.[11] There is no overall pattern across countries relating frequency of contact to gender. In quality of contact however, a clearer pattern emerges. More women rate quality of contact very positively (7 and above on a scale of 1–10) than men in the seven countries in our comparison (except Germany), though the differences are small.

Further studies are needed to shed more light on the relationship between people's attitudes to religious and cultural diversity in society, and their liberal/post-materialist or traditional-authoritarian political orientation and gender. Nevertheless, the general tendencies and differences revealed in our survey set the stage for how contestations over religion are played out in the media and how various individuals in the population engage with them. In this way, the survey findings provide an important contextualization for the case studies in the coming chapters of this book.

Bibliography

Bakker, Ryan, Erica Edwards, Liesbet Hooghe, Seth Jolly, Gary Marks, Jonathan Polk, Jan Rovny, Marco Steenbergen, and Milada Vachudova. 2015. "2014 Chapel Hill Expert Survey." Version 2015.1. Chapel Hill, NC: University of North Carolina, Chapel Hill. http://ches.web.unc.edu/

Davie, Grace. 2005. "The Changing Nature of Religion in Northern Europe: Some Implications for the Study of Welfare." In *Welfare and Religion: A Publication to Mark the Fifth Anniversary of the Uppsala Institute for Diaconal and Social Studies*, edited by Anders Bäckström, 133–144. Uppsala: Publications of the Uppsala Institute for Diaconal and Social Studies 10.

European Commission Against Racism and Intolerance (ECRI). 2012. Report on Denmark (fourth monitoring cycle). Strasbourg: ECRI Secretariat. https://www.coe.int/t/dghl/monitoring/ecri/Country by country/Denmark/DNK CBC IV 2012 025 ENG.pdf

Flanagan, Scott, and Aie-Rie Lee. 2003. "The New Politics, Culture Wars, and the Authoritarian–Liberal Democracies." *Comparative Political Studies* 36 (3): 235–270.

Gullestad, Marianne. 2002. "Invisible Fences: Egalitarianism, Nationalism and Racism." *Journal of the Royal Anthropological Institute* 8 (1): 45–63. DOI: 10.1111/1467-9655.00098.

Lundby Knut, Henrik Reintoft Christensen, Ann Kristin Gresaker, Mia Lövheim, Kati

---

[11] Questions about contact were phrased 'How often do you have any contact with people who are of a different race or ethnic group from most [country] people when you are out and about?' and 'Thinking about this contact, in general how bad or good is it?'. Answers given on a scale from 1 (extremely bad) to 10 (extremely good).

Niemelä, and Sofia Sjö – with Marcus Moberg and Árni Svanur Daníelsson. 2018. "Religion and the Media: Continuity, Complexity, and Mediatization." In *Religious Complexity in the Public Sphere: Comparing Nordic Countries*, edited by Inger Furseth, 193–249. Basingstoke: Palgrave MacMillian.

Lundby, Knut, Stig Hjarvard, Mia Lövheim, and Haakon H. Jernsletten. 2017. "Religion Between Politics and Media: Conflicting Attitudes to Islam in Scandinavia." *Journal of Religion in Europe* 10 (4): 437–456 (open access). DOI: 10.1163/18748929–01004005

Lundby, Knut, and Salve Jortveit. 2015. Dokumentasjon av CoMRel survey april 2015. [Documentation of the CoMRel survey April 2015]. Accessed 23 Aug 2017 http://www.hf.uio.no/imk/english/research/projects/comrel/survey.html

Lövheim, Mia, Jonas Lindberg, Pål Ketil Botvar, Henrik Reintoft Christensen, Kati Niemelä, and Anders Bäckström. 2018. "Religion on the Political Agenda." In *Religious Complexity in the Public Sphere: Comparing Nordic Countries*, edited by Inger Furseth, 137–191. Basingstoke: Palgrave MacMillian.

Smith, Buster. 2007. Attitudes Towards Religious Pluralism: Measurements and Consequences. *Social Compass* 54 (2): 333–353.

Trägårdh, Lars. 2011. "Rethinking the Position of Civil Society in the Nordic Social Contract: Social Trust and Radical Individualism." In *Nordic Civil Society at a Cross-Roads: Transforming the Popular Movement Tradition*, edited by Filip Wijkström and Annette Zimmer, 313–333. Baden-Baden: Nomos.

Vertovec, Steven, and Susanne Wessendorf (eds.). 2010. *The Multiculturalism Backlash: European Discourses and Practices*. London: Routledge.

Stig Hjarvard, Knut Lundby
Chapter 3
Understanding Media Dynamics

Abstract: Mass media and social media afford a communicative environment providing a horizon of orientation for citizens about conflicts relating to religion, and provide social actors with the tools to engage in such conflicts. Media may insert various dynamics into conflicts and may occasionally become actors themselves in contestations over religious issues. This chapter applies a typology that distinguishes among three different media dynamics: (1) media's ability to *amplify* the communication and the ramifications of the reported events, (2) how the world is represented, *framed*, in the media, and the ways in which the media bestow the communication of events with a certain narrative and dramaturgy and work as arenas for the *performative agency* of various involved actors, and (3) the various ways in which media as social and communicative environments come to *co-structure* communication and actions. The terror attack on the French satire magazine *Charlie Hebdo* is used as an illustrative example.

Keywords: media dynamics, framing, mediatization, mediatization of religion, Charlie Hebdo

In this chapter, we will provide a conceptual framework for understanding the active interplay between media, religion and society, with a special emphasis on the various media dynamics that come into play during social and cultural conflicts involving religion. The framework will also serve as a reference for the subsequent chapters' analyses of conflicts in mediatized religious environments.

3.1 Heated Debates

In March 2016, the Danish public service broadcaster TV2 aired a series of three documentary programs with the title *Mosques Behind the Veil*. Through the use of hidden camera and actors working undercover pretending to be Muslims who were seeking guidance from imams in eight different mosques, the documentary revealed that the advice given by some of the imams was in sharp contrast to existing Danish laws and norms: In some of the mosques, they were taught about Islamic rules for stoning and whipping, were encouraged to punish their children physically if they did not pray, and a woman was advised to stay with her violent husband and learned she could not deny him having sex with her. The documentary series spurred wide attention and discussion in other media about the problems of a 'parallel society' that is governed by religious rules and the series was the immediate cause of a political initiative to stop 'hate preachers' as these imams became labelled in the political agreement between a majority of the Danish political parties (Kirkeministeriet 2016).

The documentary series also met with severe criticism. Representatives of Muslim organizations and mosques accused TV2 of presenting a very biased picture of the practices of imams in Denmark, and for destroying years of work by the mosques in support of integration in Denmark (Westersø 2016). However, criticism also came from other quarters. The Danish talk radio station Radio24syv examined parts of the raw tape recordings and criticized TV2 for deliberately producing a much more one-sided picture of the imams' practices than the actual material had provided evidence for (Graversen 2016). When the documentary, a year later, was nominated for the prestigious award for Danish journalism, the Cavling Prize, it again met with severe criticism, this time from four university researchers. In a lengthy newspaper article, Suhr et al. (2017) raised eight questions to TV2 challenging the television station's account of the apparent misconduct of the imams in the mosques, for instance its use of undercover agents. In its present form, the researchers argued, the documentary was 'very one-sided and in several instances it directly misrepresented the circumstances'. Television documentaries using hidden camera and microphones have also created discussions about Islam in other Scandinavian countries, for instance, the documentary *The State of the Nation* (*Rikets tilstand*) from 2000, made by Norwegian TV2, about the circumcision of Muslim women in Norway, and the Swedish *Mission Investigation* (*Uppdrag granskning*) from 2012, made by SVT, about Swedish imams' advice to women about male suppression.

These cases not only bear witness to the heated public debates about Islam in Scandinavian countries, but also illustrate how various media are implicated, not only in reporting about these issues, but also in the very development of conflicts about religion. Danish TV2 not only tried to influence the public agenda, but also paved the way for political action, including new legislation that narrowed the freedom of speech for all religious actors and caused a change in public administrative and financial procedures regarding religious institutions. Media occasionally become active participants in such conflicts, for instance, by pursuing a particular agenda and by becoming the target of severe criticism. In short, the role of the media in the domain of religion has become a frequent public issue in itself, in this case, TV2's representation of reality became an important part of the dispute about Islam.

3.2 The Mediatization of Religion

The integral role of media in the interactions between religious actors and organizations and the wider culture and society has been subject to theoretical considerations within the framework of mediatization theory. Generally speaking, mediatization, as a concept, denotes the 'long-term interrelation processes between media change on the one hand and social and cultural change on the other' (Hepp, Hjarvard, and Lundby 2010, 223). Applying this framework to the institutional domain of religion, the mediatization of religion denotes the processes 'through which religious beliefs, agency, and symbols are becoming influenced by the workings of various media' (Hjarvard 2016, 8). Such changes take place at both a structural level, i.e. the interdependencies between institutional domains, such as religion, politics, and the media, and at the level of social interaction, i.e. the practices of individuals and organizations. For a series of studies on the mediatization of religion in the Nordic countries, see Hjarvard and Lövheim (2012).

In his study of historical mediatization processes in relation to the Protestant Church of Norway, Lundby points out that it still enjoyed a relatively autonomous position in the early 1970s, and also that vis-à-vis the public service broadcaster NRK, 'there was still such a respect in NRK towards the Christian tradition carried by the Church of Norway that very little media-adapted editing was applied to "religious programmes"' (Lundby 2016, 32). Gradually, the various Norwegian media, including NRK, acquired a more professional and independent stance towards religion, as well as towards other societal institutions, such as politics, and increasingly actors in the church and politics became dependent on the media as a resource for communicating with their constituencies. Following this, various media became an important source of information for the general population about religious issues, and public discussions about religious issues were increasingly influenced by the agenda of the news media, and only to a lesser extent the agenda of religious institutions. In order to gain public attention through the news media, religious issues should fit the media's news values, and frequently religion became an issue when religious communities appeared to be out of sync with the values of secular society, for instance, in relation to gender, sexual orientation, freedom of speech, etc. (Christensen 2012; Hjarvard 2013).

The proliferation of the Internet and various forms of portable, interactive, and online media, such as mobile phones and tablets, and the subsequent spread of social network media, such as Facebook and Twitter, have intensified and altered the media's influence. The traditional mass media have been supplemented by networked forms of communication that allow individuals and groups to engage with each other more directly. This has changed the conditions for social interaction: it has allowed official representatives of various religious communities (pastors, imams, etc.) to engage more directly with both their followers and the wider public, but it has also provided a new communications infrastructure giving the authority to both ordinary people and media celebrities to voice opinions about religion independently of traditional religious authorities (Clark 2011). The new media landscape has also altered the conditions for the public's engagement in political and religious conflicts. In their study of the role of various forms of digital media for mobilizing protest (for instance, the Occupy Movement) Bennett and Segerberg (2013) distinguish between collective action and connective action. The former concerns the traditional kind of protests organized by high-resource organizations, such as political parties and interest organizations. Connective action is, to a much lesser extent, or not at all, underpinned by formal organizations, and relies instead on crowd enabled networks of likeminded individuals who use various digital media to organize and communicate their protests.

Although social network media allow for individual and personal engagement, they also operate by collective and institutional logics. Dijck and Poell (2013) point to programmability, popularity, connectivity, and datafication as underlying logics, i.e. the norms, strategies, mechanisms, and economies of social network media that co-structure the interactions between people in them. In this way, social interaction becomes a hybrid social and technological phenomenon. The structuring influence of social network media on social interaction and opinion formation is reflected in the emergence of communicative 'filter bubbles' (Pariser 2011) and network patterns of 'polarized crowds' (Smith et al. 2014). We will return to such implications of the social network media for opinion formation and for citizens' willingness to discuss controversial issues, but first we need to specify some general media dynamics that are at play during various forms of conflict.

3.3 A Typology of Media Dynamics

In what follows, we will use mediatization theory as our point of departure from which to understand the influence of various media dynamics in social and cultural conflicts involving religion (Eskjær, Hjarvard and Mortensen 2015; see also Driessen et al. 2017). By using the word 'influences' in relation to the media we are explicitly avoiding the term 'media effects', i.e. the idea that media, at the level of individual messages, may have a definitive influence on audiences' opinion and behaviour. This may be the case under specific circumstances, but this is not our point of interest here. Our perspective is not primarily a question of dissemination, of spreading the 'message' but rather how the media environment conditions religious activity and influences religious representations. Our claim is at once more modest and more comprehensive. More modest, because we will not posit that media may have a determining influence on the outcome of social interaction, including opinion formation or the escalation or downscaling of conflicts. More comprehensive, because we locate the level of influence at a structural level, i.e. the mediatized social environment and the conditions it sets for human agency.

From the perspective of mediatization theory, the question about the influence of media on social interaction may more aptly be described as the ways in which the integration and presence of media in social and cultural domains come to condition, but not determine, the encounters between actors in everyday life. Media have been institutionalized in different contexts as resources of interaction. From the point of view of the individual actor, a person or organization, the media are the available tools that enable, limit, and structure communicative interaction in various ways. These conditions will certainly vary according to the media and social context in question, but at a more general level, we will in what follows suggest that these conditions insert certain dynamics into the way in which social interaction come to be spelled out, in our case, in relation to conflicts involving religion. These dynamics are, conceptually speaking, positioned at the intersection between mediatization and mediation processes. The dynamics are a result of the mediatized conditions, the institutional interdependencies between media, religion, and society, but they concern the way in which actual communicative interactions are performed and come to have a bearing on, for instance, political and religious affairs.

Following Hjarvard, Mortensen, and Eskjær (2015) we may discern three different media dynamics: (1) amplification, (2) framing and performative agency, and (3) co-structuring. This typology is inspired by a distinction by Meyrowitz (1993) on different metaphors of the media, each focusing on different aspects of their workings: (1) Considering the media as conduits draws our attention to the media's ability to influence the magnitude of communicative interactions; (2) looking at the media as languages addresses the media's formatting of meaning during conflicts; (3) and considering the media as an environment focuses our attention on the structural influences of the media environment, for instance, as regards access to communicative resources (see Table 3.1). In order to further specify the three dynamics, we will use the terror attack on the French satire magazine *Charlie Hebdo* as an illustrative example, since this major and tragic event encompassed all of these dynamics and may be more familiar to international readers than a national event in one of the Scandinavian countries. The case of *Charlie Hebdo* also contextualizes this book within a wider European setting.

Table 3.1 The influences of media dynamics in mediatized conflicts.

Media metaphor	Dynamics	Influence
Media as conduits	Amplification	Volume, speed, reach, level of involvement
Media as language	Framing and performative agency	Representation, performance, and dramaturgy
Media as environment	Co-structuring	Media practices both embedded in, and constitutive of, structural relations of power

Source: Hjarvard, Mortensen, and Eskjær (2015, 10)

3.4 Amplification

If we look at the media as conduits or channels of communication, an important dynamic of the media is their ability to *amplify* not only communication, but also the ramifications of the reported events. As such, it concerns the volume, speed, and reach of communication and the subsequent level of involvement by people. The violent attack on *Charlie Hebdo*'s editorial offices in Paris by two radical Islamists on 7 January 2015, clearly demonstrates this dynamic. The attack immediately became breaking news on a global scale. The subsequent police hunt for the perpetrators and the additional attack, and hostage crisis in a Jewish supermarket in Paris, were followed intensely by news media and on the social media in many countries, and the extremely high media attention helped to mobilize worldwide demonstrations to protest against terrorism and in support of *Charlie Hebdo* and free speech.

The target of the attack, the magazine *Charlie Hebdo*, also helped to amplify the event and the controversy: The first issue of *Charlie Hebdo* after the attack had a drawing of the Prophet Muhammad on the front page posing with a sign that said 'I am Charlie'. The magazine usually prints each issue in 60,000 copies, but this issue was printed in 7 million copies and it was distributed to numerous countries and translated into several languages (Stelter 2015). The worldwide attention to these happenings also created counter reactions to the Western media's reporting, in particular in the Arab and Muslim world. Here, the media coverage, demonstrations, and various political reactions, did not all follow the Western media's framing of the controversy as a question of terrorism, and in Turkey and Egypt authorities took various measures to ban and limit the distribution of the *Charlie Hebdo* drawing and of articles concerning the matter, in order to de-escalate the conflict within their countries, but they were only partly successful in this (Moore 2015; YaLibnan 2015). The global spread of the news of the happening re-contextualized the conflict and gave it many more interpretations. In the Philippines, for instance, Muslim demonstrators focused on *Charlie Hebdo* as the perpetrator due to its new depiction of the Prophet Muhammad on the cover of the magazine (Agence France-Presse 2015).

3.5 Framing and Performative Agency

The second media dynamic reflects the fact that the media are not neutral vehicles of information exchange, but involve a particular construction of the message in terms of meaning and aesthetics. In a metaphorical sense, the media are also languages through which the world is represented, *framed*, in particular ways at the same time as the media bestow the communication of events with a certain narrative and dramaturgy, and also work as arenas for the performative agency of various involved actors. In the case of the *Charlie Hebdo* attack, the Western news media almost unanimously framed the incident as a terrorist act against the freedom of expression, clearly supporting the official responses, not least, of Western-oriented governments. This framing of the attacks was, in a sense, over-determined by a series of existing and overarching frames that were developed in relation to similar attacks on freedom of speech, such as the death threats against the author Salman Rushdie, and the cartoonists of *Jyllands-Posten*'s Muhammad drawings.

'Framing', as a concept, has both psychological and sociological meanings, including cognitive, social, and normative dimensions. Within media studies Entman's (1993) definition of framing highlights the selection of aspects of a perceived reality and the salience these aspects are given; through these acts of selection and salience-giving, media come to promote a 'particular problem definition, causal interpretation, moral evaluation, and/or treatment recommendation' (ibid. 52). Following this perspective, we should not only pay attention to the manifest textual frames, but we must also consider 'framing' as sense-making *processes* that involve discursive struggles between competing frames, of which some may have a dominant position. As reflected in several of the studies in this book, the discursive couplings between 'terrorism' and 'Islam' seem to be a dominant aspect of the 'problem definition' in relation to Islam across class room settings, the news media, and social network media.

The various Western mass media were not only framing the *Charlie Hebdo* attack in particular ways, but were also actors in the conflict. As media, they aligned themselves with the magazine under attack and its defence of freedom of speech. On the day after the attack on *Charlie Hebdo,* many European newspapers had removed all traditional news coverage in favour of a more artistic statement expressing their contempt for the perpetrators and their support for free speech. Newspapers became demonstrators. The perpetrators also tried to use the mass media as a platform from which to express their own cause. Similarly to other terrorist attacks, it did not just aim to cause damage and fear among particular people, but also served to maximize media attention; as a terrorist act it also had a performative dimension, exploiting the mediatized condition of contemporary society (Cui and Rothenbuhler 2017). During the subsequent hostage crises in France, two of the terrorists phoned the French radio station BFM RMC to present their side of the story to a wider audience. The social network media also helped to dramatize the events. Not least during the police hunt after the perpetrators, social network media became not only the forums for discussion and the expression of feelings, but also tools for people who were trying to contribute to the hunt by collecting information about the perpetrators' whereabouts. Framing and performative agency are intertwined with each other. Using the media to perform in a particular way conveys the framing of the message with a certain authority. When a significant number of state leaders marched arm in arm in Paris in protest against the *Charlie Hebdo* attack, they were not only performing an act of protest that was reported by the news media, they were also giving authority to their own framing of the events, including their treatment recommendations, i.e. the policies to fight terrorism.

3.6 Co-Structuring

If we finally look at the media as social and communicative environments we can discern various ways in which media come to *co-structure* communication and actions. As mentioned above, the media may be understood as resources for interaction, but media resources are not evenly distributed though they are embedded within power relationships. The ability to influence the agenda of news media thus depends on your prominence as a news source, and, as many studies have demonstrated, political elites and other power holders in society typically have much easier access to the news media if compared to other sources. These power relationships are, for instance, conceptualized in the elite-driven media theory (Hallin 1986), and this may, in the present case, explain why the mainstream press in Europe was very strongly aligned with the mainstream political parties. These power relationships are, however, not set in stone, but may – depending on the specific circumstances and context – be challenged and circumvented by stakeholders who can acquire new legitimacy as sources. In the case of the magazine *Charlie Hebdo*, before the terrorist attack it had been considered a somewhat marginal and radical voice in the French media landscape, but because of the attack and the existing discursive fault lines around immigration and Islam, it emerged overnight as a privileged voice and a unifying symbol of French and European political forces that were rallying for freedom of speech, and for democracy in general.

If the mainstream journalistic media presented a rather unified voice during this conflict, other media allowed for a larger diversity of reactions to be heard. Internet-based blogs, websites and social network media, such as Twitter and Facebook, made it possible for laymen and less professional stakeholders to engage with the conflict. A variety of Muslim voices were heard on social network media, not only those expressing condemnation of the attack, but also those questioning why they, as Muslims, were expected to voice a particular excuse for such atrocities in which they had had no part. The structuring influence on who gets to have a voice was also spelled out through legal means. The French authorities were not at all happy with their level of information control during the hunt for the perpetrators. The declaration of martial law was a means with which to enforce their ability to also manage information flows.

3.7 Social Network Media, Participation, and Contentious Issues

Above we have tried to sketch out how the mediatized conditions of contemporary society introduce three general dynamics into the ways conflicts are spelled out. In addition to such general dynamics, we may also discern more specific patterns of influences from media. Recently, several studies in the USA (Hampton et al. 2014), Denmark (Kulturstyrelsen 2015), and Norway (Fladmoe and Steen-Johansen 2017) have examined how social network media may influence the ways that users engage with controversial issues in such media. These studies are methodologically fairly similar and provide empirical evidence for the existence of a 'spiral of silence' in relation to social network media. The 'spiral of silence' is a middle-range theory that was developed by Noelle-Neumann (1984), which suggested that citizens' willingness to participate in debates about controversial issues depends on their perception of the extent to which others share their opinion on the issue. If an individual person perceives her own argument to be in the minority, she will be less inclined to discuss the issue openly with others, and vice versa. At an aggregate level this implies that people sharing this perceived minority position will engage less in discussions and thereby their position will, overall, appear to be even more marginal. In this way, a spiral of silence is gradually making majority positions more pronounced and minority positions less pronounced. People perceiving themselves to be in the minority do not necessarily change their opinion on an issue, but they abstain from letting their voice be heard, and thus their argument will not carry weight in the debate.

The abovementioned studies examine citizens' willingness to use social network media for debate about controversial issues, as opposed to other contexts of communication, such as discussions in private at the dinner table, attending public meetings, and in public media. The controversial issues used as test examples differ in topic: the US study poses questions about Edward Snowden's revelation of national security information (Hampton et al. 2014), the Danish study concerns Denmark's participation in military warfare in foreign countries (Kulturstyrelsen 2015), and the Norwegian study uses the publishing of religious cartoons as its test case (Fladmoe and Steen-Johansen 2017). All three studies confirm that fewer citizens would prefer to discuss such controversial issues on the social network media, while they would be much more inclined to discuss them in more private and intimate settings. This is confirmed in our own survey from 2015. More than 1 in 4 Scandinavians said that they discuss news on religious extremism daily or weekly (see Chapter 2). This primarily takes place in closed circles, e.g. at home and with friends, as shown in Table 3.2.

An important factor is the extent to which people can anticipate whether or not their audience or co-discussants share their opinion on an issue. In private settings, citizens usually perceive other participants to have more similar views and they are more sure about other participants' viewpoints, i.e. the level of uncertainty about others' arguments is lower. The US and Danish studies also suggest that a higher level of uncertainty about others' opinions, not only perceptions of a majority against one's own viewpoint, may constrain participation in debates. The Norwegian study, furthermore, points to the fact that the general willingness to participate in such debates on social network media resembles the situation in relation to other public media, such as newspapers, radio, and television.

Table 3.2 In which contexts have you discussed news on religious extremism in the last 12 months? Percentages. From CoMRel survey, April 2015.

	Denmark	Norway	Sweden
At home with the family	66%	69%	63%
With friends	73%	70%	69%
At work or at school	49%	54%	51%
On social media (e.g. Facebook or Twitter)	9%	8%	9%
In the commentary fields of net newspapers, or in net discussion forums	2%	3%	4%
In church or other religious meeting places	3%	3%	3%
In cafés or similar locations	8%	13%	5%
N	816	953	857

Base: All of the respondents who had discussed news on religious extremism during the year before they were interviewed.

Social network media have been mentioned as possible venues for ordinary citizens' discussions about public issues in contrast to mass media's debates, which are often criticized for being populated by elite voices. It seems, however, that social network media, in practice, are not such a democratic venue for discussions about controversial issues. Social network media may allow for more voices to be heard, but they may – similarly to mass media – be prone to various dynamics that inhibit many people from debating controversial issues and that may reinforce the already existing divides between minorities and majorities, creating 'filter bubbles', etc. Perhaps a final lesson to be learned from these studies is that we cannot take the opinions articulated on the social network media as being representative of general public opinion, particularly not when it comes to controversial issues. The often fierce debates on social network media are not necessarily one of the voices of an otherwise silent majority, since many people abstain from taking part in debates here. Social network media may amplify certain viewpoints, but it is exactly the amplification of a particular framing of an issue that may cause other people to refrain from offering counter-framings.

3.8 Media Dynamics and Human Agency

As demonstrated in this chapter, media may insert various dynamics into conflicts and media may themselves sometimes become actors in contestations over religious issues. In these ways, media may condition conflicts about religious issues, but they neither determine the particular framings of the conflicts nor the outcomes. Instead, the media afford a communicative environment that provides an important horizon of orientation for citizens about these conflicts and provides partisan social actors with the tools to engage in such conflicts in order to push the public agenda in directions that are suitable to their standpoints, politically, religiously, or otherwise. As the following studies in this book also demonstrate, human actors are not just subject to the mediatized conditions of conflicts, but are, to some extent, also knowledgeable about the various media dynamics conditioning the framing of issues and the construction of public attention. This human reflexivity about the role of media has made the media into a kind of meta-issue in many conflicts: The very representation of religion in various media, the mass media as well as the social network media, has become a regular, sometimes even a dominant aspect of such conflicts. To engage with contentious issues in the public realm involves not only the use of media, but increasingly also an awareness of the various media dynamics that amplify or silence particular voices, that frame issues in particular ways, and that invest conflicts with a particular dramaturgy.

In conclusion: The framework on mediatized conflicts laid out above will prove useful and relevant in forthcoming chapters. Contested religion in media dynamics of cultural conflicts in Scandinavia could well be studied through media's amplification, their framing and performative agency, and through the co-structuring of communication and actions through the social environment.

Bibliography

Agence France-Presse. 2015. "Muslims in Philippines March Against *Charlie Hebdo*." *Daily Mail*, 14 Jan. Accessed 29 June 2017. http://www.dailymail.co.uk/wires/afp/article-2909953/Muslims-Philippines-march-against-Charlie-Hebdo.html.

Bennett, Lance W., and Alexandra Segerberg. 2013. *The Logic of Connective Action: Digital Media and the Personalization of Contentious Politics*. Cambridge: Cambridge University Press.

Clark, Lynn Schofield. 2011. "Religion and Authority in a Remix Culture: How a Late Night TV Host Became an Authority on Religion." In *Religion, Media and Culture: A Reader*, edited by Gordon Lynch, Jolyon Mitchell, and Anna Strhan, 111–121. London: Taylor and Francis.

Christensen, Henrik. 2012. "Mediatization, Deprivatization, and Vicarious Religion: Coverage of Religion And Homosexuality in the Scandinavian Mainstream Press." In *Mediatization and Religion: Nordic Perspectives*, edited by Stig Hjarvard and Mia Lövheim, 63–78. Gothenburg: Nordicom.

Cui, Xi, and Eric Rothenbuhler. 2017. "Communicating Terror: Mediatization and Ritualization." *Television & New Media*, online ahead of print 1–8. Accessed 20 June, 2017: DOI: 10.1177/1527476417715685.

Dijck, José van, and Thomas Poell. 2013. "Understanding Social Media Logic." *Media and Communication* 1 (1): 2–14.

Driessens, Olivier, Göran Bolin, Andreas Hepp, and Stig Hjarvard, eds. 2017. *Dynamics Of Mediatiztion. Institutional Change and Everyday Transformation in a Digital Age*. Basingtoke: Palgrave Macmillan.

Entman, Robert M. 1993. "Framing: Toward Clarification of a Fractured Paradigm." *Journal of Communication* 43 (4): 51–58.

Eskjær, Mikkel Fugl, Stig Hjarvard, and Mette Mortensen, eds. 2015. *The Dynamics of Mediatized Conflicts*. New York: Peter Lang.

Fladmoe, Audun, and Kari Steen-Johansen. 2017. "Willingness to Discuss the Publishing of Religious Cartoons. Spiral of Silence in the Private and Public Spheres," In *Boundary Struggle: Contestations of Free Speech in the Public Sphere*, edited by Arnfinn H. Midtbøen, Kari Steen-Johnsen, and Kjersti Thorbjørnsrud, 77–108. Oslo: Cappelen Damm (open access). https://press.nordicopenaccess.no/index.php/noasp/catalog/book/16

Graversen, Mathilde. 2016. "Lydfil rejser debat om udeladte oplysninger i TV 2s moské-dokumentar." [Sound file creates debate about omitted information in TV 2's mosque documentary]. *Berlingske*, 11 March. Accessed 29 June 2017. https://www.b.dk/nationalt/lydfil-rejser-debat-om-udeladte-oplysninger-i-tv-2s-moske-dokumentar.

Hallin, Daniel C. 1986. *The "Uncensored War": The Media and Vietnam*. New York: Oxford University Press.

Hampton, Keith N., Lee Rainie, Weixu Lu, Maria Dwyer, Inyoung Shin, and Kristen Purcell. 2014. "Social Media and the 'Spiral of Silence.'" *Pew Research Center, 26 Aug*. Accessed 29 June 2017. http://www.pewinternet.org/files/2014/08/PI_Social-networks-and-debate_082614.pdf.

Hepp, Andreas, Stig Hjarvard, and Knut Lundby. 2010. "Mediatization – Empirical Perspectives: An Introduction to a Special Issue." *Communications· The European Journal of Communication Research* 35 (3): 223–228.

Hjarvard, Stig. 2016. "Mediatization and the Changing Authority of Religion." *Media, Culture & Society* 38 (1): 8–17.

Hjarvard, Stig, and Mia Lövheim, eds. 2012. *Mediatization and Religion: Nordic Perspectives*. Gothenburg: Nordicom.

Hjarvard, Stig, Mette Mortensen, and Mikkel Fugl Eskjær. 2015. "Introduction: Three Dynamics of Mediatized Conflicts." In *The Dynamics of Mediatized Conflicts*, edited by Mikkel Fugl Eskjær, Stig Hjarvard, and Mette Mortensen, 1–27. New York: Peter Lang.

Kirkeministeriet. 2016. "Aftale mellem regeringen og Socialdemokraterne, Dansk Folkeparti og Det Konservative Folkeparti om initiativer rettet mod religiøse forkyndere, som søger at undergrave danske love og værdier og understøtte parallelle retsopfattelser." [Agreement between the government and the Social Democrats, the Danish People's

Party, and the Conservative People's Party about initiatives aimed against religious preachers who try to undermine Danish laws and values and support parallel conceptions of law]. *Kirkeministeriet,* 31 May. Accessed 29 June 2017. http://www.km.dk/fileadmin/share/kursus/Aftalepapir.pdf.

Kulturstyrelsen. 2015. "Sociale medier – brug, interesseområder og debatlyst." [Social media – usage, areas of interest and desire for debate]. *Agency for Culture and Palaces.* Accessed 29 June 2017. http://www.kulturstyrelsen.dk/mediernes-udvikling-2015/specialrapporter/.

Lundby, Knut. 2016. "Mediatization and Secularization: Transformations of Public Service Institutions – The Case of Norway." *Media, Culture & Society* 38 (1): 28–36.

Meyrowitz, Joshua. 1993. "Images of Media: Hidden Ferment – And Harmony – In The Field." *Journal of Communication* 43 (3): 55–66.

Moore, Kelvin. 2015. "How Middle East and North Africa Governments and Political Leaders Reacted to the *Charlie Hebdo* Attacks." *Almiraah,* 11 Jan. Accessed 29 June 2017. https://almiraah.wordpress.com/2015/01/11/how-middle-east-and-north-africa-governments-and-political-leaders-reacted-to-the-charlie-hebdo-attacks/.

Noelle-Neumann, Elisabeth. 1984. *The Spiral of Silence: Public Opinion – Our Social Skin.* Chicago: Chicago University Press.

Pariser, Eli. 2011. *The Filter Bubble: What the Internet is Hiding from You.* New York: Penguin.

Smith, Marc A., Lee Rainie, Itai Himelboim, and Ben, Shnediermann. 2014. "Mapping Twitter Topic Networks: From Polarized Crowds to Community Clusters." *Pew Research Center,* 20 Feb. Accessed 29 June 2017. http://www.pewinternet.org/files/2014/02/PIP_Mapping-Twitter-networks_022014.pdf.

Stelter, Brian. 2015. "*Charlie Hebdo* Now Printing 7 Million Copies." *BBC,* 17 Jan. Accessed 29 June 2017 http://money.cnn.com/2015/01/17/media/charlie-hebdo-seven-million/.

Suhr, Christian, Hjarn V. Zernichow Borberg, Kirstine Sinclair, and Niels Valdemar Vinding. 2017. "Cavling-nomineret dokumentar er unuanceret og meningsforvridende." *Politiken,* 3 Jan. http://politiken.dk/debat/kroniken/art5771535/Cavling-nomineret-dokumentar-er-unuanceret-og-meningsforvridende.

YaLibnan. 2015. "New *Charlie Hebdo* Cartoon Condemned in Muslim World." YaLibnan, 16 Jan. Accessed 29 June 2017. http://yalibnan.com/2015/01/16/new-charlie-hebdo-cartoon-condemned-in-muslim-world/.

Westersø, Rikke Struck. 2016. "Udmelding efter moské-dokumentar: Imamer fordømmer TV 2." [Statement after mosque documentary: imams condemn TV 2]. *TV2,* 13 March. Accessed 29 June 2017. http://nyheder.tv2.dk/samfund/2016-03-13-udmelding-efter-moske-dokumentar-imamer-fordoemmer-tv-2.

Mia Lövheim, Liv Ingeborg Lied
Chapter 4
Approaching Contested Religion

Abstract: Religion has become a matter of intensified public concern in contemporary Scandinavia, and the various media are the main arena in which Scandinavians encounter such controversies. Historically-rooted understandings of religion that are based on the Lutheran Church as both a public utility and cultural resource, and the secular state as the regulator of religious freedom and equality, have become re-articulated in newly emerging frames such as the politicization, culturalization and securitization of religion. This chapter presents the current volume's overall approach to religion in contemporary Scandinavia as a mediatized and contested social phenomenon. The chapter advocates a perspective from which ongoing contestations and negotiations among a larger spectrum of actors are explored through an application of both substantive and moderate social constructionist approaches to religion. The various applications and interplays of these approaches to religion may fruitfully contribute to the further development of the theory of the mediatization of religion.

Keywords: mediatized religion, contested religion, social constructionist approach, substantive definition, public sphere

In April 2016, the Swedish politician Yasri Kahn was interviewed on TV4 by a female reporter. At the end of the interview, he refrained from shaking her hand with reference to his values and upbringing, since such physical contact between men and women was considered to be 'very intimate'.[1] Kahn is a practicing Muslim and was, at the time, nominated for the national board of the Swedish Green Party. During the weeks that followed, the 'handshake affair' dominated both the Swedish media and political debate. At the core of the debate was the question of whether Kahn's refusal to shake hands with a woman could be seen as being an expression of gender discrimination and therefore incompatible with democratic values, or whether a liberal, pluralistic society should be able to tolerate a variety of ways of greeting and showing respect for other people. Khan referred to his action as a 'personal choice', but his Muslim faith and his position as a

---

1 Yasri Kahn, 'Nu lämnar jag alla mina uppdrag för Miljöpartiet' *Nyheter24*, 20 April, 2016, accessed 19 June 2017, http://nyheter24.se/debatt/840404-yasri-khan-nu-lamnar-jag-alla-mina-uppdrag-i-miljopartiet

OpenAccess. © 2018, Mia Lövheim, Liv Ingeborg Lied. [CC BY-NC-ND] This work is licensed under the Creative Commons Attribution-Non Commerical-NoDerivs 4.0 License.
https://doi.org/10.1515/9783110502060-009

leading politician quickly turned the discussion into a debate about the boundaries of the expression of religious beliefs in the public sphere.

This case illustrates how, during the first decades of the new millennium, religion has become a contested topic in public debates in Scandinavia, and how the media orchestrate tensions around the place of religion in the public realm. As the Swedish example aptly shows, it is when religious organizations or individuals 'assume, or try to assume, a public character, function, or role' (Casanova 2003, 111) that religion also becomes a matter of intensified public concern. In such cases, religion becomes a site for tensions between the values that are based on secular–humanistic ideals, such as gender equality, plurality, and freedom of religion, and religion as a carrier of cultural values in the Scandinavian countries.

This book explores how the media condition engagement with contested issues regarding the legitimate expressions of religion in Scandinavian public settings. The aim of this chapter is to discuss how such contestations can be approached, against the backdrop of theories about the public role of religion and on the mediatization of religion. On the basis of these discussions, the chapter presents an approach to analysing religion as a contested and mediatized social phenomenon.

4.1 State Church and Secularity: Models for Understanding Religion

The relationship of the Scandinavian populations to religion is shaped by a strong historical connection between the Lutheran Church and the state (see Chapter 1; Furseth 2018). The British sociologist Grace Davie (2015, 135) has argued that Scandinavian populations refer to the church as a 'public utility'. This notion seeks to capture the seemingly paradoxical situation that is expressed in our survey (see Chapter 2) of the low levels of religious self-identification combined with a strong cultural affiliation to Lutheran Christianity. As 'public utilities', churches are expected to perform public functions and social roles that are related to a religious faith that is recognized to some extent, but which is not actively practiced by the larger population (ibid.).

The notion of the church as a public utility can also be useful for understanding how Lutheran Christianity has acted as a model for the ways in which Scandinavians perceive religion in general, and also its place in society. Secularity, in the sense of a separation of state administration and the legal and political systems from the influence of religious dogmas and authorities, and of religion as personal faith that is expressed in private life and within particular religious communities, is a strong feature of modern Scandinavian societies (Furseth 2018; Lövheim et al. 2018). As described in Chapter 1, the state is, nevertheless, involved in regulation and the financial support of religion, belief, and worldview organizations (see Chapter 11), as well as in approving the curriculum for religious education (see Chapters 13 and 15). This model of a secular state that supports the Lutheran majority churches as public utilities still persists, despite being challenged by religious diversity and critiqued by humanist–atheist groups. This model further implies that Scandinavians typically rely on the state to legally balance religious freedom and the equality of all citizens with regard to private expressions of faith, as well as its public manifestations (Kühle et al. 2018).

4.2 Religion in Public Space: A Contested Issue

The conception of the Lutheran state church as a public utility, religious faith as expressed in personal life and certain organizational forms, and the secular state as a guarantee for religious freedom and equality, have become normative models that shape attitudes to, and controversies around, the growing religious diversity in Scandinavia. Our survey (see Chapter 2) shows that attitudes to religious diversity in public spaces are complex and that opinions differ depending on the various levels of public visibility and forms of religion (see Beckford 2015). A large majority, 70 percent, of Scandinavians agree that all religions should be respected, and more than 50 percent strongly or partially agree that all religious groups should be entitled to the same rights in society. It seems, however, as if this acceptance towards religious beliefs primarily refers to religion as an individual right or as a part of civil society. Previous studies show that a majority of Scandinavians are more sceptical towards the expression of religious arguments and symbols, for example, in politics (Lövheim et al. 2018). Our survey confirms this, since most Scandinavians accept the public visibility of religious symbols, such as a cross, church tower, and even signs showing the location of a mosque and minarets, but oppose the right of religious leaders to express their views in public. Expressions of Christianity are also more accepted than those relating to Islam, both among public servants and in public settings, including public service media.

4.3 Politicization, Culturalization, and Securitization of Religion

Recent studies show that references to religion have become more diversified and debates about religion have increased in Scandinavian media in the past decades (Niemelä and Christensen 2013; Lövheim and Linderman 2015; Døving and Kraft 2013). However, these debates tend to cluster around two issues in particular. The first concerns tensions between religious diversity and what are perceived as core social values, such as the rights of women, LGBTQ persons, and children. In the media, these issues have become linked emblematically to Islam and, to some extent, to conservative Christianity through topics such as the hijab, circumcision, and the rights of young people to choose life partners. The second issue concerns the legitimacy of various religious expressions, where some expressions become portrayed as being 'bad' or as 'pseudo' forms of religion. Such claims are typically made about Islam, but also about religious expressions in the New Age spectrum, particularly when religious and economic interests are assumed to overlap, and when key national traditions or institutions are challenged. Debates in the Norwegian context about the so-called 'Angel School' (Astarte Education/Soulspring) that was initiated by the Norwegian Princess, Märtha Louise, is an example of this (Døving and Kraft 2013).

These debates show how historical models of the role of religion in society have become re-articulated in response to new challenges. They are expressed in the increasing tendency to politicize religion in parliamentary debates, which started in the late 1990s (Lindberg 2014; Ivanescu 2010). In these debates, it is primarily the right-wing nationalist and populist parties that criticize Islam as a threat to security and to national identity, and thus mobilize Christianity in defence of cultural values. This use of religion to drive a political discussion about national values and identity can be seen as part of what Brubaker (2017) terms a shift from a nationalist to a 'civilizationist' position among nationalist–populist parties in Western Europe. Here, the traditional opposition between the 'people' and the 'elite' is combined with an opposition between 'the nation' and those groups that are characterized as threatening the nation, re-conceived in civilizational terms. While Islam becomes framed as a threat towards national culture, Christianity is framed as a cultural and civilizational identity, connected to modern, progressive, and liberal values, primarily those regarding gender and sexual identity. In this process, Christianity is selectively embraced 'not as a religion but as a civilizational identity, a matter of belonging rather than believing' (Brubaker 2017, 14). In a similar way, liberalism and secularism are selectively embraced and are used to legitimize 'our' way of life in opposition to Islam. Brubaker argues that the combination of Christianity and secular liberalism to construct and defend national identity is distinctive in Northern European debates (ibid.).

This use of religion to imagine the characteristics, as well as the boundaries, of national identity and values is also connected to a securitization of European public discourse, in which Islam, and Muslims in general, are framed as a potential threat to national security. This discourse has become established in the media following the 9/11 attack in New York (Flood 2012), and it is reinforced through frequent reports that connect Islam to social problems and political violence (see Knott et al. 2013; Niemelä and Christensen 2013; Hjelm 2015). Securitization, as a media discourse, is also shaped by a country's history of involvement in international conflicts and political debates on immigration and integration. In the contemporary Scandinavian situation, with experiences of migration and terror attacks in major cities, such frames become reactivated and mobilized, and contribute to negative portrayals of Islam as a threat to national security and culture in the media, as well as in political debates.

4.4 Media – A Major Site for Encountering Religion

In the Scandinavian countries religion can be seen as a mediatized phenomenon, in the sense that the various mass media have become the primary source of information about religious issues, rather than religious organizations (Lundby et al. 2018). This is one of the main arguments in the theory of mediatization as applied to religion (Hjarvard 2012, 2013; see Chapter 3). Hjarvard argues that in this process religious symbols also become disembedded from their traditional context, and they are circulated and reinterpreted according to the purpose of various media actors.

Our survey confirms that when asked about encounters with religion and belief, Scandinavians most frequently choose television and newspapers. Next in ranking come family, friends, and school or work. As the table below shows, the Internet and social media are less frequent sites; somewhat more than 10 percent encounter religion through these media. Churches and other religious sites are the least frequent options.

Table 4.1 Contexts for the encounter with, or information about, questions related to religion and belief. Percentages. From CoMRel survey, April 2015.

	Denmark		Norway		Sweden	
	Yes	No	Yes	No	Yes	No
In the family	26%	74%	30%	70%	38%	62%
Among friends	24%	76%	25%	75%	34%	66%
School or workplace	16%	84%	16%	84%	24%	76%
Through TV	33%	67%	36%	64%	40%	60%
Magazines (paper or digital)	29%	71%	35%	65%	37%	63%
Social media (Facebook, Twitter etc.)	10%	90%	14%	86%	17%	83%
Other websites	11%	89%	13%	87%	13%	87%
Radio	18%	82%	20%	80%	22%	78%
Church, mosque, other religious place	7%	93%	8%	92%	8%	92%
N	1006		1099		999	

The mediatization of religion, then, interacts with, and enhances, the processes of social and cultural change in which the meaning and legitimacy of religious beliefs, to a greater extent than before, become a matter for negotiation and contestation. This underlines a second aspect of mediatization, namely, that mediated accounts of religion provide a 'horizon' for communication and interaction about religion (Lundby 2013, 199). Such interactions take place between actors with varying interests, such as media producers, religious and belief organizations, but also political parties, enterprises, and individuals. This situation increases the possibility of tension between various, and perhaps conflicting, interests and values relating to the public role of religion. A further implication is that the processes of 'managing and producing consensus' in line with views that are consensually accepted by a particular audience, become more important (Clark 2012, 113).

4.5 Forms of Mediatized Religion

Stig Hjarvard (2012) has described three main forms of mediatized religion in contemporary society, and these are defined by the extent to which religious actors and the logics of various media genres shape the public visibility of religion:

- *Religious media* refers to media organizations and productions that are primarily controlled and performed by religious actors
- *Journalism on religion* refers to the ways that secular media, primarily news media, bring religion to the political public sphere
- *Banal religion* concerns the ways that various forms of entertainment media make religion visible in the cultural public sphere

Hjarvard's approach to mediatization starts from an institutional level and emphasizes the 'structuring influence of the media' for social interaction and meaning making (2014, 127). The implications of mediatization for changes in the significance of religion in society is a question of continuous debate (see Lövheim 2014). On the one hand, mediatization can contribute to secularization, in the sense that the public and collective role of religion as a social institution is weakened. On the other hand, new ways in which various forms of media increasingly make religion visible in late modern society can also be interpreted as a re-enchantment of the media, as increased agency for religious actors, and as the production of new tools for religious creativity in media audiences. Studies of religious change in contemporary society show that, in order to grasp this spectrum of the various outcomes of mediatization for individual and collective forms of religion, the theory needs to be based on an understanding of religion that recognizes new varieties of institutionalized forms and aspects that go beyond cognitive belief (Lövheim 2011; Lied 2012). A salient part of this criticism concerns the way that the concept of 'banal religion' might reinforce the hierarchies of religious expressions in society in regard to what qualifies as 'proper' or 'pseudo-' religion (Axelson 2015; Kraft 2017).

These debates show that a more nuanced grasp of contemporary religion and its complexities, as well as a more dynamic approach to the interplay between media development and religious change, is needed. This implies events where increased engagement with religion can lead to changes within media forms and genres (Lövheim and Axner 2014, 43). Siv Ellen Kraft (2017) argues that phenomena that are categorized as 'banal religion' are New Age plots and storylines that are taken over by the media, rather than the media production of religion. Another example is how the increasing use of religion in debating political issues in editorials and columns contributes to the challenging of a strict secularist discourse that separates religion and politics in the media (Lövheim 2017). By using and discussing various forms of mediatized religion, this book is part of an ongoing process in developing the theory of a mediatization of religion (Hjarvard and Lövheim 2012; Lundby 2013).

4.6 A Combined Analytical Approach

In a review of current research on the increased visibility of religion in western societies, Titus Hjelm (2015, 8) points to the risks of confusing visibility and debate over religion – as portrayed in, for example, the media – with an increasing importance of religion among individuals, or of religious organizations in society. The mediatization of religion implies that the contemporary media supply people with symbolic resources for individual meaning making, as well as for collective conflicts relating to religion. In this book, our focus is to study *interactions* with representations of religion in the media among various publics, how various media enable and structure these interactions, and how these interactions relate to a larger debate about the place of religion in Scandinavian societies. It is, however, not to evaluate how mediatized religion affects individual beliefs or particular religious organizations.

Our focus on interactions with the public and mediatized expressions of religion requires an approach to religion that is able to capture an interplay between previously established, institutionalized forms of religion and challenges to the meaning and legitimacy of these forms that increased mediatization brings, in the form of contestation and negotiation among a larger spectrum of actors. As discussed in the previous section, a definition of religion that privileges certain historical institutional forms of, primarily, Christianity, is too narrow to account for this interplay alone. Likewise, a 'culturalist' ethnographically inspired approach to religion as any form of meaning making that 'moves beyond the mundane to the level of particular significance' (Hoover 2006, 23) makes it difficult to differentiate between various forms of meaning making, and to account for how institutional forms of religion inform such interactions (Hjarvard 2011; Lövheim 2014).

A way to meet the analytical challenge of analysing how the mediatized visibility of religion informs interactions in various public settings that are explored in this book, is to combine two interrelated approaches to religion. Previous studies of changes in the public visibility of religion on an institutional level in the Scandinavian countries have used the classical, substantive definition of religion that is offered by Michael Hill (see Furseth 2018):

> The set of beliefs which postulate and seek to regulate the distinction between an empirical reality and a related and significant supra-empirical segment of reality; the language and symbols which are used in relation to this distinction; and the activities and institutions which are connected with its regulation. (Hill 1973, 42–43)

This kind of definition specifies religion to be a particular form of meaning making that is expressed in beliefs, language, and symbols that concern a 'supra-empirical segment of reality'. Furthermore, it specifies that religion is expressed in social 'activities and institutions', such as churches, mosques, prayer, or the wearing of a hijab. For the present discussion, this kind of definition serves the purpose of identifying when certain institutionalized forms of religion emerge in the public debate, and how these become reinforced or challenged in these interactions. As the following case studies show, media producers and audiences in mediated contestations of religion in Scandinavia often refer to particular discursive and social forms of religion, such as fundamentalism, Islam, or the Lutheran Church. A substantive definition is useful in identifying such forms through words, symbols, images, and claims that refer to a transcendent or supra-empirical dimension. Furthermore, such a definition is useful in identifying actors that claim to represent, or become associated with, particular social forms of religion, such as Christian, Muslim or interfaith organizations (see Chapters 11 and 12).

The substantive approach to religion is, however, less useful for analysing how religion becomes contested in social interactions. References to Christian values or Muslim practices in political debates or in populist arguments for a civilizationist position can take a substantive form, as in explicit references to particular organized forms of religion, such as the Islamic extremist group ISIS or the symbol of the Christian cross. 'Common sense' references to religion that circulate in conversations at the workplace or among friends and family can also refer to substantive elements albeit in a more implicit or general form. However, the meaning of these references cannot be decided solely on the basis of a substantive definition of religion. As the survey findings indicate, Scandinavian respondents may discuss mediatized representations of Islam as a way of articulating sentiments of a threat to national culture, rather than a concern with beliefs in transcendent beings, or the meaning of certain practices.

Several studies in this book analyse such situations, where symbols, traditions, practices, and artefacts *are given* meaning as being 'religious' through various uses, contestations, and negotiations, and how social identities and relations are formed from such interactions. In order to analyse such interactions, a definition that focuses on the substance of religion must be combined with an approach that focuses on the meaning and role given to religion, when this term is used in a particular situation of social interaction.

Birgit Meyer and Annelies Moors, in their introduction to the book *Religion, Media, and the Public Sphere,* argue that religion needs to be studied as 'practices of mediation' that 'claim to mediate the transcendental, spiritual, or supernatural and make these accessible for believers' (2006, 7). By emphasizing the practices of mediation this brings into focus that the meaning and legitimacy of certain forms of religion is an outcome of how – through different material forms and practices – it is mediated. This approach thus makes mediation an intrinsic part of what constitutes religion.

Approaching religion as an intrinsically mediated phenomenon has many parallels to James Beckford's social constructionist[2] approach to religion (2003: 3). Beckford starts from the deregulation of religion in advanced industrial societies, where religion has come 'adrift from its former points of anchorage but is no less potentially powerful as a result' (Beckford 1989, 170). His conclusion is not that historical, institutionalized forms of religion lose significance in this situation, but that such expressions of religion remain a 'potent cultural resource or form which may act as the vehicle of change, challenge or conservation' (ibid.). However, the meaning and function of such expressions of religion in society have become more contested, and therefore less predictable. Fitting with the focus in this book on how religious meaning and authority, through mediatization, become contested, Beckford argues that questions about what religion is, and about its place in society, become a '"site" where boundary disputes are endemic and where well-entrenched interest groups are prepared to defend their definition of religion against opponents' (2003, 13; see Hjelm 2015, 10).

This kind of social constructionist approach underlines that the meanings of religious beliefs and practices, the ways in which they claim to mediate the transcendent and regulate social relations, is subject to change through processes of social interaction. Previously institutionalized or 'sedimented' meanings associated with religion in a society constitute 'authoritative guides not only to usage of the term but also to social action' (Beckford 2003, 4). Nevertheless, new ways of using such forms, and disputes about their proper use and meaning, also mean that they are changing. In this way, the meaning of religion is not fixed, but is constructed in particular social settings, in negotiations between various meanings and interests that are articulated by religious authorities, actors in media, voluntary organizations, teachers, and politicians. The task of researching religion from such an approach thus becomes to 'analyse the processes whereby the meaning of religion is, in various situations, intuited, asserted, doubted,

---

[2] The terms social 'constructionism' and 'constructivism' for conceptualizing human construction of meaning in modern society are used in various ways in literature. In choosing the term 'social constructionist' we emphasize the importance of social interaction and material aspects for the construction of meaning rather than focusing on individual cognitive processes (see Hjelm 2014:6–7). Couldry and Hepp (2017:21) uses the term 'social constructivism' but argues in a similar manner for the significance of social and material aspects in order to understand the role of the media in the social construction of reality.

challenged, rejected, substituted, re-cast, and so on' (ibid., 3). The emphasis on relations of power and material conditions in particular situations of social interaction also means that the strength of various constructions, in terms of their implications for structuring individual perceptions and actions, varies and needs to be part of the analysis.

4.7 Studying Contested and Mediatized Religion

The case studies in this book approach religion through the combined analytical approach outlined in this chapter in various ways depending on the authors' disciplinary perspective, empirical material, and level of analysis. In this way, the book as a whole captures various aspects of how religious expressions in public spaces become thematized and enacted through the media as objects of conflict, or as resources to handle social and cultural tensions.

The following chapters analyse how particular religious organizations and practices become represented in the media, and situations where symbols connected to a certain religious tradition, such as the Muslim hijab or the Christian cross, become the subject of contestation in social interactions. Chapters 7, 8, and 10, discuss questions as to how particular media affordances in public service media and local newspapers influence the ways in which religion is represented in the public realm; this includes the representation of religion through certain frames, the selection of actors for representing various claims, and the strategies that are used to present alternative images of religion.

In other chapters, the combined analytical approach to religion is used to study settings in which mass mediated representations of religion become objects of contestation, negotiation, and reinterpretation in situations of social interaction, such as social media (Chapter 6), classrooms (Chapters 14 and 15), and local civic settings (Chapters 11 and 12). Here, the authors analyse assumptions and discussions *about* religion and religious people, and social relations and positions formed *on the basis of various understandings of religion*, for example, where 'religion' is used to articulate 'common' values among and differences between various social groups in society.

The interplay between a substantive and a social constructionist approach to 'religion' that is proposed here can, through these various applications, be fruitful in developing the theory of the mediatization of religion. It aligns with the discussion around how to relate an institutional and a social constructionist tradition in mediatization theory through a common focus on social interaction and media's role in the communicative construction of socio-cultural reality (see Lundby 2013, 196, 200; Couldry and Hepp 2017). The social constructionist perspective emphasizes that forms of mediatized religion – such as journalism on religion, religious media, and banal religion – need to be approached as continuous and always (re-)situated processes. While recognizing media as an important agent in the shaping of such expressions of religion, it shifts attention to the process of the continuous reshaping and reinterpretation of such expressions – in which a variety of actors take part – as they circulate and are engaged in new environments. By focusing on how religion is given meaning in social interaction, we can also refine the theory on the mediatization of religion in relation to the role that media users play in the communication dynamic.

Finally, an analysis of mediatized religion that combines a substantive and a social constructionist approach may contribute to the discussion about the visibility and significance of religion in the public sphere. The heightened visibility of religion in the media means that religion becomes 'more visible, present and hence available for mobilization, contestation and criticism in the public sphere' (Herbert 2011, 627). Approaching religion through a combined focus on institutional forms and the contestation of these in mediatized situations of social interaction can enable a better understanding of when, how, and with what implications such processes unfold in contemporary Scandinavia.

Bibliography

Axelson, Tomas. 2015. "Vernacular Meaning Making: Examples of Narrative Impact in Fiction Film Questioning the 'Banal' Notion in Mediatization of Religion Theory." *Nordicom Review* 36 (2): 143–56.

Beckford, James A. 1989. *Religion and Advanced Industrial Society.* London: Unwin Hyman.

Beckford, James A. 2003. *Social Theory and Religion.* Cambridge: Cambridge University Press.

Beckford, James A. 2015. "Re-thinking Religious Pluralism." In *Religious Pluralism: Framing Religious Diversity in the Contemporary World,* edited by Guiseppe Giordan and Enzo Pace, 15–29. London: Springer.

Brubaker, Rogers. 2017. "Between Nationalism and Civilizationism: The European Populist Moment in Comparative Perspective." *Ethnic and Racial Studies* 40 (8): 1191–1226.

Casanova, José. 2003. "What Is a Public Religion?" In *Religion Returns to the Public Square: Faith and Policy in America,* edited by Hugh Heclo and Wilfred M. McClay, 111–139. Baltimore, MD: Johns Hopkins University Press.

Clark, Lynn S. 2012. "Religion and Authority in a Remix Culture: How a Late Night TV Host Became an Authority on Religion." In *Religion, Media and Culture: A Reader,* edited by Gordon Lynch, Jolyon Mitchell, and Anna Strhan, 111–119. London and New York: Routledge.

Couldry, Nick, and Andreas Hepp. 2017. *The Mediated Construction of Reality.* Cambridge: Polity Press.

Davie, Grace. 2015. *Religion in Britain: A Persistent Paradox.* 2nd ed. London: John Wiley & Sons, Ltd.

Døving, Cora A., and Siv Ellen Kraft. 2013. *Religion i pressen*. [Religion in the press]. Oslo: Universitetsforlaget.
Flood, Christopher. 2012. *Islam, Security and Television News*. Basingstoke: Palgrave Macmillan.
Furseth, Inger, ed. 2018. *Religious Complexity in the Public Sphere: Comparing Nordic Countries*. Basingstoke: Palgrave MacMillian.
Herbert, David 2011. "Why Has Religion Gone Public Again? Towards a Theory of Media and Religious Re-Publicization." In *Media, Religion, Culture: A Reader*, edited by Gordon Lynch, Jolyon Mitchell and Anna Strhan, 89–97. London and New York: Routledge.
Hill, Michael. 1973. *A Sociology of Religion*. London: Heinemann.
Hjarvard, Stig. 2011. "The Mediatisation of Religion: Theorising Religion, Media and Social Change." *Culture and Religion* 12 (2): 119–135.
Hjarvard, Stig. 2012. "Three Forms of Mediated Religion: Changing the Public Face of Religion." In *Mediatization and Religion: Nordic Perspectives*, edited by Stig Hjarvard and Mia Lövheim, 21–44. Gothenburg: Nordicom.
Hjarvard, Stig. 2013. *The Mediatization of Culture and Society*. London and New York: Routledge.
Hjarvard, Stig. 2014. "From Mediation to Mediatization: The Institutionalization of New Media." In *Mediatized Worlds*, edited by Andreas Hepp and Friedrich Krotz, 123–139. New York: Palgrave/Macmillan.
Hjarvard, Stig, and Mia Lövheim, eds. 2012. *Mediatization and Religion: Nordic Perspectives*. Gothenburg: Nordicom.
Hjelm, Titus. 2014. *Social Constructionisms: Approaches to the Study of the Human World*. Basinstoke: Palgrave/Macmillan.
Hjelm, Titus. 2015. "Is God Back? Reconsidering the New Visibility of Religion." In *Is God Back? Reconsidering the New Visibility of Religion*, edited by Titus Hjelm, 1–16. London: Bloomsbury.
Hoover, Stewart M. 2006. *Religion in the Media Age*. New York: Routledge.
Ivanescu, Carolina. 2010. "Politicised Religion and the Religionisation of Politics." *Culture and Religion* 11 (4): 309–325.
Knott, Kim, Elizabeth Poole, and Teemu Taira. 2013. *Media Portrayals of Religion and the Secular Sacred: Representation and Change*. Farnham: Ashgate
Kraft, Siv Ellen. 2017. "Bad, Banal and Basic: New Age in the Norwegian News Press and Entertainment Media." In *New Age in Norway*, edited by Ingvild S. Gilhus, Siv Ellen Kraft, and James R. Lewis, 65–78. London: Equinox.
Kühle, Lene, Ulla Schmidt, Brian Arly Jacobsen, and Per Petterson. 2018. "Religion and State: Complexity in Change." In *Religious Complexity in the Public Sphere: Comparing Nordic Countries*, edited by Inger Furseth, 81–135. Basingstoke: Palgrave.
Lied, Liv Ingeborg. 2012. "Religious Change and Popular Culture: With a Nod to the Mediatization of Religion Debate." In *Mediatization and Religion: Nordic Perspectives*, edited by Stig Hjarvard and Mia Lövheim, 183–201. Gothenburg: Nordicom.
Lindberg, Jonas. 2014. "Politicisation of Religion in Nordic Parliamentary Debates 1988–2009." *Politics, Religion and Ideology* 15 (4): 565–582.
Lundby Knut, Henrik Reintoft Christensen, Ann Kristin Gresaker, Mia Lövheim, Kati Niemelä, and Sofia Sjö – with Marcus Moberg and Árni Svanur Daníelsson. 2018. "Religion and the Media: Continuity, Complexity, and Mediatization." In *Religious Complexity in the

Public Sphere: Comparing Nordic Countries, edited by Inger Furseth, 193–249. Basingstoke: Palgrave MacMillian.
Lundby, Knut. 2013. "Media and Transformations of Religion." In *Religion Across Media. From Early Antiquity to Late Modernity*, edited by Knut Lundby, 185–202. New York: Peter Lang.
Lövheim, Mia. 2011. "Mediatisation of Religion: A Critical Appraisal." *Culture and Religion* 12 (2): 153–166.
Lövheim, Mia. 2014. "Mediatization and Religion." In *Mediatization of Communication*, edited by Knut Lundby, 547–571. Handbooks of Communication Science 21. Berlin: De Gruyter Mouton.
Lövheim, Mia. 2017. "Religion, Mediatization and 'Complementary Learning Processes' in Swedish Editorials." *Journal of Religion in Europe* 10 (4): 366–383.
Lövheim Mia, and Marta Axner. 2014. "Mediatised Religion and Public Spheres: Current Approaches and New Questions." In *Religion, Media, and Social Change*, edited by Kennet Granholm, Marcus Moberg, and Sofia Sjö, 38–53. London & New York: Routledge.
Lövheim, Mia, and Alf Linderman. 2015. "Religion, Media, and Modernity: Editorials and Religion in Swedish Daily Press." In *Is God Back? Reconsidering the New Visibility of Religion*, edited by Titus Hjelm, 32–45. London: Bloomsbury.
Lövheim, Mia, Jonas Lindberg Pål Ketil Botvar, Henrik Reintoft Christensen, Kati Niemelä, and Anders Bäckström. 2018. "Religion on the Political Agenda." In *Religious Complexity in the Public Sphere: Comparing Nordic Countries*, edited by Inger Furseth, 137–191. Basingstoke: Palgrave MacMillian.
Meyer, Birgit, and Annelies Moors. 2006. "Introduction." In *Religion, Media, and the Public Sphere*, edited by Birgit Meyer and Annelies Moors, 1–25. Bloomington, IN: Indiana University Press.
Niemelä, Kati, and Henrik Reintoft Christensen. 2013. "Religion in the Newspapers in the Nordic Countries 1988–2008." *Nordic Journal of Religion and Society* 26 (1): 5–24.

Part II: **Controversies**

Public Service Media

Knut Lundby, Stig Hjarvard, Mia Lövheim, Mona Abdel-Fadil
Chapter 5
Perspectives: Cross-Pressures on Public Service Media

Abstract: Through online services, the Scandinavian public service broadcasters have managed to retain strong positions as public service media (PSM) among the audiences in Denmark, Norway, and Sweden. Social and political changes in the Scandinavian populations influence the ways PSM involve themselves in conflicts that relate to religion. The growing cultural and religious diversity of the Scandinavian countries, along with digitalization and commercialization, shape PSM publics with varying, and perhaps conflicting, interests and needs. This has put the PSM under political pressure to alter their programming. On the one hand, their obligation to provide a common, and perhaps even a unifying, public space for the whole nation, in some cases, has become more pronounced. On the other hand, they are encouraged to take into account the multiplicity of voices and subcultures that exist among their audiences and users.

Keywords: public service media, radio, television, religion, culture

Public service media (PSM) occupy a strong position in the Scandinavian countries and they continue to play important roles in the dissemination of information and discussions about issues of public interest and contestation involving religion. In some cases, PSM may become the subject of such conflicts when controversies develop around the representation of religion. Our empirical analyses concerning the roles of PSM in such conflicts are spelled out in detail in the subsequent three chapters, with a case study from each of the three countries.

'Public service media' are national 'broadcasting' corporations that have developed a presence on the Internet alongside 'linear' radio and television transmissions. PSM companies may be commercially or publicly funded. In both cases, they have a public mandate that is derived from the national parliaments, and they report their activity to national bodies.

The purpose of this chapter is threefold. Firstly, we will characterize the historical origins and institutional contexts of the present Scandinavian public service organizations and their obligations, and compare these to other media systems. Secondly, we consider the contemporary challenges that PSM face in view of both a changing media environment and a more diverse population, in terms of religion and culture. Thirdly, we provide a framework for the case studies (in Chapters 6, 7, and 8).

5.1 Historical Origin and Institutional Context

Although media with public service obligations may be found in many countries around the globe, they clearly have a different and more prominent position in the media systems in Scandinavia compared with, for instance, the role of the public service media in the US or Eastern Europe. In contrast to countries where PSM play minor roles, PSM programmes have historically been utilized by a majority of the populations in Scandinavia. Although there today is competition with other providers, public service radio and television still hold a strong position in the national media landscapes. The historical, institutional, and political contexts of PSM in Scandinavia are important to consider in order to understand the possibilities and dilemmas that public service media face when political, social, and cultural conflicts are increasingly interpreted through religious frames.

The PSM in Scandinavia are the continuation of state-owned corporations under specific broadcasting guidelines and policies that are monitored by bodies appointed by the governments. In effect, there was a radio and television monopoly in all three Scandinavian countries until the latter part of the 20th century. Following digitalization and the spread of the Internet, these corporations have expanded their public service activities to most digital media platforms, for instance, computers, tablets, and mobile phones. The public service broadcasting corporations in Scandinavia have thus moved from PSB, public service broadcasting, to PSM, public service media (Lowe and Bardoel 2007), as these corporations now operate on cross-media platforms (Carpentier, Schrøder, and Hallett 2014). The Scandinavian corporations were ahead with these developments. We apply the term PSM to the multi-platform services that emanate from the established 'broadcasting' corporations.

PSB in Scandinavia was inspired by the BBC, which was developed in Britain in the 1920s by the first General Director, John Reith. The BBC was founded on the idea that it should not be for-profit, like the private radio companies in the US, nor should it be directly state controlled, as was the case in authoritarian regimes, such as the Soviet Union. Public service also meant national coverage and a national monopoly (Briggs 1995). This was during the early days of radio. Reith considered religious programming to be part of the public service mission and put religion under the national public service monopoly. He introduced religious talks and the broadcast of church services on Sundays, but kept a tight grip on them. Speakers had to submit their manuscripts to the BBC in advance. The senior clergy were sceptical, as they found the broadcasting of church services to be an invasion of a secular body into a theological domain. Reith answered by developing a church service designed and delivered specifically for radio which became very popular among the audience, but which was contested by the leaders of various religious groups (Wolfe 1984, 3–17). In the BBC's editorial shaping of religious rituals and messages, an early mediatization of religion (see Chapter 4) can thus be observed.

Since the inception of the BBC, the meaning of the concept of 'public service' has changed over time. It has been applied in relation to shifting policy purposes on the role of broadcasting in society, or for various ideological stances. The distinction between American and Scandinavian radio was continued when television was introduced (Linderman 1993). There has been a sliding away from Reith's sense of 'public service' as a public utility, to one where broadcasting is carried out in the service of the public sphere and, further, to broadcasting in the service of the individual listener or viewer (Syvertsen 1999). This latter meaning of the term is strengthened by the intensified commercialization and the many media user options that are given by digitalization, and by the general individualization of society.

5.2 The PSM Companies in Scandinavia

It is typically the former monopolies and publicly owned PSM corporations that are listed as 'public service' entities in scholarly works (Syvertsen et al. 2014; Hujanen, Weibull, and Harrie 2013). However, it is reasonable to include commercial corporations with a government-issued mandate and public service obligations.

Denmark's TV2 has public service obligations for both its main national television channel and the regional network, and they form the advertising-funded counterpart to the purely license-financed DR (formerly Danmarks Radio) television outlets. Both companies offer Internet based services. DR also runs public service radio channels. Radio24syv is a licence funded private public service national talk radio channel with public service obligations.

In Norway, NRK (Norsk rikskringkasting), with television and radio channels and Internet services, is the state-owned PSM. There are commercial companies with public service mandates and obligations as well: TV2 offers television channels and applications on the Internet. The radio companies P4 and Radio Norge are both listed as public service (*allmennkringkasting*).

In Sweden, the radio broadcaster SR (formerly Sveriges Radio) and the television branch, SVT (formerly Sveriges Television), are separate public service companies, alongside the educational broadcaster UR (Utbildningsradion), which all also provide Internet services. The three companies are owned by an independent foundation. The Swedish Parliament decides on the mandate of the companies, but is not represented on the boards. There is no acknowledged commercial PSM in Sweden. TV4, the only commercially funded media company that can broadcast from Sweden, pays a yearly fee to the state.

5.3 Scandinavian PSM in a Comparative Perspective

In Northern Europe, PSM have been regarded as a cornerstone of and as a contributor to democracy. However, technological, economic, and political changes challenge the position of PSM (Ibarra, Nowak, and Kuhn 2015). Reality may not match the ideals. Based on a study of 56 countries around the world Damian Tambini (2014) points out the problems that are occurring for the public service media: dwindling political support, governmental interference, declining audience rates, disputes on the PSB remit with private interests, and the contentious transition into digital PSM solutions.

In the Nordic 'media welfare states', public service broadcasting and its extension into PSM stands strong on all of the four pillars that are pointed out by Syvertsen et al. (2014): They are considered public goods, enjoy editorial freedom, are part of a wider cultural policy, and they work in cooperation with the state, the media industries and the public as main stakeholders. However, this strong position is challenged by national market competition and the international media environment, and editorial autonomy is always at stake in Nordic public service media (Nissen 2013).

Within the Nordic region, we concentrate on the three Scandinavian countries (see Chapter 1). With the proactive move to public service multimedia companies, the Scandinavian PSBs have defended their position and legitimacy. The political challenge is to maintain a viable balance between demands from the state, the market, and the civil society, e.g. in questions on whether the licence fee should be kept or replaced by another form of funding (Lund and Lowe 2013). The Scandinavian PSBs have managed to keep high user attendance during the transition into PSMs (Nissen 2013). They still dominate listening and viewing figures, but are, at the same time, fighting against dwindling attention among young people and are trying to compete with the growing interest in streaming services, like Netflix and HBO.[1] The multiplatform series *Skam* from NRK, on young people's identity struggles in relation to love and religion, captured huge audiences in Norway, Denmark, and beyond (Bjerkan and Aanstad 2017, 2), demonstrating that the PSM are able to attract a new generation (Sundet 2017).

Social media and other new media services may mould the meaning and shape of public service media, as 'publics are brought into being through historically specific media practices' (Hirschkind, de Abreu, and Caduff 2017). Contemporary public service media are 'public' primarily as a result of their public mandate, which is issued by the national government to reach the entire population. However, they extend their publicness by inviting their users to actively participate on PSM digital platforms (Lowe 2010), thus catering to collective publics among their audiences (Livingstone 2005; Moe 2010). In sum, they remain public by demonstrating their 'public value' in a competitive media market (Lowe and Martin 2014; Donders and Moe 2011).

5.4 Contemporary Challenges to Public Service Media

The ongoing changes with digitalization and commercialization towards a more competitive media environment and the growing differences in the sociocultural background of the public, put cross-pressure on PSM. On the one hand, they are increasingly prompted to cater to audiences as consumers in a media market, and therefore seek to maximize audience ratings. On the other hand, they are obliged to provide cultural programming that primarily caters to minorities or to high-brow segments of the population. While experts may be invited to discuss religious conflicts, audience interests may be geared towards popular coverage of religious topics. The Swedish media scholar Gunilla Hultén points, in a similar vein, to the conflicting pressures on public service media as they balance between the ambition to increase diversity and ensure market shares, and at the same time keep democratic commitments and relate to issues critical for immigration (Hultén 2016, 336).

PSM have to handle the dilemmas that arise of inclusion and exclusion and find strategies to include minority groups without reproducing stereotypes. The logics of the media market, national political considerations, and social and cul-

---

[1] Relevant statistics are available from Nordicom, http://nordicom.gu.se/en/statistics-facts/media-statistics

tural developments thus interact with each other in various ways, providing both possibilities and constraints through which PSM can engage actively with religious conflicts.

5.5 Public Service Under Emerging Diversity

There is a built-in tension in the PSM between facilitating critical discussion and contributing to common cultural points of reference. This also applies to the coverage of religion. The growing cultural and religious diversity of the Scandinavian countries make the public to which PSM cater increasingly diverse, with varying and perhaps conflicting interests and needs. This put PSM under political pressure to alter their programming. On the one hand, their obligation to provide a common, and perhaps even a unifying, public space for the whole nation has, in some cases, become more pronounced while, at the same time, they are also encouraged to take into account the multiplicity of voices and cultures that actually exist among their audiences and users.

Politically, these developments have led to demands for the public service media to strengthen their commitments to the national culture, as a form of cultural defence against globalism and multiculturalism. This has been supported, not least by right-wing national populist parties, such as the Danish People's Party, the Norwegian Progress Party and the Sweden Democrats. At the same time, more liberal and left-wing cultural and political actors have argued for the public service media to acknowledge the growing diversity in these societies and to provide more culturally and religiously inclusive programming. The mixed pressures on the PSM have had varying outcomes: The balancing act between PSM serving a common national culture, together with a culturally diverse population, has been spelled out somewhat differently and also reflects the political situation in each of the Scandinavian countries.

The formal obligations of the key PSM organizations NRK, SVT and DR, demonstrate these differences in relation to the ways in which they balance different, and potentially oppositional, considerations. In the current stipulations of the Norwegian NRK's obligations (*NRK-plakaten*), it is clearly stated that 'NRK must strengthen the Norwegian language, identity, and culture' and therefore 'a large part of its offerings must have a Norwegian background and reflect Norwegian realities' and 'communicate the cultural heritage of Norway'. At the same time, it also states: 'NRK must communicate knowledge about different groups and the diversity of Norwegian society. NRK must create arenas for debate and information about Norway as a multicultural society'. With regard to religion, we also see obligations that point in the directions of both unity and diversity:

'NRK must reflect Norway's religious heritage and the diversity of outlooks and religions in the Norwegian society' (NRK 2014).

In the case of the Danish DR, we find similarly ambiguous obligations that point towards both unity and diversity in the 'Public service contract 2015–18', which is a contract between the state and DR. Here, it is stipulated that 'DR must put special emphasis on its role as the promoter and communicator of Danish art and culture and the Danish cultural heritage, including the Christian cultural heritage.' As a new addition to the public service contract it has, for example, been explicitly stipulated that DR, in its annual overview, must report on 'DR's communication of the Christian heritage', a demand supported by the Danish People's Party. DR must also 'gather the Danes in big and small communities with content, experiences, and shared events' at the same time as it must 'reflect the diversity of culture, philosophy of life, and living condition between the various parts of the kingdom'. It is furthermore stipulated that DR must support integration into Danish society (Kulturministeriet 2014). The official obligations of the Danish DR seem to emphasize national culture and a national unifying role (at the expense of cultural diversity), a focus which is somewhat less evident in the Norwegian NRK.

The official obligations for Swedish SVT put less emphasis on the culturally unifying dimension. The responsibility to cater to the national language, Swedish, is clearly visible, but, generally, the 'Licence for Swedish Television AB' (Kulturdepartementet 2013) puts more emphasis on diversity. It states, for instance, that 'SVT must reflect the many different cultures and cultural expressions existing in Sweden' and 'programming activities must as a whole be based on perspectives of equal rights and pluralism'. In general, Swedish public service broadcasters have a mandate from the Swedish government to provide education and entertainment to all citizens, and that includes guidelines about independence, impartiality, and factuality, and the value of freedom of speech. Swedish public service radio has, since 2008, been commissioned to represent the variations in the Swedish population from a perspective of equality and plurality, within a framework of impartiality and factuality. Cultural plurality is to be seen as a 'natural part' of the planning and evaluation of SR's and SVT's activities. During 2015, Swedish public service television (SVT) also renewed its policy on plurality. Religion, faith, and other life views are to be included among the perspectives from which SVT is to carry out its coverage of Swedish society. In the balancing act between serving a common national culture and multiculturalism, the Swedish SVT thus seems to be more obligated to consider cultural diversity if compared to the two other Scandinavian PSM companies.

Changes in policies towards increasing the diversity in PSM show that during the latter part of the 20th century these were often focused on providing special programming services (e.g. news and cultural affairs) for minorities, sometimes in the languages of the minorities in question. This type of minority programming still exists, typically for indigenous minorities, such as the Sami or the Greenlandic minorities, but such policies have increasingly been criticized for supporting ghettoization within the national culture. During recent years, diversity has instead been stimulated within the overall programming for, in principle, all audiences, since this is seen as a way to both encourage integration and to make minorities visible. This 'mainstreaming' (Horsti and Hultén 2011) of cultural diversity policies in the PSM has also been a reaction to religiously based controversy and concern in the Nordic countries. As Horsti and Hultén argue (2011), the non-integration of some minorities has become a major concern in the early 21st century after a number of events that seemed to create a polarization between 'Muslim' and 'European' values.

The 'mainstreaming' approach to diversity has, in some cases, had the effect of making PSM managers more conscious of questions relating to diversity, because the visibility of minorities in mainstream programmes has become a more pertinent issue when compared to the strategy that was based on minority programming. In Swedish SVT, the so-called headscarf episode from 2002 prompted the development of diversity policies. The episode concerned a Muslim woman who was denied a position as a television programme host because she wished to wear her hijab. The head of SVT's corporate responsibility department, Johan Hartman, argued that this incident revealed the need to update SVT's policy on diversity, saying, 'These types of questions are not always highly prioritized, but the headscarf debate placed diversity concerns into focus in a new way' (quoted from Horsti and Hultén 2011, 219). It is, however, not only PSM managers and programme producers, but also audiences and politicians who may react to the visibility (or lack of visibility) of religious minorities and majorities in the PSM. As our case studies in the following chapters will demonstrate, the question about how to represent and frame cultural and religious diversity in the PSM may be the cause of controversy in and of itself (Lövheim and Axner 2011).

5.6 Genres and User Interest

The public service media encompass several media forms (radio, television, and Internet-based services) with a range of genres that cover news, current affairs, and entertainment, with a particular responsibility for minorities and children's programming. Within this wide repertoire, the Scandinavian public service media are involved in all three forms of mediatized religion (Hjarvard 2012).

There is critical journalism on religion within news and actuality programmes. Entertainment programming contains what Hjarvard (2012) has termed 'banal religion', the popular cultural uses of bits and pieces of religious symbols and references remixed into drama series and other popular programmes. The third form of mediatized religion is 'religious media', usually produced by religious organizations on their premises.

Within the Scandinavian PSM, the continued practice, inspired by the early BBC, of transmitting Christian worship services and of keeping space for devotions based on a Christian tradition come close to the category of religious media. These genres are usually regarded as classical 'religious programmes', along with psalms and music programmes with a Christian reference. The category is now renamed 'life stance' programmes. However, the diversity is still limited. Although the PSM company has editorial responsibility, most of these programmes are dominated by the Christian religious tradition (and primarily the Lutheran majority churches). In this sense, these programmes could, to some extent, be regarded 'religious media' (see Lundby et al. 2018).

Table 5.1 Should proclamation programmes in DR/NRK/SVT refer to several religions or only to Christianity? Percentages. From CoMRel survey, April 2015.

	Denmark	Norway	Sweden
The PSMs should not transmit such programmes from any religion	29	33	27
All religions should have the same share of such programmes	8	8	18
The programming should relate to the number of members	10	12	13
Most of such programmes should refer to Christianity	22	26	20
All such programming should refer to Christianity	17	10	6
Do not want to answer / Don't know	15	10	17
Sum	101	99	101
(N)	(1005)	(1099)	(996)

User expectations may differ according to genre. For instance, in a debate programme or talk show with online audience interaction, audiences may expect a certain level of tension, and may be disappointed if the invited speakers are too cordial towards one another. Similarly, some audiences may have very strong opinions that religious devotional programmes have no place on PSM and that religion should only feature in the news or in educational programmes. Yet others may believe that there is too little religious programming across all genres, and demand that Christianity receive far more positive exposure. In our survey (see Chapter 2) we asked about people's attitudes towards the 'religious programmes'. In Denmark and Norway, the question was related to DR and NRK, respectively, both carrying radio and television channels. In Sweden, the question was restricted to the television company SVT. The proclamation programmes are themselves contested among the audiences, as seen from Table 5.1.

Due to journalistic standards in the regulations of the Scandinavian PSMs which require unbiased and objective coverage, one might expect the PSM users to share this intention. This is not the case when it comes to the coverage of the world religions, where there is a similar pattern in attitudes on the coverage of Islam, Judaism, and Christianity. Although a majority, around half of the population, fully or partially agree that their PSMs should cover all three religions in an unbiased and objective way, there is a considerable portion of Scandinavians who do *not* think these religions deserve such coverage. One in 4 Danes fully or partially disagrees that the coverage needs to be unbiased and objective. This applies regardless of which religion is at stake. Among the Swedes this is the case for 1 of 5, with the Norwegians positioned in between. (See Figure 5.1).

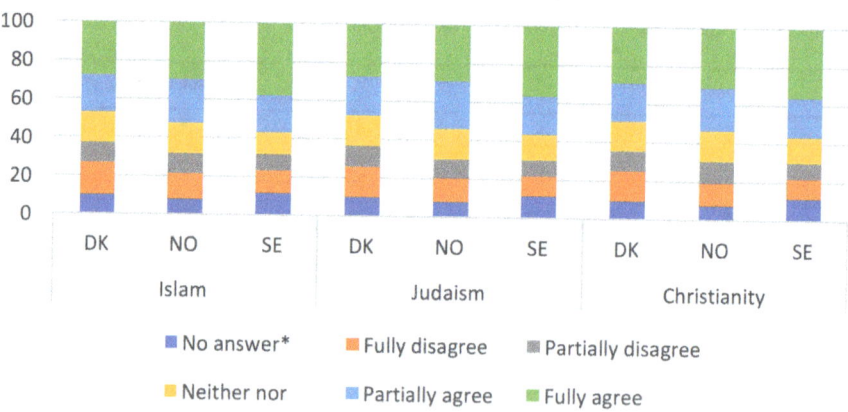

Figure 5.1 Public Service Media should only cover Islam/Judaism/Christianity in an unbiased and objective way. Percentages. From CoMRel Survey, April 2015.

Notes: For the Danes both DR and TV2 are included as PSM. The Norwegian answers are about NRK only, covering radio as well as television, while the Swedish answers are on SVT television only. Number of responses (N): Denmark 1003, Norway 1090, Sweden 990.
* 'Do not want to answer' plus 'Don't know'

It seems, thus, that Scandinavians take a stance that leans against religion in general in public service media, regardless of which religious tradition in question.

5.7 Implications for Authority

The previous sections outline the conditions offered by PSM in mediating the increased visibility of religious diversity in Scandinavia, in particular with regard to conflicts that concern the public role of religion. Religion is increasingly becoming a diverse and contested phenomenon in the Scandinavian societies, influencing the production of programmes on religion in PSM, and shaping the conditions for their reception and for interaction among media users.

With the change to multi-media platforms, public service media have gone through a transformation, from being monopoly broadcasting to competing cross-platform media companies, which is parallel to the transition José Casanova (2003) describes for public religions in the modern world. They need to accommodate to a shift from the idea of a unitary morally homogeneous nation that is grounded in an (assumed) moral consensus, to a morally, culturally and religiously pluralistic society that must strive for common ground, and a fragile consensus, through public deliberation (Casanova 2003, 128).

The transfer of authority and of an assumed consensus on values and identity are the links between these changes in public religion and the transformations of the public service media. To release audience participation in contemporary PSM, the religious actors appearing in the media must be able to express themselves quickly and clearly in debates and must also relate to a common interest in the public good.

Our studies, to a large extent, draw upon mediatization theory (see Chapter 3), and in particular on the mediatization of religion (see Chapters 3 and 4) and the dynamics of mediatized conflicts (Hjarvard, Mortensen, and Eskjær 2015). Mediatization, in general, challenges existing religious authorities and introduces new or alternative bases for knowledge and authority. 'Changing media structures challenge existing forms of religious authority at the same time as they allow new forms of authority to emerge – forms that have a more individualized and temporary character and rely on popular cultural forms' (Hjarvard 2016, 15). This applies to Scandinavian PSM which still allow designated space for worship and devotions in their programming schedules but mostly cover religion as a contested phenomenon in news and in diffuse forms of 'the religious' in entertainment programmes. The case studies in this section of the book demonstrate the complexity of the implications of mediatization on authority, which is a global phenomenon (Hoover 2016). In the study of *People and Belief* in SR (Chapter 8), media producers mainly reinforce, rather than challenge, traditional religious authority (chairpersons, imams, professors, mostly men). In the Danish case relating to the documentary series *Rebellion From the Ghetto* (Chapter 7), DR brings in new voices, offering them authority through the careful planning of the debate across media platforms. In the Norwegian 'cross case' (Chapter 6), media users turn to a Facebook group to massively critique – or defend – the visibility of religion in PSM news bulletins and in society at large.

Media users seem to react in very similar ways across very different mediatized conflicts (Abdel-Fadil 2016). The following chapters deal with the contested visibility of religion in public service media. To what degree, and in what ways, have these Scandinavian media institutions become actively involved in representing a more diverse spectrum of religious actors and opinions? How do the media users actively respond to the programmes through interactions and interpretations? These are the questions explored in the three case studies on controversies over religion in the public service media.

Bibliography

Abdel-Fadil, Mona. 2016. "Conflict and Affect Among Conservative Christians on Facebook." *Online – Heidelberg Journal of Religions on the Internet* 11. http://heiup.uni-heidelberg.de/journals/index.php/religions/article/view/23625/17350

Bjerkan, Lorns, and Kristine Hellem Aanstad. 2017. "43 millioner treff på Skam." [43 million hits on Skam]. *Aftenposten*, 21 June 2017.

Briggs, Asa. 1995. *The Birth of Broadcasting.* 5 vols. Vol. 1, *The History of Broadcasting in the United Kingdom.* Oxford: Oxford University Press.

Carpentier, Nico, Kim Christian Schrøder, and Lawrie Hallett, eds. 2014. *Audience Transformations. Shifting Audience Positions in Late Modernity.* Routledge Studies in European Communication Research and Education. New York: Routledge.

Chadwick, Paul. 2014. "Prologue." In *The Value of Public Service Media*, edited by Gregory Ferrell Lowe and Fiona Martin, 11–18. Gothenburg: Nordicom.

Donders, Karen, and Hallvard Moe, eds. 2011. *Exporting the Public Value Test. The Regulation of Public Broadcasters' New Media Services Across Europe.* Gothenburg: Nordicom.

Hirschkind, Charles, Maria José A. de Abreu, and Carlo Caduff. 2017. "New Media, New Publics? An Introduction to Supplement 15." *Current Anthropology* 58 (Supplement 15).

Hjarvard, Stig. 2012. "Three Forms of Mediatized Religion. Changing the Public Face of Religion." In *Mediatization and Religion. Nordic Perspectives*, edited by Stig Hjarvard and Mia Lövheim. Gothenburg: Nordicom.

Hjarvard, Stig. 2016. "Mediatization and the changing authority of religion." *Media, Culture & Society* 38 (1): 8–17. DOI: 10.1177/0163443715615412.

Hjarvard, Stig, Mette Mortensen, and Mikkel Fugl Eskjær. 2015. "Introduction. Three Dynamics of Mediatized Conflicts." In *The Dynamics of Mediatized Conflicts*, edited by Mikkel Fugl Eskjær, Stig Hjarvard and Mette Mortensen, 1–27. New York: Peter Lang.

Hoover, Stewart M., ed. 2016. *The Media and Religious Authority*. Pennsylvania: The Pennsylvania State University Press.

Horsti, Karina, and Gunilla Hultén. 2011. "Directing Diversity. Managing Cultural Diversity Media Policies in Finnish and Swedish Public Service Broadcasting." *International Journal of Cultural Studies* 14 (2): 209–227.

Hujanen, Taisto, Lennart Weibull, and Eva Harrie. 2013. "The Challenge of Public Service Broadcasting in the Nordic Countries. Contents and Audiences." In *Public Service Media from a Nordic Horizon. Politics, Markets, Programming and Users*, edited by Ulla Carlsson, 17–50. Gothenburg: Nordicom.

Hultén, Gunilla. 2016. "Den sårbare mångfalden." In *Människorna, medierna & marknaden. Medieutredningens forskningsantologi om en demokrati i förändring*, 329–350. Stockholm: Statens offentligga utredningar. Wolters Kluwer.

Ibarra, Karen Arriaza, Eva Nowak, and Raymond Kuhn, eds. 2015. *Public Service Media in Europe. A Comparative Approach, Routledge Studies in European Communication Research and Education*. London: Routledge.

Kulturdepartementet. 2013. Tillstånd för Sveriges Television AB att sände tv och sökbar text-tv. Stockholm: Kulturdepartementet.

Kulturministeriet. 2014. DRs public service kontrakt for 2015–2018. København: Kulturministeriet.

Linderman, Alf. 1993. Religious Broadcasting in the United States and Sweden. A Comparative Analysis of the History of Religious Broadcasting with Emphasis on Religious Television. In *Lund Research Papers in Media and Communication Studies*. Lund: University of Lund.

Livingstone, Sonia. 2005. "Introduction." In *Audiences and Publics: When cultural engagement matters for the public sphere*, edited by Sonia Livingstone, 9–16. Bristol: Intellect.

Lowe, Gregory Ferrell, ed. 2010. *The Public in Public Service Media*. Vol. RIPE@2009. Gothenburg: Nordicom.

Lowe, Gregory Ferrell, and Jo Bardoel, eds. 2007. *From Public Service Broadcasting to Public Service Media*. Vol. RIPE@2007. Gothenburg: Nordicom.

Lowe, Gregory Ferrell, and Fiona Martin, eds. 2014. *The Value of Public Service Media*. Vol. RIPE@2013. Gothenburg: Nordicom.

Lund, Anker Brink, and Gregory Ferrell Lowe. 2013. "Current Challenges to Public Service Broadcasting in the Nordic Countries." In *Public Service Media from a Nordic Horizon. Politics, Markets, Programming and Users*, edited by Ulla Carlsson, 51–73. Gothenburg: Nordicom.

Moe, Hallvard. 2010. "Notions of the Public in Public Service Broadcasting Policy for the Digital Era." In *The Digital Public Sphere. Challenges for Media Policy*, edited by Jostein Gripsrud and Hallvard Moe, 99–115. Gothenburg: Nordicom.

Nissen, Christian S. 2013. "What's so Special about Nordic Public Service Media?" In *Public Service Media from a Nordic Horizon. Politics, Markets, Programming and Users*, edited by Ulla Carlsson, 9–16. Gothenburg: Nordicom.

NRK. 2014. NRK-plakaten. Oslo: NRK.

Syvertsen, Trine. 1999. "The Many Uses of the "Public Service" Concept." *Nordicom Review* 20 (1): 5–12.

Syvertsen, Trine, Gunn Enli, Ole J. Mjøs, and Hallvard Moe. 2014. *The Media Welfare State. Nordic Media in the Digital Era.* Ann Arbor: The University of Michigan Press.

Wolfe, Kenneth M. 1984. *The Churches and the British Broadcasting Corporation 1922–1956. The Politics of Broadcast Religion.* London: SCM Press.

Mona Abdel-Fadil
Chapter 6
Nationalizing Christianity and Hijacking Religion on Facebook

Abstract: *Yes to wearing the cross whenever and wherever I choose* (YWC) is a Facebook group that was established in November 2013 to campaign for the right of a television news anchor to wear a cross pendant. YWC with its more than 100,000 likes, swiftly became a locus for discussing religion in society in general. A range of participants, with various agendas and modes of interaction are drawn to YWC: conservative Christians, nationalists, humanists, fervent secularists, and ardent atheists – 'hijacking religion' in multiple ways. Among those positive to Christianity, it is for the most part construed as either a religion of 'identity' or 'compassion'. This chapter builds on ethnographic research and focuses on the generic positions, repetitive patterns of communication, writing styles, and modes of enacting the conflict(s). There is a particular emphasis on how people's emotions, narratives, and worldviews shape the way they engage with mediatized conflict and play into the internal group dynamics.

Keywords: mediatized conflict, hijacking religion, Christianity, social media, nationalism

6.1 Introduction

A Norwegian TV news anchor called Siv Kristin Sællmann wore a bejewelled cross pendant while presenting the news in the autumn of 2013. Little did Sællmann know that this deed would spark a huge controversy about religion and public service media (PSM), or that more than 120,000 people would 'like' a Facebook group that supports her right to adorn herself with the cross while reading the news.

The Facebook group *Yes to wearing the cross whenever and wherever I choose*[1] (hereafter abbreviated to YWC) was created as a campaign group, but swiftly developed into a multifaceted online space where conservative Christians and other concerned citizens continue to discuss religion. YWC provides both a window into what PSM audiences think about the NRK news anchor neutrality

---
[1] *Ja til å bære korset når og hvor jeg vil* in Norwegian.

policy and their varying opinions about what religion's position in society ought to be. There is a clear tendency that the YWC participants' specific stance on the initial cross controversy correlates with a parallel stance on religion in society. For instance, those who advocate for the visibility of the cross on PSM, also rally for the increased visibility of religion in general – and vice versa (Abdel-Fadil, 2017). It is also clear that antipathies towards a particular religion may serve to conflate positions on religion and immigration, a tendency that is not exclusive to YWC (see chapters 1, 2, 9, 10, 11, 12).

Wearing a cross was swiftly deemed a breach of NRK neutrality policy for news anchors. The policy prohibits the use of all religious and political symbols, a fact that is often neglected by many participants in YWC. Thus, the NRK cross-verdict only served to fuel the discussions in YWC. At the peak of the conflict in November and December of 2013, YWC had more than 120,000 likes. The number of likes has since fluctuated up and down as people have joined and left the group in protest. Among those actively expressing their opinions in YWC, I have identified five main clusters of participants: conservative Christians (CC), nationalists (N), humanists (H), fervent secularists (FS), and ardent atheists (AA). Some individuals may be betwixt and between clusters. The categorizations are based on my analysis of statements and interaction patterns and function as analytical tools.

In this chapter, I will illustrate how participants from these clusters typically engage with conflict(s) and with one another in YWC. As will be elucidated, at the very core of the performance of conflict(s) are struggles over religion. I will focus on constructions of and contestations of Christianity in particular. Before delving into the empirical examples, I situate the study by sharing a few reflections on methodology.

6.1.1 Methodology

This is an online ethnography of YWC, i.e. it is an in-depth and longitudinal research of YWC as an online environment. Since observation is the main method, I am able to also focus on participants' conduct and interactions with one another, and not only on the words they utter. Due to the overwhelming amount of YWC data, the study is delineated in time. The time period under study runs from November 2013 when the page was created to December 2013, covering a six-week period during which activity on the page reached its peak. Data collection was conducted in 2015 and comprises all posts, comments, and replies during these six weeks. I observed, logged, and coded all verbal interactions, repetitive communication patterns, positions, and roles in the group. In ethnographic research, data collection and analysis is a highly immersive process which does not abide by the 'data saturation' principle. Instead, 'more of the same' type of data is highly valued and seen as an opportunity to subject initial patterns discovered in the data to further rounds of coding, to deepen the analysis. The advantage of this approach became clear when I stumbled across a small cluster of ardent atheists a couple of months into the analysis. I subsequently discovered that this group left a huge mark on the debates they threw themselves into.

In order to systematize my data, I kept a field diary, which includes: 1) a 'methods log' of methodological challenges and solutions, 2) 'observations notes' which includes preliminary analysis and reflections, and 3) a 'coding log' containing tweaks and adjustments of substantive codes. I coded the data within four main parent codes – themes, roles, styles, and arguments – using the qualitative analysis software program Nvivo. I will write in ethnographic present.

Tricia Wang's adaptation of Clifford Geertz' iconic notion of 'thick descriptions' is a good fit for what I do:

> Thick Data is data brought to light using qualitative, ethnographic research methods that uncover people's emotions, stories, and models of their world (Wang 2016).

I was particularly interested in how people's emotions, narratives, and worldviews shape the way they engage with mediatized conflict (see Chapter 3) and the internal group dynamics of YWC. The longer I observed variations of interactions and bursts of emotion in YWC, the more I realized that the term 'flaming' is not very useful as an analytical category unless it signifies something more specific or elaborate than simply passionately stirring up a debate. My understanding of the term 'flaming' deepened during the ethnographical study.

Quotes in this chapter are reconstructions based on generic positions, repetitive patterns of communication, writing styles, and modes of enacting the conflict(s). The decision to reconstruct rather than quote verbatim is based on 1) my interest in generic narratives and typical group dynamics, for which reconstructions suffice, and 2) ensuring the anonymity of those who participated in the debates. This methodological choice is available to me, because generic narratives are ubiquitous in YWC.

Critics may view reconstructions as tampering with the data. Yet, the idea that verbatim quotes are pure, or unspoiled by the researcher's selective choices and subjectivities is an illusion. Reconstruction is already in much of what ethnographers do. Most notably, those of us who translate quotes from one language to another are very much involved in reconstructing narratives, and adapting words, stylistic choices, and arguments in ways that we best believe represent that individual's worldview in another language. But, we also reconstruct when we omit ughs, spelling mistakes, punctuation mishaps, or cut and paste from various parts of an interview or dialogue in order to provide a more succinct slice of data. Speaking of which, I have, save for a couple of examples, not included any spelling mistakes or CAPSLOCK, extreme punctuation!!!!!!! or emoticons (in this case, mostly smileys, crosses, hearts, and angry faces) in my reconstructed quotations. This is because I have not systematically coded and analysed the patterns in which such visual embellishments occur.

Quotes are twinned with pseudonyms and the first letters of the cluster that I code such a statement within, for instance 'CC' for 'conservative Christian'. At times it is difficult to determine which cluster a statement belongs to. Therefore, some quotes are assigned a double label such as 'N/CC'. The frequency with which each pseudonym appears in a reconstructed exchange is intentional, and aimed at giving the reader a taste of the different sizes of the clusters, their gender compositions and how many people from one cluster are typically active in a debate.

Technologically, Facebook is structured in a way that gives rise to a particular set of media dynamics. Pinned posts are not always read, and the same question or comment may be made repeatedly without any regard for what the person(s) just before may have said. Typically, users' responses cross each other, partially due to the Facebook structure 'reply to reply', which can be chaotic in terms of who is replying to what – and whom – especially when hundreds or thousands of comments are involved. Users who are not seasoned Facebook users will be unaware of the difference between replying to a comment and replying to a reply, contributing to random placement of their replies. There is also a time lag, and when many people are responding to a post, comments may be delayed before appearing, creating a mismatch with regards to which reply a comment belongs to. This slight chaos may help explain why many comments go largely unnoticed in the maze of Facebook comments. This chapter gives the reader a unique insight into typical types of exchanges and the internal dynamics of YWC, and what the various types of participants are fighting for and believe in.

6.2 Various Enactments of Conflict in YWC

6.2.1 Protesting the Cross Ban

> Olga/CC: Norway is a Christian nation. We cannot accept that the cross is banned here. It makes no sense. This is Norway. We are Christian.

Rudolf/CC: I'm outraged! How can they ban the cross? It is a very important symbol of our Christian identity.

Christian/N: Muslims can't just come here and demand that we have a cross ban in Norway. We have to protect our heritage from immigrants. What will they demand next? Erasing the cross from the Norwegian flag?

Heidi/H: Holy moly! There is a lot of anger in this group because of this misunderstanding. I repeat: There is no cross ban in Norway.

Magdalene/CC: I refuse to abide by this ridiculous verdict. I shall wear my cross with pride, and nobody can stop me.

Laila/CC: I can't believe that I am not allowed to wear the cross anymore in Norway. What is the world coming to?

Rita/N: If they don't like the cross they should go home.

Heidi/H: Take a deep breath. Unless you are an NRK news anchor, you can wear a cross pendant anytime and anywhere you like.

Conservative Christians and nationalists are the largest clusters and contain both women and men, with no noteworthy gender imbalance. Their enactment of the conflict can be said to dominate the page, and hence conservative Christians and nationalists play an active role in shaping the conflict(s). Conservative Christians, nationalists, fervent secularists, and ardent atheists often employ the language of 'speaking out' and 'speaking the truth' (Abdel-Fadil 2016). They also claim to be the silent majority or the real voice of the people, which is a characteristic of other mediatized conflicts too (Figenschou et al. 2015). Particularly among the conservative Christians and the nationalists, the idea that YWC provides a platform to say what needs to be said, but is often dismissed by politicians, journalists, etc., circulates. Conservative Christians (and at times nationalists) claim to speak *for* the Christian nation. This starting point is significant in terms of affect, and shapes much of their emotive engagement with the mediatized conflict. Papacharissi (2015) speaks of 'affective publics' which is an apt description of how participants in YWC respond to the postulate that there is general cross ban in Norway. Such claims mobilize strong emotional responses. Similarly, nationalists evoke emotive engagement based on fear of loss of nationhood. Yet such claims do not stand uncontested. Humanists, ardent atheists, and fervent secularists ferociously battle against this reading of their nation and national identity.

The quotes illustrate how the various clusters of debaters perform the conflict *for* each other, but do not always interact *with* each other in a way that involves 'listening' to other perspectives. Trigger themes, emotional cues, and emotive reactions fuel the dynamics of mediatized conflict and push the buttons of individual debaters (Abdel-Fadil 2016). Conservative Christians typically reinforce the idea that there is a cross ban or proclaim that they plan to defy the (alleged) cross ban just seconds after humanists have pointed out that there is in fact no general cross ban in Norway. The idea that there is a general cross ban in Norway is emotional ammunition for many conservative Christians, causing them to react and repeat this postulate as if it were true. The sense of a threatened Christian identity and a fear of the extinction of Christianity are tangible. The focus becomes on preserving Christianity in Norway. Nationalists tend to spur emotions and amplify the conflicts, by transforming the conflict into one about the nation. They typically contribute to an escalation of the conflict by engaging in spiralling argumentation and by evoking a series of worst-case scenarios well suited to trigger emotive reactions from conservative Christians, declaring that the cross will be obliterated from everything including the Norwegian flag itself (ibid.). Both conservative Christians and nationalists can be said to adhere to 'Christianity of identity'.

Notably, nationalists lament Muslims and immigrants taking over Norway and tend to direct their emotive triggers towards fellow nationalists and the conservative Christians in an attempt to fuel their fury and entice them into buying into the narrative of threatened nationhood. Stylistically the nationalists can be said to erupt into the 'enraged fan' level of negative emotion in their outbursts (Michailidou and Trenz 2015).

At the opposite end of the emotional spectrum, the humanists perform the role of mediators. Humanists, unlike the majority of other debaters, generally do not get entangled in highly emotionally charged renditions of the conflict. Instead, humanists attempt to defuse tensions, debunk myths, and create space for a constructive debate – although they do at times display signs of exasperation with other debaters' efforts to trigger one another. Unlike other clusters, humanists are a small cluster, in which a handful of women are extraordinarily active. Humanists leave a mark on practically all of the selected debates, displaying what appears to be a tireless dedication to remediate the conflicts in a reconciliatory manner. A couple of the humanists copy and paste the same lengthy answer time and time again, but others tailor their responses to each exchange. Notably, humanists primarily address conservative Christians, presumably in the hope of disrupting the partial overlap between conservative Christians' and nationalists' narratives. Humanists promote Christianity as compassion as a counter-narrative to Christianity as identity.

6.2.2 Saving Christianity and the Nation

Torgrim/CC: We must protect our Christian heritage before it is lost forever.

Rita/N: Wake up!!!! Protect Christianity in Norway before it's too late. Muslims and immigrants are taking over. Politicians are giving away our country. WAKE UP before it's too late.

Georg/N: For me personally, Christianity is not important. But, Christianity is part of Norwegian heritage and we cannot deny that.

Sonia/CC: I wear my cross with pride and I don't think anybody has the right to tell me not to wear the cross. This is Norway. Norway is a Christian country.

Georg/N: Christianity is the cornerstone of Norway. Nobody, not Muslims, atheists, or secularists can change that.

Olga/CC: I will wear my cross wherever I please and there ain't nothing anyone can do to stop me!

Rudolf/CC: If we do not wake up now – and protect our Christian heritage – there may not be any traces of Christianity left.

Christian/N: Protect Norway before it's too late. Muslims and immigrants are taking over. Politicians are GIVING AWAY our country.

Therese/CC: Muslims are not to blame, it is the secularists and atheists who have de-Christianized Norway.

Frida/CC: Are we really not allowed to wear the cross anymore in Norway? I haven't had any bad experiences and I wear my cross every single day.

Oskar/AA: Most Norwegians are far too rational to believe in Christianity or religion. You're trying to sink the nation with your stupidity.

Oskar/AA: In order to believe in god, you have to close your eyes to facts and have half a brain. You Christians are delusional.

Rudolf/CC: Your passionate anger about this proves that deep down you know that He exists.

This exchange illustrates how protecting Christianity is often conflated with protecting the nation, particularly for the nationalists but also to a certain degree for the conservative Christians. It also provides a glance at how the participants take turns in blaming a variety of others, which in fact is a recurring dynamic in mediatized conflicts in general (Abdel-Fadil 2016; Eskjær et al. 2015).

An overwhelming majority of conservative Christians (and nationalists) appear to either fuel or express no resistance to the postulate that there is a general cross ban in Norway. Yet, the occasional conservative Christian interjects with a sincere question (and some confusion) inquiring whether there is in fact a ban and if others experience negative incidents. Such lone comments rarely provoke a response. Nationalists produce a significant number of emotive comments that appear to be designed to either heat up or derail conversations, by transforming the conflict into one about immigrants/Muslims threatening the nation. Likewise, ardent atheists, a tiny, exclusively male cluster, specialize at stirring up emotions among conservative Christians.

Conservative Christians' main concern is the preservation of Christianity. They rally for more visibility of Christianity in public spaces, and often equate the nation with themselves. The sense that wearing the cross is an act of defiance, and a brave act of standing one's ground, is a claim repeated by several conservative Christians, and lends authority to the postulate that there is a cross ban. Conservative Christians in their own rendition exhibit resolution and agency when both wearing the cross, and when arguing passionately for the right to wear the cross. These are considered heroic acts of taking a stand against injustice and hence very important steps towards preserving Christianity from complete extinction.

At times conservative Christians express an unveiled disdain for the ardent atheists and fervent secularists. Other times they see the aggressive attacks from the ardent atheists as a sign of a believer in denial, which may well be the worst possible insult to ardent atheists. Yet I do not believe that the intention of the conservative Christians in those instances is to cause offence. Based on my analysis of a number of such exchanges (and the context they appear in) I believe that such projections are sincere, if somewhat bizarre.

Nationalists repeatedly mention how they do not consider themselves Christian, but that Christianity goes hand in hand with 'Norwegianess'. Nationalists focus extensively on the preservation of 'Norwegian heritage'. In their own rendition, conservative Christians and nationalists see themselves as representing the majority of Norwegians, and consider Norway as a 'Christian nation' founded on 'Christian cultural heritage'. Christianity thus becomes a religion of identity even for nationalists who do not believe in God.

Ardent atheists, much like the humanists, are only a small group of individuals. But unlike the humanists who have managed to engage with practically all the debates, ardent atheists only leave a mark (albeit a significant one) on a tiny fraction of debates. Ardent atheists appear to only sporadically visit the Facebook group, while humanists comment on practically all the debates. It is invariably the ardent atheists who pair their narrative with 'flaming' behaviour and exploit the full potential of emotive cues. Ardent atheists are unique in that they enter a debate, bellow antagonistic commentary or insults, and then disappear into thin air. The conduct of ardent atheists is distinct from the behaviour of all other types of participants, and warrants being described as 'flaming' behaviour. This is also the only cluster composed nearly exclusively of men. The fiery debates ardent atheists ignite rage on long after they're gone.

6.2.3 Religion of the Nation

> Olga/CC: Norway is Christian. But, atheists and secularists are willing to deny our Christian heritage.
>
> Jenny/FS: Norway ain't Christian! It is a secular state.
>
> Rudolf/CC: We religious people of different faiths need to stick together. We have common interests in preserving religion in society, unlike secularists and atheists who would be happy to see religion disappear altogether.
>
> Alfred /CC: Secularists and leftists think they own the country. But, they don't. Christianity is the state religion and most Norwegians are Christian.
>
> Jenny/FS: Actually Christianity is not the state religion any more and the stats don't back up the argument that most Norwegians identify as Christian.
>
> Christian/N: Muslims threaten Norway's Christian heritage.
>
> Niklas/FS: Hell no. The majority of Norwegians don't believe in anything! And stop this racist spew. Muslims and immigrants have nothing to do with the NRK verdict on the cross.
>
> Rita/N: I don't consider myself Christian, but Christianity is part of our Norwegian heritage. We can't stand by while foreigners take over Norway and push away Christianity.
>
> Niklas/FS: Racist pricks!
>
> Thor/AA: Clinging on to archaic, violent, make-believe gods is not gonna save Norway. It is you who need saving. From your own stupidity.
>
> Geir/AA/FS: You lot are holding Norway back. It is a good thing you are not actually a majority.
>
> Georg/N: Christianity is a Norwegian religion.
>
> Thor/AA: This goes to show you how ignorant you are. Christianity is not made in Norway, you dimwit. Neither do most Norwegians consider themselves Christians.
>
> Magdalene/CC: They've banned the cross, Christmas celebrations. What will they ban next? Alcohol? Pork????? This nonsense has to STOP!!!!.

When conservative Christians talk about the Christian nation and how the majority of Norwegians are Christians, ardent atheists and fervent secularists protest, and often refer to recent statistics on the matter to back up their claim. Fervent secularists are a much smaller cluster than the nationalists and conservative Christians, but appear similarly gender-balanced.

Sometimes comments can fit into more than one analytical category as exemplified in this reconstructed exchange. For instance, the generic argument that Norway isn't Christian can be classified as fervent secularist or ardent atheist. Much like how there may be overlap between some conservative Christians and nationalists, or humanists and conservative Christians.

Ardent atheists are primarily concerned with protecting the nation from the stupidity of religion. They talk to all Christians but specifically target conservative Christians. The uniqueness of the ardent atheists lies in their mode of performance: they often participate briefly in a debate, by dispensing an antagonistic atheist agenda and decrying all believers as a bunch of imbeciles, before disappearing. This suggests that the ardent atheists may be more intent on performing the conflict in a manner that leaves a mark on the debate and the other media users than actually engaging in an exchange of positions over time. Their main point of departure is that all religions are bad, and believing in God is irrational.

Nationalists in the Facebook group talk among themselves in a way that fuels and intensifies the existing conflict, but also in a way that that tries to tempt conservative Christians with their worldview by transforming the conflict into one about protecting the nation from its demise and introducing new conflicts, between Muslims and Christians, and foreigners and Norwegians. Muslims (and to a lesser extent immigrants) are singled out as the archenemy of the nation.

Indifference characterizes nationalists' personal affiliation to religion. To nationalists, Christianity is good because it is 'Norwegian', and by default everything Norwegian is good. The presumed 'Norwegianess' of Christianity is contested and also ridiculed by others in YWC. The postulate that Christianity as 'Norwegian' is dismantled by those who see Norway as a secular, atheist, or a multi-confessional nation. Fervent secularists, ardent atheists, humanists, and even conservative Christians may be critical of this claim and mock the territorial claims of 'Christianity being made in Norway'.

6.2.4 Defining Christianity

Rita/CC: Muslims are a threat to Christianity.

Henrik/CC: To me Christianity is about compassion. It is about spreading the love and treating your fellow human with compassion. You cannot single out Muslims and say that this doesn't apply to them. That is not how Christianity works.

Therese/CC: It makes me sick to my stomach that some people in here use Christianity as an excuse to spread hatred and scapegoat Muslims and immigrants. I can't think of anything less Christian.

Tina/HC: To me Christianity is about compassion. For all humankind.

Ingrid/CC: As Christians we are supposed to love one another as part of God's grace.

Jacob/CC: I don't think that Muslims are our enemy. On the contrary we share many of the same values and concerns. Muslims are not the problem. Atheists and secularists are. They're the ones who want to do away with religion all together.

Georg/CC/N: Muslims threaten our Christian values, demanding special rights and forbidding our Christian traditions like Christmas celebrations.

Heidi/H/: What happened to 'love thy neighbour'? Did you miss that Sunday school class?

Jonathon/FS: This is seriously the most conspiratorial, nonsensical racist spew I have ever read. If anybody is ruining Norway it is you lot of fucking imbeciles. For instance you 'Anders Nordson' you spew out a lot of unintelligent xenophobic bullshit and expect us to take you seriously.

Nancy/CC: Muslims are fellow believers. We have no fight to pick with Muslims or vice versa.

Thor/AA: Christianity is peaceful, my ass. You've got blood on your hands. That cross you are so passionate about represents centuries of violence and ignorance.

Edvard/AA: Religions are dumb and nonsensical. Christianity is a far cry from enlightenment. You are all delusional.

Magdalene/CC: I wear the cross I inherited from my grandmother with pride.

Teodor/N: Muslims are cockroaches infesting our society. We must get rid of them immediately before it is too late.

Wilhelm/N: Immigrants and Muslims are violent criminals, who want to rape our women, yet you keep letting them in. They want to force their intolerant sharia law on Norwegians.

Edvard/AA: YOU are a threat to HUMANITY!!

Magdalene/CC/N: It just makes no sense. Muslims cannot come here and prance around in their hijabs and what not, and we're expected to cover up our crosses. MADNESS!

Selma/FS: You call yourself Christian but you are all raging racists. I have had it with you lot. There is no hope for you.

Tina/HC: Christianity is about being compassionate towards everyone. Twisting Christianity to spread an anti-Islamic message is profoundly un-Christian.

The range of positions that may be expressed in a simple short exchange such as the one above is – remarkable. The exchange illustrates the typical dynamics of debates, how the various participants' comments at times get posted in a zigzag pattern. Only an alert or cautious reader will realize who is answering whom, and about what. In addition, some participants turn a blind eye to what others think and dedicate their undivided attention to hammering their own perspective. The result is a somewhat confusing collection of perspectives that appear in random order. The example of a conservative Christian recounting how wearing her grandmother's cross is of personal significance is a very typical comment. Such comments act as both an affirmation of faith, and signal an affective value to the cross itself (including through who it belonged to previously). Here, the personalized relationship to religion is evident in that the cross becomes a source of everyday comfort. Still, the comment appears random and unrelated to the other comments next to which it appears – which is also a typical characteristic of the group dynamics.

There is an obvious tension between Christianity as a religion of identity, and Christianity as a religion of compassion (see chapter 10).[2] Some conservative Christians' approach to Christianity overlaps with nationalists' in the sense that they too adhere to Christianity as a religion of identity – and link its significance and preservation to the nation. In such instances, the main difference between conservative Christians and nationalists is that the conservative Christians avow a personalized faith thereby embracing both a national and a personal Jesus –whilst the nationalists stay clear of any personal faith-based commitment to Christianity. Humanists, especially those with a Christian leaning, share common ground with conservative Christians. Still, some conservative Christians have overlapping ideas with nationalists. Christians of various leanings make multiple claims about Christianity. Their performance of the conflict unravels tensions within those who believe that Christianity – however they define it – is worthy of preservation. As a result, YWC functions as a space for negotiating what the essence of Christianity is, or ought to be, and why.

For a subset of conservative Christians, the 'religiousness' of Muslims is singled out as a positive shared experience and pitted against the secularization of Norway. For those conservative Christians, Muslims are considered an ally in their efforts to prevent Norway from becoming entirely secularized. Most of the conservative Christians are summoned to perform the conflict(s) based on their fear of extinction of Christianity. A sub-strand of the conservative Christians fear for all religions, and move to protect religion in the public sphere, because they worry that religion will have to make way for either an entirely atheist or an entirely secular outlook. In this sense the conservative Christians are divided in

---

2 Ádám and Bozóki (2016, 146) operate with a seemingly similar distinction between 'National Christianity' and 'Christianity as a religion of love', but do not go into great detail about what this means.

their fears. While the majority of conservative Christians in this online milieu fear the possible extinction of Christianity, some conservative Christians fear for the death of religion.

Ardent atheists repeatedly claim that Christianity is irrational and violent, as are all religions. But it is Christianity and particularly conservative Christians that are the target of the ardent atheists' wrath. And conservative Christians take the bait. The conflict lines erupt and conservative Christians continue to fall into the trap of intensified conflict performance, long after the ardent atheists have left the 'room'.

6.3 Understanding the Dynamics of Conflict(s) in YWC

6.3.1 Who Talks to Whom?

Fervent secularists talk mainly to nationalists (and the conservative Christians who resemble them) and try to fire them up – but often become unhinged in the process. Nationalists primarily talk to conservative Christians, and attempt to entice them with their 'us vs. them' worldview. Ardent atheists exclusively address the conservative Christians and repeatedly tell them what pinheads they are. While ardent atheists allegedly hate all religions in equal measure, in practice they single out Christians as their primary target of disdain, but reserve their most impassioned performances for very conservative Christians. Conservative Christians for their part talk to all the other clusters – mainly because they respond to how they are being portrayed, attacked, or befriended by others. They may at times respond to atheists, humanists, and nationalists, but their primary audience appears to be fellow Christians, who they hope will be seduced into joining their cause of preserving Christianity.

While several of the clusters are gender-balanced, there are two exceptions with highly distinct forms of interaction. Firstly, the predominantly male cluster of ardent atheists who only pick a few small corners of the online debates to repeatedly lash out at conservative Christians – before making a run for it. Secondly, the handful of humanist women who are highly prolific and leave a unique reconciliatory mark on nearly all the selected debates, exhibiting a prolonged commitment to the mediator role. Humanists also primarily address the conservative Christians (and the odd nationalist). They debunk myths and attempt to soothe and engage in dialogue with the conservative Christians, in contrast to the diametrically opposite 'drop a bomb and run' approach of ardent atheists.

Still, some of the Facebook users are far less concerned with what other participants write, and mostly focus on what they themselves *feel*. As I have written about in detail elsewhere, affect is abundant in the Facebook discussions and a recurring component of mediatized conflicts in general (Abdel-Fadil 2016). As illustrated in this chapter, all of the participants display emotions in the modes in which they engage with both the conflicts and one another. Nationalists, fervent secularists, and ardent atheists voice their anger. Such venting appears to simultaneously function as a form of entertainment – particularly for ardent atheists who mostly direct their rage at the conservative Christian participants. Conservative Christians predominantly express anger, intermingled with fear. Humanists convey exasperation, albeit in a patient manner, but their aim is to stir up feelings of compassion among fellow debaters.

6.3.2 Contesting the Essence of Christianity

A striking feature of the debates in the Facebook group is the detailed negotiation of what Christianity is all about, and of the symbolic meaning it holds in the various participants' eyes. Christianity is interpreted, brokered, and adhered to in a multitude of ways. For instance, some of the conservative Christians convey the personal meaning Christianity holds for them through their emotional attachment to a particular cross pendant that brings them closer to God. Nationalists see Christianity as a signifier of Norwegian nationhood and identity – but their understanding of religiosity is void of personal faith. Ardent atheists consider Christianity the cradle of ignorance and irrationality. Fervent secularists regard Christianity a threat to a healthy state and society. Humanists view Christianity as a (non-exclusive) source of positive values on which a compassionate and just society can be modelled upon. In most clusters there is a tangible internal cohesion when it comes to the big issues. The participants within a cluster may well have different degrees of embracing and expressing a stance, but their core beliefs are similar. For example among nationalists, 'Muslims should go home' is a much milder version of 'Muslims are cockroaches and infesting our land', but they are de facto variations of the same standpoint, namely: 'Muslims do not belong in Norway'.

Conflicts in YWC are enacted in a way that pits Christians not only against Muslims, atheists, and secularists, but ultimately pits Christians against Christians. Those who self-identify as Christians in YWC perform the conflicts in diametrically opposite ways based on their adherence to Christianity as either a religion of identity – or – compassion. One of the central tropes of 'Christianity as identity' is 'Christian heritage', coupled with Muslims and immigrants being perceived as a threat. It is a narrative of identity preservation and defence. Adhering to Christianity as compassion entails making an effort to put an end to the vilifying of Muslims and immigrants and is reminiscent of what Woodhead and Heelas call (2000, 71–72) 'religions of humanity', in which 'compassion' is a central trope. Humanists, both those who explicitly identify and don't identify as Christian, are united by the idea that Christianity as a religion dictates compassion to all humankind, and that compassion is a core Christian value. A strand of conservative Christians join forces with humanists in this reading of Christianity. Rather than animosity, these conservative Christians feel an affinity with pious Muslims who are believed to share a common moral outlook. To these conservative Christians (and humanists), attacking Muslims in the name of Christianity is seen as the antithesis of the foundational values of Christianity. This is a narrative of faith and love.

Similar findings surface in the book *Saving the People: How Populists Hijack Religion*, which collects case studies in several European countries (Marzouki, McDonnell, and Roy 2016). The term 'hijack religion' is used to connote how Christianity is increasingly infused with particular traits that serve specific ideological goals. A core finding is that when populists hijack religion, they focus only on 'belonging', rendering 'belief' superfluous. Moreover, populist religion revolves around the tropes 'restoration' and 'battle', and is adamant about the preservation of Christian heritage from the threat of extinction or foreign takeover (Marzouki and McDonnell 2016, 2). In this way, Christianity is viewed as an identity but divorced from both faith and Christian values, which are deemed either too leftist or too conservative (Roy 2016a, 91). Populists are only interested in 'Christianity in its cultural form' argues Peace (2016, 104). According to Roy (2016b, 186) Christianity is predominantly expressed in terms of national identity and its proponents 'are Christian largely to the extent that they reject Islam'. Roy (ibid., 190) makes the intriguing argument that while populists speak of identity, churches speak of faith. Based on the European case studies of populism, Roy (ibid.) argues that Christianity functions as a marker of identity, and serves as a platform to 'distinguish between good "us" and bad "them"'. Roy goes on to assert that: 'when evoking the Christian identities of their nations populist leaders tend to refer to symbols such as the cross, rather than theological dogma' (ibid., 186). Taken together then, the conclusion from *Saving the People* seems to be that the more one identifies with Christianity as culture, the less likely it is that one will identify with Christian values or faith.

This argument is a good fit for the nationalists in YWC, but does not necessarily hold true for the bulk of the conservative Christians. What characterizes them is precisely the entanglement of Christianity as identity and Christianity as faith. Conservative Christians may well be more interested in symbols than dogma, but they most certainly also articulate genuine expressions of 'belief'. Therein lies a potential theological tension with the faith-based Christianity of compassion (see chapter 10). Still, the conservative Christians who embrace Christianity as identity in YWC seem to do so wholeheartedly. In contrast, several active members of Norway's newly established conservative Christian Party (*Partiet De Kristne*) have expressed a combination of anxiety about the survival of Christianity and remorse about adopting a selective love that only extends to particular neighbours (Brekke n.d.). In this sense several members of the Christian Party appear to be betwixt and between Christianity as identity and Christianity as compassion. This discrepancy may perhaps be related to politicians being better versed in reflexive conversations than 'ordinary people' online, or it might be a result of methodology and the medium of expression, or a combination. Certainly Christianity of identity is pitted against Christianity as compassion in YWC, but not by a single individual who claims to adhere to both. Rather, scores of 'others' criticize nationalists and conservative Christians who adhere to Christianity as identity for replacing the core value of 'love thy neighbour' with 'hate thy neighbour'.

6.3.3 Sacred Values

Religion in itself is a trigger theme that pushes participants into affective modes of enacting conflicts. For many of the participants a number of the themes of discussion very close to the heart. Participants are at times protecting their foundational worldview or values they consider sacred. This raises the emotional stakes in the conflict, and renders its enactment important at both the personal and symbolic level. To the nationalists it is Norway as a nation that is held sacred and must be protected from contamination. Conservative Christians consider Christianity/Christian heritage sacred, and strive to preserve Christianity from extinction. To fervent secularists it is anti-racism which is at stake. They fiercely oppose building a xenophobic sense of belonging. For humanists, human compassion and knowledge are both held sacred. Forming informed decisions that benefit humankind and promote compassion is the overarching goal. To the ardent atheists, it is ultimately rationality and their own perceived superiority for being non-believers which trumps all other concerns, and is the sacred value worth fighting for. Fervent secularists unleash their anger on both conservative Christians and nationalists, but it is xenophobia and not religion per se that winds them up. Against this backdrop, it seems evident that many parallel conversations take place, fuelled with competing and at times diametrically opposite concerns.

Sacred values can also be used for leverage. For instance, ardent atheists repeatedly exclaim that Christianity is nonsense and Christians are imbeciles. While I do not question the sincerity of such attacks, I think the point not to be missed is that these are highly intentional efforts to cause rupture and attack the core beliefs and sacred values of conservative Christians. Baumgartner's (2013) analysis of blasphemy as a 'profound offence' and a form of 'inter-subjective violence' appears highly fitting for the both the intent and the effect ardent atheists have on conservative Christians. Baumgartner (2013, 58) describes how 'blasphemy functions as a tool to produce and enforce negative stereotypes of followers of a particular religion'. Crucially, ardent atheists enact the conflict in that particular way precisely *because* it is a profound offence and does psychological harm to the conservative Christians. I would add two observations. First, dispensing 'profound offenses' may in itself be a form of entertainment. Sometimes people are drawn to conflict because its enactment is a cherished pastime (Abdel-Fadil, 2017). Second, a value need not be religious for it to be held sacred or attacked in a blasphemous way. For instance, the fervent secularists go ballistic about racist and overly religious content precisely because it constitutes a 'profound offence' to what they hold sacred, namely an anti-racist, unequivocally secular state.

6.3.4 Who Hijacks Religion?

Will the populists' hijacking of religion receive legitimacy from Christianity's various churches or 'rightful owners'? and who ultimately owns the 'copyright' of religion? asks Roy (2016b, 190). These types of questions latch onto longstanding discussions about the authority of religion, the legitimacy of lay interpretations, and the societal role of religion. In YWC, it seems evident that both 'Christianity' and 'religion' can be hijacked and infused with the sacred values of a spectrum of people who have vested interests in particular readings of religion. For instance, I would argue that ardent atheists also hijack 'religion', imbuing the concept with all shades of bad. For the ardent atheists religion is equated to imbecility. Humanists paint Christianity as a religion of compassion. For most conservative Christians the fear of extinction dictates their religious outlook, placing them within a religion of identity understanding of Christianity – where Christianity is simultaneously seen as the true path to salvation, and superior to other religions. Against this backdrop, I do not think it is accurate to state that Christianity has been *exclusively* hijacked by a very conservative agenda or an exclusivist approach to religion only. The concept 'hijacking religion' can be critiqued for erroneously connoting that religion can be stripped of its 'true' meaning or purest form. Yet, particularly in the case of the mediation of very specific or absolutist definitions of religions I believe 'hijacking religion' is analytically useful. In employing 'hijacking religion' in a broader conceptual sense one may elucidate how various understandings of religions are often infused with a range of political agendas, that may range from 'leave me be' to fantasies of 'world domination'.

This online ethnography of YWC complements previous quantitative and qualitative approaches to mediatized conflicts. The strength of this study lies in in its methodology. In delving into the particular specifics and thick descriptions of YWC, it becomes possible to draw new conclusions, that may be generalizable and may nuance – and add to – our body of knowledge about how media users engage with conflicts about religion. In this chapter, I have highlighted how various clusters of YWC participants behave and express their emotions in a multitude of ways, and I illustrate how these enactments and interactions, in turn, play into the mediatized conflict(s) about religion. The stubborn ethnographic determination to analyse huge chunks of data from one particular community may yield surprising and very valuable results, such as the unearthing of an entirely new cluster of participants, in this case – the ardent atheists – who left a significant mark on YWC. This discovery may serve to widen scholarly understandings of the spectrum of worldviews that may entangle with one another, even in highly particular milieus such as YWC, and may thus balance out viewing online spaces as mere 'filter bubbles'. It also points to the importance of observing and analysing online *behaviours* and emotive responses within a group. Similarly, this chapter sheds light on how the participants' gender may play into the intensity and type of enactment of conflict, and – the emotional labour involved. As evidenced by the case of YWC, gender may also be constitutive of an entire cluster, and at times a small cluster of women can do the work of an entire army of men. Together these findings, nuance and add a layer of empirical detail to claims that men participate 'more' in online debates about contentious issues (see chapter 2 & 16). Future qualitative studies must therefore pay close attention to – and flesh out – gender-specific ways of engaging with mediatized conflicts about religion. Similarly, future studies ought to take into consideration that a range of social actors, be they secular, atheists, secular religious, or radically religious may seek to hijack both their own religion, and the religion of their selected 'other(s)' in an attempt of political gain and as part their enactment of conflict. Rather than consider 'hijacking religion' unique to nationalists and conservative Christians, it may be more fruitful to view the 'hijacking of religion' as a more universal phenomenon and an integral part of the performance of mediatized conflicts about religion, across the globe.

Acknowledgments

I am especially grateful to Birgit Meyer, Louise Lund Liebmann, Audun Toft and Mia Lövheim for their valuable feedback on an earlier draft. I would also like to thank my colleagues at the Centre for the Study of Political Communication (POLKOM) and the Centre for Research on Extremism (C-REX) for engaging discussions that have shaped my analysis.

Bibliography

Abdel-Fadil, Mona. 2016. "Conflict and Affect Among Conservative Christians on Facebook." *Online – Heidelberg Journal of Religions on the Internet* 11. http://heiup.uni-heidelberg.de/journals/index.php/religions/article/view/23625/17350

Abdel-Fadil, Mona. 2017. "Identity Politics in a Mediatized Religious Environment on Facebook: Yes to Wearing the Cross Whenever and Wherever I Choose." *Journal of Religion in Europe* 10 (4): 457–486 (open access). DOI: 10.1163/18748929–01004001

Ádám, Zoltán, and András Bozóki. 2016. "The God of Hungarians: Religion and Right-Wing Populism in Hungary." In *Saving the People: How Populists Hijack Religion*, edited by Nadia Marzouki, Duncan McDonnell, and Olivier Roy, 129–47. New York: Oxford University Press.

Baumgartner, Christoph. 2013. "Blasphemy as Violence: Trying to Understand the Kind of Injury That Can Be Inflicted by Acts and Artefacts That Are Construed As Blasphemy." *Journal of Religion in Europe* 6 (1): 35–63.

Brekke, Torkel. n.d. "Love Thy Enemy! Christian Politics and Attitudes to Muslim Immigrants in Norway." Unpublished article in review process.

Eskjær, Mikkel Fugl, Stig Hjarvard, and Mette Mortensen, eds. 2015. *The Dynamics of Mediatized Conflicts*. New York: Peter Lang.

Figenschou, Tine Ustad, Kjersti Thorbjørnsrud, and Anna Grøndal Larsen. 2015. "Mediatized Asylum Conflicts: Human-Interest Framing and Common-Sense Public Morality." In *The Dynamics of Mediatized Conflicts*, edited by Mikkel Fugl Eskjær, Stig Hjarvard, and Mette Mortensen, 129–145. New York: Peter Lang.

Marzouki, Nadia, Duncan McDonnell, and Olivier Roy, eds. 2016. *Saving the People: How Populists Hijack Religion*. New York: Oxford University Press.

Marzouki, Nadia, and Duncun McDonnell. 2016. "Populism and Religion." In *Saving the People: How Populists Hijack Religion*, 1–11. London: Hurst & Company.

Michailidou, Asimina, and Hans-Jörg Trenz. 2015. "Mediatized Transnational Conflicts: Online Media and the Politicisation of the European Union in Times of Crisis." In *The Dynamics of Mediatized Conflicts*, edited by Mikkel Fugl Eskjær, Stig Hjarvard, and Mette Mortensen, 51–69. New York: Peter Lang.

Papacharissi, Zizi. 2015. *Affective Publics: Sentiment, Technology, and Politics*. Oxford Studies in Digital Politics. Oxford: Oxford University Press.

Peace, Timothy. 2016. "Religion and Populism in Britain." In *Saving the People: How Populists Hijack Religion*, edited by Nadia Marzouki, Duncan McDonnell, and Olivier Roy, 95–108. London: Hurst & Company.

Roy, Olivier. 2016a. "The French National Front: From Christian Identity to Laïcité." In *Saving the People: How Populists Hijack Religion*, edited by Nadia Marzouki, Duncan McDonnell, and Olivier Roy, 79–93. New York: Oxford University Press.

Roy, Olivier. 2016b. "Beyond Populism: The Conservative Right, the Courts, the Churches and the Concept of a Christian Europe." In *Saving the People: How Populists Hijack Religion*, edited by Nadia Marzouki, Duncan McDonnell, and Olivier Roy, 185–201. New York: Oxford University Press.

Wang, Tricia. 2016. "Why Big Data Needs Thick Data." *Ethnography Matters*. Accessed 28 Aug 2017. https://medium.com/ethnography-matters/why-big-data-needs-thick-data-b4b3e75e3d7

Woodhead, Linda, and Paul Heelas, eds. 2000. *Religion in Modern Times: An Interpretive Anthology*. Oxford: Wiley-Blackwell.

Stig Hjarvard, Mattias Pape Rosenfeldt
Chapter 7
Planning Public Debate: Beyond Entrenched Controversies About Islam

Abstract: The contentious public debates about Islam in Scandinavia may to some extent be characterized as an entrenched conflict, upheld by stereotypical framings and fixed rhetorical positions. This case study examines public service media's ability to facilitate public debates that move beyond such ingrained positions. Through interviews with key professionals behind the TV documentary *Rebellion from the Ghetto*, we examine the strategies for generating public debate about cultural and religious problems. We furthermore analyse online and offline debates, with particular focus on the inclusion of minority voices and how framings of religion enter and influence the discussion. By consciously downplaying the role of 'religion' and framing conflicts in terms of personal experiences and universal themes, the documentary managed to set the scene for a debate in which young Muslims' various experiences were given authority, thereby allowing the debate to transcend the usual 'us–them', 'majority–minority' framing of these issues.

Keywords: debate, Facebook, Islam, minority voices, public service

7.1 Introduction

In this chapter, we address the role of public service media in generating and facilitating public discussions about controversial issues related to Islam in Denmark. Existing research has often demonstrated that news media tend to focus on religious conflicts and frame Islam in stereotypical ways that may reinforce rigid juxtapositions between the majority of ethnic Danes, 'us', versus the ethnic minority of immigrants with a Muslim background, 'them' (Madsen 2002; Yilmaz 2016). As a result, news media may at times reproduce and reinforce existing discourses and conflicts among ethnic Danes and Muslim immigrants rather than challenge these entrenched positions. Research into public opinion concerning Islam also reveals that critical attitudes towards Islam are not only or primarily a feature of media discourses. Both in Denmark and other Scandinavian countries, a majority of citizens feel that Islam poses a threat to their national culture (Lundby et al. 2017). We should take care to not regard this opinion as synonymous with a general resentment towards immigrants since a majority of citizens who consider Islam a threat to their national culture do not endorse hostility towards foreigners. That said, public criticism of Islam has been actively used by right-wing populist parties in all Scandinavian countries to mobilize against immigration in general and from Muslim countries in particular. This political strategy has been fairly successful, with the result that over the past couple of decades, populist parties have become major political parties in Scandinavian parliaments (although with different roles in the individual countries) and have exerted issue ownership over the immigration agenda (Rydgren 2011; Lindroth 2016). In light of this and other major political conflicts that have become intertwined with the immigration issue, such as the international war on terror and the Muhammad cartoon crisis, most of the mainstream political parties in Denmark and other Scandinavian countries have gradually adopted more critical attitudes towards immigration in general and Islam in particular.

It is against this backdrop that we wish to examine whether and how it is possible to engage the public in discussing potentially controversial issues involving Islam and Muslim immigration without necessarily reproducing stereotypes of Muslims among ethnic Danes. We do not aim to provide yet another analytical 'deconstruction' of existing dominant discourses and media's role in reproducing negative stereotypes but seek instead to thread a more 'constructive' path. On the basis of a single case study, we examine how conscious awareness of the existing discursive landscape and deliberate debate planning may play important roles in creating public debates that move beyond entrenched positions concerning religion, Islam, and immigration. Specifically, we examine the television documentary series *Rebellion from the Ghetto* (*Oprør fra ghettoen*), broadcast in 2015 by the Danish public service broadcaster DR on its niche channel DR2. The documentary tells the stories of four ethnic minority youths and their relationships to the cultural and religious norms of their parents' generation. The documentary generated public debate across various media platforms, focusing on controversial topics, such as concealed love affairs and homosexuality as well as broader debates concerning the role of minorities and minority religion in Danish society.

In our analysis of the public debate, we look at the interlocking of a generalized public sphere constituted through mass media and a series of sub-publics, which are often articulated through various social network media such as Facebook. We wish to study how discussions in both mass media and social network media framed the problems presented in the documentary series and to what extent discussions also involved a more diverse set of voices, including ethnic minority voices. To summarize, our three main research questions are as follows: (1) What are the intentions and strategies of the producers (the commissioning broadcaster DR and the production company Plus Pictures) in terms of generating and moderating public debates about religious and cultural problems? (2) To what extent did the public debate involve ethnic minority participants? (3) Which framings became prominent in the debate following the documentary series *Rebellion from the Ghetto*?

Figure 7.1 New voices in Danish television. Saja, 'Sami', Muna, and Moe from the Danish television documentary series *Rebellion from the Ghetto*. It was produced by Plus Pictures and broadcast on DR2 in 2015. 'Sami' appeared anonymously in the programme. (Photo: Plus Pictures / Photographer: Simon Dixgaard.)

Methodologically, the study is based on qualitative and semi-structured research interviews (Kvale 1996) and textual framing analysis (Entman 1993) of the debate in publicly accessible media. The analysis builds upon a theoretical typology of mediatized conflicts (Hjarvard, Mortensen, and Eskjær 2015; see Chapter 3) that highlights the role of media in framing and co-structuring conflicts. In the case of *Rebellion from the Ghetto*, the mediated debate involved not only particular framings of religious and cultural conflicts but also conscious efforts by the producers to take into account pre-existing public framings of contentious issues, which to some extent enabled them to co-structure the discussions beyond entrenched positions of existing debates about Islam.

The programme and our analysis also address the borders between religion and culture. Ever since Clifford Geertz' (1966) work on religion and culture, it has been common in scholarly circles to view religion as a dimension of culture. A more popular understanding may regard religion as distinct from culture, distinguishing between what is true, essential, and eternal (e.g. Islamic religion) and what is manmade, contextual, and historical (e.g. Islamic culture). However, in the public debate on *Rebellion from the Ghetto*, such clear distinctions do not seem to exist. To the contrary, the two concepts are often used interchangeably and as containers for the same content. This may in part be a result of the documentary series' initial framing of problems as secular, cultural, and universal, rather than as religious and specific.

7.2 Producer Intentions

In December 2015 and January 2016, we carried out four interviews with key actors involved in the production of and public communication surrounding *Rebellion from the Ghetto*. The interviews focused on expectations, intentions, and relationships in the production phase as well as evaluations of the effects and the roles of various actors in the debate. From the production company, we interviewed one of the two directors, Louise Detlefsen, as well as producer Mette Heide. The communication specialist Line Bilenberg, who was hired externally to promote the documentary, was our third informant. We also interviewed DR senior editor and head of documentaries Mette Hoffmann Meyer, focusing on DR's role in the initial production phase and public discourse surrounding *Rebellion from the Ghetto*.

The DR editor provided the initial idea for the documentary, wishing to explore what she perceived as a more general problem of social control and everyday violence in immigrant families. She got the inspiration for this topic and framing from the poems of the young Danish writer Yahya Hassan, who has fiercely criticized the parental generation of immigrants in Denmark on the basis of his own experience (Hassan 2013). Despite Hoffmann Meyer's power as commissioning editor, the relative autonomy of the production company should not be overlooked. The initial objectives of the documentary seem to have gradually changed after the project was adopted by Plus Pictures. Executive producer Mette Heide describes a process in which the directors – through a lengthy and 'academic' research process – developed a more nuanced understanding of the social reality they intended to describe. Heide continues:

[The directors] were casting and talking to people, and in their 'fieldwork' they could see there were softer values and some themes that would be relevant for a larger group of people, namely who you can partner up with in your love life. As directors of the documentary, they were very clear on this. It's of no use if we make another 'us versus them' story with this violent image of immigrant culture. It's important that we make a film where they [the ethnic minority youth] can recognize themselves and that at the same time gives insight for Danish-Danish viewers. You might say we changed what we'd originally been asked to produce along the way.

Producer, Mette Heide, Plus Pictures. Interviewed by authors on 18 December 2015

The production company did not, however, have completely free rein, and the commissioning editor interfered when she found it necessary. This became particularly clear when deciding on the title of the series, with the DR editor insisting on *Rebellion from the Ghetto*. No one from the production company was happy with this title since it revived negative 'us versus them' stereotypes, but they had to live with it. This disagreement about the title reveals DR's 'business as usual' logic when it comes to representing Islam and Muslims. The DR editor does speak of approaching the topic with an open mind, but her focus is the conflict between immigrant, minority norms and those of the majority society. In contrast, the directors are more interested in making a television series in which the conflicts take on a universal character concerning love, sex, and generational conflict while differences between majority and minority groups become less divisive.

DR has a longstanding professional relationship with independent production companies, including this company, Plus Pictures. In the case of *Rebellion from the Ghetto*, we see a dynamic relationship between DR and Plus Pictures, with the public service broadcaster taking part in several steps of shaping and producing the documentary. Plus Pictures naturally influences the shaping of the programme, but we also see the production company playing an important role in orchestrating initiatives designed to generate public debate about the themes of the documentary series. It is important to note that the professionals in question from Plus Pictures articulate a strong personal commitment to public service values: Public service ideals seem just as deeply embedded in the private company as in the public organization.

7.3 Talking About Islam

The director of the documentary Louise Detlefsen says that the team was 'talking a lot about religion [Islam]' throughout the production. There is clear awareness that Islam is a controversial and difficult subject. In the eyes of the production team, the main difficulty seems to be the polarized range of pre-existing stances that dominate public conversations about Islam – Islamists on the one side and Islam-bashers on the other – and that it is hard to avoid being pushed into one of these positions. The communication specialist Line Bilenberg argues that it was important to deal with this problem in advance in a very explicit way when talking to the various people involved in the documentary: 'If there's an elephant in the corner of the room, then say it. Don't pretend it's not there. So, say it out loud: "My biggest fear is that this is going to be about Islam".' The young characters in the film did not want their problems to be interpreted in light of Islam and instead regarded problems with their parents and wider social network as cultural issues. The production team wanted to replace the scornful criticism of first-generation immigrant parents they had experienced in, for instance, the poems of Yahya Hassan with a more mature and nuanced critique. In the eyes of the communication specialist, this was the documentary's new and ground-breaking feature: The main characters take centre stage as (part of) the rational and compassionate mainstream 'we', instead of standing outside as either victims or aggressors. The strategy was to focus on showing the participants' problems as more general – or even universal – instead of something specific to Muslims. This approach was designed to create space for a conversation that would be less easily hijacked by the usual polemic positions in the debate about Islam.

DR editor Mette Hoffmann Meyer does not have the same concerns. She is not particularly interested in downplaying the role of Islam and religion but instead simply states that she tries 'to treat this as I would any other topic', tying this to general claims of balance and impartiality. Furthermore, she explicitly distances herself from activist documentary films with a particular message, which seek to persuade audiences to think in particular ways:

> I actually don't believe activist documentary films have any great impact. If you sense right from the start that there's a hidden agenda, or as often the entire programme is cut to make you stop eating pork or drinking French wine, you get bored and intimidated. Do they think I am stupid, or what? If you make activist film, you want to twist the story to brainwash the viewer – want to guide people toward something in particular. I actually don't think activism is a public service role. I think we need to create knowledge and understanding and insight. And then, I suppose, it's up to the individual to take a position on it. Perhaps even seek further knowledge. In other words, I believe in making people curious and asking 'Why?'

Senior Editor Mette Hoffmann Meyer, DR. Interviewed by authors on 1 December 2016

The production team from Plus Pictures does not necessarily disagree with this. Executive producer from the production company, Mette Heide, supports an impartial position, saying 'we're not promoting any particular position' and 'you can't – and shouldn't – try to control and manipulate opinion'. She thus positions herself between a traditionalist and impartial role of public service broadcasting as merely a forum for public debate and a more activist conception of public service media as an actor that intervenes to make a difference in public debate. This latter position does not necessarily entail that the television series carries a persuasive message, which is what DR's editor argues against. The activist position does, however, seek to engage audiences to discuss problematic issues in new ways.

7.4 Engaging the Audience: Building Public Debate

The director and the communication specialist are strikingly clear in their explanations of the purpose of the programme. The programme seeks to engage ethnic minority youth in the debate surrounding the themes of the documentary: homosexuality and individual freedom to choose the partner you want. Bringing these themes to the ethnic youth and engaging them in dialogue became the documentary's *raison d'être* for director Louise Detlefsen:

> It wasn't the typical DR2 audience we were looking for. It's wonderful that the programme is shown on the Danish TV channel DR2, and they are the ones we produced it for, etc. But clearly, our own motivation was that it was the young people with a non-Danish ethnic background who we wanted to talk about these themes. We wanted to have a discussion internally. Could we start a conversation? This was clearly what we wanted to do.
>
> Director, Louise Detlefsen, Plus Pictures. Interviewed by authors on 18 December 2015

On a more general note, the director points out that the interest in ethnic minority youth and Islam comes from a general social commitment, and it is in a sense 'accidental' and comparable with the interest she has in other social issues, such as poverty.

The producer is largely in agreement with the director on this issue. A freelance communication specialist was hired to plan and organize the debate, and with special focus on moving it into the realms of Danish ethnic minority youth. There were two steps in this strategy. First, to gather a diverse group of existing young ethnic minority debaters (role models) and engage them in debating the themes of the documentary on various media platforms. Second, to arrange a series of screenings of the documentary in typical 'ghetto areas', thereby taking the debate back to the environment the documentary explores. Engagement with the ethnic minority community was important for the subsequent marketing of the television series and the framing of the debates following the broadcast. This priming of ethnic minority opinion leaders to engage with the issues raised by the television series ensured there would be people and arguments to build upon when the programmes were eventually broadcast and when the debate in the general news media and social media took off. As communication specialist Bilenberg states, 'you can't set an agenda if only the media write about it, and no one pays attention to it in social media. You can't set the agenda if you only have what is called a journalistic approach. You also need to have debaters or politicians or some other people'. The initial screenings with young ethnic debaters also allowed Bilenberg to get an early account of possible frames and criticism that could arise when the programme was broadcast. On this basis, she was better equipped to stimulate the subsequent debate in line with the original intentions of Plus Pictures.

Curiously, the strategy was based not only on a professional evaluation of how to maximize the programme's reach but also fuelled by personal frustration on the part of key members of the production team. This sense of indignation seemed to drive even the communication specialist in her professional efforts:

> Both instructors felt... – and I felt – an indignation that we haven't got any further [with integration]. It's important that these [young ethnic minority] voices come out. Quite simply, because they're voices we've lacked in the debate. If we can reach out to this target group, the effect will be that it may be more legitimate to talk about these things. So it's a huge help. This thing when something is being said on TV – nationwide – that you in one way or another suddenly create a space where it's permitted to talk about things.
>
> External communications specialist Line Bilenberg. Interviewed by authors on 7 January 2016

The statement by Bilenberg also bears witness to the strategy of using the authority of television to create space for discussions in civil society, both online and offline. The aim was thus less to attract the attention of political decision makers than to allow new voices to emerge.

In addition to the task of stimulating debate in general, the communication specialist was hired to take care of various forms of crisis communication. Experiences from other Plus Pictures productions had shown that debates could become very harsh, including hate mail and death threats targeted at the main characters in the documentary. Especially when dealing with young and non-professional sources, it is important to have a support function for these kinds of debates, including professional advice for the characters about when to engage – or not engage – in social media debates. As a whole, the production company's strategy seems to reflect a public service ethos of a more activist variety; it is less concerned with usual parameters of success in the broadcasting industry, such as higher viewer ratings (popularity) and professional recognition. Instead, the strategy bears witness to a much more idealistic approach and suggests a conviction that the documentary can initiate real societal change.

7.5 Minority Voices in the Debate

The critical question is, then, to what extent the television series managed to create a public debate in mainstream news media and social network media with a greater representation of minority actors' voices (MAV). In this analysis, we distinguish between strong and weak MAV representation. Inspired by Jacobsen et al. (2013), we define strong MAV representation as when the primary actor in the commentary has a visible minority background. In most cases, this is when the author/host has a visible minority background, but we have also coded interview protagonists as strong MAV. Weak MAV is when a minority actor is mentioned and quoted or paraphrased in a comment.

Representation of MAV is often regarded as a measure of media outlets' success at including minorities (Jacobsen et al. 2013). There may, however, be other factors behind a particular frequency of MAV representation than the media's openness to diversity and minorities. Nadim (2017) reports from a Norwegian study that individuals with minority backgrounds do not necessarily find it difficult to access public debate but may nevertheless be reluctant to participate because they are often ascribed a fixed role in such contexts as being representative of a particular minority group. Based on these insights, we propose a theoretical understanding of MAV representation that takes into account the willingness of and ability for minority voices to make themselves heard.

We use a recent study of news and current affairs debates about Islam and Muslims as a benchmark for comparing the representation of minority voices in the debates about *Rebellion from the Ghetto* with the more general pattern of MAV representation. In their study of minority actor voices in four Danish newspapers' coverage of Islam, Muslims, and racism, Jacobsen et. al. (2013) find 11 percent weak MAV representation and 13 percent strong MAV representation, resulting in a total of 24 percent MAV representation. The study concludes that 'the reporting was rather one-sided and exclusive of minority voices, and when Muslims were given voice, the same few publicly visible and vocal actors appeared. At the same time, the lives and opinions of the less visible majority of Muslims more or less vanished in the Media coverage' (Jacobsen et al. 2013, 53). Not only were no minority actors represented in three-quarters of the articles about Islam,

Muslims, and racism, but news media seem to present a narrow range of minority sources.

In order to acquire an overall understanding of the media debate, we screened and collected material from a broad range of online, broadcast, and print media, compiling a sample of debate and opinion pieces explicitly addressing *Rebellion from the Ghetto*. We found relevant material from roughly two weeks leading up to the TV premiere at the start of December 2015 until one week into January 2016, thus covering a period of approximately seven weeks. In this period, we registered 10 opinion pieces from six different national print papers. From broadcast radio, we look at three long-format debates. One of these is from DR and has a general reputation of being critical, devoting time to background and counter-perspectives. The other two long-format radio debates were derived from two episodes of *Rushy's Roulette*, a weekly debate programme focusing on integration and immigrant culture and hosted by the public service Radio 24/7. Our evaluation of the online debate material singled out the official Facebook site of the show *Rebellion from the Ghetto* (40 posts, 184 comments) as well as from the official site of DR2 (the channel that aired the film; 1 post, 40 comments) and the official Facebook page of the daily newspaper *Politiken* (1 post, 338 comments) as central online hubs for the public discussion. The Facebook sites were all lightly moderated, e.g. removing hateful commentary.

The coding of MAV representation in the debates about *Rebellion from the Ghetto* in the printed press and broadcast radio reveals an extraordinarily high representation of minority voices. Table 7.1 shows the representation of minority voices in ten opinion pieces in the press and in three radio debates.

Table 7.1 The distribution of Minority Actors' Voices (MAV) in debates about *Rebellion from the Ghetto* in the press and broadcast radio.

	Press (10 items)	Broadcast radio (3 items)
Weak MAV	50%	0%
Strong MAV	40%	87%
Total MAV	90%	87%

With nine out of ten of the items including a MAV in the press debate, and with 40 percent having a minority representative as the primary voice, it is clear that MAV representation is high in this part of the debate. A condition of unusually high representation becomes even clearer when we consider the debate in broadcast radio, where nearly nine out of ten debate participants/hosts have minority backgrounds. The debates found online also feature high MAV representation, though not quite on the same level as in press and broadcast radio. An analysis of 562 comments from the three Facebook sites in the study show that MAV is represented in well over half the total comments (61.5 percent). On *Rebellion from the Ghetto's* Facebook site (*Oprør fra Ghettoen*), MAV representation in 74 percent of the comments is remarkably high, and somewhat comparable to the level in the press debate, whereas the two other websites have MAV representation in approximately half the comments. MAV representation in the online debates is summarized in Table 7.2.

Table 7.2 The distribution of Minority Actors' Voices (MAV) in debates about *Rebellion from the Ghetto* on three Facebook sites.

Facebook pages:	DR2 (40 comments)	Politiken (338 comments)	*Oprør fra Ghettoen* (184 comments)	All (562 comments)
Weak MAV	5%	1%	20%	7.5%
Strong MAV	45%	55%	54%	54%
Total MAV	50%	56%	74%	61.5%

The debate about *Rebellion from the Ghetto* has a significantly higher occurrence of minority actors' voices compared with in the average news and current affairs debate. We note that the established and edited media outlets (the daily press and broadcast radio) have a significantly higher number of minority actors' voices than we find on broad spectrum Facebook pages. Also, when considering the 'public visibility' of the actors present in the debate, it is clear that many new voices are making themselves heard, especially online, where only few of the minority voices contributing to the debate are individuals who are familiar from the ongoing public debate. It is also interesting to note that, in quite a few of these online and radio conversations between different minority actors, we find no non-MAV participants. The public service radio debates presenting a full panel of ethnic minority voices are good examples of this. The result is a debate that, at least on a structural level, challenges traditional 'us versus them' and 'majority–minority' juxtapositions.

7.6 Public Debate About *Rebellion from the Ghetto*

In order to analyse the main arguments and discursive positions in the various debates, we apply framing theory as developed by Entman (1993) and others. According to Entman (1993), frames provide texts with a specific perspective by implicitly or explicitly proposing a problem definition, causal interpretation, moral evaluation, and/or treatment recommendation. We distinguish between two types of framings, each operating at a different level of generalization: specific frames and general frames. Specific frames are more definitive articulations of 'problems', 'explanations', 'moral evaluations', 'recommendations for action', or any combination of these. Since our textual material in some cases includes very short interventions, it is not possible to identify all these dimensions in every intervention, and in some cases these dimensions are present in only rudimentary form. General frames are central organizing principles that are socially shared (Reese 2001), i.e. that occur persistently across larger sections of textual discourses and represent a general 'interpretative package' (Gamson and Modigliani 1989). Both general and specific frames are understood as issue-specific frames, in contrast to generic frames that may be used across various thematic domains (de Vreese 2005).

Our textual analysis revealed three general frames in the debate. The first typical general frame is what we have dubbed *Immigrant culture (religion) is oppressive*. Here we find immigrant culture and/or religion singled out as a critical problem. This problem definition is sometimes substantiated with reference to reports and social research focusing on immigrant ghettos. In other cases, problems are explicitly linked to qualities inherent in the immigrant and/or Muslim culture, thereby explaining the problem with a more explicitly essentialist understanding, as expressed in this letter to the editor from a *Berlingske* reader:

> The young people feel frustrated, split between the interests of their cultural background with a very purely patriarchal, male-dominated culture, and the culture of freedom and independence that we in Denmark are so proud of, and which the young people in the film long to be able to live in.
>
> Jan Hald, 'Integration' letter in *Berlingske*, 13 December 2015

Some of these specific frames lack solutions to the proclaimed problems of immigrant culture, ending in vague, sometimes sentimental formulations of hope that 'the young Muslims will see change' (P.A. Pedersen 2015) or that they will 'continue so that their children will be able to live the dream we all have' (Hald 2015). The debates do not clearly distinguish between culture and religion; to the contrary these concepts tend to be used interchangeably. This may in part be a result of the documentary series' attempt to downplay the explicitly religious aspects of the issues.

Other comments do come up with solutions or calls to action: One frequent recommendation is that heterogeneous immigrant and religious culture should be promoted and accepted more broadly (Piil 2015). This recommendation is perhaps unsurprising, given that it aligns with the central theme of the documentary. Another recommendation for action is part of a recurring theme in the material, namely a meta-perspective in which media involvement is part of the focus. Here it is stated that critical media representation of immigrant culture and Islam is an important tool for countering social problems within immigrant environments. Some of these discussions are remarkably nuanced, weighing and assessing the various arguments. One example is a long post on *Rebellion from the Ghetto*'s Facebook site that acknowledges the generally negative media representation of Islam but also warns against keeping this media critique on autopilot. This post recommends normalization of the representation of Islam and Muslims, and from this follows a reasonable inquiry into, for example, social problems (Oprør fra Ghettoen 2015).

The second general frame precisely concerns media representation of young Muslims. Here the central problem is that the representation of young Muslims in *Rebellion from the Ghetto* is stereotypical. According to this frame, the television series is basically another victim story, lacking nuance. The story does not make the Danish audience confront its own violence and social control but confirms the fiction that this phenomenon belongs to immigrant families:

> Precisely by avoiding the exploration of the nuances, the documentary turns Muna [a central character] into a hand puppet delivering a cliché victim story typical of Danish TV's representation of ethnic minorities. This is sad because [Muna's] story deserves to be told in full, with all its ambivalence and despair. That would generate identification instead of fascinated outrage and might even remind Danish viewers of the power relations in their own families, instead of confirming that social control only exists among Muslims.
>
> Johanne Mygind, 'Egen stemme' in *Weekendavisen*, 4 December 2015

One solution to this problem is to let the young Muslims represent themselves – as artists and producers. Another recommendation is to involve Muslims in the everyday media landscape as subjective individuals with expertise in many other subject areas, such as the economy – and not to constantly single them out as outsiders or 'the other' (Piil 2015). This general frame obviously has a meta-quality as well since it evaluates the media's representation of Islam and Muslims.

The third general frame also has a self-reflexive meta-layer. Here, however, the reflexivity concerns the debate itself. One aspect of this framing focuses on new female voices, which seem more frequent and more diverse. The moral here is that it is important that young women start speaking for themselves in public debates, and the recommendation is for continued recognition and support for this new development. Another aspect of this frame focuses on homosexuality among immigrants as an important topic. The young ethnic minority homosexuals represent an extremely vulnerable group that can be helped and normalized if the public debate sheds light on this taboo topic. Some debaters also speak of increasing discord among young Muslims. Some Muslim youths take part in shaming and social control of other young Muslims, making their lives miserable:

> On the one hand, we find young 'new Danes' who can no longer keep up appearances or want to compromise their own freedom and liberal rights. And on the other hand, we find the young 'new Danes' who surpass even their parents' ability to abide by conservative values, and thereby interpret any deviation from the parents' cultural and religious customs as a final departure from the tradition. It's the youth rebellion fighting itself.
>
> Geeti Amiri, 'Nydansk ungdomsoprør svigtes af sine egne' in *Ekstra Bladet*, 7 December 2015

This divide, it is asserted, is a huge problem, obstructing more rapid integration of the young generations. Instead, it is suggested, young Muslims should stand together in solidarity and defend each other's rights to individual choice (Oprør fra Ghettoen 2015). Religion is also considered in this moral evaluation: One debater asserts that the young Muslims who use religious arguments to target documentary participants as sell-outs are in fact being hypocritical: These critics lack real religious conduct or knowledge. Their lack of empathy and solidarity with young peers who are facing social difficulties is disturbing and should be seen for what it is, nasty bullying (M.C. Pedersen 2015). A final aspect of this framing is constituted by new citizen-driven organizations *The Neighbourhood Mothers* (Bydelsmødrene) and *Baba – Fathers for Change* (Baba – Fædre for Forandring). Both seek to involve the parental generation in the younger generation's social problems through dialogue. These organizations are typically active in local areas – arranging meetings and community events – but are usually absent from the media debate. They try to make a difference locally, including by recognizing the horizons and sensibilities of the parental generation.

To summarize, the debate that surrounded *Rebellion from the Ghetto* is characterized by the following: First, we find a relatively limited number of general framings. This testifies to a focused debate that stays on the track proposed by its initiators, although the debate also involves critical voices against the framings of the documentary's producers. Second, there are remarkably few radical and aggressive standpoints. As noted above, the specific topic of integration and Islam is by default synonymous with contentious conflict in the media, and public debates often feature a very aggressive tone. This is not the case for this documentary. The debate about *Rebellion from the Ghetto* is on the whole quite sober. Third, debaters seem interested in discussing how different media and public figures act with regard to religion and minority culture. We call this meta-talk, which is characterized by two aspects in particular: 1) There is a focus on (classic) media representation, typically formulated as a critique of the established media's ability to adequately represent minorities. It should be noted that we also find a defence of the established media's right and duty to scrutinize all citizens regardless of ethnicity or religion. 2) New actors in the debate are highlighted: the young female voices, the sexual minorities, and the parental generation. These new actors in the debate become a separate topic of discussion. Broadcast radio in particular is working on this framing. This brings us to a fourth point: The production team's intentions seem to materialize in reality. There is extensive reflection on the quality and nature of the debate from different angles, and ethnic minority youths play a prominent role in the discussions, often as active protagonists.

7.7 Conclusion

Public service media are under special obligations to both engage with critical issues in society and provide forums for informed public debate, and in the case of Danish public service media under a specific obligation to work for integration (see Chapter 5). Often these obligations are fulfilled by communication of already existing critical positions in the debate and giving voice to traditional and well-established voices in the field. As this case study has demonstrated, public service media may also – occasionally – succeed in raising critical issues independently of traditional political actors and at the same time engage other and less frequent heard voices in the debate. To succeed with this in an already established – and to some entrenched – political conflict requires not only an interesting programme with a series of selected and well-researched stories to ground the argument, but also a conscious effort to develop and organize discussions in particular ways among different audiences, online as well as offline, and a strategy to create synergy between debates in different kinds of media and between different actors.

This conscious approach is certainly not a guarantee of success, and the debates surrounding *Rebellion from the Ghetto* could easily have taken another course. The production team also expresses a certain relief that the debate about the programme was not significantly affected by some of the traditional positions in the public debate concerning Islam and immigration. The producer Mette Heide mentions that if, for instance, the Danish right-wing populist party Dansk Folkeparti had entered the debate, it could have gone in very different direction. An interesting lesson from the case study seems furthermore to be that, by consciously downplaying Islam as a religion, the series allows discussions to follow a somewhat different path than might otherwise have been the case. The result is not that religion or Islam are neglected in the debate; to the contrary, religious issues are frequently addressed. But because critical issues are not initially framed as a critique of Islam as such, more immigrants with Muslim backgrounds felt inclined to enter the debate.

Our analysis also demonstrates how the mediatized conditions of contemporary cultural and religious conflicts may not only or always deepen conflicts. Through critical awareness of the role of media in public controversy, it is possible to use media to stimulate new ways of engaging with such conflicts. The media dynamics of mediatized conflict, amplification, framing and performative action, and co-structuring (Hjarvard, Mortensen, and Eskjær 2015; see also Chapter 3) can also be mobilized to support a more sensitive and nuanced debate about controversial issues. The advance screening of the documentary series among ethnic minority groups and particularly among individuals with a recognized position within these communities worked to amplify and frame the documentary's arguments in a particular way, which helped set the scene for subsequent interventions. The conscious framing of the problems as not being about religion but as individual, cultural, and universal issues also helped make the debate diverse. The combined professional resources of DR and Plus Pictures allowed these media actors to influence the overall structure of the debate as it occurred in broadcast radio and the documentary's official Facebook page. The public service media's ability to raise such discussions is not limited to factual genres such as documentary but may also involve entertainment genres such as comedy shows (Hjarvard and Rosenfeldt 2017).

The mediatized conditions of the debate were, however, evident to more than just the people behind the documentary. As our framing analysis shows, meta-discussions about the (problematic) role of media in relation to these issues are integral to public discussions about integration and Islam. This reflects a growing public awareness of the mediatized conditions of such conflicts, yet as our analysis demonstrates, these conditions do not necessarily intensify conflicts or get participants to dig deeper into even more entrenched positions. Nevertheless, moving a debate out of entrenched positions requires not only good will but also professional media expertise, resources, and an institutional framework – such as public service – that can deploy expertise and resources in practice.

Bibliography

Amiri, Geeti. 2015. "Nydansk ungdomsoprør svigtes af sine egne." [The Youth Rebellion of the New Danes is Betrayed by their Own]. *Ekstra Bladet*, 7 Dec. http://ekstrabladet.dk/opinionen/geetiamiri/Nydansk-ungdomsopr%C3%B8r-svigtes-af-sine-egne/5861555

de Vreese, Claes H. 2005. "News Framing: Theory and Typology." *Information Design Journal + Document Design* 13 (1): 51–62.

Entman, Robert. 1993. "Framing: Toward Clarification of a Fractured Paradigm." *Journal of Communication* 43 (4): 51–58.

Gamson, William A., and Andre Modigliani. 1989. "Media Discourse and Public Opinion on Nuclear Power: A Constructionist Approach." *American Journal of Sociology* 95 (1): 1–37.

Geertz, Clifford. 1966. "Religion as a Cultural System." In *Anthropological Approaches to the Study of Religion*, edited by Michael Banton, 1–46. London: Tavistock Publications.

Hald, Jan. 2015. "Integration." Letter to the editor. *Berlingske*, 13 Dec.

Hassan, Yahya. 2013. *Digte*. Copenhagen: Gyldendal.

Hjarvard, Stig, Mette Mortensen, and Mikkel F. Eskjær. 2015. "Introduction: Three Dynamics of Mediatized Conflicts." In *The Dynamics of Mediatized Conflicts*, edited by Mikkel F. Eskjær, Stig Hjarvard and Mette Mortensen. New York: Peter Lang.

Hjarvard, Stig, and Mattias P. Rosenfeldt. 2017. "Giving Satirical Voice to Religious Conflict: The Potentials of the Cultural Public Sphere." *Nordic Journal of Religion and Society*. 30 (2): 136–152. DOI 10.18261/issn.1890-7008-2017-02-03

Jacobsen, Sara Jul, Tina Gudrun Jensen, Kathrine Vitus, and Kristina Weibelet. 2013. "Analysis of Danish media Setting and Framing of Muslims, Islam and Racism." Working Paper 10: 2013. Copenhagen: SFI (The Danish National Centre for Social Research).

Kvale, Steinar. 1996. *Interviews: An Introduction to Qualitative Research Interviewing*. Newbury Park, CA: Sage.

Lindroth, Bengt. 2016. *Väljarnas hämnd. Populism och nationalism i Norden*. [The revenge of the voters. Populism and nationalism in the Nordic countries]. Stockholm: Carlsson

Lundby, Knut, Stig Hjarvard, Mia Lövheim, and Haakon H. Jernsletten. 2017. "Religion Between Politics and Media: Conflicting Attitudes to Islam in Scandinavia." *Journal of Religion in Europe* 10 (4): 437–456 (open access). DOI: 10.1163/18748929-01004005

Madsen, Jacob G. 2002. *Mediernes konstruktion af flygtninge- og indvandrerspørgsmålet*. [The Media's Construction of the Refugee and Immigration Issue]. Aarhus: Magtudredningen.

Mygind, Johanne. 2015. "Egen stemme." [In their own voice]. *Weekendavisen*, 4 Dec.

Nadim, Marjan. 2017. "Ascribed Representation: Ethnic and Religious Minorities in The Mediated Public Sphere." In *Boundary Struggles: Contestations of Free Speech in the Public Sphere*, edited by Arnfinn H. Midtbøen, Kari Steen-Johansen, and Kjersti Thorbjørnsrud, 229–256. Oslo: Cappelen Damm Akademisk (open access). https://press.nordicopenaccess.no/index.php/noasp/catalog/book/16

Oprør fra Ghettoen. 2015. Facebook.com. *Rebellion from the Ghetto*'s official movie page. Accessed 29 August 2017. https://www.facebook.com/Oprør-fra-Ghettoen-133032013724952/.

Pedersen, Marie C. 2015."Vi er en stærk generation, og vi er villige til et oprør." [We are a strong generation and we are willing to rebel]. *Politiken*, 17 Nov.

Pedersen, Poul A. 2015."Forbudte følelser i Ghettoland." [Forbidden feelings in the land of the ghetto]. *Politiken*, 6 Dec.

Reese, Stephen D. 2001. "Prologue – Framing Public Life: A Bridging Model for Media Research." In *Framing Public Life: Perspectives on Media and our Understanding of the Social World*, edited by Stephen Reese, Oscar Gandy, and August Grant, 7–31. Mahwah, N.J.: Lawrence Erlbaum.

Piil, Sarah. 2015. "Hvornår ser vi en etnisk minoritetsdansker være økonomiekspert." [When will we see an ethnic minority Dane as an expert on economy?] *Information*, 11 Dec.

Rydgren, Jens. 2011. "Radical Right-Wing Populism in Denmark and Sweden: Explaining Party System Change and Stability." *The SAIS Review of International Affairs* 30 (1): 57–71.

Yilmaz, Ferruh. 2016. *How the Workers Became Muslims: Immigration, Culture, and Hegemonic Transformation in Europe*. Ann Arbor: University of Michigan Press.

Mia Lövheim, Linnea Jensdotter
Chapter 8
Contradicting Ideals: Islam on Swedish Public Service Radio

Abstract: Cultural and religious diversity are contested topics in Swedish public debate. This chapter analyses how the radio programme *Människor och tro* (People and belief) enables and structures the actors and issues that become heard in this debate, particularly with regard to Islam and Muslims. The programme aims to present an alternative to the dominant negative media discourses by equally representing Christianity and Islam in reports, inviting Swedish Muslims to present experiences and opinions on various news events, and enabling debate between religious organizations, experts, and listeners through phone-in sessions and social media. Despite these efforts, the programme tends to reconstruct, as well as challenge, the dominant frames of Islam as a problem for Swedish society and for the relations of power between the majority and minority voices in public debates. The chapter explores how contradictions between the traditional ideals and formats of public service radio and its ambitions to produce a more nuanced and diverse image of religion contribute to this outcome.

Keywords: public service radio, Sweden, Islam, phone-in session, women

Public service media (PSM) faces challenges both regarding changes within the media landscape and due to the enhanced religious and cultural diversification of the "public" that it is commissioned to service. As described in Chapter 5, Swedish public service broadcasters seem, in comparison with Norway and Denmark, more obliged to consider this dimension in the balancing act between serving a common national culture and enhancing cultural pluralism. *Människor och tro* (People and belief), the programme which is the focus of this chapter, has been broadcast weekly in its current format on Swedish public service radio since the 1990s. This long history makes it unique in a Swedish, as well as in a Nordic context, as a current affairs programme that is focused on religion. The P1 channel features high-quality news about politics, science, and art and it reaches an audience of about 14 percent of the population (Kantar Sifo 2017). As part of this genre, *Människor och tro* is a programme that primarily serves an educated, middle-aged segment of the public, and its audience numbers a few percent of the Swedish public. This, however, makes the programme an interesting example of how public service media seek to manage the cross-pressures between, on the one hand, obligations to service the traditional segment of high-brow listeners and, on the other, the need to attract a new and younger audience with a more diverse cultural background and expectations of popular coverage of religious topics. As shown in a recent survey (see Chapter 2), Swedes stand out among the Scandinavians as being more tolerant towards public expressions of religious diversity, in particular of Islam. In recent years, migration to Sweden has increased, particularly since 2015 as a result of the escalating war in Syria. Combined with growing support for right-wing nationalist political opinions, cultural and religious diversity have become highly contested topics in Swedish public debate.

Through its mandate to serve all citizens, public service radio plays an important role in enabling and structuring the visibility of issues and of various perspectives concerning religion in the public sphere. This also means that public service programmes on religion can become arenas for enacting controversies about the legitimate place of religious values and actors in society. In this chapter, we ask how the programme *Människor och tro* represents religious diversity in Sweden, with a particular focus on the visibility of actors, perspectives, and issues related to Islam.

8.1 Public Service Media and Religion in Sweden

As in the other Scandinavian countries, public service media have a strong position in Sweden. Despite challenges from other media providers, 58 percent of the population still listen to public service radio (SR) daily (Nordicom 2016). More than 60 percent trust public service media and have a positive view of the broadcasters (Ipsos 2016). The change from minority programming to a mainstreaming of cultural diversity policy, which is described in Chapter 5 (see also Horsti and Hultén 2011) is reflected in a renewed policy, brought into being in 2015, in Swedish public service television and radio. Religion, faith, and other life views are to be included among the perspectives from which Swedish PSM are to carry out its coverage of Swedish society.

Studies of the coverage of Islam in Swedish news media (Axner 2015; Brune 2006) show that Islam, Muslim believers and Muslims as a social category are predominantly represented in connection with international conflicts, terrorism, and extremism. News about Islam in Sweden tends to focus on tensions between Islam and the rights of women, and discrimination against Muslims. Although exceptions exist, the everyday life of Muslim believers and the variety among various traditions and ways of practicing Islam is less often portrayed. Brune

(2006, 91) argues that Swedish news media therefore produces a powerful and repeated othering, primarily of Muslims, who are turned into the carriers of characteristics that are seen as being unwanted in Swedish culture. These dominant trends are reported in studies that focus on news media and that use quantitative methodologies based on search words such as 'Islam'. In order to get a fuller understanding of the representation of Islam and Muslims in Swedish media it is, therefore, important to study different kinds of media and to analyse representation in particular media formats in-depth.

The general guidelines of Swedish public service radio emphasize plurality and an ambition to counter prejudices and stereotypes, as well as to look for 'new and unexpected voices'.[1] The specific policy formulations for representing ethnicity and religion, or life views (*livsåskådningar*), state: 'We allow in all contexts participants from different ethnic and cultural backgrounds to be presented as individuals and not primarily as representatives of a particular group.' The policy goes on to say that religious affiliation should not be stated unless 'relevant for context', and words such as 'fundamentalist', 'militant', or 'Islamist' should be used with great care.

8.2 *Människor och tro:* Current Affairs and Insider Perspectives

The programme *Människor och tro* is presented as a 'current affairs program about societal issues that concern religion and politics in Sweden and the world'.[2]

The programme aims to provide in-depth coverage and historical, as well as future-oriented, perspectives and comments. *Människor och tro* comes under the editorial unit that produces programmes on society (*samhällsredaktionen*). The editorial staff for *Människor och tro* consists of two to three people (one programme host, one producer and/or a researcher). About 40 reports in a year are commissioned from freelance journalists. A typical programme is 44 minutes long and consists of a couple of longer reports, including interviews or discussions with invited guests, a brief presentation of the current news on religion,

---

[1] Sveriges Radio, "Mångfald," 2011, accessed 3 July 2017, http://sverigesradio.se/sida/grup psida.aspx?programid=3113&grupp=20752&artikel=5790804
[2] Sveriges Radio, "Om Människor och tro," 2012, accessed 3 July 2017, http://sverigesradio.se/sida/artikel.aspx?programid=416&artikel=5285914.

and reports by international correspondents. The programme is moderated by a programme host and includes possibilities for listeners to interact with the editorial staff, and with each other, through phone-in sessions, email, Facebook, and Twitter.

The policy document (*programbeställning*) of 2016 for *Människor och tro* specifies that the programme should examine the impact of religion on individuals and society and identify and debate upon crucial topics that concern religion and values. It also prescribes that the programme should 'take part in people's everyday reality', and that the 'insider perspective should saturate the programme'. Individuals who are 'experts on their own situation' should be given a salient role. During 2015, the programme was commissioned to interact with the audience and to try out a format of broadcasting discussions from places outside of the studio, such as libraries and other public spaces.

This chapter will focus on the representation of Islam and Muslims in *Människor och tro* in all of the broadcast programmes between January 2014 and April 2015 (62 programmes in total). Starting from the theory of mediatization and religion, we will analyse how the media logic of a current affairs programme on public service radio conditions the programs' engagement with contested issues about religion. We will discuss the relationship between the policy and the aim of the programme, the format of reports, interviews, phone-in sessions, and the Facebook group, and the outcome, in terms of different representations of Islam and Muslims in the programme. We have also interviewed the editorial staff and the producer who worked on the programme during the timespan of our analysis. The interview took place at Sveriges Radio's (SR) headquarters in Stockholm in September 2016.

8.3 Mediatization of Religion and Conflict

As discussed in Chapter 4, the mediatization of religion takes several forms. One of these, journalism on religion, refers to how news media and opinion journalism bring religion to the political public sphere. This implies that religious actors, beliefs, and practices will be presented in a way that conforms to the criteria of newsworthiness and critical inquiry.

Simon Cottle (2006, 3) argues that a mediatized conflict is a part of the process through which a democratic society can define, challenge, and defend important values in the public sphere. In Cottle's understanding, the role of the media in this process is performative, rather than passive and reflective. To understand the role of the media in tensions and controversies involving religion, we use the framework presented by Hjarvard, Mortensen, and Eskjær (2015; see Chapter 3).

They suggest that the way in which the media add a dynamic to a conflict can be analysed through three processes: *amplification, framing and performative agency,* and *co-structuring.* In this chapter, we will primarily focus on the dynamics of framing and performative agency, which concern ways in which the media influence the representation of a conflict, its dramaturgy, and how various actors can perform in a situation. *Framing* describes the process through which media producers 'select some aspects of a perceived reality and make them more salient' in order to 'promote a particular problem definition, causal interpretation, moral evaluation, and/or treatment recommendation' (Entman 1993, 51–52). Frames are produced through the use of certain keywords, phrases, stereotyped images, sources of information, etc., that 'provide thematically reinforcing clusters of facts or judgments' (ibid.). Frames work through referring to, and reinforcing, social conventions, or the 'stock of commonly invoked frames', in a particular context. Framing has implications for the *performative agency* of the various actors involved. Different frames construct different kinds of positions for acting, and different possibilities for the presenting of arguments in the media. These positions for agency are also structured by the formats and genres of a particular form of media.

In news media, events are framed according to what Kent Asp describes as the institution of 'news media logic'. This institutional logic works as 'a constraint on action since its values and rules reduce uncertainty and provide an overall structure that shapes the behaviour of both the news organizations and individual news journalists' (Asp 2014, 259). News media logic works through a combination of shared professional norms, values, and standards for the production of news. Two important values underpinning the power of news logic (Figenschou, Thorbjørnsrud, and Larsen 2015, 130) is a belief in the significance of news, and the role of journalists as the watchdogs of democracy. These values make journalists into privileged interpreters of 'what goes on in the world and how to talk about it' (ibid.). News media logic builds on, and reproduces, certain *generic news frames*, such as conflict, economic consequences, and the attribution of responsibility. These frames are often constructed as *narratives*, which include the roles of both antagonists and protagonists as the actors in a conflict.

Brune (2006, 93–94) identifies four kinds of discursive discrimination in the representation of migrants in the daily press. These are: exclusion from the discourse, often through invisibility; negative representation; objectification by the exclusion of needs and interests; and the normalization of discrimination. These categories reflect how framing can normalize or legitimize problem definitions or treatment recommendations that discriminate against certain groups of people, based on their religious beliefs and practices. In Swedish news media, Muslims and presumed Muslims are predominantly represented as the perpetrators or the victims of violence. In very few cases are Muslims portrayed as actors who are willing and able to make a constructive contribution to Swedish society (Axner 2015, 28).

A particular kind of news frame is the *human-interest frame*. This frame works through making social and political issues interesting through personalization, individual cases, and model stories (Figenschou, Thorbjørnsrud, and Larsen 2015, 131). As Figenschou, Thorbjørnsrud, and Larsen (2015) show in their analysis of asylum conflicts in Norwegian media, these stories tend to focus on the idealized victim, in the form of individuals displaying innocence, morality, and a pleasant personality. The human-interest framing, on the one hand, represents an alternative to the dominant news logic frames of negative representation and objectification. On the other hand, human-interest stories tend to construct one-dimensional characters and hide the complexity of a situation. This may disfavour individuals who fail to display the characteristics of ideal cases, and contribute to a differentiation between "good" and "bad" cases within minority groups. In this way, the human-interest frame can be seen as a form of mediatization of societal conflicts and tensions, in which more complex, structural, or group-based arguments are superseded by a focus on singular events and persons (ibid. 2015, 141).

8.4 Representing and Framing Islam: Reports

The first step in our analysis of how the ideals of diversity and nuance are implemented in *Människor och tro*'s representation of Islam, was to analyse the programming time for topics on Islam in relation to those on other religions from January 2014 to April 2015. This was followed by an analysis of how Islam was connected to other societal issues that were addressed in the programmes. Each report in the programmes was categorized by religious tradition, theme, and region. Invited guests and interviewees who were either presented or self-identified as Muslims were categorized by religious affiliation, profession, and gender. We have also categorized the roles that guests or interviewees were given in the programme as 'expert', 'religious leader', or 'ordinary believer'.

In looking at the representation of different religions, Christianity and Islam are most frequently presented, with an almost equal share of reports during the period. Judaism is covered in 10 percent of the reports. Almost half of the reports focus on Sweden, 19 percent on the Middle Eastern region, and 16 percent on Europe. In terms of themes, the programme lives up to its aim to cover 'the intersection between religion and politics': the most frequent theme, 22 percent of the reports, was political issues. Nine percent focussed on terrorism, and an equal amount on theology and culture. Other themes are much less frequent. Looking at co-occurrences between the themes, we see that reports on Christianity also take up issues that are related to politics and theology, culture, and LGBTQ rights. Reports on Islam tend to focus primarily on religious extremism and politics in both the Middle East and Europe, followed by resistance to, and harassment of, Muslims in Sweden and Europe. Turning to invited guest and interviewees, our analysis shows that the Christian denominations are more often represented than the Muslim denominations. Of the persons invited to discussions in the studio during the time period, 32 came from a Christian context and 9 from a Muslim context.

Even if topics such as international conflicts and terror attacks by violent and extremist Islamist groups dominate, several programmes also discussed the situation of Muslims living in Sweden. Frequent topics are the discrimination against Muslim women by members of their own community, as well as by ethnic Swedes; attitudes toward politicians with a Muslim background; discrimination and islamophobia; and radicalization among young Muslims. Three of the programmes on these themes were broadcast from public places outside the studio, where a live audience entered into the debate with reporters and a panel of invited guests from political parties and civil society.

8.5 Critique and Nuances: Contradicting Demands?

Människor och tro has a mandate to debate on crucial topics that concern religion and values, but also to counter stereotypes about religion through focusing on people's everyday reality and an 'insider perspective', not least concerning Islam. Our interviews with the producer who is responsible for current affairs programmes, Louise Welander, the programme editor, Tithi Hahn, and the reporter, Jalal Lalouni, revealed some dilemmas that relate to the ways in which these ambitions should be realized. One of these was that religion has generally become a more visible issue in the media during recent decades. When other current affairs programmes and news journalism increasingly focus on religion related news, such as the war and the terror attacks that are carried out by the so-called Islamic State, this increases the demand for *Människor och tro* to produce a more profound analysis and to find alternative perspectives to the dominating news logic. However, this demand was not matched with the resources to enable it to 'dig deeper' into current news events, or to produce longitudinal, scrutinizing research on particular issues. Furthermore, the fact that religion is becoming more of a hot topic in the regular news flow made it more difficult to find participants for interviews and debates in the studio. Several issues, they remarked, were perceived as being controversial, and representatives of some religions felt overly exposed and vulnerable to criticism.

Our analysis reveals the efforts of the editorial team to give voice to a broad range of Muslims in Sweden, such as women, youth, and lay people. Nevertheless, in looking at the profession and gender of these guests, it is clear that male imams and chairpersons of Muslim organizations in Sweden, along with researchers, politicians, and activists in public debates, dominate among the invited guests in the studio (21 of 32). Individuals presented as Muslims were also interviewed, for example in connection with the attacks in Paris, Belgium, and Copenhagen in 2014 and 2015, or about the situation of Muslims in Sweden. Among these interviewees, young women and mothers dominate (19 of 28). A common format in reports is that experiences of such 'ordinary Muslims' are followed by comments and discussion among invited religious leaders and experts in the studio. This format can be seen as a kind of framing, in that such comments privilege particular problem definitions, interpretations, evaluations, or recommendations for the treatment of events and experiences. This framing also affects the performative agency of the actors involved in the programmes. The subject position of an interviewee who shares her or his experiences is changed into a position of object or example in a discussion in which this person is not able to take part on equal terms. However, two programmes break from this format in giving young Muslim women the role of commentators on recent media debates about Muslim men controlling young women's dress and behaviour in suburban communities.

8.6 Giving Voice to 'Ordinary People': Phone-In Sessions

The phone-in sessions are presented as an important strategy through which *Människor och tro* can achieve the purpose of including insider perspectives on religion, and strengthen dialogue with listeners. Phone-in programmes, as a genre in public service media, invite listeners to participate in a radio programme through sharing their views and opinions on a specific topic (Nordberg 2006; Thornborrow 2001). Our analysis in this section focuses on the organization of the interaction between participants in phone-in sessions, and what implications this has for the performative agency of the different categories of participants. Does the dynamic of the phone-in sessions in *Människor och tro* differ from the framing that is commonly used in reports about Islam and Muslims in Swedish society? Do they provide for other forms of performative agency for actors who come from minority religious groups to present their perspectives on the presence of religion in the public realm?

Six phone-in sessions took place between January 2014 and April 2015.[3] Three of these addressed the role of Islam in Swedish society: 'Humor, scorn, hate speech or blasphemy?' (October 2014), 'In what spaces should religion be allowed?' (April 2015), and 'Should religious free schools be allowed?' (October 2015[4]). In *Människor och tro*, the programme host moderates the phone-in sessions. Listeners are encouraged to call in either before or during the session, and to send emails to the programme. Staff at the switchboard of SR perform a first sorting of callers, off air.[5]

The call-in sessions are organized following a similar pattern. The host opens the session by referring to a current news event that is related to the chosen theme. One or two calls from listeners, or occasionally emails and Facebook posts, are presented. These comments or questions from listeners are followed by responses from a panel of invited guests, followed by a few more calls, or emails and Facebook posts. In two of the programmes short clips from previous radio programmes are inserted. The first session, on humour and blasphemy, opens with a mix of examples from previous programmes, such as a recording of Pussy Riot's performance 'A Punk Prayer' in Moscow's Cathedral of Christ the Saviour in 2012, a news clip about the Muhammad cartoons controversy in 2005, and a song from the film *Life of Brian* (1979). The host presents the theme of 'the increasingly multifaceted debate on what is allowed to be said, and what not, about religion'. Listeners who 'may have reflected on, or who have experiences with this topic' are invited to call in. Five callers participated in the programme: one man who self-identified as a Sikh, one women identifying as Christian, and one woman and three men representing a secular standpoint. The callers' opinions on the need for criticism of religion and their experiences of disrespect and violation of religious faith were commented on by two guests: Mona Samadi, a university lecturer in civic law and Islamic law, and Jakob Heidbring, university lecturer in civil law and freedom of speech. Furthermore, Christer Sturmark, the chairperson of the Swedish Humanist Association, and Tuve Skånberg, of the Christian Democratic Party, were invited to call in and dis-

---

[3] The other sessions concerned euthanasia, freedom of consciousness and abortion, the new female Archbishop of the Church of Sweden, and prenatal diagnosis.
[4] This session was added to the original period of study due to its relevance.
[5] This sorting was not part of the study.

cuss the theme, due to recent political initiatives that had been taken by these organizations.

The second programme, on the space that religion should be allowed in public, opens with references to whether police officers should be able to wear religious symbols, the allowance of church bells or the muezzin's calls to prayer in public spaces, and end-of-school celebrations in churches. Six callers participated in this session – three men and three women. Two of these had names that signal that they have origins from a country other than Sweden. Arguments ranged from claims about Sweden being a Christian country, the importance of the plurality of religious expressions in the public sphere, and opinions that religion should be expressed in private life or within assigned buildings, and not in other public spaces. Invited guest commenting on the topic and calls were Göran Greider, editor-in-chief of the Social-Democratic leaning newspaper *Dala-demokraten*, Tara Twana, from the Swedish Humanist Association, and Carl-Henric Jaktlund, the then editor-in-chief of the Christian daily *Dagen*.

The third session, on allowing religious free schools in Sweden, opened with a provocative question from the host about whether these are to be seen as a 'a unique possibility for integration, or a tax-financed obscenity'. Nine listeners participated through calls and email. Six of these were women, of which the first – a religious education teacher – argued against religious schools, on the basis that they contradict the law relating to the provision of equal education for all pupils. Two men who self-identified as Muslims, also called in. Both of them argued that religious schools are needed, by reference to their own experience of a lack of understanding for the importance of religious plurality in regular Swedish schools. These opinions were commented upon and discussed by Elisabeth Sandberg, the opinion editor of the Christian daily *Dagen*, Christer Sturmark, of the Swedish Humanist Association, and Claes-Göran Aggebo, from the Swedish National Agency for Education.

8.7 Dynamics: Moderation, Commentators, and Space

Previous research on phone-in programmes has shown a high degree of structural regularity in terms of the pre-allocated turns to talk and the distribution of such turns between speakers. This framework both enables and limits the possibilities for participation, in terms of who can speak to whom, when, and for how long (Thornborrow 2001, 119, 121). Our analysis of the interactions in the phone-in sessions of *Människor och tro* shows that the intermediary role of the host is a salient feature. The host opens the programme and moderates the exchange between the callers and the invited guests by inviting opinions, asking questions, or interrupting and closing down other participants' speeches.

The regular pattern is that callers comment on the theme only, but invited guests comment on both the theme and the opinions of callers. All the programmes include exchanges between callers. However, these exchanges are brief, and when debates or quarrels arise they are interrupted by the host, for example through call closings such as: 'I am sorry to interrupt, but many more people are waiting to share their opinions,' or 'I just need to say that our programme time is coming to an end, but I hope this debate will continue.' In the sessions on the public place of religion and on religious schools, there are examples of brief direct exchanges between a caller and an invited guest. Nevertheless, it is clear that the host directs these exchanges through follow-up question, or by inviting another speaker to speak. Furthermore, the phone-in sessions in the studio usually end with a round of comments from the invited guests and a summing-up comment from the host, which strengthens this pattern.

Phone-in sessions in *Människor och tro* differ from those in other phone-in programmes broadcast on Swedish public service radio (Nordberg 2006) in a number of ways. They are brief and are structured as part of a programming time of less than one hour. They also differ in the frequent use of invited guests, who function as commentators on calls. Our analysis shows a pattern in regard to whom the callers and invited guests represent. Guests are representatives of secular humanist associations, Christian politicians, newspaper editors, researchers, and state officials. Callers predominantly represent native Swedish people (men more than women), who often identify as being secular or Christian. Of the 22 people who participated through calls, mail, or Facebook posts in the three sessions that we analysed, only two self-identify as Muslims, and one as a Sikh. Muslims, however, often become represented by other callers, or guests who speak *for* them, in statements such as: 'I think Muslims are thinking that ...'. This pattern of representation means that Islam and other minority religions are primarily commented on by representatives of native Swedish people, by secular social institutions, or by Christians.

An additional feature which adds to this dynamic is the access to space. The host and invited guests share the studio space, while callers only share air space for a limited time. Being in the studio or on the telephone also affects the possibility of having a voice in the discussion. Callers' talk is often of poorer sound quality than the talk of the host and the panellists. Comments such as, 'I cannot hear you properly – can you repeat or speak up, please? Are you with us? We lost contact with X' are frequent in the host's interactions with callers.

David Herbert, Tracey Black, and Ramy Aly (2013, 536) point out, in an analysis of discussions about religion in the online forum 'Have Your Say' on the BBC World Service channel, that in spite of constraints to interactivity by the technology and the news media discourses, these debates illustrate the potential to enable complex dialogue among individuals from different contexts about common concerns. Joanna Thornborrow (2001, 134), in her study of phone-ins to BBC Radio 1, discusses how the possibility of callers debating with politicians, or other authorities in society, gives the caller the position as a questioner of authorities and dominant discourses.

Our analysis shows that the format of the phone-in sessions in *Människor och tro* made it difficult for listeners to interact directly, and also to actively react to the framing discourses and production processes which structure the programmes. The host and the invited guests had more speaking time and shared the studio space, and thus had an ability to express their opinions that was greater than that of the listeners who called in. Furthermore, the prominent role of the host in directing follow-up questions and inviting speakers into the conversation, defuses the potentially powerful role of the ordinary person as a questioner of people in institutional positions of power in society. Interviews with the editorial team revealed another aspect that contributes to this pattern. This concerned the tension between combining a plurality of perspectives with a qualified analysis of a topic. While the team strived to find representatives from other groups than 'academics' who tended to be male, middle-aged and of Swedish origin, and who might contribute with everyday experiences of religion, they also argued that guests had to 'fit the format', meaning that even if some people might have had very interesting and relevant experiences they had to be able to articulate these in a short timeframe and during a heated debate. This illustrates the significance of an ability to express arguments in a clear, rational, discursive form in order to participate in the programme.

These aspects contribute to an asymmetrical, rather than a symmetrical, framework of mediated interaction in the programme. The pattern of representatives from majority groups in society who comment on other religious groups, contributes to the framing of minority religions, here, primarily Islam, as the issue or problem at stake in the debates. This framing can contribute to, rather than challenge, a normative understanding in Swedish society that a secular or Christian model for public expressions of religion can be tolerated, but that other religious expressions are an anomaly or problem that must be solved (see Chapter 4). The asymmetry between callers and invited guests also risks reinforcing, rather than reversing, the institutionally inscribed roles of elites and common people in the public discourse. This pattern, as well as the importance of expressing arguments in a particular linguistic form, is probably reinforced by the fact that *Människor och tro* is a public service programme, with an aim to supply an educated, middle-aged segment of the population with high-quality news and in-depth perspectives.

8.8 Positive Role Models and Identification: A Hijab on Facebook

A second forum for interactions with the audience is *Människor och tro*'s Facebook page. As pointed out in Chapter 5, PSM are challenged to reach out to younger audiences through digital media. Facebook and Twitter are recent additions to the programme, and the editorial team expressed to us that they still struggled somewhat to integrate these platforms into their work. They found it difficult to get a dialogue going between posters and, due to the lack of time for moderation, they often refrained from promoting more controversial topics from the radio programme, since this might generate antagonistic discussions that they were not equipped to handle.

The most liked and shared posting on the Facebook page during the study concerned a police student named Donna Eljammal. The posting, made on 1 April 2015, followed an earlier interview in the programme (3 April 2014) and included an image of her wearing a hijab and a police uniform:

> Donna Eljammal is the first student at the Swedish National Police Academy who wears a headscarf. When the media drew attention to this in a 2011 debate, support and hateful comments online followed. More than three years later, Donna is representing Södertälje Police Office as a receptionist. 'The response here has been surprisingly positive,' she says.

The post received 1,385 'likes' and 61 comments, and it was shared 63 times from the Facebook page. In addition, the post was shared from the archives of text published by sverigesradio.se over 3,000 times in various social media. In comparison, the second most noticed posting, about a teaching student in training who was harassed for wearing a headscarf received 55 'likes', zero comments, and was shared five times.

Only two of the comments expressed criticism of the veiled police student. The majority are positive, short statements that thank and encourage Donna Eljammal. The following is one of the longest and most elaborate:

> You are a role model for many women who do not dare to fight for for the profession of their dreams, and you are a strong woman who shows what your heart chose!! Fight on, even if it

might be hard sometimes. You change society by showing what you chose and how strong you are! Very nice, mashalah.

The names of posters and the frequent adding of 'mashallah'⁶ at the end of posts indicate that the majority of posters come from, or affiliate themselves with, a Muslim religious tradition. A few of the commenters also engaged in brief discussions about the professions that Muslim women can take up, and how they should dress in public. The editorial team of *Människor och tro* posted four short statements expressing appreciation for the positive comments, and invitations to listen to the programme. Donna Eljammal herself posts once, saying, 'Thanks everyone for the nice comments. They strengthen and warm my heart. (Feel proud after all these nice comments.)'

The form and content of the Facebook interaction differs in many ways from the patterns discerned in the phone-in sessions. The Facebook interactions have a low degree of moderation and are not commented on by the invited on-air guests. The majority of posters seem to be identifying with Donna Eljammal as young Muslims in Swedish society, and various opinions on Muslim women's dress in public spheres are expressed. The posting is widely 'liked' and shared. However, there is a low degree of interaction between posters.

This example illustrates how *Människor och tro* seek to realize the policy of Swedish public service radio to counter prejudices and give voice to individuals as 'experts on their own situation'. As pointed out in our analysis of the reports, young Muslim women are often chosen as interviewees, and, on two occasions, as invited guests, to give their perspective on issues raised in the programme. This strategy can, on the one hand, be seen as an alternative to the 'discursive discrimination' of minority groups in news media framing. In the original posting, the 'surprisingly positive response' at the police office to a veiled police woman is contrasted with previous 'hateful comments' in media and online debates. Giving voice to the experiences and opinions of young Muslim women counters invisibility and the stereotypical representation of Muslim women as victims derived of agency. On the other hand, the young Muslim women who are fronted in the programme are, like Donna Eljammal, representatives of Islam in a way that aligns with an established model of religion in Sweden: as an expression of personal belief and as a human right that is also compatible with democratic values, such as gender equality (see Chapter 4). Donna Eljam-

---

6 The Arabic expression 'mashallah' can be used in a literal religious sense, as a neutral generic saying (detached from its religious roots), or even ironically. Due to the context of commenting on wearing the hijab as a religious symbol, we surmise that it is here being used religiously.

mal thus becomes a symbol of how a young Muslim woman ideally should take part in, and contribute to, Swedish society. This strategy is also an example of the ambiguous implications of using a human-interest frame in media representations of Islam. By fronting a particular ideal case, this frame aligns with dominant secularist media discourses that tend to dichotomize between religion as personal faith or as an ideology with political claims (Lövheim 2017). While religion is seen as being problematic for a democratic society in both of these discourses, religion as an expression of individual human rights can be accepted, as expressed in the uses of the human-interest frame. This kind of conditioned acceptance of religion as a public expression in Swedish society can, on the one hand, be seen as an example of how the media contribute to the processes of negotiating important values in a democratic society – in this case, how to accommodate religious freedom and certain values of the (secular) majority of society (see Lövheim and Axner 2011; Cottle 2006, 3). On the other hand, it shows how 'alternative' media frames can contribute to upholding a distinction between 'good' religion, as practised by individuals in the private sphere, and 'bad' religion, as public expressions that generate tensions between various opinions and groups.

8.9 Conclusion: Balancing Contradictory Ideals

Cultural and religious diversity have become increasingly contested topics in Swedish public debate. As part of the public service media, *Människor och tro* enables and structures what actors, perspectives, and issues are expressed in this debate, particularly with regard to controversies that relate to Islam. Swedish public service radio has high ambitions to present an alternative to the dominant media discourse that represents Islam as being connected to terrorism and extremism as social problems, and to provide a nuanced insider perspective, rather than repeating the stereotypes of particular groups.

This chapter has shown that *Människor och tro* provides an equal representation of Christianity and Islam, in terms of programming time, but that Islam is still largely placed in the context of extremism and terrorism. The programme's editorial team strive to counter stereotypes by allowing 'ordinary' Swedish Muslims to comment on such events and to present their experiences and opinions. These are often women, which indicates an effort to give a voice to a minority group. The Facebook posting about the police student, Donna Eljammal, shows an ambition to give a voice to practising Muslims who have found a way to present their religion in public, which has resulted in 'positive' responses and has challenged stereotypes about Islam among the Swedish public. The ambition of the phone-in sessions, to provide a more nuanced public discussion than those seen in the established news formats, is hindered by the structure of the interaction, where the voices of ordinary Muslims are few and, to a large extent, they become framed by the dominant discourses on Islam, which see it as a 'problem' in democratic secular societies. In the words of Sonya Sherefay, a participant in *Människor och tro*'s public hearing on radicalization in the Stockholm suburb Tensta: 'I think you should not just come to us when there is a problem, radio. You should come also when things are good!'

The editorial staff and producers are well aware of the generally negative media image of Islam, and they also know that their way of reporting can reproduce this. However, in response to our finding that most of the reports repeat the image of Islam as being connected to conflicts and terrorism, they responded that it is not their assignment to portray 'everyday Islam'. There has to be a story, they argued, in order for the programme to portray Islam 'in a good way'. This difficulty of combining critical reporting with a more nuanced image of Islam was enhanced by reactions from listeners who, most prominently, were critical of the programme for focusing too much on Islam and covering up 'dark sides' of religion such as conflicts.

The producers also emphasized the need to differentiate between journalistic programmes on religion, and 'religious programmes', such as worship in religious communities. *Människor och tro* belongs firmly to the first category, and it is thereby commissioned to report on religion in a critical and factual manner. This tension between an ambition to nuance the news media's framing of Islam and the ideals of good journalism is mirrored in the editorial teams' experiences of communication with what they termed 'religious people'. They had experienced the ways in which 'religious people' felt that they were asked the wrong questions, or were forced into unknown and awkward territory by journalists. One of the reporters explained, 'Religious people do not accept debate as a format, where various opinions are tested against each other. They are reluctant to enter into a format where they cannot control what is being communicated.'

In sum, our analysis of the reports, the interactive formats, and the interviews with the editorial team of *Människor och tro* illustrate several aspects of the dilemmas that public service media face in balancing traditional ideals and formats, and the ambition to communicate a nuanced image of religion. As a current affairs programme that is traditionally catering for elite segments of the population, the editorial team of *Människor och tro* follows the traditional journalistic ideals of public service media. The frequent use of invited guests, such as researchers, politicians, other journalists, and leaders from religion and belief organizations, to comment on the experiences and opinions of listeners, follow an attempt to present a critical, in-depth analysis that differs from ordinary news media. However, as these experts often refer to explanatory frames that present public expressions of Islam as a problem in Swedish society, they tend to strengthen a division between 'good' and 'bad' public religion. This tendency is strengthened by journalistic ideals and standards, the 'gut feeling' of what makes a 'good debate', in the phone-in sessions, which tend to privilege the voices of established experts, rather than ordinary listeners. In this way, our analysis of *Människor och tro* reveals some of the dynamics of the ways in which public service radio enables and structures the visibility of issues, actors, and perspectives that represents Islam and Muslims in contemporary Sweden. These dynamics are shaped by, and contribute to, the public sentiments against religion, in particular, Islam. Swedish citizens may be more tolerant towards expressions of Islam in the public sphere than their Scandinavian neighbours, but, as our analysis shows, the possibility for Muslim citizens to make their voices heard is still structured by the traditions, rules, and values that are formed by the majority of the participants in this public discourse.

Bibliography

Asp, Kent. 2014. "News Media Logic in a New Institutional Perspective." *Journalism Studies* 15 (3): 256–270.

Axner, Marta. 2015. "Representationer, stereotyper och nyhetsvärdering. Rapport från medieanalys om representationer av muslimer i svenska nyheter."
[Representations, stereotypes and news values. A media analysis of representation of Muslims in Swedish news]. Stockholm: DiskrimineringsOmbudsmannen (DO). Accessed 30 June 2017. http://www.do.se/om-diskriminering/publikationer/representationer-stereotyper-och-nyhetsvardering/.

Brune, Ylva. 2006. "Den dagliga dosen. Diskriminering i Nyheterna och Bladet." [The daily dose. Discrimination in the news and the paper]. In *Mediernas vi och dom. Mediernas betydelse för den strukturella diskrimineringen*, edited by Leonor Camauër and Stig Arne Nohrstedt, 89–122. SOU 2006: 21.

Cottle, Simon. 2006. *Mediatized Conflict: Developments in Media and Conflict Studies.* Maidenhead: Open University Press.

Entman, Robert M. 1993. "Framing: Toward Clarification of a Fractured Paradigm." *Journal of Communication* 43 (4): 51–58.

Figenschou, Tine Ustad, Kjersti Thorbjørnsrud, and Anna M. Grøndahl Larsen. 2015. "Mediatized Asylum Conflicts: Human-Interest Framing and Common-Sense Public Morality." In *The Dynamics of Mediatized Conflicts*, edited by Mikkel Fugl Eskjær, Stig Hjarvard, and Mette Mortensen, 129–145. New York: Peter Lang.

Herbert, David, Tracey Black, and Ramy Aly. 2013. "Arguing about Religion: BBC World Service Internet Forums as Sites of Postcolonial Encounter." *Journal of Postcolonial Writing* 49 (5): 519–538.

Hjarvard, Stig, Mette Mortensen, and Mikkel Fugl Esjkær. 2015. "Introduction: Three Dynamics of Mediatized Conflicts." In *The Dynamics of Mediatized Conflicts*, edited by Mikkel Fugl Eskjær, Stig Hjarvard and Mette Mortensen, 1–27. New York: Peter Lang.

Horsti, Karina, and Gunilla Hultén. 2011. "Directing Diversity. Managing Cultural Diversity Media Policies in Finnish and Swedish Public Service Broadcasting." *International Journal of Cultural Studies* 14 (2): 209–227.

Ipsos. 2016. "Stort förtroende för Sveriges Television och Sveriges Radio." [Strong trust in Swedish Television and Swedish Radio]. Accessed 3 July 2017 http://ipsos.se/160401-DN-Ipsos-Mediefortroende

Kantar Sifo. 2017. Accessed 10 January 2018 https://www.kantarsifo.se/rapporter-under sokningar/radioundersokningar/radioresultat-nationell-radio-ppm

Lövheim, Mia. 2017. "Religion, Mediatization and 'Complementary Learning Processes' in Swedish Editorials." *Journal of Religion in Europe* 10 (4): 366–383.

Lövheim, Mia, and Alf Linderman. 2015. "Religion, Media, and Modernity: Editorials and Religion in Swedish Daily Press." In *Is God Back? Reconsidering the New Visibility of Religion*, edited by Titus Hjelm, 32–45. London: Bloomsbury.

Lövheim, Mia, and Marta Axner. 2011. "Halal-TV: Negotiating the Place of Religion in Swedish Public Discourse." *Nordic Journal of Religion and Society* 24 (1): 57–74.

Nordberg, Karin. 2006. *Folkhemmets nya röster. Ring P1 – en alternativ offentlighet?* [New voices of the people. Call P1 – an alternative public?]. Stockholm: Stiftelsen Institutet för mediestudier.

Nordicom. 2016. The Media Barometer. Accessed 10 January 2018 http://nordicom.gu.se/en/statistics-facts/media-barometer

Thornborrow, Joanna. 2001. "Questions, Control and the Organization of Talk in Calls to a Radio Phone-In." *Discourse Studies* 3 (1): 119–143.

Local Civic Settings

David Herbert
Chapter 9
Perspectives: Theorizing Mediatized Civic Settings and Cultural Conflict

Abstract: This chapter reflects on how the interplay between national media frames and discourses, social media, and user-generated content works out in practice in civic settings. It argues that while social media in theory break national elites' representational monopoly, in practice successful challenges (which would shift mass media frames and overall public opinion) are rare; rather, voicing of alternative views mostly results in the formation of networked counter-publics, with potential to challenge mainstream views but also to increase polarization. These dangers may be exacerbated by an increasingly uneven spatial distribution of both religious diversity and anti-immigrant sentiment, shown in levels of religious participation by ethnicity and voting patterns by region. The challenges posed for local governance by this situation are outlined, and possible solutions briefly considered, drawing on evidence from the literatures on superdiversity, contact theory, and political participation.

Keywords: mediatized civic settings, spatial distribution of diversity, digital hybridization, agency, networked crowd

9.1 Introduction

This chapter sets the scene for the case studies of mediatized cultural conflict in the three chapters that follow. None are neighbourhood studies in a classic ethnographic sense, but rather range across scales to capture the interplay between them created by intensified media communications. Hence Repstad (Chapter 10) examines connections (and disconnections) between national media frames, political discourse, and local media representations in his study of the discourse on refugees amongst churches in Southern Norway; Liebmann (Chapter 11) traces links between national media frames, social media posts, the funding of local inter-faith groups, and the experiences and actions of residents in multi-ethnic neighbourhoods in Eastern and Southern Norway; and Hansen and Herbert (Chapter 12) investigate how Muslims in the Greater Copenhagen area in Denmark respond to a negative national media frame, and reflect on the conditions shaping the formation and acceptance of multiple identities as a key ingredient in cooperative community relations.

The aim of this chapter is to situate these case studies in the broader context of theories and empirical work relevant to the relationship between mediatization and other processes of social change at work in local civic settings. While there are studies of various relevant factors including the role of transnational media networks in the lives of diasporic minorities (Gillespie, Herbert, and Anderson 2010; Rinawwi 2012), citizens' use of media for a sense of public connection (Couldry and Markham 2008), and the mobilizing capacities of Web 2.0 social media for social protest (Theocharis 2013), the impact of mediatization on relationships and experience in local settings remains relatively underdeveloped, creating a gap between locality (and especially urban, as the main locus of religious diversity in contemporary European societies) studies and media studies. This section of the book, drawing on both CoMRel and its sister project *Cultural Conflict 2.0: The Dynamics of Religion, Media and Locality in North European Cities*,[1] seeks to address that gap.

In their introduction to media dynamics in Chapter 3, Hjarvard and Lundby provide a framework for conceptualizing media as embedded in and partly constitutive of social relations, outlining three types of dynamics through which media permeate and reshape them (amplification, framing and performative agency, co-structuring). They also emphasize, especially in their conclusion, that individual agency can still make a difference to outcomes, despite the powerful structuring forces at work. This chapter seeks to build on that account by examining how civic dynamics interact with media dynamics, and the conditions under which this interaction occurs, drawing on perspectives from a range of resources to conceptualize mediatized civic settings and the forms of agency emergent within them.

9.2 Mediatized Civic Settings

> The city ... does not end with the visibly observable. ... Urban spaces are becoming hybridized, meaning they are composed through a combination of physical and digital properties. (Gordon and de Souza e Silva 2011, 1, 14)

> In mediated societies – societies where media institutions have a dominant role and most, if not all, of our information about what is going beyond our immediate locality on comes from media – it is impossible to separate the recognition individuals get from each other from the way media resources are distributed. (Couldry 2011, 48)

---

[1] Grant No. 231344. Our thanks to the Research Council of Norway for funding this project.

How people experience their own neighbourhood of residence, and those they work in, pass through or visit, has always been mediated by the impressions of others, whether through local gossip, newspaper accounts, or perhaps by travel guidebooks in the case of larger cities and favoured tourist destinations. However, changes in media technologies and their uses have significantly altered and arguably intensified the role of the media in shaping our experience of locality.

First, the combination of digital mapping, geo-locating, and social media technologies has changed how we perceive and negotiate our way around local areas, especially but not exclusively in cities, because of the dense networks of digital information available for users to navigate the urban environment, using smartphones and other networked devices. Thus, as Gordon and de Souza e Silva (2011) argue in the first opening quotation, localities and especially urban spaces are becoming 'hybridized', with digitized layers of information interposed between us and the physical environment by navigation tools, often embedded with commercial recommendations, photos and videos posted on platforms such as YouTube and Instagram, and commentary in blogs and on platforms such as Twitter. Indeed, this abundance of information creates the need to filter out what is most useful, attractive, or entertaining, producing selection processes enabled by social media platforms which may, ironically for technologies which are often widely available, intensify existing patterns of social segmentation, stratification, and inequality (Boy and Uitermark 2016).

Second, this production and circulation of urban imagery and other user-generated content breaks the representational monopoly of local and national leaders, as well as that of the one-to-many media platforms which have helped leaders disseminate their messages and secure consent for their policies – platforms ranging from parish magazines and political pamphlets to regional newspapers and national television and radio (Watt 2008). Using social media, audiences may become not mere observers but participants who can contest and challenge received understandings, as they fill comment sections on websites, tweet their thoughts, share their ideas on Facebook, post YouTube videos, or recirculate content (which, at scale, can generate the phenomenon of content 'going viral'). And yet the evidence of our case studies suggests that local actors still have limited power to challenge national media frames; indeed, social media may function predominantly rather as channels to reinforce dominant stereotypes, both by recirculating stereotypically framed material, and by producing new material framed in terms of dominant stereotypes.

In Chapter 11 Liebmann draws on fieldwork from Groruddalen, an East Oslo suburb with a large ethnic minority population, and Kristansand in Southern Norway. In opening, she uses a vignette from Groruddalen which provides a good example of both the digital hybridization of locality and the unintended stigmatizing effects of a potentially emancipatory technology. She describes the injured response of local resident 'Zunair' to a video posted on social media by another young man, an ethnic Norwegian from the other side of town, who recorded his apparently 'horrific' experience of an accidental visit to Groruddalen when he overslept on the train. While the stigmatizing video, posted by a member of an ethnic majority and feeding into existing media stereotypes (ECRI 2015), may readily gain traction in the social media marketplace, minority views may struggle to attract similar levels of attention. Hence while social media offer new vistas on localities and in theory the possibility to challenge mainstream and official representations, in practice minority voices may be drowned out by a torrent of re-hashed stereotypes, and the weakening of official representations mainly serve to remove barriers that once obstructed this flow.

Similarly, the findings of Chapters 10 and 12 tend to support the view that while Web 2.0 technologies in theory offer media audiences opportunities to participate in, and hence potentially co-construct, emergent media landscapes, in practice, at least in these cases, the sense of a national media frame, fed by powerful transnational media discourses, remains dominant, offering limited opportunities for interruption, let alone co-construction. Thus, in his study of local church discourse on refugees in Chapter 9, Repstad finds no warrant for national media and politicians' claims that church leaders' liberal views on asylum are at odds with those of local congregations. Yet neither the preponderance of positive attitudes of active local Christians towards refugees, at least as presented on church websites and in newsletters, nor their practical mobilization to support refugee welfare, nor the liberal statements of the national leadership of the most powerful religious institution in Norway, the Lutheran church, appear sufficient to interrupt dominant national media and political discourses. Indeed, this case fits with the narrative of historical mediatization described by Hjarvard and Lundby in Chapter 3, which holds that 'in order to reach public attention through the news media, religious issues should fit the media's news values.' On the other hand, Repstad's case shows that the national negative media frame does not determine the content of local discourses; while the local may not interrupt the national, at least the local retains some autonomy.

In Chapter 12, Hansen and Herbert report that ethnic Danish and minority heritage Muslims in Copenhagen often expressed exhaustion at their experience of an unrelenting flow of negative mainstream representation, and most experienced apparently little sense of empowerment flowing from their social media participation. However, some research has found social media significant in providing space for minority empowerment. For example, in the Netherlands Leurs, Midden, and Ponzanesi (2012) report on how the social media platform *Hyves* was used by Dutch Moroccan women to organize street protests against Dutch politician Geert Wilders' proposal for a *'kopvoddentax'* ('head-rag tax'), announced to Parliament on 16 September 2009. Organized online under the heading *Wij Willen Geen Hoofddoek Verbod!* (We want no headscarf ban!), the site attracted 15,000 followers and led to protests in several locations across the Netherlands before the proposal was dropped. The researchers locate this activity in the broader context of Internet discussion platforms providing 'hush harbours' for sharing experiences of hostility and offering mutual support in the context negative public framing of Islam and Muslim practice in the Netherlands. For example, one platform for Dutch Moroccans, Marokko.nl, 'is estimated to reach a remarkable 70 to 75 percent of Moroccan-Dutch youth in the age category of 15 to 35' (ibid., 159). The researchers conclude that these online spaces:

> not only offer an important critique of mainstream media debates on multiculturalism, but also create space for alternative bottom-up interpretations of everyday practices of multiculturalism in the Netherlands. (ibid.)

Internet forums and social media platforms have also provided the organizational infrastructure for acts of inter-religious solidarity in Denmark and Norway, including the human ring formed around the synagogue in Oslo organized by young Muslims in the wake of the shootings at a synagogue in Copenhagen in February 2015 (Hovland 2015). Social media use enables rapid and widespread mobilization across space; thus, the ring of solidarity idea was a response to an attack in Denmark which led to action in Oslo, Norway, then was re-used in Bergen, and an earlier 'March Against Terror' in September 2014 in Oslo was re-used in Kristiansand.[2] In such mediatized events, the use of urban space is both enabled through the digital infrastructure supporting its organization and amplified in impact by the circulation of the images generated. Thus, while our case studies show some negative impacts of social media on minority stigmatization, there are clearly other sides to the story.

Such social media networks may be understood as constituting 'counter-publics', meaning 'parallel discursive arenas where members of subordinated social groups invent and circulate counter-discourses ... to formulate oppositional interpretations of their identities, interests and needs' (Fraser 1990, 67), and which may produce 'offline' social and political action. This role of social media does not seem to fit easily into the typology of media dynamics in mediatized conflicts supplied by Hjarvard and Lundby in Chapter 3 (Table 3.1; see also Hjarvard, Mortensen, and Eskjær 2015, 10). Perhaps it best fits the metaphor of 'media as environment' and the dynamic of 'co-structuring', as the affordances

---

2 Observed by Sivin Kit for the Cultural Conflict 2.0 project, field notes September 2014.

of the social media platform structure the form that contributions to debates take (a kind of formatting – Instagram enables curated visual representations, Twitter favours aphoristic sloganeering etc.). However, while the platforms used operate in a broad commercial environment shaped by relations of power (Facebook, Instagram, and Twitter are all monetized commercial platforms), so that the media practices of users are in some sense 'embedded in … structural relations of power', it is not clear how this influences them, and social media practices displayed on these platforms do not seem necessarily to reinforce these 'relations of power', but rather, may, under some conditions (modestly) redistribute power across networks, and indeed at a local level (by virtue of the concentration of network participants within a locality), for example by distributing counter-images, as with the positive representations of refugees in local church communications found by Repstad (Chapter 10).

While Hjarvard, Mortensen, and Eskjær recognize that 'the relationship between media and conflict does not constitute a one-way street from media to social actors' (2015, 10), and write of social actors 'using' media and media being 'implicated in stratified systems of social power' (ibid.), neither 'use' (by an intending agent) nor 'implication' within a stratified system seems to quite capture the networked dynamics of social media power. Rather, the power of social media is somehow more 'distributed' – not so much under the control of powerful individual (or corporate) actors as mass media power – yet capable of being activated by the posting of a single image, as the term 'going viral' suggests. Maybe this is a kind of 'co-structuring', though not of an incremental, gradual kind, as that term may suggest, but something more rapid and volatile; such power is the product neither of individual will nor of institutional formation, but rather of the networked crowd. Perhaps then, Hjarvard, Mortensen, and Eskjær's (2015) model could use an extra, fourth media metaphor, that of the 'network', with its characteristic dynamic of 'circulation' and 'influence' of 'increased volatility' which creates 'potential for disruption of dominant representations, but also for their retrenchment'.

The counter-publics enabled by social media – whether ethnic minority hush harbours or regional subcultures (such as Repstad's churches in Chapter 10) – also suggest a mechanism which might disrupt the 'spiral of silence' dynamic (Noelle-Neumann 1984) identified by Hjarvard and Lundby (Chapter 3), whereby majority viewpoints become more dominant in public discussions as dissenters become reluctant to contribute, once a dominant position is established. Certainly, our Danish interviewees (Chapter 12) illustrate this spiral, as interviewees expressed reluctance to contribute to public forums due to the overwhelmingly negative responses received. However, the formation of social media networks might also interrupt this process, by providing forums in which minority opinions form a critical mass empowered to challenge dominant positions. While this might contribute to a 'filter bubble' effect (Pariser 2011), increasing fragmentation of public opinion, this is unlikely for minorities, who are not likely to be unaware of dominant media frames. Rather, such counter-publics can enable the strengthening of minorities through the development of solidarity, and may empower them to intervene in the public sphere at opportune moments (as with the anti-head scarf ban protest, or the human ring initiatives).

Furthermore, both Scandinavian and Dutch counter-publics discussed suggest the importance of spatial relations for grasping the dynamics of interaction between media and locality. In several cases, online activity galvanizes protest enacted at specific significant sites; and in Groruddalen we see an example of the uneven spatial distribution of religious diversity in Scandinavia, which, it will be argued, is central to understanding the dynamics of mediatized civic conflicts in this region.

9.3 Place Matters: The Uneven Spatial Distribution of Religious Diversity, Practice, and Fear of Difference in Scandinavia

> Non-European immigrants tend to be more religious – typically Muslims or Christians – than their host populations. ... The limited evidence for second-generation minority populations suggests that religious decline will occur more slowly (if at all) among them than it has among the majority population. ... We may begin to see 'de-secularization' in Western Europe in the coming decades. Indeed, this is already visible in the continent's religiously vibrant immigration cities. (Kaufmann, Goujon, and Skirbekk 2012, 71–86)

> Debates for or against the banning of the construction of mosques and/or minarets reveal the tumultuous transition of Muslims from the status of the invisible migrant worker to that of visible Muslim citizenship. ... Public visibility is approached therefore as a radically disruptive, transgressive, provocative form of transformative agency that is intrinsically related to the political process of becoming citizens. (Göle 2011, 383)

The presence and hence experience of religious diversity in Scandinavia, as elsewhere in Europe, is not evenly distributed spatially. Rather, it is the major cities which are the sites of significant religious diversity, due both to initial immigrant settlement patterns and ongoing residents' constraints and choices. Thus, it is in the Scandinavian capitals of Oslo, Copenhagen, and Stockholm, and some larger regional cities such as Malmö, that higher concentrations of visible minority populations exist, often focused residentially in particular neighbourhoods. It is here that Pentecostal churches and mosques are mostly located (where planning permission can be obtained), and it is on these neighbourhoods that media attention is often focused, with coverage of religion uneasily mingled with anxieties about public safety, urban disorder, and criminality, and prone to proliferate into periodic moral panics (Bangstad 2011). While immigrant, especially asylum seeker, settlement policies to some extent offset these patterns, for example creating settlements of Sri Lankan Tamils (mostly Hindu) in the coastal towns of Arctic Norway (Guribye 2011), the pattern of urban concentration predominates.

Indeed, it is not just religious diversity that is unevenly distributed spatially, but religious participation. As pointed out in Chapter 1 and Chapter 2, Scandinavians have amongst the lowest levels of religious observance in the world, but the immigrants, and especially refugees, arriving in Scandinavia's major cities come from some of the most religiously observant societies globally, notably from Africa and the Middle East. While it should not be assumed that all will wish or choose to maintain this observance, assumptions informed by secularization theory that minorities will rapidly assimilate to Northern European norms in this respect are not supported by empirical studies.

Thus, van Tubergen (2006) found that British and Dutch immigrants (from several major religions, and 12 percent with no religious affiliation) had a weekly congregational attendance rate of 34 percent and 33 percent respectively (ibid., 10), compared with national rates of 17 percent and 12 percent, suggesting considerable differences between migrant and majority populations. Amongst Muslims, Güveli and Platt (2010, 1027) found weekly mosque attendance rates for British and Dutch Muslims of 67 percent and 47 percent respectively, roughly four times higher than amongst the national population in both countries. Supporting these findings, Maliepaard, Lubbers and Gijsberts (2012) found that amongst Dutch Muslims, whereas data before 1998 suggested a 'linear trend towards secularization over time and over generations', evidence from 1998–2006 shows a 'striking revival among the second generation', leading them to conclude that, 'forces of secularization such as educational attainment and generational replacement gradually lose their predictive power' (2012, 359).

Similar patterns may be found in Scandinavia. Certainly, fear of the consequences of religious diversity also seems to be unevenly distributed spatially here, paradoxically highest in areas of least diversity, especially where these are near major urban centres; a 'halo effect' of media-driven anxiety about the ethnic other. One source of evidence for this is voting patterns: support for anti-immigrant political parties is strongest in areas with fewer immigrants and ethnic minorities. Thus, in Denmark in the 2015 elections support for the Danish People's Party (Dansk Folkeparti, DF) was strongest in the areas of

Southern Jutland (Sydjylland) and Sjælland, located away from the major urban centres (*Politiken*, 2015³). In Norway, support for the Progress Party (Fremskrittspartiet, FrP) in the 2013 elections was strongest in rural and small-town areas close to major urban areas (e.g. Vestfold with 19.5 percent and Telemark with 19 percent, compared to Oslo with 11.7 percent [Statistics Norway 2015]⁴). This pattern repeated in Sweden's 2015 elections, where the Swedish Democrats were strongest outside Stockholm in Södermanlands län (13.4 percent) and outside Malmö in Blekinge län (14.1 percent), while in Stockholm proper the party received 5.8 percent and in Malmö, 8.9 percent (Statistics Sweden 2017⁵). These lower rates in the major cities are more than the effect of minorities themselves not supporting these parties – as these groups constitute small minorities in most areas, and tend to vote less (Scuzarello, 2015), these voting patterns mostly reflect differing majority population preferences in urban and rural areas.

So, why are people living in areas with fewer immigrants more worried about immigration than those living in areas with more immigrants? Survey evidence points to the processes which might be involved. Duffy and Frere-Smith analysed Ipsos-MORI polls conducted in the UK from 2006–2011, finding that immigration was consistently perceived as a much greater problem nationally (69–76 percent) than locally (15–28 percent; 2014, 90). This suggests a dominant role for the national media in the production of anxieties about immigration (closely associated with religious diversity in the Scandinavian context). The mechanism could be that those who live in areas of lower immigrant concentration fear what they perceive through the media, which tend to over-represent conflict in general (due to its higher 'news value', Jewkes 2011), and especially conflict relating to immigration and Muslims (ECRI 2015). In this context, short-term encounters such as visits to major cities tend may be read in the light of dominant media narratives. In contrast, residents in major cities, accustomed to living with diversity, are less fearful of it but aware (again, through the media) of concerns elsewhere in society. Either way, we find an uneven pattern of concern, with media coverage likely to be the major factor shaping it.

This evidence of the power of media frames to shape our perceptions of other localities – beyond our immediate neighbourhood where we must rely

---

3 *Wikipedia*, s.v. Wahlkarte Folketing Dänemark 2015, last modified 19 June 2015, https://commons.wikimedia.org/wiki/File:Wahlkarte_Folketing_D%C3%A4nemark_2015_da.svg

4 Statistics Norway, "Storting election 2013: Valid votes, by party/electoral list and county," http://www.ssb.no/196612/storting-election-2013.valid-votes-by-party-electoral-list-and-county.per-cent-sy-7

5 Statistics Sweden, "General elections, results," http://www.scb.se/en/finding-statistics/statistics-by-subject-area/democracy/general-elections/general-elections-results/

on mediated sources – comes from the UK, but there are good reasons to think that similar mechanisms are at work in Scandinavia. While concerns about immigration are higher in the UK, concerns about religious diversity run at similar levels – for example, the wish to restrict Muslim immigration runs at the same level in Denmark and the UK (46 percent agree with the statements 'allow few' or 'no' Muslim immigrants), at comparable level in Norway (34.4 percent), though significantly lower in Sweden (19 percent, European Social Survey 2014). Thus, the scale of public concern is broadly similar. But more importantly the key ingredients – powerful negative media frames shaping perceptions of immigration and Islam, and an inverse relationship between local experience of diversity and anxieties about it – are present in each case; in the UK, residents in 'low migration small towns and rural areas' are twice as likely to want to restrict immigration as residents in 'superdiverse' London (Duffy and Frere Smith 2013, 22), similar to the distribution suggested by voting patterns in Scandinavia.

9.4 Governance and Challenges for Civic Leadership

> Mediatisation changes the logic of governance. It introduces new stakes for governance actors as their actions are ... perceived through a media gaze. (Uitermark and Gielen 2010, 1327)

In the kind of mediatized civic environments described, local (as well as national) leaders face new challenges in the management of cultural conflicts. As national and international conflicts percolate through different media channels, they may create or amplify local tensions. When satellite and digital communications transcend national borders, local disputes may escalate rapidly into international incidents, as with the Danish Muhammad cartoons controversy in 2005–2006 (Lindekilde, Mouritsen, and Zapata-Barrero 2009). Similarly, since people are entangled in extensive and complex media landscapes, local civic relations may be affected by distant events, or even by their anticipation. For example, Uitermark and Gielen (2010) found in their study of the Amsterdam neighbourhood De Baarjes in aftermath of the murder of Theo van Gogh in 2004, that local government officials were strongly influenced by their anticipation of national media coverage, adopting a kind of proactive media-oriented stance, more than they were informed by a detailed grasp of local civic dynamics, with damaging consequences for the latter in the long run.

This mediatization of local politics needs to be understood in the context of the neo-liberalization of governance in Northern European cities, part of a global pattern. While Scandinavian societies may be less affected than others, due to the strength of social welfare model of democracy, they are not exempt. Neoliberalism is understood here as 'a series of contemporary projects of capital accumulation that, beginning in the 1970s, sought to reconstitute social relations of production including the organization of labour, space, state institutions, military power, governance, membership and sovereignty' (Glick-Schiller 2011, 213–4). Neo-liberal ideologies advocate increasing the scope of market logics, bringing purchaser–provider relationships into areas of social provision previously dominated by the welfare state and professional norms, and emphasizing the exchange value of urban space at the expense of its multiple use values (Lefebvre 1991).

In the field of local governance, as elsewhere, this is has led to a disruption of established relationships between residents, welfare institutions, and local authorities. For example, analysing the case of the Dutch national community development agency *Wijkalliantie* (Neighbourhood Alliance), which they see as indicative of trends across Western Europe to bring private entrepreneurial organizations into local governance, Uitermark and Duyvendak argue that 'fragmented and transparent institutions have to compete in a new landscape dominated by periodical evaluations and quick shifts in policy ... Flexibility for financers, including politicians, administrators and charities, has at the same time meant instability for professionals and citizens' (2008, 117).

So, in contrast to previous practice where, through processes of consultation and discussion, 'residents defined which discourses were legitimate', now 'governmental organizations formulate a discourse that primarily reflects the concerns of ... their financially and politically powerful partners ... and subsequently try to find residents who are willing and able to ground this discourse institutionally in disadvantaged neighbourhoods' (ibid., 115).

Parallel impacts of mediatization and neo-liberalism are suggested by Liebmann's study of organized cultural encounters in an Oslo neighbourhood (Chapter 11). First, local projects must compete for funding in a competitive environment (neoliberalism), then mediatization shapes what funding is available, especially national media-driven frames of reference formed by anxieties related to security, which influence the cultural programmes of local organizations. Thus, the influence of media frames may be refracted both through local government policies (as in the Dutch examples) and national funding programmes (as in Groruddalen and Kristiansand), impacting local civic dynamics.

9.5 What Makes Diverse Neighbourhoods Work? Converging Evidence, and a Research–Policy Rupture

> A feature common to many European countries is that the body of scientifically based knowledge on immigrant integration has increased substantially, while at the same time public authorities seem to have become less interested in making use of the assembled knowledge. ... Although the idea of 'evidence-based policymaking' has gained wide recognition discursively, strong evidence also exists that politicians and policymakers often use scientific research for symbolic rather than instrumental purposes. (Scholten 2015, 2)

In concluding this introduction to shaping cultural conflicts in mediatized civic settings, and given the challenges facing local leaders implied by this account, it may be useful to consider briefly empirical evidence and theories on what makes diverse neighbourhoods 'work', and, given the problem of the spatial distribution of anxieties about cultural difference, to ask, what might reduce fears in less diverse regions? In addressing these topics, on the one hand there is good news that several theoretical perspectives and a range of empirical studies converge on which features help make diverse neighbourhoods work (and may be transferable to less diverse areas), and on what impacts on the anxieties that underlie prejudices. On the other hand, as Scholten argues, it is unfortunate that across Europe, precisely because of the dominant media frames concerning immigration and Islam that they must negotiate and the political dynamics these have generated, politicians and policy makers are reluctant to act on such evidence-led recommendations.

First, several theories (superdiversity, Vertovec 2007; contact, Al Ramiah and Hewstone 2013; political participation, Scuzzarello 2015), are both well-grounded in empirical studies and concur that development and public recognition of multiple, intersecting, and overlapping roles and identities is critical to successful social integration. In other words, seeing that others who are different in some respects (e.g. religion, ethnicity) also have overlapping interests and roles (e.g. as parents, neighbours, school governors, tenants, etc.), combined with a basic level of civility in public contact, seems sufficient to form the basis of mutual recognition necessary for the development of trust between neighbours and a localized sense of a shared public good, even in very diverse neighbourhoods (Wessendorf, 2014). On this basis engagement with and acceptance of divergent aspects of identity may develop.

In fact, it seems that conditions in more diverse neighbourhoods, with an established history of migration and with many immigrants from different backgrounds, seem work in favour of civic integration (Hickman and Mai 2015). This may be because in these conditions it is difficult for the binary categories around which prejudice is formed (us and them, long-time resident and newcomer, Muslim and Dane, as we shall see in Chapter 12), to develop. And this may be why less diverse regions pose greater challenges, as it is easier for such binary categories to take hold. Nonetheless, programmes which build on contact and para-contact theory show that even in some of the most unpromising conditions (e.g. in Israel–Palestine, where 'natural' inter-ethnic contact is limited and binary categorization reinforced by most social processes), school programmes which combine education with extended contact and constructive interaction can have a major impact on attitudes (Berger et al., 2016).

9.6 Conclusion

This survey of evidence on the relationship between the changing media landscape, civic settings and cultural conflict, framing Scandinavia in a European context, suggests complex challenges facing both future research and policy. While macro, structural factors have always impacted local civic relations, which in turn have their own logics not reducible to structure, and national and regional media have long been a significant link between scales, the evidence reviewed suggests social media significantly intensifies and complicates these links, introducing new dynamics whose effects are hard to predict, as they include both amplifying the dominance of national media frames (e.g. mediatization of local governance in Amsterdam), and empowering marginalised groups to resist the political effects of such framing (the Dutch Muslim anti-headscarf ban campaign). For researchers, this implies the need for constant attention to factors operative at different scales and their mediated interconnection. For policy makers and advisers, the challenge has the added difficulty that the field has become not just intensely mediatized but politicised by populist discourses which frame relations between majorities and minorities antagonistically, mobilizing a divisive binary worldview which 'pits a virtuous and homogenous people against a set of elites and dangerous "others" who are depicted as depriving ... the sovereign people of their rights, values, identity, and voice' (Albertazzi and McDonnell 2008: 3). Furthermore, this competitive framing may be intensified by the neo-liberalization of local governance. Under these conditions, evidence based policies of inclusion meet a sceptical reception, even when based on well-grounded theories, as both may be dismissed as mere 'expert opinion' in populist rhetoric. But, surely in Scandinavia, with its traditions of social equality, high value placed on education and inclusivity, they may yet prevail?

Bibliography

Al Ramiah, Ananthi, and Miles Hewstone. 2013. "Intergroup Contact as a Tool for Reducing, Resolving, and Preventing Intergroup Conflict." *American Psychologist* 68 (7): 527–542.

Bangstad, Sindre. 2011. "The Morality Police Are Coming! Muslims in Norway's Media Discourses." *Anthropology Today* 27 (5): 3–7.

Berger, Rony, Joy Benatov, Hisham Abu-Raiya, and Carmit Tadmor. 2016. "Reducing Prejudice and Promoting Positive Intergroup Attitudes Among Elementary-School Children in the Context of The Israeli–Palestinian Conflict." *Journal of School Psychology* 57: 53–72.

Boy, John, and Justus Uitermark. 2016. "How to Study the City on Instagram." *PLoS ONE* 11 (6): 1–16.

Couldry, Nick, and Tim Markham. 2008. "Troubled Closeness or Satisfied Distance? Researching Media Consumption and Public Orientation." *Media Culture & Society* 30 (1): 5–22.

Couldry, Nick. 2011. "Media and Democracy: Some Missing Links." In *Media and Social Justice*, edited by Sue Curry Jansen, J. Pooley, and L. Taub-Pervizpour, 45–54. London: Palgrave.

Duffy, Bobby, and Tom Frere-Smith. 2014. *Perceptions and Reality: Public Attitudes to Migration*. Ipsos-MORI Social Research Institute.

European Commission Against Racism and Intolerance. 2015. *ECRI Report on Denmark (Fifth Cycle)*. Strasbourg: European Commission.

European Social Survey (ESS). 2014. *European Social Survey Data*. Accessed 17 April 2017. http://nesstar.ess.nsd.uib.no/webview/

Fraser, Nancy. 1990. "Rethinking the Public Sphere: A Contribution to the Critique of Actually Existing Democracy." *Social Text* 25/26: 56–80.

Gillespie, Marie, David Herbert, and Matilda Anderson. 2010. "The Mumbai Attacks and Diasporic Nationalism: BBC World Service Online Forums as Conflict, Contact and Comfort Zones." *South Asian Diaspora* 2 (1): 109–129.

Glick-Schiller, Nina. 2011. "Localized Neoliberalism, Multiculturalism and Global Religion: Exploring the Agency of Migrants and City Boosters." *Economy and Society* 40 (2): 211–238.

Göle, Nilüfer. 2011. "The Public Visibility of Islam and European Politics of Resentment: The Minarets-Mosques Debate." *Philosophy and Social Criticism* 37 (4): 383–392.

Gordon, Eric, and Adriana de Souza e Silva. 2011. *Net Locality: Why Location Matters in a Networked World*. Blackwell: Oxford.

Guribye, Eugene. 2011. "Sacrifice as Coping: A Case Study of the Cultural–Political Framing of Traumatic Experiences Among Eelam Tamils in Norway." *Journal of Refugee Studies* 24 (2): 376–389.

Güveli, Ayşe, and Lucinda Platt. 2011. "Understanding the Religious Behaviour of Muslims in the Netherlands and the UK." *Sociology* 45 (6): 1008–1027.

Hjarvard, Stig, Mette Mortensen, and Mikkel F. Eskjær. 2015. "Introduction: Three Dynamics of Mediatized Conflicts." In *The Dynamics of Mediatized Conflicts*, edited by Mikkel F. Eskjær, Stig Hjarvard, and Mette Mortensen, 1–27. New York: Peter Lang.

Hovland, Kjetil. 2015. *Norway Muslims Encircle Synagogue to Support Jews*. Accessed 4 July 2016. http://search.proquest.com/docview/1657100028?accountid=9851. See also https://www.nrk.no/norge/1.300-people-formed-_ring-of-peace_-outside-oslo-synagogue-after-young-muslims-initiative-1.12222956 (Accessed 28 Sept, 2017).

Hickman, Mary, and Nicola Mai. 2015. "Migration and Social Cohesion: Appraising the Resilience of Place in London." *Population, Space and Place* 21 (5): 412–432.

Jewkes, Yvonne. 2011. *Media and Crime*, 2nd ed. London: Sage.

Kaufmann, Erik P., Anne Goujon, and Vegard Skirbekk. 2012. "The End of Secularization in Europe?: A Socio-Demographic Perspective." *Sociology of Religion* 73 (1): 69–91.

Lefebvre, Henri. 1991 [1974]. *The Production of Space*. Translated by Donald Nicholson-Smith. First published in 1974 as La production de l'espace. Oxford: Blackwell.

Leurs, Koen, Eva Midden, and Sandra Ponzanesi. 2012. "Digital Multiculturalism in the Netherlands: Religious, Ethnic and Gender Positioning by Moroccan-Dutch Youth." *Religion and Gender* 2 (1): 150–175.

Lindekilde, Lasse, Per Mouritsen, and Richard Zapata-Barrero. 2009. "The Muhammad Cartoons Controversy in Comparative Perspective." *Ethnicities* 9 (3): 291–313.

Maliepaard, Mieke, Lubbers, Marcel, and Gijsberts, Merove. 2012. "Generational Differences in Ethnic and Religious Attachment and Their Interrelation: A Study Among Muslim Minorities in the Netherlands." *Ethnic and Racial Studies* 33(3): 451–472.

Noelle-Neumann, Elisabeth (1984). *The Spiral of Silence. Public Opinion – Our Social Skin*. Chicago: Chicago University Press.

Pariser, Eli. 2011. *The Filter Bubble: What the Internet Is Hiding from You*. New York: Penguin Press.

Scholten, Peter. Ed. 2011. *Framing Immigrant Integration: Dutch Research–Policy Dialogues in Comparative Perspective*. Amsterdam: Amsterdam University Press.

Scuzzarello, Sarah. 2015. "Political Participation and Dual Identification Among Migrants." *Journal of Ethnic and Migration Studies* 41 (8): 1214–1234.

Rinnawi Khalil. 2012. "'Instant Nationalism' and the 'Cyber Mufti': The Arab Diaspora in Europe and the Transnational Media." *Journal of Ethnic and Migration Studies* 38 (9): 1451–1467.

Theocharis, Yannis. 2013. "The Wealth of (Occupation) Networks? Communication Patterns and Information Distribution in a Twitter Protest Network." *Journal of Information Technology & Politics* 10 (1): 35–56.

Uitermark, Justus, and Jan Willem Duyvendak. 2008. "Citizen Participation in a Mediated Age: Neighbourhood Governance in The Netherlands." *International Journal of Urban and Regional Research* 32 (1): 114–34.

Uitermark, Justus, and Amy-Jane Gielen. 2010. "Islam in the Spotlight: The Mediatisation of Politics in an Amsterdam Neighbourhood." *Urban Studies* 47 (6): 1325–1342.

van Tubergen, Frank. 2006. "Religious Affiliation and Attendance Among Immigrants in Eight Western Countries: Individual and Contextual Effects." *Journal for the Scientific Study of Religion* 45 (1): 1–22.

Vertovec, Steven. 2007. "Super-Diversity and its Implications." *Ethnic and Racial Studies*, 30 (6): 1024–105.

Watt, Paul. 2008. "The Only Class in Town? Gentrification and The Middle-Class Colonization of the City and the Urban Imagination." *International Journal of Urban and Regional Research* 32: 206–211.

Wessendorf, Susanne. 2014. "'Being Open, But Sometimes Closed': Conviviality in a Super-Diverse London Neighbourhood." *European Journal of Cultural Studies* 17 (4): 392–405.

Pål Repstad
Chapter 10
Moral Involvement or Religious Scepticism? Local Christian Publications on Asylum Seekers

Abstract: Norway's Christian leaders have been directing a stream of almost unanimous criticism at the present (2017) Conservative and populist government's increasingly restrictive policy on refugees and asylum seekers. Some have claimed that the criticism from Christian leaders is an elite phenomenon, and that local Christians are more positive to the adopted restrictions, as well as to proposals for an even more restrictive policy. This chapter presents results from a study of local Christian publications from August 2015 to April 2016. Publications online and on paper from 52 local organizations and congregations in a region in Southern Norway have been analysed. The results indicate that local Christian congregations and organizations welcome and support arriving refugees and asylum seekers, and to the extent that they comment on political issues, they support the criticism coming from their national leaders. The local publications studied can be seen as a kind of counter-information to national right-wing populist politicians and media trying to create 'official fear'.

Keywords: refugees, migration, local publications, local Christianity

10.1 A More Restrictive Policy

After the general election in autumn 2014, Norway got a so-called blue–blue government, a coalition between the Conservatives (Høyre) and the Progress Party (Fremskrittspartiet). The Progress Party in particular, has placed scepticism toward immigration very high on their agenda (Fangen and Vaage 2014). Progress Party member Sylvi Listhaug, serving the government since December 2015 as Minister of Immigration and Integration, has been criticized for using harsh language against immigrants and asylum seekers.[1] While still Minister of Agricul-

---

[1] From January 2018, Listhaug was no longer Minister of Integration, but Minister for Justice, Public Security and Immigration. In March 2018 she resigned from Government after heavy criticism from the opposition.

ture and Food, she told the press that she, a Christian, considered leaving the Church of Norway because she disliked the bishops' criticism of the government's refugee policy. In an interview in the Christian daily *Vårt Land* on 4 November 2015, she criticized the bishops directly, referring to 'a tyranny of goodness' haunting Norway. Later, on 5 February 2016, she followed up on her criticism in the newspaper *VG*, stating that the church is not for everyone, as it has become a political actor for leftists, a player likely to destroy the welfare society due to its stance in favour of free immigration. In response to another bout of criticism from bishops, she said in an interview with the weekly *Morgenbladet* on 8 April 2016: 'It is not for the bishops to define who is a Christian and who is not, or who has the right form of Christianity and who does not'. Furthermore, in an interview with the newspaper *Aftenposten* on 7 January 2016, she expressed concern about the future of her children if immigration to Norway gets out of control. When presenting some restrictive reforms in Norwegian refugee policy in an interview with the newspaper *VG* on 29 December 2015, Listhaug used an old Norwegian metaphor, stating that refugees cannot expect 'to be carried into Norway on a chair of gold'.[2] According to the *Atekst* software program for retrieval and analysis of newspaper material, Listhaug's statement about the chair of gold was quoted and commented on 360 times in Norwegian newspapers and magazines in paper format from the time when it was published until the end of 2016. She even got international attention, for example in the *Independent* on 21 October 2016, after posting a statement on Facebook the day before attending a conference on integration that Norwegians 'eat pork and drink alcohol', and those who come to Norway should adapt to that.

Clearly, Sylvi Listhaug, has been a central figure in the immigration debate since she took over as minister, but it should be noted that the government has been standing behind her proposals, and that some of the restrictions have been supported by some of the political parties outside the government as well. On a less rhetorical and more concrete level, Sylvi Listhaug, on behalf of the government, sent for consultation several proposals for a more restrictive policy toward refugees and asylum seekers in December 2015 (Ministry of Justice and Public Security 2015). The proposals included a stricter policy on family reunion, and limitations concerning unaccompanied minor asylum seekers. According to the new proposals, instead of a permanent permission, minor adolescents would only get a temporary permission to stay in Norway. The consultation process resulted in protests from several organizations, lawyers, and even administrative agencies

---

[2] It should be added that all the newspapers quoted so far are independent of political parties and considered mainstream media in Norway.

under the government. Many of the consultation responses claimed that some of the proposals contradicted international law and human rights conventions. However, the government decided to maintain almost all the proposals (Ministry of Justice and Public Security 2015–2016). When presenting the news in media interviews, among them in *Aftenposten* on 6 April 2016, Sylvi Listhaug expressed as a positive quality of Norwegian immigration policy that it would be the strictest in Europe. The proposals were discussed in the Parliament in June, and many of the proposed restrictions were formally adopted, such as permission for the police to stop asylum seekers at the border in times of crisis. However, the most controversial ones, concerning unaccompanied minor asylum seekers and a more restrictive family reunion policy, were not.[3]

10.2 Protests from Church Leaders

Five or six decades ago, many church leaders, especially in minority churches, argued against Christian involvement in politics, recommending individual Christian conversions and Christian upbringing of new generations as better strategies for a better world, rather than political efforts. Exceptions from the rule of political non-involvement were Christian 'core issues' such as abortion and financial state support for Christian schools.

Gradually Norwegian church leaders have approached the political field on a broader scope of issues, such as socio-economic equality, climate, and pollution. In the 1990s, churches found on their literal doorsteps the politics of refugees and immigration, as several asylum seekers responded to their cases being rejected by seeking asylum in churches. Most of these refugees and asylum seekers were Kosovo Albanians. During the peak year of 1993, about 140 local churches of various denominations had asylum seekers in their church buildings for short or long periods, a practice that church leaders generally accepted as legitimate in acute situations (Vetvik and Omland 1997). In 1997, 25 Norwegian church leaders from various denominations presented a common statement warning against fear of Muslims (Haugen 2010).

Today general warnings against political involvement are almost non-existent in churches, except among Jehovah's Witnesses and a few small faith communities. Reservations against direct church support for specific parties are still widespread, but for the past three or four decades, church leaders in Norway have often placed themselves in a centre-to-left position in many socio-political

---

[3] See the newspaper *Dagsavisen*, 11 June 2016, for an overview of the Parliament's decisions.

issues. They are concerned with climate and environmental issues, as well as equality and justice, nationally and globally. Many also claim that public immigration policies are too restrictive. Leaders are more conservative in matters of family policy and sexuality, as well as in bio-ethical issues. This is shown in an interview study of Norwegian national religious leaders from 2011 (Furseth et al. 2015, 153–157). However, especially the Church of Norway has seen a recent liberalization of attitudes, including in the matter of same-sex marriages. In April 2016, the Church of Norway General Synod accepted same-sex marriage ceremonies in churches, and in February 2017, a new liturgy was introduced.

A similar centre-to-left socio-political profile is documented in a previous study of 118 national and regional leaders in the Church of Norway (Gulbrandsen et al. 2002). This study showed that the church elite turned out to be the most politically radical group of all Norwegian elites. They preferred environmental concerns to economic growth, they were the strongest proponents of increased wage equality, and they opposed regulation of immigration based on labour market needs.

Many individual bishops and other church leaders have issued criticisms of Norwegian asylum politics. The website of the Church of Norway, as well as the websites of many minority churches and umbrella organizations, like the Council for Religious and Life Stance Communities (STL) and the Christian Council of Norway, show a centre-to-left engagement in many current socio-political issues, including criticism of the present government's restrictive immigration policies. Together with several humanitarian and political organizations, the Christian Council of Norway, with most Christian faith communities as members, takes part in the so-called Forum for Asylum Politics, a meeting place for organizations involved in asylum politics. In November 2016, this forum issued a joint statement, strongly criticizing restrictive decisions made recently or planned by the government. The forum protested against initiatives such as plans to remove refugee status for Somalian refugees, reduction of economic support for families with children in refugee reception centres, and an increasing number of returns of refugees to Afghanistan (Asylpolitisk forum 2016).

The involvement by Norwegian Christian leaders was summed up by columnist Sven Egil Omdal some years ago, in the newspaper *Stavanger Aftenblad* on 1 March 2014:

> Christian leaders have turned into a humanitarian vanguard. When someone feels cold, weeps or is afraid of Norwegian state power, more and more often a bishop or Christian general secretary is nearby, offering warmth, comfort and vigorous protest.

10.3 Criticism from the Churches – An Elite Phenomenon?

As we have seen earlier in this chapter, Christian leaders have been overwhelmingly critical to government policy. In 2016, however, a few Christian leaders voiced scepticism toward the profile of churches and Christian organizations in these matters. One of them was Vebjørn Selbekk, the editor of the conservative Christian newspaper *Dagen*. In an interview with the newspaper *VG* on 6 February 2016, he stated that he sympathizes with Sylvi Listhaug, claiming that the question of immigration must be solved politically and that the church has no special competence in the field. Erik Furnes, general secretary of Indremisjonsforbundet, a conservative, low-church inner mission organization, expressed similar views. In an editorial in the organization's magazine *Sambåndet* in April 2016, Furnes reminded readers that it is the politicians who have a responsibility to 'take care of the totality of concerns' and criticized church leaders for having voiced statements that were too specific against the policy of the government. In an interview in *Vårt Land* on 6 February 2016, Furnes warned against one-sidedness from the church, stating that he, to some extent, understood Sylvi Listhaug.

In early 2016, *Vårt Land* published a couple of interviews pointing to an alleged cleavage between Christian leaders and the local grass roots. A local politician from the Christian Democrats, Torolf Nordbø, claimed in an interview on 2 February that the lack of immigration control is worry number one among many people at grassroots level, and author Lars Akerhaug told a journalist on 1 February that, while visiting some local Christian communities to present his books on extremism in Norway, he noticed an undercurrent of scepticism toward Muslims. Akerhaug quoted statements like 'all Muslims can lie; it is part of their religion', and 'the Muslims have come to take over Norway'. As the Christian leaders have a different view, these opinions are seldom voiced in public, he said, adding that these views come from the grass roots members and from visitors who may not be members of the congregation.

So, my question is whether the Christian criticism of the government's refugee policy is just an elite phenomenon, while Sylvi Listhaug and the government have broad support at the local and grassroots level in the Christian communities.

10.4 A Study of Six Municipalities

My study is based on local Christian websites, Facebook pages, parish magazines and local organizations' publications in the town of Kristiansand in the southernmost part of Norway, as well as in five surrounding municipalities: Birkenes, Lillesand, Søgne, Songdalen, and Vennesla. In total, these six municipalities, situated in the Agder region, have about 130,000 inhabitants and is part of an area sometimes referred to as Norway's Bible Belt, known for its vital and diverse Christian involvement in the majority Church of Norway and in a wide range of minority churches and Christian organizations. Christian faith and participation in organized Christianity are more widespread here than in other areas of Norway (Botvar, Repstad, and Aagedal 2010). Although a softening of the strictest and most pietistic religious traditions has been observed in recent decades, active Christians still seem to be more conservative and restrictive in matters of morality in the region of Agder than elsewhere in Norway (Repstad 2009; Magnussen, Repstad, and Urstad 2012; Repstad 2014). Hence, it is not unreasonable to believe that if Christians in this relatively conservative region are critical towards the government's restrictive policy against refugees and asylum seekers, the same will be the case for Christians in other regions.

I have systematically studied websites, Facebook pages, and printed publications from 52 local congregations and Christian organizations, using a combination of counting and a more hermeneutic qualitative analysis. There is no comprehensive overview of the number of such publications available in these municipalities, but I believe I have reviewed most of the material published from August 2015 to March 2016. Not all local faith communities and organizations publish electronically, but most of them do, so I would dare to say that my study captures the general sentiment in local Christian publications in the area during the period in question. Like many other European countries, Norway experienced a considerable increase in the number of asylum seekers during these months, followed by a marked decrease. At some point during this time frame, there seemed to be a marked national change in rhetoric about refugees and asylum seekers, in the media as well as in public opinion. From October to November especially, there was a shift from empathy and care to more concern for strictness and control. It will be interesting to note whether this shift is reflected in the local Christian publications as well.

10.5 A Widespread and Stable Local Christian Concern

What did I find? Publications from 28 of the 52 congregations and organizations – over half of them – mentioned refugees and asylum seekers during the eight months analysed. Most statements are connected to local humanitarian efforts, and there are many recommendations to take part in such volunteer work. These projects are sometimes organized by the congregations or organizations themselves, sometimes in cooperation with others, either municipal bodies, other Christian communities, or humanitarian organizations like the Red Cross.

A main finding is that not one single statement from the 52 local Christian organizations expressed support for the government's asylum politics and its proposals for a more restrictive policy. This does not mean that many of the publications explicitly objected to the restrictive policy, but some did voice a protest. An employee in the Salvation Army in Kristiansand was invited to speak at an event in one of Kristiansand's largest minority churches, the Evangelical Lutheran Free Church, and according to the report in the magazine of this faith community, *Frikirkeaktuelt*, in November 2015, she had 'much to say about what, in her opinion, is an unsuccessful policy'. She criticized several concrete proposals for a more restrictive line of action. A pastor in the Pentecostal congregation Filadelfia in Kristiansand quoted Angela Merkel's statement that fear is a poor adviser. He concluded by asking whether we in Norway are meant to be only five million inhabitants: 'Could we not be seven? We have enough space, and we have an economy enabling us to meet the challenges of our continent', he wrote in *Filadelfiamagazinet*, March 2015. The local congregation of the Church of Norway in Søgne some miles west of Kristiansand encouraged its members on its Facebook page in September to take part in a demonstration outside the town hall to show the politicians that they 'welcome the refugees to Søgne'. This was before a meeting where the local council was to decide how many refugees (if any) the municipality should receive. The Christian social welfare organization Blue Cross housed many asylum seekers in Kristiansand during an acute period in the early autumn of 2015, when several refugees arrived on the night ferry from Denmark. Twice that autumn, the Blue Cross organized benefit concerts for refugee help, and a well-known singer-songwriter in Norway, Ole Paus, was interviewed on the Blue Cross website, encouraging people to turn their backs on the attitudes of the Progress Party. On the website of the Pentecostal congregation Betania, we found before Christmas 2015 a feature article on Budget Hotel in Kristiansand, which served as a temporary home for 82 refugees. Here the authors took issue with the oft-used term *lykkejegere* (fortune hunters): 'Had we been in the same situation, we too would probably have stopped at nothing in our hunt for happiness and a better life'. Finally, City Mission pastor Bjarte Leer-Helgesen in Kristiansand has a much-read Facebook page where he, on 16 December 2016, wrote ironically about Sylvi Listhaug and her use of the term 'tyranny of goodness'.

There are some more statements with a political sting, but most of the 28 congregations and organizations writing about asylum seekers mention various humanitarian initiatives, inviting members and others to take part in these. Examples are refugee cafés with low-threshold language training and social contact, football for young asylum seekers, collection of clothes for asylum seekers living in temporary emergency centres, and organized systems of refugee hosts. As mentioned, many initiatives were the results of cooperation, such as the welcome centres for refugees in Vågsbygd Church and in the parish hall of the Cathedral in Kristiansand. Christian social welfare organizations such as the Blue Cross, the Salvation Army, Christian Intercultural Work (KIA), and the Church City Mission in Kristiansand are doing their share, and so are several minority churches, such as the Evangelical Lutheran Free Church and local Pentecostal congregations.

The lowest level of activity was found among low-church organizations often associated with so-called 'prayer halls' (*bedehus*). These have a long tradition of being 'within, but not controlled by' the Church of Norway. Only two out of 13 organizations in this category mentioned refugees or asylum seekers in their publications. This part of the Norwegian Christian landscape has shrunk in numbers and resources recently. Furthermore, they have a religious tradition characterized more by words and dogma than by a focus on 'good deeds'. However, there were exceptions: According to their website, the local branch of the Norwegian Lutheran Mission established a café with language training and homework assistance for immigrants every Tuesday.

The minority churches are at least as active as the Church of Norway, possibly because active members in the minority churches are used to taking initiatives themselves. They have less bureaucracy and a shorter distance between thought and action. I do not have direct evidence of such an explanation in my empirical material; it should be considered as a hypothesis for further research.

There is no significant change in frequency or content of the texts about refugees during the period analysed. Neither is there any indication that the efforts to help are a kind of disguised missionary or conversionist project. Here, the activists at the local level seem to follow the recommendations given in a statement from the Christian Council of Norway (2009) about baptism of asylum seekers, where it is stated that 'no one should be manipulated to adopt a faith through some exploitation of their vulnerable situation or their wish for protection'. Such exploitation may exist, especially in some charismatic milieus (Stene 2016), but there were no traces of it in the publications analysed. The reasons given in every case for encouraging people to help were a combination of general ethics and the occasional reference to Biblical recommendations to help people in need, such as the Pentecostal congregation Betania's reference on their website to Matthew 25:35–40[4] when asking people to bring winter clothes for asylum seekers to Betania's office for further distribution.

How are the refugees and asylum seekers presented? In general, these publications are rather modest and ascetic in their use of pictures and advanced layout. That said, Norwegian helpers are presented more often than the asylum seekers with names and pictures, and those who are quoted in the text are nearly always Norwegian helpers. However, the texts are dominated by care and respect for asylum seekers, presenting them as human beings in need of help, and characterizing them more as motivated people with resources than as pitiful, calculating or selfish creatures.

How valid are the findings? The study covers a limited area, so the potential for mechanical generalizations to Norway is limited. However, unsystematic visits to websites in other parts of Norway (including Oslo and the county of Hordaland) seem to confirm the tendencies found in the south. And, as mentioned before, Agder is a comparatively conservative region in Norway, both politically and religiously, so it is a reasonable hypothesis that we may find even stronger criticism of the government's immigration policy elsewhere.

We cannot rule out the possibility that there is some informal and hidden support for a restrictive immigration and refugee policy among grassroots Christians. The same can be said about a possible scepticism against Muslims. Most of the texts that I have looked at were written by employees or volunteers at the local level; some might call them members of local elites, or at least local opinion leaders. Be that as it may, there are no indications of such scepticism in the analysed material, and I can add that the threshold for member response on the organizations' Facebook pages does seem to be quite low. Support for my conclusions can also be found in the fact that very few Norwegian priests or pastors in local congregations have expressed negative attitudes against asylum seekers and immigrants (Haugen 2014).

---

4 'For I was hungry and you gave me food....'

10.6 A Change of Sentiment

I have not found a massive and unanimous, explicit support for a more liberal policy. 24 of the 52 organizations, mainly in the low-church milieus, were silent about asylum seekers and refugees, and most of those who mentioned them recommended local humanitarian projects without political comments. However, all the statements within the field of politics clearly went against restrictions proposed by the government and/or criticized government rhetoric, especially from Immigration Minister Sylvi Listhaug. Furthermore, the strong recommendations to help can also be interpreted as indirectly political in the heated debate in 2015–2016, when Christian leaders were stigmatized as 'tyrants of goodness', although my interpretation here should not be stretched too far.

The study gives no indication that organized Christianity at the local level followed the change from generosity and empathy to control and fear that took place some weeks before Christmas in 2015 in some media, among some politicians, and in parts of public opinion. Many indications of this change can be mentioned. A change from a concern to help to a sceptical attitude seems to have been a general European phenomenon. Researchers behind a content analysis of newspapers from eight European countries (not including Scandinavia) summarize their findings like this:

> Temporal trends: the narratives of the coverage changed dramatically across Europe during 2015. The sympathetic and empathetic response of a large proportion of the European press in the summer of 2015 and especially in the early autumn of the same year was replaced by suspicion and, in some cases, hostility towards refugees and migrants, following the November attacks in Paris. (Chouliaraki et al. 2017, 2)

A study of regional and local newspapers and regional TV in the south and north of Norway showed a similar shift, although not as dramatic as the European study. The authors have analysed 10 local and regional media from August 2015 until July 2016. What they call the perspective of help was the most prominent one, but the relative number of items with this perspective decreased from November 2015. The total number of articles about refugees also decreased significantly from January 2016 (Hognestad and Lamark 2017, 12).

A similar change took place in the Liberal–Conservative *Aftenposten*, Norway's biggest newspaper. Charlotte Åsland Larsen (2016) has conducted a quantitative and qualitative study of this newspaper during two periods of time, August–September 2015, when many asylum seekers started to arrive, and January 2016, when Norwegians looked back on a year with a large influx of asylum seekers, and before it was clear that immigration was on the decline. Solidarity and care for refugees dominated the newspaper's news coverage during the first period, while what Larsen calls a discourse of burden became more frequent in the second period. There was also a sharper focus on refugees as individuals during the first period. For example, refugees were more often presented by name and picture during this period. During both periods, Norwegian journalists, politicians and experts were the chief speakers rather than the refugees themselves. Discourse about refugees as threats was also present in *Aftenposten*, but in very few cases. This approach was presumably more widespread in other media, not least in social media.

10.7 Influential Media – But There are Countermoves

Some politicians, especially members of government from the Progress Party, have tried to trigger worries about uncontrolled immigration and radical Islam after the relatively large number of refugees that came to Norway in 2015. As for the media's more general role, they no doubt have the power to influence popular opinion, especially in alliance with national politicians. In the terms of Zygmunt Bauman (2016), the fear that is a general trait in all human existence can be translated into *official fear*, where those who are different are marginalized through a number of mechanisms, such as stereotyping, scapegoating, and moral paralysis. On a more concrete level, media studies often conclude that reports about refugees tend to be stereotypical, and that they feature in the news in connection with negative topics and events (for an overview, see Figenschou, Thorbjørnsrud, and Larsen 2015, 129). These three Norwegian media researchers have analysed several Norwegian media's presentations of asylum politics and asylum seekers from 2011 to 2014. Their picture of the media coverage is ambiguous. They claim that Norwegian politicians and bureaucrats get a lot of space in the media to promote what they call a strict, but fair immigration and refugee policy. At the same time, they note that concrete narratives about specific individuals are often told as well.[5] A typical example is when individuals are introduced and encouraged to tell their dramatic stories, often when they are refused refugee status by Norwegian authorities. According to the researchers, these narratives can function as criticism of a strict policy, as they resonate with and appeal to an intuitive, common-sense morality. However, at the same time, the events narrated are presented mainly as isolated single events, and

---

5 See also Chapter 3.

not related to any political context. Therefore, these stories can contribute to greater division between those who deserve to stay and those who do not. Thus, they may end up as slightly idealized narratives about people who deserve to stay, without any critical searchlight on the rules and their interpretation.

The results of my study may be conceived as a sign of the limited power of national media and national politicians. The profile of the local publications can be considered a kind of counter-information, stressing humanitarian and Christian responsibility. Such counter-information can probably be of more significance if individuals relate to each other than if they are more isolated media users. Moreover, direct contact with refugees – something many of the local Christian activists have – will probably dismantle some stereotypes about Muslims and refugees in general. The old contact hypothesis formulated by Gordon Allport (1954), claimed exactly that: Personal encounters will reduce prejudice and increase mutual understanding. The thesis has often been criticized, but it seems robust, especially when the situation is not strongly conflictual to begin with. A large meta-study including more than 500 studies confirmed this some years ago (Pettigrew and Tropp 2006). In the words of the famous composer and record producer Phil Spector's first hit: 'To know, know, know him is to love, love, love him'. More recent studies from Denmark have also strengthened the contact hypothesis: Personal contacts at work and in neighbourhoods increase tolerance toward ethnic minorities, as members of the minorities appear less threatening, and majority members who gain more concrete knowledge of minority people also understand their situation better (Thomsen 2012; Rafiqui and Thomsen 2014).

Local media seem to be quite vital and important in Norway, possibly because of a general ideology in many regions in the direction of decentralization.[6] The media that I have studied fall in the category of religious journalism, that is publications edited by religious institutions (Hjarvard 2012; see also Chapter 3). This probably limits the scope of influence to Christian in groups. On the other hand, such publications tend to spread their own message without necessarily following trends in the national and more secular media, and may be important for the identity-forming in the groups.

So, if there are worries among Christians in and around Kristiansand about Islam and immigration, such worries seem overshadowed by a simple Christian ideal of helping those who need help. It is interesting that this moral commitment is found in very broad parts of the Christian landscape, not only among mainstream and comparatively liberal adherents of what Nancy Ammerman

---

[6] See Chapter 1 on the territorial dimension in Scandinavian politics.

(1997) in her studies in America called 'Golden Rule Christianity', but also among conservative Evangelicals.

The main findings in this study can be discussed in a broader class perspective. Active Christians in Norway belong mainly to the middle class (Repstad 2010, 384). In an interview study of middle class morality and values in Norway, the researchers find that representatives of this class state 'that they dislike racists, the intolerant, the dishonest, those who are judgmental etc.' (Skarpenes, Sakslind, and Hestholm 2016, 14). The authors claim that such statements reflect a value hierarchy culturally rooted in Christianity and humanism. The hero in this Christian-humanist repertoire resembles the Good Samaritan, they claim. Another hero is the socially responsible citizen. The discourse in the local Christian publications that I have studied, is in accordance with this middle-class moral profile.

A final point: a trend toward a more sensual Christianity, an aestheticization of religion in a wide sense, is reported in several recent research reports from Norway (Repstad and Trysnes 2013; Løvland and Repstad 2014). These reports point to an increasing significance of religion's experiential and emotional dimension, and less weight on dogmatic and theological aspects. Processions are getting longer, sermons are getting shorter. In preparation for confirmation, young people learn fewer commandments and light more candles. Sometimes an interest in aesthetics is read as a sign of superficiality and of a noncommittal attitude. Søren Kierkegaard's criticism in that direction still has some influence in Scandinavia. However, aesthetics in a wide sense – that which appeals to the senses and the emotions – can be important resources to form sentiments and encourage practices. Our study indicates that this shift in lived religion does not necessarily empty Christianity of its immediate ethical content.

Bibliography

Allport, Gordon. 1954. *The Nature of Prejudice*. Cambridge, MA.: Perseus Books.
Ammerman, Nancy. 1997. "Golden Rule Christianity: Lived Religion in the American Mainstream." In *Lived religion in America*, edited by David Hall, 196–216. Princeton: Princeton University Press.
Asylpolitisk forum. 2016. "Felles uttalelse fra asylpolitisk forum." [Joint statement from the Forum for Asylum Politics]. Accessed 30 June 2017. https://antirasistisk.no/felles-utta lelse-fra-asylpolitisk-forum/
Bauman, Zygmunt. 2016. *Strangers at our Door*. Cambridge: Polity.
Botvar, Pål Ketil, Pål Repstad, and Olaf Aagedal. 2010. "Regionaliseringen av norsk religiøsitet." [Regionalization of Norwegian religiosity]. In *Religion i dagens Norge*, edited by Pål Ketil Botvar and Ulla Schmidt, 44–59. Oslo: Universitetsforlaget.

Chouliaraki, Lilie, Myria Georgiou, and Rafal Zaborowski, with Wouter Oomen. 2016. *The European 'Migration Crisis' and the Media: A Cross-European Press Content Analysis*. Project Report. London: London School of Economics.

Christian Council of Norway. 2009. *Dåp av asylsøkere*. [Baptism of asylum seekers]. Accessed 30 June 2017. http://www.norgeskristnerad.no/index.cfm?id=142309.

Fangen, Katrine, and Mari Våge. 2014. "FrP-politikeres innvandringspolitikk i posisjon og opposisjon." [Progress Party politicians' immigration policy in position and opposition]. *Agora* 3–4: 30–63.

Figenschou, Tine, Kjersti Thorbjørnsrud, and Anna Grøndahl Larsen. 2015. "Mediated Asylum Conflicts: Human Interest Framing and Common-Sense Public Morality." In *The Dynamics of Mediated Conflicts*, edited by Mikkel Fugl Eskjær, Stig Hjarvard, and Mette Mortensen, 129–145. New York: Peter Lang.

Furseth, Inger, Pål Repstad, Sivert Skålvoll Urstad, and Ole-Edvin Utaker. 2015. "Tros- og livssynssamfunnene og deres ledere – innadvendte eller utadvendte?" [Faith and life stance communities and their leaders – introvert or extrovert?]. In *Religionens tilbakekomst i offentligheten?* Edited by Inger Furseth, 139–168. Oslo: Universitetsforlaget.

Gulbrandsen, Trygve, Fredrik Engelstad, Trond Belo Klausen, Hege Skeie, Mari Teigen, and Øyvind Østerud. 2002. *Norske makteliter*. [Norwegian power elites]. Oslo: Gyldendal.

Haugen, Hans Morten. 2010. "Den norske kirke og de flerkulturelle utfordringer." [The Church of Norway and the multicultural challenges]. *Tidsskrift for teologi og kirke* 81 (3): 208–224.

Haugen, Hans Morten. 2014. "Hvorfor har Den norske kirkes ledere advart mot å stemme Fremskrittspartiet?" [Why have the leaders of the Church of Norway warned against voting for the Progress Party?]. *Teologisk tidsskrift* 3 (1): 4–18.

Hjarvard, Stig. 2012. "Three forms of mediatized religion." In *Mediatization and Religion: Nordic Perspectives*, edited by Stig Hjarvard and Mia Lövheim, 21–44. Gothenburg: Nordicom.

Hognestad, Liv Iren, and Hege Lamark. 2017. "Flyktningene kommer! Lokale mediers dekning av flyktningkrisen." [The refugees are coming! Local media's coverage of the refugee crisis]. *Norsk medietidsskrift* 24 (2): 1–19.

Larsen, Charlotte Åsland. 2016. "Fra offer til ansiktsløs? En kritisk diskursanalyse av Aftenpostens fremstilling av flyktninger." [From victim to no face? A critical discourse analysis of Aftenposten's representation of refugees]. Master thesis, University of Agder.

Løvland, Anne, and Pål Repstad. 2014. "Playing the Sensual Card in Churches: Studying the Aestheticization of Religion." In *Sociological Theory and the Question of Religion*, edited by Andrew McKinnon and Marta Trzebiatowska, 179–198. Farnham: Ashgate.

Magnussen, May-Linda, Pål Repstad, and Sivert Skålvoll Urstad. 2012. "Skepsis til likestilling på Sørlandet – et resultat av religion?" [Scepticism to gender equality in Southern Norway – a result of religion?]. *Tidsskrift for kjønnsforskning* 36 (3–4): 204–222.

Ministry of Justice and Public Security. 2015. "Høring. Endringer i utlendingslovgivningen (innstramminger II)." [Consultation. Changes in Immigration Act (austerities II)]. 29 December, 2015.

Ministry of Justice and Public Security. 2015–2016. "Prop. 90 L. Endringer i utlendingslovgivningen mv. (innstramminger II)." [Draft resolutions and bills 90 L. Changes in the Immigration Act etc. (austerities II)].

Pettigrew, Thomas, and Linda Tropp. 2006. "A Meta-Analytic Test of Intergroup Contact Theory." *Journal of Personality and Social Psychology* 90 (5): 751–783.

Rafiqui, Arzoo, and Jens Thomsen. 2014. "Kontakthypotesen og majoritetsmedlemmers negative stereotypier." [The contact hypothesis and the negative stereotypes of majority members]. *Tidsskrift for samfunnsforskning* 55 (4): 415–438.

Repstad, Pål. 2009. "A Softer God and a More Positive Anthropology: Changes in a Religiously Strict Region in Norway." *Religion* 39: 126–131.

Repstad, Pål. 2010. "Fra lov til lønnkammer? Religion og livssyn i dagens Norge." [From law to closet? Religion and world-views in contemporary Norway]. 6th ed. In *Det norske samfunn*, edited by Ivar Frønes and Lise Kjølsrød. Oslo: Gyldendal, 371–392.

Repstad, Pål. 2014. "When Religions of Difference Grow Softer." In *Christianity in the Modern World. Changes and Controversies*, edited by Giselle Vincett and Elijah Obinna, 157–174. Farnham: Ashgate.

Repstad, Pål, and Irene Trysnes (eds.). 2013. *Fra fortapelse til feelgood. Musikk, sang og dans i religiøst liv.* [From perdition to feelgood. Music, song and dance in religious life]. Oslo: Cappelen Damm Akademisk.

Skarpenes, Ove, Rune Sakslind, and Roger Hestholm. 2016. "National Reportoirs of Moral Values." *Cultura* 13 (1): 7–27.

Stene, Nora. 2016. "Christian Missionaries and Asylum Seekers: A Case Study from Norway." *Nordic Journal of Human Rights* 34 (3): 203–221.

Thomsen, Jens. 2012. "How Does Intergroup Contact Generate Ethnic Tolerance? The Contact Hypothesis in A Scandinavian Context." *Scandinavian Political Studies* 35 (2): 159–178.

Vetvik, Einar, and Torunn Omland. 1997. *Kirkeerfaringer med kirkeasyl.* [Church experiences with church asylums]. Trondheim: Tapir.

Louise Lund Liebmann
Chapter 11
Media, Muslims and Minority Tactics: Compelling Dialogues in Norway

Abstract: The chapter investigates dynamics of minority–majority religious interaction in two localities in Norway with a strong Muslim presence and considers the ways in which media, based on conflictual representations, comes to co-structure interaction relating to lived religion and conduct of citizenship. The chapter asks: How do Muslims active in interreligious initiatives in Kristiansand and Oslo relate to the media portrayals of Islam and in what ways does the coverage influence their engagement? The study argues that attending, and participating in, interreligious forums can be understood as a minority strategy to cope with, counter, and calibrate perceived negative media portrayals since these actions are ways of performing belonging to the Norwegian nation and conducting citizenship. As the interreligious forums provide an occasion for the Muslims to self-present in ways that allow them to demonstrate their Norwegian belonging, the Muslims' public conduct and self-representations, nonetheless, becomes restricted by the forums' diversity governance.

Keywords: Norwegian Muslims, banal securitization of Islam, cultural citizenship, interreligious dialogue, Muslims and media.

11.1 Introduction

Zunair[1] is a young, male Muslim from Groruddalen in eastern Oslo. I met him to talk about a film project that he was involved in on former Syrian fighters from Norway [*syriakrigere*][2] and, more generally, his view of media and being Muslim in Norwegian society. Visibly upset, Zunair recounted how on social media he had recently come across a video featuring a young, ethnic Norwegian man from West Oslo who divulged how he had accidently ended

---

[1] All names in this chapter has been changed by the author due to reasons of anonymity.
[2] These are sometimes synonymously referred to as 'foreign fighters' (*fremmedkrigere*) and comprise Norway-based Muslims, often affiliated with IS, who travel to Syria or Iraq to become trained by and participate in the civil war on behalf of IS or less frequently, Al-Qaeda. If they return, these Muslims are considered a threat to the nation due to their radicalized religious worldviews, militant training and acquisition of social networks among international terrorists (PST 2016, 13).

OpenAccess. © 2018, Louise Lund Liebmann. [CC BY-NC-ND] This work is licensed under the Creative Commons Attribution-Non Commerical-NoDerivs 4.0 License. https://doi.org/10.1515/9783110502060-016

up at Vestli station in Groruddalen as he had fallen asleep on the tube. Zunair clearly took offense to the video as the man talked about his allegedly horrific experience of suddenly finding himself in an unknown yet highly stigmatized part of town. (Field notes, June 2016, Oslo)

To many Norwegians, Groruddalen has become a metaphor for cultural, ethnic, and religious diversity, but to critics it symbolizes a piece of 'anti-Norway', notions that figure frequently in media coverage (Eide and Eriksen 2012, 7). Located in the outskirts of the eastern part of Oslo, Groruddalen constitutes a suburban area, which due to its numerous social housing blocks and high number of immigrants has gained a reputation of social deprivation and 'white flight'.[3] Yet, as for many other Norwegian Muslims, Groruddalen is the place Zunair, his friends, and family call home.

Over the last 45 years, Norway has become an increasingly diverse society due to immigration. But even as the country from the 1970s and onwards has seen a religious pluralization due to an influx of immigrants and refugees, Christianity clearly continues to dominate the religious scene. Christianity also enjoys a privileged position in relation to the extant political system, and it constitutes the largest religion in terms of followers. The second largest religion is Islam, brought about by recent decades' immigration from Muslim majority countries such as Pakistan and Somalia. As Norway enshrines the principle of freedom of religion in government legislation, all registered faith and life stance communities receive public funding equivalent to their number of members, and religious minorities are basically free to operate as they wish. However, issues related to multiculturalism, Islam, integration, gender equality within minority religions, social cohesion, and the extent to which Norway shall be(come) 'multicultural' are much-disputed topics, and tensions between the newly secular state, Christian–secular majority society, and religious minorities certainly exist (Fox 2008).

According to a survey by the state Directorate for Inclusion and Diversity (IMDI), in recent times Muslims have received more coverage in Norwegian mass media than any other topic,[4] and Muslims are depicted in almost exclusively negative ways, regularly portrayed as posing a threat to the Norwegian nation (IMDI 2009). Another recent study shows that in Norwegian news bulletins during 2015, Islam was mentioned more than nine times as often as Christianity (Mi-

---

3 Nowadays, Groruddalen is usually categorised along two topical axes in public debates: social problems and an increasing number of immigrant residents (Eriksen and Vestel 2012, 18).
4 The prime minister excluded.

chelsen 2016, 6).[5] When it comes to religion featured in mass media, debate material on Islam such as opinion pieces has replaced the everyday mentioning of Christianity and the latter's roles and values within society (Michelsen 2016, 7). The same pattern may appear in social media (see Chapter 9). Correspondingly, the ComRel survey (see Chapter 2) shows that in 2015, 47 percent of the Norwegian respondents perceived Islam as a threat to 'Norwegian culture' whereas, for instance, only 12 percent thought of Judaism and 8 percent of Christianity in such terms (Lundby 2017, 8). While the Norwegian media environment around Muslims is far from the hostility projected in Danish media frames, the findings do support the notion of Islam being overrepresented in the media compared to the relatively low number of Muslims living in the country – estimates suggest less than 4 percent (Østby and Dalgard 2017). Likewise, the findings also indicate a widespread tendency of associating Islam with conflicts and tensions and illustrate how mediatized radical and far-right discourses on essential cultural differences have had an impact on the population (see Mårtensson 2014, 238).

11.2 The Study and Its Context

Departing from the way in which media shapes conflictual frames on Islam and Muslims in Norway and beyond, this chapter engages with how Norwegian Muslims, active in various interreligious forums, relate to media portrayals of Islam and come to engage, and self-present, in local civic settings. Interreligious initiatives such as public dialogue meetings offer idealized conversations that display harmonious multi-religious diversity as a reaction to transformations and (potential) tensions in society.[6] Thus, a growing number of studies focus on citizenship as subjective experiences of inclusion or exclusion and as a process through which people may come to affirm or contest their belonging to the community through different practices (see van Es 2016; Yuval Davis 2011).

---

[5] The growing focus on Islam in the Nordic countries' news media is additionally documented by the NOREL research project comparing religion in the daily press in Denmark, Finland, Iceland, Norway, and Sweden (see Niemelä and Christensen 2013).

[6] Thereby, the meetings serve as exemplars of inclusive religiosity as civilized behaviour in cross-religious encounters. As shown elsewhere (Liebmann 2017), the formation of a cultivated form of religiosity links closely to civilizing processes, and through these mechanisms to the formation of moderate and liberal citizens who, peacefully, can interact and co-exist. Then, what is ultimately performed and 'rehearsed' in many interreligious forums is the conduct of formations of cultural citizenship through enactment of respectable, proper, and inclusive religiosity.

The present case study investigates the dynamics of minority–majority religious interaction in localities in Kristiansand and Oslo with a strong Muslim presence and considers the ways in which media, based on the conflictual representations, co-structures interaction relating to lived religion and conduct of cultural citizenship. It asks: How do Muslims active in interreligious initiatives in Kristiansand and Oslo relate to the perceived media portrayals of Islam and in what ways does the coverage influence their engagement? The chapter argues that attending, and participating in, cross-cultural interreligious forums and initiatives can be understood as a minority strategy to cope with, counter, and calibrate negative media portrayals since these actions are ways of performing belonging to the Norwegian nation and conducting Norwegian citizenship.

Qualitative in its scope, the study is based on ethnographic fieldwork conducted at and around interreligious initiatives in Kristiansand and Groruddalen in Oslo during 2015 and 2016, including 26 interviews with people active in various interreligious forums and informal conversations with local citizens and journalists. Organizational documents and media coverage are also included in the analysis. Whereas Groruddalen is part of the Norwegian capital and is culturally, ethnically, and religiously highly diverse due to its high number of residents with immigrant backgrounds, Kristiansand is the municipal and county capital of the West-Agder region in the religiously rich Sørlandet (The Southern County), which has mainly experienced immigration from Pakistan, Chile, Vietnam, and, more recently, Poland.

11.3 Targeted Muslims in Norway

An ethnic Norwegian woman in her 60s, whom I interviewed in Groruddalen where she had been living her entire adult life, and where she is active in various interreligious initiatives, also noted how Muslims she knew personally inadvertently risked becoming the centre of negative and inaccurate media attention by way of local media coverage:

> Brynhild: When we partake in The Ellingsrud Days, it's often young people who act as convenors. And this year it was a young man, he was 17 years old, and he was interviewed by the local newspaper. They requested a picture of him, and he took a picture of himself wearing [his ancestral] national costume with white layers, a tunic. That was the photograph, and he was bearded too [in the picture]. And subsequently, the photograph was shared in a web forum called *document.no*. And they said, 'Is this the best Ellingsrud has to offer? A picture of someone wearing a night gown and being hate-bearded? That is siding with...' And then they compared it [the photograph] to IS and extremists, so, that was unfair. And I know the guy [in the photograph] and he stands for totally different values.

In this excerpt, Brynhild refers to how the media can transform certain content and generate a mediatized conflict (see Hjarvard, Mortensen, and Eskjær 2015) around Islam. These conflicts might occur even when the Muslim in question is simply being active and engaged in an intercultural, local community festival set to promote community participation and generate social cohesion at the local level – a task that is otherwise held in high regard and considered very much in sync with values held to be at the core of Norwegian majority society (Eide and Eriksen 2012, 10; for a discussion of the role of Norwegian festivals, see Ryan and Wollan 2013). This way, Brynhild's experiences testify to the way in which the media plays both performative and constitutive roles for the development of conflicts in contemporary society aside from merely reporting on pre-existing conflicts (Cottle 2006, 9). Moreover, the case referred to by Brynhild substantiates that lots of Muslims in Norway experience stigmatization in their everyday lives and that they, at different levels of society, are treated as members of 'suspect communities', singled out as devious by the media and the state (Manchanda 2010).

Speaking to Zunair, who in the introduction to this study disclosed the discomfort he felt when his neighbourhood was perceived as a dangerous place for members of majority society, he also highlighted a documentary film project, originating from a mosque in Groruddalen, as a response to the media's – and majority society's – linkage of violent religious extremism with Islam. Furthermore, he stressed how religious extremism and radicalization especially have during the last few years come to be associated almost exclusively with Islam by authorities and mass media in Norway, including on occasions in which Muslims had nothing to do with the perpetrated attacks in question. Perhaps this tendency was most lucidly displayed in the immediate aftermath of the events of 22 July 2011, when for a few hours, the fatal attacks in Utøya and government buildings in central Oslo were connected to Islam and perceived as being acts of radical Muslims when, as it turned out, Anders Breivik a white, far right and then self-proclaimed Christian, was behind the attacks (see Andersson 2012, 418).

Another male Muslim from Groruddalen, affiliated to a different Islamic organization undertaking dialogue work, likewise reflected on the way in which Muslims are being depicted and perceived, and he explained his, and his organization's, involvement in dialogue efforts to counter the fact that religious extremism is routinely connected to Islam:

> Farid: But during the last year there has been so much conflict and unrest in society attached to religion that we think it's important to bring up things that unite and which point to the potential for tolerance and comprehensive things.
>
> Interviewer: Which conflicts are you referring to?

> Farid: You see, right? It is - we did have the cartoon crisis for example. We have IS, we have terrorism attached to Islam. It is Islam that essentially is being linked to a lot of these things. For example, after the cartoon crisis, right? So, what we did, as a starting point – we also held conferences about it, we had *Charlie Hebdo*, we had a conference called 'Je suis Charlie', and then we posed a lot of questions – and we had some experience with it as we're devoted to those exact things, concerns, with blasphemy, and people feeling insulted, who want to kill somebody because of something.

Farid describes how during the last few years his organization has been occupied with arranging various conferences and facilitating dialogue around tensions and conflicts that repeatedly emerge between Muslims and non-Muslims, in this case primarily outside Norway. Doing so, Farid indicates how Muslims are frequently induced to take a defensive stance, which compels them, and especially those involved in interreligious efforts, to constantly navigate, and strive to prevent, Islamophobic prejudices from increasing and cross religious-conflicts from escalating. Correspondingly, Farid characterizes the situation of societal tensions and heightened media awareness, in this case referring to the attack on the French satirical magazine, *Charlie Hebdo*, as 'playing Monopoly and moving back to Start. Whether it is Theo van Gogh or Je Suis Charlie or whatever, we [repeatedly] have to pull out the same pamphlets and start all over'.

Wagas is a male Muslim born and raised in Kristiansand where he now lives and works. Describing how Wagas himself used never to experience anything discriminating in his hometown of Kristiansand, he recalled how he was recently verbally attacked by an elderly ethnic Norwegian woman: as Wagas was on a casual Sunday trip to a local beach to feed the ducks with his young children, he, it appears, had missed a sign post that prohibited animal feeding. While the children were enjoying themselves and the ducks eagerly ate the food, a woman approached the dark-skinned family and 'screamed and yelled' at them in English for not being able to read a simple sign post and not abiding by the rules when 'coming here [to Kristiansand]'. Apparently, and mistakenly, she had assumed that Wagas and his children were part of the refugee group, which had come to Norway in 2015 and been given huge media coverage. Wagas was subsequently able to rebuke her in eloquent Norwegian. Nonetheless, incidents like this one clearly influence Wagas and his sense of belonging in the local and national community. He says:

> Wagas: To me, since I was born and raised here, I feel that Norway is my country. When I go to Pakistan, it's like going on a holiday. When I return home from Pakistan, I feel like coming home. It's not until recently that I started to feel a little disapproved of, and a bit labelled, and I've never felt that way before. Now, during the last two to three years, in terms of the refugee crisis, I feel a little bit like: 'Shit!' You feel as if – even though you've lived here and you're here – you're still not a part of this society. And I see myself as quite resourceful

in many respects, so when I feel that way, I'm sure many other [Muslims] feel the same. [...] I don't have to dwell on it, but still, I've got this feeling, and I only just got it. I'm 39 years old, and I just got it recently. That's a little sad!

As illustrated by their various accounts, Waqas, Brynhild, Zunair, and Farid all point to how macro events also play out at the civic and individual levels in terms of psychological insecurities that condition diverse ways of societal belonging and participation. In other words, they address how securitization of issues, such as migration, Islam, and ethnic minorities, is not only a tool in the hands of politicians but occurs in the broader political culture on an everyday basis and is closely linked to psychological and media frames and to various citizenship strategies (see Kinnvall and Nesbitt-Larking 2011, 272). As noticed by several studies of the nexus between media frames and social interaction, political discourses and media frames do much more than simply reflect and depict (Mårtensson 2014; Entman 1993). As will be further elaborated upon later (see Chapters 14 and 15), the selection and activation of media frames in the coverage of a given issue structures and impacts the way in which audiences come to think of the issues in question; that is, frames are not only essential to formations of identity but also to the way in which people interact with each other as social interaction tends to occur around prescribed and pre-structured formations.

11.4 Banal Securitization of Islam: Dialogues and De-Securitization

Across religious divides, most of my interlocutors who were engaged in interreligious initiatives mentioned their participation in interreligious dialogue efforts as a way of accommodating lesser antagonisms between religious (and secular) fractions, and thereby prevent immoderate and extremist views. In this respect, some reflected on the media's emphasis on ethno-religious tensions in order to sell its stories; negative media depictions of Muslims were emphasized by half of the interviewees, though this was not necessarily part of their motivation in volunteering in various interreligious initiatives. However, nearly all Muslims stressed negative media portrayals of Muslims as a key factor to their engagement within these initiatives. A characteristic that they to a certain extent shared with representatives of the other minority religions. Yet, as media and politics are highly interrelated (Meyen, Thieroff, and Strengeri 2014), media inadvertently comes to influence funding opportunities and interreligious solution models, and, thereby the way in which certain social problems are framed and associated with Islam.

Gro, a young woman representing a new religious movement and actively participating in and leading different interreligious initiatives in Oslo, described how Islam and Muslims constitute a significant object of media representation and how she had noticed that Muslims, consequently, are posited at the core of various de-radicalization measures:

> Interviewer: How come that topic [extremism] takes up so much space?
>
> Gro: In our case, it's because we got funding to work with it. And, in addition, because it's a topic we have selected due to our work with faith and life stance dialogue. Essentially, we felt that majority society demands from us that we bring up extremism as extremism is attached to religion. [...] What we have done is to focus on religious extremism, on what it is, and what extremism as a phenomenon entails, and to show that it exists within all religions; it's not just in Islam. [...] So, we have, when applying for funding, it's that kind of funding that is announced at this point; that is, funding to work with extremism. So, we have jumped on that wave. [...] And often, this is my personal opinion, it's implicit within the call that you're dealing with Islam. [...]
>
> Interviewer: How do you get the sense that it's really about Islam?
>
> Gro: Because it's a lot like 'today's challenges', 'integration', 'radicalization of youth', and the only thing the media – since this is what you're trying to deal with – everything that is part of the news coverage today, I think, is just Islam, Islam, Islam and everyone, everyone has forgotten about Breivik being Norwegian, everyone has forgotten that Breivik was active just a few years ago.

In the interview, Gro effectively links the media coverage of Islam to governmental announcements of various funding opportunities related to cross-religious dialogue and de-radicalization; she points to the way in which authorities' growing interest in interreligious dialogue is intermingled with negative media coverage of immigrants and especially Muslims – a fusion I suggest calling 'banal securitization of Islam.' The concept 'securitization of Islam' (see Cesari 2013) refers to the central rhetorical tropes, partly induced by the media, which portray Muslims as threats to national security in Western societies. Furthermore, as observed by political scientists Catarina Kinnvall and Paul Nesbitt-Larking (2011, 275), securitization is also an everyday phenomenon and 'banal securitization' thus refers to the everyday practices in which issues or people are categorised in stereotypical terms in response to macro-logical events with local ramifications. In these processes, it is not only phenomena, objects, or identifications that become securitized, but also subjectivities (ibid.). Thus 'banal securitization of Islam' refers to the way in which Muslim citizens, in Norway and beyond, are, on a daily basis, rendered as potentially suspicious by being demarcated and stigmatized.

Elaborating on whether Farid's organization had convened any interreligious events that were less successful, Farid highlighted an increased level of general attentiveness towards dialogue initiatives and came to focus on the interest that Norwegian authorities recently have taken in interreligious dialogue:

> Farid: Yes, absolutely! We have had very few attendants as well, so it's up and down. ... Lately [people's interest] has increased as many see the need for interreligious dialogue exactly because the world has become a more dangerous place in many respects. And religion is a factor in that, and that's why many see the usefulness, right? Many asylum seekers have arrived in Norway, there's been some murmuring among religious groups, some extreme groups such as Profetens Ummah and others who have made themselves noticed, right? And in that regard, it's also important, and I clearly see that authorities emphasize interreligious dialogue in that they organize more in that direction, they encourage [people] to [participate in] it. ... Actually, at this point, the climate is well-suited for religious dialogue.

Here, Farid touches on how authorities link interreligious initiatives with de-radicalization. The authorities' coupling of interreligious initiatives with de-radicalization constitutes an interesting, yet rather camouflaged, instance of religious diversity management:[7] As interreligious events are based on the implicit assumption that there is an incompatibility that threatens the intended peaceful interaction between the dialogue partners if disagreements are not reduced or resolved (Malik 2013, 500), from an outer perspective, interreligious forums help create platforms from which public parties are able to conduct and transform religious minorities into moderate and liberal citizens of the modern nation state (Amir-Moazami 2011, 13–14, 25).

As the populist discourse has increased the pressure on young Muslims especially to take a stand in the perceived conflict between 'Norwegianness' and 'Islam', there is, however, at the same time an institutional structure that strives to guarantee important rights for individual and community members: Norway is among a number of European welfare states that enable a certain degree of cultural and religious diversity, and the country has facilitated, and often promoted,

---

[7] Since 2014, the Ministry of Culture has announced annual funding opportunities, ranging from 50,000–400,000 NOK (about 5,000–43,000 Euros), for interreligious events held to create mutual acceptance and respect between faith and life stance communities and to promote the societies' common values such as democracy, rule of law, and human rights, and to prevent radicalization. These funding opportunities are consistent with the government's *Action Plan against Radicalization and Violent Extremism* (Justis- og beredskapsdepartementet 2014, 3).

cultural diversity instead of demanding full assimilation from new citizens. An important aspect of Norwegian diversity management is the funding of organizations by and for ethnic minorities, either in the form of project subsidies or structural funding (Ghorashi, Eriksen, and Alghasi 2009). These funding opportunities also apply to interreligious forums that can get financial support from the municipality, the county, and the state.

As Muhammad, a young Muslim man from Kristiansand, argued in response to a question of what he wanted to gain from his involvement with interreligious dialogue initiatives, being engaged in interreligious efforts affords him a feeling of social inclusion and belonging:

> Muhammad: In a way - to become acquainted with one another. Again, this has to do with prejudices, right, prejudices. That I'll come across a Christian, and then we'll chat at the [interfaith] meeting. And then I'll become acquainted with him. We have a lot in common, at least when it comes to peace efforts. Here in Kristiansand. We can do something good for our town. I'll greet a Buddhist, and then I'll find out that he has been a teacher, for example, he's been a teacher at my school, and then I'll get to know him. When I'll meet a Christian or a Buddhist, in a way, I'll feel more secure when talking to them. ... I felt that when we, Muslim youngsters, handed out peace pamphlets produced by FTL.[8] We feel that, okay, we're part of society, also, we work to obtain peace. Just the fact that we went out, I felt that it was good for us, because then we feel that we're a part of this society, and that we do something good, we contribute to something good. That in itself - then I don't feel isolated, right?

By being active in an interreligious forum, Muhammad feels that he is doing something 'good', considers himself included in society and less isolated. This is supported by Akmal Ali, former imam in the Kristiansand Mosque and current member of the mosque board committee and actively involved in a local interreligious organization. In an op-ed on the topic in a widely read local-regional newspaper, Ali writes: 'It is very important that Muslims, Christians, Humanists, Buddhists, Ahmadiyyas, Bahais, and people from all faith and life stance communities sit together in dialogues. Because, essentially, it is about cooperating to support beneficial values. [...] Dialogue builds upon trust that, again, leads to your own faith and viewpoints being listened to.' (Ali 2017, 28). In other words, engagement in interreligious forums is an investment that will lead to the recognition of minority religions and giving them a voice, and a place, in Norwegian society.

Several research projects on first- and second-generation ethnic minority youth in Norway have concluded that reactions against essentialist categories

---

8 Forum for Tro og Livssyn (Forum for Religious and Life Stances), in short: FTL.

and negative media portrayals of migrant, ethnic, and religious minorities are among the central drivers for identity work, that is, processual experiences of identity, belonging, and recognition (Andersson 2005, 2010; Jacobsen 2006; Fangen 2008; van Es 2016).[9] As illustrated throughout this chapter, many Muslims clearly feel stigmatized and stereotyped by the media and, thus, their engagement in various interreligious initiatives can be understood precisely as part of a tactic to overcome and disrupt these negative portrayals. People disrupt or subvert stereotypes when they present themselves in ways that contradict these stereotypes. Disruption can be a deliberate strategy, but people may also subconsciously challenge popular perceptions simply by behaving differently from what is commonly expected (van Es 2016, 14). This way, the studied Muslims' engagements in interreligious forums and embedded self-representations can be understood as a way of creating acceptance for Muslims in the society in which they live. Sociologist Anna Halafoff, too, has noted how multi-faith participants recounted that interreligious initiatives in Australia provide a platform for Muslim communities to differentiate themselves from terrorists, to dispel negative stereotypes, and to affirm their commitment to non-violent principles (2011, 460). As will be elaborated below, engaging in interreligious initiatives constitutes a way of coping and aspiring to counter the 'banal securitization of Islam'.

Speaking to a highly placed employee within a central interreligious forum, Ingunn, she explicitly referred to the nexus between core values in Norwegian society and the scope and efforts of the national interfaith body, Council for Religious and Life Stance Communities in Norway (STL):[10]

> Ingunn: You see, what's up with this interreligious dialogue is, essentially, that it's a training in community participation, and in a way, it is participation training in democracy development, and in that way, it's training in the Norwegian model. ... STL is a secular project. It's not a religious organization. It's a secular project working with politics as well as dialogue, right? Between the faith- and life-stance societies. And – as within all projects – you have got to have some root concerns, and in STL it's 'democracy', 'co-determination', 'participation', and 'human rights'.

Sociologists Grete Brochmann and Anne Grødem argue that in many respects the Norwegian welfare model constitutes a grand societal integration project with three central components: democracy, modernization, and citizenship (2013,

---

9 The term 'identity work' addresses the dialectics between 'outer' categorical aspects and 'inner' personal aspects in these processes (Andersson 2000, 291).
10 Name in Norwegian: Samarbeidsrådet for tros- og livssynssamfunn, in short: STL.

59).[11] This perception supports Ingunn's observation on the nexus between STL's scope and core values in Norwegian society such as democracy, co-determination, (community) participation, and human rights and, furthermore, that secularly informed interreligious dialogue essentially consists of participation training in democracy development, and consequently, that engagement in these forums basically revolves around conducting Norwegian citizenship through education and training in the Norwegian welfare model.

Adding to this, sociologist Willem Schinkel illustrates that citizenship as a legal status does not guarantee being perceived as belonging to the (imagined) community. Migrants and their descendants must prove to majority citizens that they have acquired certain 'essential' virtues to be accepted as part of society – an acceptance which Schinkel refers to as acquiring 'moral' or 'virtualised citizenship' (2008, 20). Yet, members of ethnic or religious minority groups are by default presumed to lack such virtues, simply because they are associated with a specific minority culture or religion. In effect, ethnic and religious minorities are to a much higher extent obliged to continuously demonstrate – or perform – their national belonging in order to not (be perceived to) pose a threat to the community or the national order.

If we invert Ingunn's statement, it is possible to see how interreligious forums provide an opportunity for the Muslims involved to self-present as peaceful, equality-orientated, democratically minded, and secular-accepting and, through this, also come to affirm their commitment to Norwegian society. As citizenship entails full membership of the nation as a community, it is much more than a matter of formal and legal rights and responsibilities. Participation in civic society and creation of a sense of belonging are not only central components in identity work, but also in subverting stereotypical notions that endorse the 'banal securitization of Islam'. In turn, such engagement can be understood as constituting part of a Muslim minority strategy to create stronger ties with majority society and conduct cultural citizenship.

---

11 If one is to maintain a societal framework, new members must be made part of society through the welfare model. Effective welfare states do not want to have large numbers of people that fall through the safety net, disturb regulated working life, burden social budgets, or eventually undermine solidarity (Brochman and Grødem 2013, 60).

11.5 Engaging in Interreligious Dialogue as a Tactic of Belonging: Muslims in Minority Contexts

Internationally, Norway is renowned for its diplomatic efforts and is regarded as an egalitarian, peace-loving nation, where concepts of human rights are historically well established (McIntosh 2014, 71). A strong welfare state, relatively small class differences, and a woman-friendly labour market are other characteristics of Norwegian society (Andersson 2012). Even as media portrayals of Muslims are framed in terms of conflict, the Norwegian public debate has nonetheless been characterized as a mellow 'consensus culture' compared to the often heated debate climate in the other Scandinavian countries (Stenius 2010), and the national self-image is characterized as innocent (Gullestad 2002; Berg Eriksen, Hompland, and Tjønneland 2003). Correspondingly, status is internally ascribed to attitudes – and performances – of being a 'good' Norwegian citizen through demonstrations of tolerance, kindness, honesty, and democratic attitudes (Skarpenes 2007).

Interreligious forums and initiatives fit into this perhaps paradoxical setting well, as they are suitably placed to, in a peaceful and patient manner, counter cross-cultural and religious ignorance, prejudice, and intolerance and ultimately foster understanding, stability, and peaceful co-existence through organised cultural encounters such as public meetings, community festivals, and other cross-religious get-togethers. Compared to the other two Scandinavian countries, interreligious forums enjoy a more profound public voice and a higher standing in Norway. For instance, interreligious forums such as STL constitute a nationally well-known interest group partaking in mainstream, accepted forms of multicultural religiosity, and STL itself holds a prominent place in society reflected by the public support of the otherwise politically neutral Royal House of Norway and by a 2015 state-funded commissioned evaluation report of interreligious dialogue efforts in civil society (see Brottveit et al. 2015).[12]

From this perspective, and through their interreligious engagement, the Muslims studied take part in identity work through which they project images of themselves as sociable and peace-seeking citizens; that is, when engaging in in-

---

[12] STL has nine local branches across the country plus a youth forum and is, to an increasing degree, frequently approached by the media when policies on religion are debated or conflicts around religious issues need contextualization and commenting on (interview with STL chairman, September 2016).

terreligious initiatives, they inadvertently cast themselves as inhabiting traits and attitudes in sync with societal values highly regarded in Norway. As noted by Schinkel, demonstrating acquisition of essential 'virtues' such as being civilized, peace-seeking, honest, kind, tolerant, caring, and democratic is a way of testifying their belonging to the Norwegian community – even as the community is imagined. Correspondingly, as members of an ethnic and religious minority group, they effectively mirror themselves in social imaginaries of ethnic Norwegians as non-radical and consensus-seeking, particularly peaceful, kind, tolerant, caring, and democratic citizens (Liebmann 2017).

In recent years, religious minority groups in Europe have adapted their discourses and strategies to a context of religious revitalization by engaging in interreligious councils or associations.[13] This also means that religious minority groups are aware of how they must adapt to the 'rules of the game' and repeatedly and actively demonstrate, or perform, being part of 'good', 'mainstream', or 'accepted' religious communities in order to be recognized (Griera 2012, 583, Liebmann 2017). Likewise, the 'religiously correct' behaviour of some religious minority leaders – such as that of Muslims – is under greater public scrutiny than the rest, which forces Muslims to play the 'religiously correct' role more intensively (Griera 2012, 583).

During the autumn of 2016, a telling case of the tacit regulations that often underlie European Muslims' public conduct arose in Kristiansand. Below the headline 'I just follow what the Quran says', in a widely read local–regional newspaper, the then local imam in Kristiansand, Abdikadir Mahamed Yussuf, was quoted saying, 'We Muslims have our religion. If the Quran or the Hadiths say it's okay to attend birthday parties, we say okay. I don't believe they say that. That's why we say, "Do not attend birthday parties". We don't say "you're wrong and it's forbidden", but "you shouldn't"' (Kristensen 2016, 16). Yussuf's views – and not least the interpretations and debates the interview generated – resulted, first, in his temporary absence of leave, shortly followed by his withdrawal from the imam position after a board meeting in the local mosque steering committee. The reaction to the imam's statement is quite telling of the cultural-religious navigation required by Muslims, and especially Muslim officials, to avoid uproar in the public realm and what a member of the Mosque committee to me described as 'a set-back' in the relations between Kristiansand-based Muslims and local authorities. A different case study shows equally well how an interreligiously

---

[13] Sociologist of religion, Mar Griera, argues that a policy paradigm based on the 'secularization thesis' has been replaced by a new paradigm grounded on the fear that the revitalization of religion would undermine urban and social cohesion (2012, 572).

convened de-radicalization seminar based in Kristiansand repeatedly came to posit Islam as an organizing principle around which the intended unpacking of violent religious extremism's generic entities revolved in spite of the seminar's religious minority-inclusive objectives (Liebmann forthcoming).

11.6 Conclusion

Based primarily on ethnographic fieldwork and interviews with people active in various interreligious forums, this chapter has explored how Muslims involved with interreligious initiatives in Kristiansand and Oslo relate to media portrayals of Islam and in what ways the coverage impacts their engagement. To capture the everyday framing, and stigmatization, of Muslims as threats to national security in Western societies – a phenomenon partly induced by the media – the chapter suggested applying the notion 'banal securitization of Islam'. The term refers to the way in which Muslim citizens are regularly rendered as potentially suspicious. The study, ensuingly, illustrated how engaging in interreligious initiatives constitutes a way of coping, and aspiring to counter and circumvent notions that endorse the 'banal securitization of Islam'. By doing so, Norwegian Muslims can both perform and affirm their commitment to Norwegian society, thus demonstrating their acquisition of essential citizenship 'virtues' such as being civilized, honest, kind, tolerant, and caring. As the interreligious forums provide a recognized platform and an occasion for the Muslims to self-present in ways that allow them to demonstrate their peacefulness, orientation towards equality, democratic-mindedness, and acceptance of secularism, the Muslims' public conduct and self-representations are accordingly managed and conditioned by the interreligious forums and their inherent governance of religious diversity.

Rather than focusing on the empowerment and freedom the forums may provide, this study has stressed the conditions and restrictions that apply to all members of interreligious initiatives – but which perhaps operate more intensely in relation to media and stigmatized groups such as Muslims. Whether to analytically emphasize agency on the one hand, or societal structures on the other, reflecting on empirical implications constitutes a research dilemma that is mirrored by longstanding scholarly discussions. Yet, as contemporary studies of interreligious initiatives tend to have an applied scope based upon the implicit assumption that interreligious forums generate empowerment and room for minority agency, this chapter has favoured a structurally informed, critical stance towards the way in which civic organizations working with, and along, media portrayals of Islam may also come to form, discipline, and restrict Muslims' behaviour and self-representations.

Bibliography

Ali, Akmal. 2017. "Dialog i et samfunn i endring." [Dialogue in a changing society]. *Fædrelandsvennen*. Accessed 23 Feb 2017. http://www.fvn.no/mening/Dialog-i-et-samfunn-i-endring-698150b.html.

Amir-Moazami, Schirin. 2011. "Dialogue as a Governmental Technique: Managing Gendered Islam in Germany." *Feminist Review* 98 (1): 9–27.

Andersson, Mette. 2000. "'All Five Fingers are Not the Same': Identity Work Among Ethnic Minority Youth in an Urban Norwegian Context." Bergen: Centre for Social Science Research, University of Bergen.

Andersson, Mette. 2005. *Urban Multi-Culture in Norway: Identity Formation among Immigrant Youth*. New York: Edwin Mellen Press.

Andersson, Mette. 2010. "The Social Imaginary of First Generation Europeans." *Social Identities* 16 (1): 3–21.

Andersson, Mette. 2012. "The Debate about Multicultural Norway Before and After 22 July 2011." *Identities: Global Studies in Culture and Power* 19 (4): 418–427.

Berg Eriksen, Trond, Andreas Hompland, and Eivind Tjønneland. 2003. *Et lite land i verden. 1950–2000*. [A small country in the world. 1950–2000]. Oslo: Aschehoug.

Brochmann, Grete, and Anne S. Grødem. 2013. "Migration and Welfare Sustainability: The Case of Norway." In *Europe's Immigration Challenge: Reconciling Work, Welfare and Mobility*, edited by Elena Jurado, and Grete Brochmann, 59–76. London: I.B.Tauris.

Brottveit, Ånund, Ann Kristin Gresaker, and Nina Hoel. 2015. *Det handler om verdensfreden!: En evaluering av rollen Samarbeidsrådet for tros- og livssynssamfunn, Norges Kristne Råd og Islamsk Råd Norge har i dialogarbeidet* [It's about the world peace!: An evaluation report]. Oslo: KIFO Report.

Cesari, Jocelyn. 2013. *Why the West Fears Islam: An Exploration of Muslims in Liberal Democracies*. New York: Palgrave Macmillan.

Cottle, Simon. 2006. *Mediatized Conflict: Developments in Media and Conflict Studies*. Maidenhead: Open University Press.

Eide, Elisabeth, and Thomas Hylland Eriksen. 2012. "Innledning: Den flerstemte drabantbyen." [Introduction: The multi-voiced suburb]. In *Den globale drabantbyen: Groruddalen og det nye Norge* [The global suburb: Groruddalen and the new Norway], edited by Sharam Alghassi, Elisabeth Eide, and Thomas Hylland Eriksen, 7–14. Oslo: Cappelen Damm Akademisk.

Entman, Robert M. 1993. "Framing: Toward Clarification of a Fractured Paradigm." *Journal of Communication* 43 (4): 51–58.

Eriksen, Thomas Hylland, and Viggo Vestel. 2012. "Groruddalen, Alna og det nye Norge." [Groruddalen, Alna, and the new Norway]. In *Den globale drabantbyen: Groruddalen og det nye Norge* [The global suburb: Groruddalen and the new Norway], edited by Sharam Alghassi, Elisabeth Eide, and Thomas Hylland Eriksen, 15–32. Oslo: Cappelen Damm Akademisk.

Fangen, Katrine. 2008. *Identitet og praksis. Etnisitet, klasse og kjønn blant somaliere i Norge*. [Identity and practice. Ethnicity, class, and gender among Somalis in Norway]. Oslo: Gyldendal Akademisk.

Fox, Jonathan. 2008. *A World Survey of Religion and the State*. Cambridge: Cambridge University Press.

Hjarvard, Stig, Mikkel F. Eskjær, and Mette Mortensen. 2015. "Introduction: Three Dynamics of Mediatized Conflicts." In *The Dynamics of Mediatized Conflicts*, edited by Mikkel F. Eskjær, Stig Hjarvard, and Mette Mortensen, 1–30. New York: Peter Lang.

Ghorashi, Halem, Thomas Hylland Eriksen, and Sharam Alghasi. 2009. "Introduction." In *Paradoxes of Cultural Recognition: Perspectives from Northern Europe*, 1–18. Farnham: Ashgate.

Griera, Mar. 2012. "Public Policies, Interfaith Associations and Religious Minorities: A new Policy Paradigm? Evidence from the Case of Barcelona." *Social Compass* 59 (4): 570–587.

Gullestad, Marianne. 2002. *Det norske sett med nye øyne: Kritisk analyse av norsk innvandringsdebatt.* [The Norwegian reconceptualized]. Oslo: Universitetsforlaget.

Halafoff, Anna. 2011. "Countering Islamophobia: Muslim Participation in Multifaith Networks." *Islam and Christian–Muslim Relations* 22 (4): 451–467.

IMDI [Integrerings- og mangfoldsdirektoratet]. 2009. "Immigrants in the Norwegian Media." Accessed 7 June 2017. http://www.imdi.no/no/Nyheter/2010/Engelsk-oversettelse-av-IMDis-arsrapport/.

Jacobsen, Christine. 2006. "Staying on the Straight Path: Religious Identities and Practices among Young Muslims in Norway." PhD Diss., University of Bergen.

Justis- og beredskapsdepartementet. 2014. *Action Plan against Radicalisation and Violent Extremism.* Accessed 7 June 2017. https://www.regjeringen.no/en/dokumenter/Action-plan-against-Radicalisation-and-Violent-Extremism/id762413/

Kinnvall, Catarina, and Paul Nesbitt-Larking. 2011. "Global Insecurity and Citizenship Strategies: Young Muslims in the West." *Distinktion: Journal of Social Theory* 12 (3): 271–290.

Kristensen, Eivind. 2016. "'Jeg bare følger det som står i Koranen.'" [I just follow what the Quran says]. *Fædrelandsvennen*, 14 Jan 2017.

Liebmann, Louise Lund. 2017. "Interfaith Dialogue in Christian Norway: The Enactment of Inclusive Religiosity as Civilized Behaviour." *Journal of Religion in Europe* 10 (3).

Liebmann, Louise Lund. Forthcoming. "Islam and Muslims as Elephants in the Interfaith Room: Frame-governance of Dialogue and De-radicalisation."

Lundby, Knut. 2017. "Mediebruk og konflikter om religion i Norge." [Media uses and conflicts on religion in Norway]. *Norsk medietidsskrift* 24 (4): 1–19.

McIntosh, Laurie. 2014. "Before and After: Terror, Extremism and the Not-So-New Norway." *African and Black Diaspora: An International Journal* 7: 70–80.

Malik, Jitendra. 2013. "Integration of Muslim Migrants and the Politics of Dialogue: The Case of Modern Germany." *Journal of Muslim Minority Affairs* 33 (4): 495–506.

Manchanda, Rita. 2010. "Media-Mediated Public Discourse on 'Terrorism' and Suspect Communities." *Economic and Political Weekly* 45: 43–50.

Meyen, Michael, Markus Thieroff, and Steffi Strengeri. 2014. "Mass Media Logic and The Mediatization of Politics: A Theoretical Framework." *Journalism Studies* 15 (3): 271–288.

Michelsen, Jaran. R. 2016. "Islam dominerer religionsdebatten." [Islam dominates the debate on religion]. *Vårt Land*. Accessed 16 Aug 2016. http://www.vl.no/nyhet/islam-dominerer-religionsdebatten-1.766627?paywall=true

Mårtensson, Ulrika. 2014. "Hate Speech and Dialogue in Norway: Muslims 'Speak Back'." *Journal of Ethnic and Migration Studies* 40 (2): 230–248.

Niemelä, Kati, and Henrik R. Christensen. 2013. "Religion in Newspapers in the Nordic Countries 1988–2008." *Nordic Journal of Religion and Society* 26 (1): 5–24.

PST [Politiets sikkerhetstjeneste]. 2016. *Trusselsvurdering 2016*. [Threat assessment 2016]. Accessed 7 June 2017. http://www.pst.no/media/utgivelser/trusselvurdering-2016/

Ryan, Anne Wally, and Gjermund Wollan. 2013. "Festivals, Landscapes, and Aesthetic Engagement: A Phenomenological Approach to Four Norwegian Festivals." *Norsk geografisk tidsskrift* 67 (2): 99–112.

Schinkel, Willem. 2008. "The Moralization of Citizenship in Dutch Integration Discourse." *Amsterdam Law Forum* 1: 15–26.

Skarpenes, Ove. 2007. "Den 'legitime kulturens' moralske forankring." [The moral anchoring of 'the legitimate' culture]. *Tidsskrift for samfunnsforskning* 48 (4): 531–557.

Stenius, Henrik. 2010. "Nordic Associational Life in a European and an Inter-Nordic Perspective." In *Nordic Associations in a European Perspective*, edited by Risto Alapuro and Henrik Stenius, 29–86. Baden-Baden: Nomos.

van Es, Margaretha A. 2016. *Stereotypes and Self-Representations of Women with a Muslim Background: The Stigma of Being Oppressed*. Cham: Palgrave Macmillan.

Yuval-Davis, Nira. 2011. *The Politics of Belonging: Intersectional Contestations*. Los Angeles: Sage.

Østby, Lars, and Anne Berit Dalgard. 2017. "4 prosent muslimer i Norge?", *Samfunnsspeilet* 4/2017, http://www.ssb.no/befolkning/artikler-og-publikasjoner/4-prosent-muslimer-i-norge

Janna Hansen, David Herbert
Chapter 12
Life in the Spotlight: Danish Muslims, Dual Identities, and Living with a Hostile Media

Abstract: We examine ethnic Danish and ethnic minority Muslim (n = 15) responses to the negative media frame they experience, and their efforts[1] to build viable dual identities – ways of being Danish and Muslim. The reported media negativity is triangulated with evidence from ECRI media reports, public opinion surveys, and reports on government policies and institutions. We find that interviewees' experiences vary with their visibility as Muslims, so hijab wearing women and men of colour report most negativity in public environments. We also find that efforts to pro-actively project a positive social media image of Islam vary by time since conversion, gradually declining. Danish Muslim challenges in forming dual identities are compared with those of Swedish (Malmö) and British (London) Muslims. We examine why London Muslims more readily construct dual identities than Malmö Muslims – despite greater negativity in national surveys and barriers to voting. The implications for cultural conflict in Scandinavia are discussed.

Keywords: dual identity, media framing, social media, visibility, conversion

Across the Western world, and especially since the terrorist attacks of 11 September 2001, Islam and Muslims tend to be viewed through a hostile, conflictual frame in media and public discourse, a frame only reinforced by the rise of the so-called Islamic State (IS) in the Middle East, and the series of recent IS inspired terrorist attacks in European capital cities, including Copenhagen in 2015. Such conditions create a challenging public environment for Muslims throughout the West. However, judging by reports from the European Commission Against Racism and Intolerance (ECRI), it seems that the media frame in Denmark is particularly negative, even by comparative European standards, a situa-

---

[1] We recognise that the conditions facing Muslims in Western societies vary greatly, and that talk of 'the West' includes hugely diverse societies. However, we use the term while recognising the risks of over generalisation for three reasons: it was used spontaneously and often by our participants; it is cumbersome to constantly qualify the term; and we contend that there are features shared by many Western societies – market economies, democratic institutions, an emphasis on the importance of freedom of speech – that are relevant to the topic.

OpenAccess. © 2018, Janna Hansen, David Herbert. This work is licensed under the Creative Commons Attribution-Non Commerical-NoDerivs 4.0 License. https://doi.org/10.1515/9783110502060-017

tion exacerbated a lack of representation of, and hence 'voice' for, Muslims in public media (ECRI 2012, 28). Furthermore, the situation is also longstanding. Thus, as early as its second report on Denmark (2001) ECRI expressed concern about the climate surrounding Muslim and Islam in Denmark (2006, 25).

By the time of third report, 2006, in the wake of the Muhammad cartoons controversy (2005), this concern had grown, to the extent that ECRI was expressing 'deep concern that the situation concerning Muslims in Denmark has worsened since its second report' (ibid.). In the fourth report (2012) these concerns persist, evidenced by accounts of bias in reporting of criminal cases: 'some media report the ethnic background of a suspected criminal when this is not necessary for understanding the information, but that criminal offences committed by Danes against groups of concern to ECRI are underplayed' (ibid. 28), and by a continuing lack of opportunities for minorities to express their views in the media.

Judging by these reports, there is clearly a negative media climate for Muslims in Denmark; this is not to say the media is exclusively negative towards Muslims or that all sections of the media are negative, but that negativity is sufficiently prevalent to be of concern for human rights groups, and part of the everyday experience of our interviewees (see also Jacobsen et al. 2013). How, then, do Danish Muslims experience this hostile media frame, and how do they cope with it? In particular, given the capacity of social media to enable 'media contraflow' (Cottle 2006), whereby individuals and groups can respond to stigmatization by developing their own counter-representations and counter-narratives, how far and in what ways do Danish Muslims engage in such practices? And, in terms of the work of self-presentation (Goffman 1959) needed to maintain group- and self-esteem in the face of stigmatization, how do they represent themselves and construct a viable public identity? In this chapter we address these questions using data from interviews with 15 Muslims from mixed ethnic majority and minority backgrounds from the Greater Copenhagen area. We also comment on the conditions which structure the formation and public acceptance of dual and multiple identities, and on how this might be linked to positive integration outcomes.

12.1 Context: Public Attitudes, Culture, and Public Institutions

> In mediated societies – societies where media institutions have a dominant role and most, if not all, of our information about what's going beyond our immediate locality comes from media – it is impossible to separate the recognition individuals get from each other and the way that media resources are distributed. (Couldry 2011, 48)

How Danish Muslims experience the negative media frame is likely to be significantly shaped by their interactions with ethnic Danes and by how they are treated by Danish public institutions. There is not necessarily a perfect fit between dominant media frames and public attitudes; audiences are active, bringing their own experiences and thinking to their interpretation of media representations (Livingstone 2015). However, as Couldry (2011, 48) points out, on issues where the public is largely dependent on the media for information, media frames are likely to play a decisive role. So how widely shared is the dominant negative media frame in Denmark by the Danish public?

Widespread negativity towards immigrants in Denmark in general, and especially towards Muslims, is evident in European Social Survey (ESS, 2014) data. Thus, 46 percent of Danes agree with the proposition that the government should allow 'few or no Muslims' to come and settle in their country, a finding consistent the YouGov figure of 45 percent of Danes having a negative impression of Muslims (Dahlgren 2015). Furthermore, 42.3 percent of Danes agree with the proposition that 'immigrants take out more than they put in' in terms of taxes and services, suggesting a competitive framing of the relationship between immigrants and the majority amongst a substantial section of the population, which is likely to reinforce societal divisions.

Danes also score highly on measures of a sense of cultural superiority. Thus, 59.9 percent of Danes agree with the proposition that 'some cultures are much better than others' (ESS 2014, second only to Norwegians, at 64.4 percent), an attitude which might provide fertile ground for forms of 'cultural racism' (Blaut 1992), and provide weak foundations for practices which value the contribution to society of culturally different others. Furthermore, 29.8 percent of Danes agree with the statement that 'having a law against ethnic discrimination in the workplace is bad for the country', the highest in Europe, with those considering having such a law as 'extremely bad' in Denmark (12 percent) more than twice that of the second placed country (Switzerland, 5.9 percent). Such strong public rejection of anti-discrimination laws may impact on Muslim minorities if they seek to challenge workplace discrimination, and contribute to a climate where Muslims feel unwelcome.

Of course, opinions expressed confidentially in surveys do not necessarily translate into publicly expressed attitudes or behaviour. However, the CoMRel survey (see Chapter 2) found that 18.2 percent of the Danes agree that 'hostile attitudes towards foreigners should be tolerated', suggesting that public expression of xenophobic views is acceptable for a significant minority. Further evidence suggests that the challenging public environment extends to Danish government policies and public institutions. Thus, researchers have argued that government policy discourse has contributed to reinforcing a binary division between 'Muslims' and 'Danes' by de-legitimizing conservative Muslims voices through an overly broad official discourse on radicalization (Kühle and Lindekilde 2012). In this process Muslims who hold conservative views on gender and sexuality, which overlap with those of some in the majority population and had been previously considered part of legitimate difference in values, are grouped together with extremists.

Barriers to inclusion in public institutions are caused not just by overt hostility, but produced also as an unintended consequence of strongly marked difference arising from a history of relative homogeneity. As Nielsen comments in his introduction to *Islam in Denmark: The Challenge of Diversity*, if one is not Lutheran or of Lutheran heritage then:

> in the Danish context, the institutional structures are such, however, that it is difficult to avoid being reminded that one is somehow different. Although one of the most secular societies in Europe, Danish society and institutions are thoroughly impregnated with Lutheran Christianity. Normally less than 3 percent of the population is in church on Sundays ... [but] 80 percent are members of the state-sponsored Lutheran church. (2012: 3–4)

Nielsen describes Danish Muslims as caught in the crossfire between 'a nationalist populism with right-wing tendencies and a more outward-looking spectrum of pluralist and cosmopolitan perspectives', which results in 'a continuous challenge for Muslims – and others, but especially non-Christians – to take advantage of the freedom of assembly and organization guaranteed by the Danish constitution' (Nielsen 2012, 4).

We interviewed Muslims from Copenhagen, the largest and most diverse city in Denmark. Although it is not necessarily the case, a range of evidence suggests that minorities in large cities often take the lead in developing new institutions and identities which help to establish a sense of belonging in society, which then spread to groups in other parts of the country. One of the reasons for this is the diversity of minority communities in large cities; whereas in small cities minority religious communities might be dominated by a single ethnic group, this is less likely in large cities, meaning that if groups are to create institutions based on a shared religious identity, they need to cooperate on multi-ethnic lines. In Copenhagen, there is evidence of this; for example, the Grand Mosque in Copenhagen (Hamad Bin Khalifa Civilisation Centre), opened in 2014, and the feminist oriented Women's Mosque, which opened in August 2016, are both organized on multi-ethnic lines (The Local.dk 2016). Reciprocally, the public authorities in large cities often also take the lead in recognizing diversity and developing practices and policies which enable migrant integration (Vertovec and Wessendorf 2010). And, as shown in Chapter 9, anti-immigrant sentiment tends to be lower in large cities. Given these conditions, one might expect Muslims in Copenhagen to be at the forefront of developing strategies to negotiate the hostile national media frame.

12.2 Sampling, Sample, and Method

This chapter draws on qualitative interviews with 15 Muslims from the Greater Copenhagen area in Denmark. Five were Muslims from ethnic minority backgrounds, while ten were ethnic Danes who had converted to Islam, for periods of between six months and 15 years before the interview. We chose to interview both groups because we hypothesized each may negotiate the media frame and handle identity challenges in different ways. Previous research had located converts on a pronounced fault line in Danish society, where a marked boundary between 'Danes' and 'Muslims' is perceived to exist (Jensen 2008, 390). Indeed, in a striking passage Jensen describes converts as having 'become ... members of the immigrant minority' in the eyes of ethnic Danes (ibid.), suggesting a remarkable process of ethnicization worthy of further study. Straddling such a boundary, converts might provide unique insights into ways of negotiating the hostile media frame. Conversely, because of their visibility and 'double otherness' (ethnically and religiously other), and potential to draw on a range of (including media) resources from transnational networks, ethnic minorities also promise to provide distinctive insights.

Among the converts, six were females and four males. Their ages ranged from 18 to 42 years, with three of the males being in their forties, the other 21. Among the females, one was 18, the others in their twenties – between 21 and 29. The three older males all converted to Islam near the millennium, one in year 2000 and two in 2002 – shortly after 9/11. One female converted in 2007, while the others had converted within the past four years. Among the ethnic Muslims, one is female and four are males. The female was 29 years old, while the age of the males ranged from 19 to 29. All five ethnic Muslims were born in Denmark, but have diverse family backgrounds from Turkey, Pakistan, Palestine, and Lebanon.

Interviewees were chosen because of their active media engagement – such as in local newspapers, and on Facebook and Instagram – where they deal in different ways with the negative media frame in Denmark in relation to Muslims and Islam. Through these media practices they publicly engage in discussions and debates about Islam and Muslims, or in other ways display their Muslim identity, e.g. by posting pictures of their hijabs and/or quotations from the Quran and Muslim teachers or philosophers on Facebook and Instagram.

The study used semi-structured interviews, conducted between August 2015 and March 2016. After initial questions about name, age, and date of conversion (where applicable), all respondents were asked the same four main questions: 1) how do you view the Danish media, especially the representation of Muslims and Islam? 2) what social media do you use? 3) how do you use social media? 4) do you think that the ways in which Islam and Muslims are presented in the Danish media has any impact on your life and/or on how you behave in public? These main questions were followed by several 'follow up' questions, e.g. about the strategies the interviewees adopted in relation to the negative media frame in Denmark.

In the following sections, the responses will be analysed around two themes. First, how Muslims from different backgrounds attempt to construct a viable identity in a hostile media environment, and second, the uses and forms of self-representation developed, both in person and using social media.

12.3 Discussion: 'In-Betweens': The Struggle to Construct Viable Identities

Based on our data, we can initially state that being a Muslim in Denmark – regardless of ethnic origin – is to a high degree to be ethnically marked. Or in other words: you are considered (and consider yourself to be) part of an ethnic minority when you are or, more strikingly, become a Muslim. Such is the binary distinction prevalent between being Muslim and being Danish experienced by our convert interviewees, and attested in previous studies (Jensen 2008), that becoming Muslim trumps being ethnically Danish; as one of our interviewees, Henrik[2] (see further below), puts it, 'Henrik … used to be Danish – or still is Danish – but in cultural terms is not Danish anymore because he is Muslim.' (Henrik, 40-year-old male convert, Copenhagen).

---

2 Subjects' names have been changed to protect their anonymity.

This is very different to the findings of studies in some other locations. For example, Alyedreessey (2016) interviewed 36 converts contacted via central London mosques, and while most reported considerable tensions with their families and other difficulties (indeed a quarter gave up their Islamic faith), none expressed this in terms of a change of ethnicity. We shall return to this puzzling contrast in the conclusion.

Further, we can initially state that all respondents have basically accepted the social fact of the mutual exclusiveness of Danish and Muslim identities as a starting point, even though they continued to struggle to overcome it. The visible Muslims (marked either by dress, self-presentation, or skin colour) experienced many tensions in this regard, mainly due to resistance from their own families and friends and/or due to the conflictual public environment towards Muslims in Denmark. In this section, we will consider how this ethnic minority status affects our respondents' identity construction.

The 'Invisible Muslims'

To construct a viable dual (Muslim and Danish) identity in a 'hostile' or 'conflictual' public environment and to negotiate the tensions between these identities is, for most of our respondents, an ongoing struggle. First, we address those respondents (white, male) whose Muslim identity was not publicly apparent to ethnic Danes (either through clothes or skin tone), hence 'invisible' Muslims. Of these, only one did not feel conflicted in his identity: 21-year-old Brian from Copenhagen.

In April 2009, at the age of 16, Brian converted to Islam, and as he stated, he has never looked back since. Prior to his conversion[3] to Islam, Brian was, in his own words, 'a wild young man', whose primary focus and favourite activity was to 'party and chase ladies'. At some point during his 16th year, he got tired of this lifestyle, and began to search for 'something' – he did not know what he was searching for, only that he wanted and needed 'something new to fill out my life with'. During this process Brian began to chat with a male convert to Islam from his neighbourhood. Every Friday the neighbour went to Friday Prayer in a local Mosque and after a couple of weeks, Brian decided to visit the Mosque. Since that day, Brian has considered himself a Muslim. He began to study Islam

---

[3] Most of our interviewees preferred the term 'reversion' to 'conversion', because the former implies a return to Islam understood as the original faith of all humanity, and hence better fits their theological view. We use 'conversion' for ease of understanding.

daily – and still does. He began to pray five times every day, he stopped drinking and chasing ladies, he stopped eating pork, and lastly, he changed his name. For Brian, there is no 'middle way': either he is a Muslim, with all that it entails, or he is not. Therefore, Brian claims that he does not experience tensions in negotiating between a Muslim and a Danish identity – simply because he has, in his words, erased his Danish identity, symbolized by his change of name:

> When I converted I was like ... the identity that I had before, I left it behind me. Because when you are convinced of something, you cannot only commit to half of if – that is, if you are convinced that this is the right thing for you. Then you have to embrace it. So, for example, if there is a discussion about 'us' and 'them', I feel I belong to 'them' in some way. I feel I belong on the other side, in a way. Because the other identity is in a way left behind. And a new identity has been constructed, in a way. And now I am Muslim. And I have changed my name. (Brian, Danish convert, 21 years old)

Like Brian, both 40-year-old Henrik, 40-year-old Jørgen, and 42-year-old John are ethnic Danish males who have converted to Islam. However, unlike Brian none of these claim to have have completely erased their Danish identity, and unlike Brian, all three say that they sometimes or often experience tensions in relation to their dual identity – not so much due to *direct* hostility towards them and their religion, but more due to what Henrik calls 'the hostile atmosphere in general in Denmark'. He says, 'The media and especially the politicians spend most of their time trying to split people. That is what burdens and saddens me'. Additionally, Henrik, Jørgen, and John say that this tension is rather new.

As mentioned in the previous section, the three male converts in their forties all converted to Islam at the beginning of this century, one in year 2000 and two in 2002, that is, shortly after the September 11 attacks on the US. Likewise, all three male converts in their forties tell that they, during the first eight to ten years after reversion, did not think so much about their 'Muslim-ness' and 'Danish-ness', or rather, their 'Muslim-ness' as opposed to their 'Danish-ness', simply because they very rarely did get confronted with their dual identity as problematic. For example, during our interview with Henrik we had a long talk about how things had changed for him as a Muslim since he converted to Islam prior to the September 11 attacks on the US. According to Henrik, he never thought about his identity during his first years as a Muslim – about whether he was Muslim and/or Dane, because 'of course, I am both'. However, during the past five years or so, with politicians, the public, and the media all focusing on the contradictions between Islam and 'Danish-ness', Henrik, as well as Jørgen and John, has been forced to reflect upon his identity in a new, different and deeper way. And for all three this reflection has meant that they all today consider themselves as belonging to the Muslim minority in Denmark – as belonging to another ethnicity and culture. However, even though Henrik does not consider himself Danish in cultural terms anymore, he still considers himself to be a Dane. That is also the reason why he experiences tensions between his Danish and Muslim identity, and why he often tries to show those around him that he is not a dangerous man – just a normal Danish man, at least by birth, who also happens to be Muslim. Thus, he expressed a wish to:

> show who you are as a person, tell the world that Henrik, who used to be Danish – or still is Danish, but in cultural terms is not Danish anymore because he is Muslim – is a good person. He is still a human being, he still has good values, he does not adhere to ISIS or other oppressive worldviews. (Henrik, Danish convert to Islam, 38 years old)

In similar ways, this is also what the two other male converts in their forties said during the interviews.

Visible Muslims: Part 1

Our data indicates that it is *especially* – though not entirely – the visible Muslims, that is the Muslims from ethnic minority backgrounds and the female converts, who all wear the hijab, who experience tensions in relations to their religion and construction of a viable dual identity. Or put differently, the data indicates that the visible Muslims face resistance in a more *direct* way than the invisible Muslims, i.e. the male converts.

Unlike Brian, Henrik, John and Jørgen, the six female ethnically Danish converts, the one female minority Muslim, and the four male minority Muslims are visibly Muslim. All females wear the hijab, and all males are dark-skinned and have dark hair, two have long beards and one wears an Islamic rope and a turban. Besides being highly aware of their visibility as Muslims, all 11 visible Muslims expressed frustration over not being fully accepted as Danes due to them being visible Muslims. However, the focus of the concern this causes, among the female converts on the one hand and the Muslims from ethnic minority backgrounds on the other hand, and the consequences the lack of acceptance has for the two groups, seems to be different. Thus, our data indicates that especially the female converts are highly preoccupied with issues related to their own families – to resistance and lack of acceptance from their own family members and their own belonging in their families – and not with lack of acceptance from society in general. This – lack of acceptance from society in general – was on the contrary what most concerned the minority Muslims. Some examples can help demonstrate this tendency in our data.

In 2008, at the age of 15, Sonja converted to Islam, meaning that, when we met Sonja at a café in Copenhagen in January 2016, she had been a practicing Muslim for eight years. With a smile on her face, Sonja referred to herself as some kind of 'Danish-Muslim closet-feminist' – in this context meaning that she silently fights for the rights of other female Muslims in Demark, inside the Muslim milieu as well as (maybe especially) outside. When we explored this theme further, Sonja began to talk about her family and about the resistance she had met in her family during the last eight years. Sonja, like several other female converts, told us about episodes in her family, at family dinners, etc., where relatives had reacted quite strongly to her conversion to Islam. When faced with reactions like these, the female converts often feel that their identity and 'belonging' is being challenged, that they do not belong anywhere – neither in their families, nor in Denmark. In this regard, Sonja said:

> Some family members of mine do not like Muslims, and say disgusting things about them. That makes me sad. Because I am also Muslim, I am just like 'them', because I have the same understanding of Islam as 'they' have. In addition, it is obvious that there is a division between me and the others in my family, because they do not like Islam. They do not know how to deal with the situation, what to say to me. (Sonja, age 23, female convert to Islam)

Even though Sonja does find it unfair that some family members and others outside her family treat her differently – or badly – because she is a Muslim, she has accepted that being a Muslim in Denmark can be challenging. Likewise, Sonja has accepted that being a Muslim includes an ongoing negotiation about identity and belonging. However, basically, Sonja does not consider Islam and Muslims to be ethnically marked, meaning that she *basically* does not consider herself as part of an ethnic minority – just a Danish Muslim. Though, due to the anti-Islamic atmosphere in Denmark in general, and specifically within certain circles in her own family, Sonja feels that she has been forced to take a stance in this regard. Therefore, for the most part, Sonja feels like an outsider, as one of 'them' – that is, as belonging to the Muslim minority in Denmark.

Like Sonja, all female converts say that they consider themselves as belonging to the Muslim minority in Denmark. But unlike Sonja, not all consider this an 'unwanted necessity', but rather something they have chosen as part of the package of being Muslim in Denmark. This is especially the point of view of recent female converts such as Kirstine and Louise, who converted six months and one year before the interview respectively. These recent women converts are also the most eager to 'fight' or try to counterbalance the hostile atmosphere towards Islam and Muslims in Denmark (see more below). Contrary to Louise and Kirstine, both Sonja, 20-year-old Kathrine and 29-year-old Maria, who converted three and five years before the interview respectively can be said to have largely given up this 'fight', or at least to have grown tired of trying to counter negative stereotypes about Islam and Muslims. The same goes for the Muslims from ethnic minority backgrounds we interviewed during this study.

Visible Muslims: Part 2

Twenty-three-year-old Omar from Copenhagen is a lively Islamic debater, who often participates in public discussions and debates about issues related to Islam and Muslims. During our interview with Omar we both asked him why he spends so much time debating these issues, and how the often negative atmosphere towards Muslims in Denmark affects him in any way. To this, he answered:

> It is ... difficult not to really belong anywhere. You know, when I am in Turkey, I am not fully accepted as a Turk. And when I am in Denmark I am not fully accepted as a Dane. So, who am I and where do I belong? I mean, this is not a question I am struggling with today. But I used to. (Omar, ethnic Muslim, 23 years old)

Similarly, 29-year-old Hadyia told us that she, due to this 'in-betweenness' straddling a Danish, ethnically foreign, and Muslim identity, had spent her entire teenage years figuring out who she is and where she belongs. Today she has come to peace with her dual identity, even though she is aware that this dual identity might not be accepted in society generally.

Due to the Danish media and her visibility as a Muslim, Hadyia is very keen on keeping some of her Islamic values – those that she knows are at risk of being labelled 'radical' – to herself, e.g. her views on the Islamic veil, halal meat, homosexuality, etc. As such, she expects that she never will be able to fully blend her two identities.

12.4 Self-Presentation: Islam as 'Project Identity'

Even though the Muslims from ethnic minority backgrounds and the female converts experience tensions in relations to their dual identity, due to their visibility as Muslims, their religion is at the same time both one of their most prominent identity markers and a means through which they can articulate their identity, feminist standpoints, and political values; in short, Islam presents as a 'project identity' in Castells' (1996) sense, meaning it is a source of critique of existing societal arrangements, pointing to an alternative social order. Our first example in this regard is 19-year-old Amman from Copenhagen.

Amman was born and raised in Copenhagen. His parents are from Palestine, but have lived in Denmark for the past 26 years. We met Amman at a small Mosque in Copenhagen, where he spends much of his free time, studying Islamic law and literature. One theme that Amman particularly focused upon during the interview was the way in which many journalists, politicians, and ordinary people see terrorism and Islam/Muslims as synonymous. For Amman, as well as for 29-year-old Adil, it is important to try to counterbalance this tendency. Therefore, Amman has decided to grow a long beard. By letting his beard grow, Amman wants to show the Danish people that the fundamentalist branches of Islam do not have a monopoly on the long beard, quite the contrary –young, well-integrated Muslims can also wear a long beard:

> Just because the Wahabi branch of Islam have long beards, that does not mean that they have a monopoly on the beard ... or that I, for that reason, have to shave off the beard. On the contrary, I have the beard to show that they do not have monopoly on specific Islamic values. (Amman, ethnic Muslim, 19 years old)

Like Amman, Adil is also very conscious about his physical appearance. Adil wears an Islamic robe and a turban every day. This was a conscious decision he made some years ago – that he is a devout Muslim, who will not hide his religion to appease the public. Thus, Amman and Adil seem to handle tensions about their religion in the same manner: They try to disrupt the stereotypical connection between displays of Islamic orthodoxy and a sense of threat by showing that devout Muslims, who wear Islamic clothes or grow long beards, can be, and should be seen as, good citizens.

In different ways, several female converts use similar strategies. For example, in the previous section, we saw that Sonja called herself a 'Danish-Muslim closet feminist'. Also, the views expressed by Louise, Kristine, and Maria suggest that they can appropriately be labelled 'Danish-Muslim feminists', even though they do not use that word to describe themselves. However, through what they say, what they do, the makeup they put on, the colourful headscarves and garments they wear, the pictures and statements they post on Instagram and Facebook, etc., they all try to express both who they are and what they believe in, and in particular that it is possible to be both a Muslim and what they see as a free, modern, woman at the same time.

During our six interviews with female converts, all six talked about the hijab/veil, and oppression and freedom. Contrary to popular opinion, our respondents maintain that wearing the hijab or veil is not the same as being oppressed, quite the opposite. For example, according to Maria, she was often treated as a 'sexual object' before she took on the hijab. Today, wearing the hijab, Maria feels relaxed and free. This was also something Louise talked about. Like Maria, Louise also felt that especially young males often used to treat her as an 'object', prior the taking on the hijab. Today, that is not the case anymore. In addition to this – and to some degree due to it – Louise also considers herself more special and feminine today than prior to conversion and especially before taking on the veil; as well as making her feel special (in the sense of positively distinctive – noticed, in a good way – but also better respected), wearing the hijab has also made Louise more conscious about her appearance in public.

When we met Louise, she had been wearing the hijab for two months. We therefore asked her whether this visibility had changed her identity and/or public appearances in any way. This she confirmed:

> After I began to wear the veil and I sit on a train ... I can put some Arabic music on, on my headphones, and then turn the volume up, so that people around me can hear it. I do not know why, but I just want people to see that it is OK – nothing bad will happen, just because I am Muslim. Moreover, if I greet someone on the train, when I get in or on my way out, then I greet them in Arabic. I probably just have a need to say, that it is OK to be a Muslim, that it is not dangerous. I just want to tell the positive story about Islam in public. (Louise, 24 years old, convert)

And lastly, besides making her feel more distinctive as a woman and as responsible for counterbalancing stereotypes about Muslims, the hijab has also become a fashion item for Louise, and, again, a tool through which she can show the public that she is still a 'normal' woman with normal interests – e.g. fashion:

> Louise: I sometimes use Instagram now that I wear the veil. Because there are so many pictures of how to arrange the veil. Therefore, I use Instagram to see how others arrange their veils and what style they have.
>
> Interviewer: Do you post similar pictures?
>
> Louise: Yes. Or no, not of clothes in general, only pictures of my veil, face and so on. I mean, after I have taken on the veil, I have become like, 'Oh, now I have to take a new picture and post it'. So that people can see that it is actually really beautiful to wear the veil.

The last example we will discuss is 18-year-old Kirstine. Kirstine is a very energetic young woman, with a fast and sharp mind and tongue. She is politically volunteering, active on several boards at school, in her neighbourhood, etc. Like several other women converts, she has faced strong resistance from within her own family. Thus, to show both her parents and surroundings in general that she is still the 'same, good old Kirstine' regardless of religion, she is still doing volunteer work at the Christian congregation where she formerly was a member and her parents still are members. In addition, she also has a feeling that people often consider her to be a 'dumb' or suppressed, young woman now that she has become a Muslim – or as if 'the veil had shot down my intelligence'. This annoys Kirstine, as she is an elite student at her school and in general is very devoted to her studies and to getting a higher university degree after high school. She considers herself to be a 'normal' young girl, and she uses Instagram to show that to her followers. Several times every day Kirstine posts pictures of herself wearing the hijab, red lipstick, and heavy makeup around her eyes. Sometimes she lets the 'pictures do all the talking', and sometimes she writes a short text to the pictures, about her being a young, modern, and free woman – certainly not a repressed or foolish woman.

12.5 Danish Muslims in Comparative Context

The impact of negative media framing seems to be dependent on the interviewees' visibility as Muslims, with those who are more visible (whether by dress or ethnicity) experiencing it more strongly and relentlessly. It is experienced as frustrating and tiring, with tiredness shown not only in reported feelings, but in a tendency amongst converts gradually to become less active in attempts to pro-actively combat negative stereotypes. However, the very visibility that results in a sense of being permanently under scrutiny can also be mobilized as part of a strategy to combat stereotyping, both amongst ethnic minority males and female converts, by combining the adoption of markedly Muslim styles of dress and grooming with behaving in exemplary ways, both by ethnic Danish and Muslim standards. For women, this includes combining hijab with makeup, using fashionable styles, and excelling in studies; for men this may mean being scrupulously polite and considerate. Thus both genders use strategies to subvert stereotypes which link Islamic dress to insularity and radicalism (for men) or submissiveness and stupidity (for women).

Our interviewees were not key organizers of online 'counter-publics' (see Chapter 9), but all belonged to and to differing extents were active in such groups (e.g. for hijab fashion), and drew social and emotional support from them. This support, as well as mosque attendance, the example of the Prophet, prayer and private study, helped them to cope with the psychological strain of 'living in the spotlight'.

Finally, we compare our findings with that of a study conducted partly on the far side of the Øresund Bridge, in Malmö, Sweden, which may shed some light on why the formation of dual (Danish and Muslim) and multiple (e.g. Danish Turkish Muslim) identities are proving so hard to achieve, and on the conditions which might more readily enable their formation. It may also illuminate the interplay of media with other factors shaping both identity formation and the integration of contemporary European societies.

Scuzzarello (2015) compared participation in elections and the formation of dual identification amongst Somalis and Poles in Ealing, West London and Malmö, Sweden, municipalities of similar size (between 310,000 and 340,000, and with high proportions of foreign-born population; 31 percent in Malmö and 57 percent in Ealing; ibid., 1221). We shall focus on the Somalis, who, as Muslims, are the most relevant comparison group for our sample. Somalis, in both municipalities, have low economic activity rates (20 percent employment), and tend to be portrayed as poorly integrated in national media. While voter registration and access to polling was easier in Malmö than Ealing, Scuzzarello found that 'Somali participants in Malmö tend to vote to a lesser degree than those in Ealing' (ibid., 1224). She concludes that this was because Somalis in Ealing were more readily able to form multiple identifications, because Muslim, Somali, and British identities were experienced as compatible, and this in turn made them feel entitled and motivated to vote (ibid., 1228). In contrast in Malmö, Somalis felt they were still viewed as immigrants and not accepted as Swedish: 'Somalis' identification with the superordinate group (i.e. Sweden) has not been socially validated by the majority society.' (ibid., 1229). For example, one interviewee, who had lived in Sweden from age three, stated:

> When I am [in Kenya] they call me Swede because I haven't lived there for years, but when I am in Sweden I'm an immigrant. [...] I cannot feel wholly Somali or wholly Swedish. (Somali man, 20–29 years old, Malmö)

The formation of multiple identities in Ealing seems to relate to a sense of acceptance into the host society mediated by what is practiced and perceived as normal at neighbourhood level, and recognized by local state institutions, for example:

> There is something called British Muslim [here] and that's normal for [the English]. Muslims having the mosque and halal meat, Eid celebrations and that's a normal thing. [It makes you feel] comfortable and ... recognized ... and that means you're also going to be part of that [country]. (Somali man, 50–59 years old, Ealing)

> In Ealing culture and religion define what you do, how you do it. I think this has a lot to do with British society allowing multiculturalism. It's not like that in other countries in Europe. (Somali woman, 20–29 years old, Ealing) (ibid.)

Acceptance at a local civic and state level seems to translate into an identification with British national identity, an identification which leads to positive affect and a desire to participate:

> What does it mean to be a UK citizen? To contribute to society and to be part of it, really, not just sitting back. (Somali woman, 20–29 years old, Ealing)
>
> To be a UK citizen [means] I don't know ... I'm quite proud of being British. (Somali man, 20–29 years old, Ealing)

This identification occurs despite a very negative media frame in the UK (similar to Denmark), and much higher levels of negativity towards immigrants and especially Muslims; 38.6 percent of Swedes agree the country should 'allow many Muslims to come and live here' compared with 11.4 percent of British; only 18.7 percent of Swedes said 'allow few' or 'no Muslims to come and live here', compared with 46 percent of British.

It may be that Scuzzarello's findings are an artefact of comparing a district in a global city (London, with 9 million population, of which white British are a minority, 2011 census), with a medium sized Swedish city; perhaps a comparison between Stockholm and a medium-sized British city with a large minority population would reverse the result. The findings for Poles support this; few Poles voted in either city (three from a total sample of 30, ibid. 1223), and their national identification remained wholly Polish; but they felt more at home in London (pre-Brexit) than Malmö. The dual identification they had developed was with London rather than Britain; in contrast with the Somalis, none of the Poles described themselves as Polish-British. But then British institutional multiculturalism, developed from the 1970s to 1990s, and still largely maintained in schools and public institutions despite its rhetorical rejection by national governments since 2001, was not built to accommodate white Europeans (a possible factor in Brexit), but South Asian Muslims, Hindus, and Sikhs, and was influenced by an American black empowerment movement which celebrated dual and multiple identities. So, battles won in previous decades – over accommodation of dress, food, and public celebration of various religious festivals – and discourses developed then – e.g. British Asian, Black British, and later, British Muslim and British Hindu – may have created a legacy from which British Somali Muslims now benefit.

This legacy is not limited to London or the UK; while specific civic and national histories shape the form which institutional multiculturalism takes (and support for it), its varieties are found globally, including in Sweden (Vertovec and Wessendorf 2010). However, a multiculturalism rooted in collective struggles for equality (UK) may prove more resilient, and have wider societal resonance, than one imposed by a liberal welfare state (Sweden). Furthermore, in more historically homogeneous societies, it may be more difficult to prevent the formation of the binary us/them, immigrant/native distinction which works against the formation of multiple identities.

12.6 Conclusion

Returning to Denmark, here we find a combination of UK level negativity towards Muslim immigrants (46 percent in both the UK and Denmark support the statements 'allow few' or 'allow no' Muslim immigrants compared with 19 percent in Sweden, ESS 2014), with a history of Lutheran hegemony and homogeneity, but less mitigated by government-led attempts to introduce institutional multiculturalism than in Sweden. Hence the challenges facing ethnic and new Muslims witnessed in this chapter. In relation to furthering understanding of mediatization in a comparative context, our findings suggest that while media are powerful structuring forces, other factors also shape national dynamics, e. g. government support for institutional multiculturalism, the historical legacies of Lutheranism (Scandinavia) and Empire (UK), and the influence of civil society-led anti-racist struggles, as seen here. This suggests that to properly understand the dynamics of mediatization in specific cases, media dynamics need to be rigorously contextualized by broader processes of historical and social change, and are best viewed comparatively.

Bibliography

Alyedreessey, Mona. 2016. "British Muslim Converts: An Investigation of Conversion and Deconversion Processes to and from Islam." Unpublished PhD diss., Kingston University London.
Blaut, James M. 1992. "The Theory of Cultural Racism." *Antipode* 23 (4): 289–299.
Castells, Manuel. 1996. *The Network Society*. Oxford: Blackwell.
Cottle, Simon. 2006. *Mediatized Conflicts*. Buckingham: Open University.
Couldry, Nick. 2011. "Media and Democracy: Some Missing Links." In *Media and Social Justice*, edited by Sue Curry Jansen, Jefferson Pooley, and Lora Taub-Pervizpour, 45–54. London: Palgrave.
Dahlgreen, Will. 2015. *Roma People and Muslims are the Least Tolerated Minorities in Europe*. Analysis of YouGov poll. Accessed 7 Jan, 2017. https://yougov.co.uk/news/2015/06/05/european-attitudes-minorities/
ECRI. 2001. *ECRI Report on Denmark*. (Third Cycle) Strasbourg: European Commission.
ECRI. 2006. *ECRI Report on Denmark*. (Fourth Cycle) Strasbourg: European Commission.
ECRI. 2012. *ECRI Report on Denmark*. (Fifth Cycle) Strasbourg: European Commission.

European Social Survey (ESS). 2014. *European Social Survey Data.* Accessed 17 April, 2017. http://nesstar.ess.nsd.uib.no/webview/

Goffman, Erving. 1959. *The Presentation of the Self in Everyday Life.* New York: Anchor Press.

Jacobsen, Sarah Jul, Tina Gudrun Jensen, Kathrine Vitus, and Kristina Weibel. 2013. "*Analysis of Danish Media Setting and Framing of Muslims, Islam and Racism.*" Working Paper 10:2013. Copenhagen: SFI (The Danish National Centre for Social Research).

Jensen, Gudrun T. 2008. "To Be 'Danish', Becoming 'Muslim': Contestations of National Identity?" *Journal of Ethnic and Migration Studies* 34 (3): 389–409.

Kühle, Lene, and Lasse Lindekilde. 2012. "Radicalisation and the Limits of Tolerance: A Danish Case-Study." *Journal of Ethnic and Migration Studies* 38 (10): 1607–1623.

Livingstone, Sonia. 2015. "Active Audiences? The Debate Progresses But Is Far From Resolved." *Communication Theory* 25 (4): 439–446.

The Local.dk. 2016. "Danish Women-Led Mosque Makes Scandinavian History." 29 Aug. Accessed 4 Jan 2017. http://www.thelocal.dk/20160829/danish-women-led-mosque-makes-scandinavian-history.

Nielsen, Jørgen. ed. 2012. *Islam in Denmark: The Challenge of Diversity.* Plymouth: Lexington.

Scuzzarello, Sarah. 2015. "Political Participation and Dual Identification Among Migrants." *Journal of Ethnic and Migration Studies* 41 (8): 1214–1234.

Vertovec, Steven, and Susanne Wessendorf. eds. 2010. *The Multiculturalism Backlash: European Discourses, Policies and Practices.* London: Routledge.

Upper Secondary Schools

Audun Toft, Maximilian Broberg

Chapter 13
Perspectives: Mediatized Religious Education

Abstract: This chapter presents two empirical case studies of religious education (RE) in Norway and in Sweden. In addition to introducing the *Upper Secondary School* section of the present volume, the chapter explores how media materials and discourses are being extensively used in a similar fashion as part of RE in both countries. Media materials and discourses serve to both contextualize the content of the subject and to legitimize RE by showing why religion is relevant for contemporary Norwegian and Swedish society; thus, they form an important part of the RE lessons. Applying a mediatization perspective, we argue that this use of media impacts both the choice of topics addressed and the way they are presented, as it inserts various media dynamics into the pedagogical practice of religious education.

Keywords: mediatization, religious education, representations of religion, media materials

As participation in institutionalized religious practice is on the decline in the Scandinavian countries, the media seem to fortify their role as the main source of information about religion (Lövheim and Bromander 2012, 16–24). The claim that what most people know about religion, they know from the media is often made (Hjarvard 2008; Lundby and Gresaker 2015). Our survey, presented in Chapter 2, supports this claim. TV and the newspapers are rated highest as the context in which people encounter questions related to religion and belief. When it comes to young people, the focus of this essay, we have to take into account another such context, and that is the school.[1] Non-confessional religious education (RE) is mandatory in both Norway and Sweden, and although not a major subject, youth still regularly encounter religion throughout primary and secondary school.

However, school is not just a source of information about religion; it is a site where religion is contested. As schools are primarily regarded as public institu-

---

[1] This is not reflected in the survey. Most respondents are over 18 years old, and are thus not in school.

tions, the role of religion in school is a controversial topic in both Norway and Sweden, and is often a matter of public debate. RE is also constantly changing to accommodate the growing diversity of contemporary Scandinavian society. On an institutional level, RE can be seen as a social arena where young people engage with religion, and as a site where the meaning of religion, and various representations of religion, are contested and negotiated.

This section of the book explores RE in upper secondary schools, through data from two empirical studies, one in Norway and one in Sweden. The purpose of the present essay is twofold. First, we will describe some aspects of the school systems in Norway and Sweden, and how RE is organized in the respective countries. This chapter will also function as an introduction to the other chapters in this *Upper Secondary School* section of this book. Secondly, we will account for some of the findings from the two studies, in which we examine the use of media within the context of RE. We approach this study with an institutional mediatization perspective. Regarding RE as a site for contestation of religion, we look at how media materials and media representations are used and engaged with in the pedagogical practice of teaching and learning about religion. Mediatization theory states that in modern society, the media are established as an institution in their own right, and other institutions come to depend on the media in their everyday practices and communication (Schrott 2009; Hjarvard 2013). This may alter institutional practices, as dynamics inherent in the operations of the media thus influence the interactions within the said institution. The integration and presence of media may thus come to condition, but not determine the encounters between actors in everyday life (see Chapters 3 and 4).

The research's focus is on the use of media in RE. Here, we employ a broad conception of media that includes media technology, platforms, materials, and discourses.[2] We examine how representations of religion and topics related to religion, in the form of media discourses and materials produced by and for the mass media, play a role in the lessons observed. We argue that media representations form an integral and consistent part of the practice of RE as a way to relate the content of the subject to contemporary society. This, however, has some ramifications for how religion is engaged with, as various media dynamics come to influence the classroom practice.

---

[2] See Chapter 14 for a detailed description.

13.1 The Swedish and Norwegian Context – Religion and School

Religious education is organized in a great variety of ways across Europe (e.g. Kuyk et al. 2007; Davis and Miroshnikova 2012). The national context seems to be one of the most important factors in how each country does RE (Schreiner 2014), and the specific relationship between church and state seems to be particularly influential in RE's organization (Loobuyck and Franken 2014, 169). The historically close ties between state, schools, and church in Norway and Sweden appear to have led to a similar process of transforming RE from denominational teaching in the state religion into a non-denominational school subject (Ferrari 2014, 29). Both countries have organized RE as an *integrative* subject,[3] meaning that children with different religious and non-religious backgrounds are taught together about different religions (Alberts 2007). RE is viewed as a regular school subject and is mandatory for all students throughout primary and lower secondary school, as well as for students in most of the upper secondary school programs.[4] One of the rationales behind this kind of RE is that knowledge about religions is an important competency in multicultural and multi-religious societies. This trend can also be seen in the recommendations from the European Council to its member states regarding the inclusion of religious and non-religious convictions within intercultural education (Jackson 2014).

The school systems in Norway and Sweden are an important part of the context here. Both countries see education as a key part of their welfare state systems, in which the state should provide citizens with equal opportunities for free education, regardless of gender, geographical, social, or economic background (Alberts 2007, 215). This means that the state plays a very active role in the educational system. The parliament and the government are responsible for education, and providing national curricula, aims, and guidelines for schools, as well as bearing most expenses, even for independent schools.[5] In Norway, only about 4 percent of students in primary and lower secondary schools and 9 percent of the students in upper secondary schools attend independent schools, while the corresponding

---

[3] As opposed to *separative* RE, where children are divided according to religious background, and taught accordingly (Alberts 2010, 276).
[4] In Norway, this means that RE is mandatory for all students in the programs that are preparatory for higher education; vocational education does not have RE. In Sweden, RE is a mandatory subject for all upper secondary school programs, including vocational ones.
[5] In Norway, independent schools have a limit on tuition fees of 15%, the remaining 85% being financed by the state. In Sweden, independent schools are completely financed by the state.

numbers in Sweden are higher at 15 percent and 26 percent respectively. These schools are required to provide education equivalent to that of the state schools. The educational systems of both countries are organized as comprehensive schools, in which the first nine years in Sweden and ten years in Norway are mandatory for all citizens, with a legal right after that to three years of upper secondary education. It is not until upper secondary school that the students choose separate programs and are allowed to choose what courses to take (Wiborg 2009). All these aspects of the educational systems of both countries could be said to constitute many of the 'dynamics' that condition much of the RE practice – dynamics, we argue, that are fundamentally different from the dynamics of the media. The case studies of this chapter are conducted on RE in upper secondary school and, although similar in many ways, Norway and Sweden differ a bit in their organization of RE at this level.

13.1.1 Norway

RE in Norwegian upper secondary school is mandatory for every student enrolled in programs qualifying for higher education. This subject is called 'Religion and Ethics' and is placed in the last year of upper secondary school, meaning that most of the students are about 18 years old. Religion and Ethics consists of four main subject areas: 1) Religion and the criticism of religion, 2) Islam and an elective religion,[6] 3) Christianity, and 4) Philosophy, ethics and views on life/humanism. The subject matter is thus not very broad in as far as learning about different religions. Christianity is given priority in relation to the amount of time, due to its historical and cultural role in Norway.[7] Islam is singled out as being especially important. Religion and Ethics is non-confessional and relies on an analytical approach that is based on methods from religious studies (Andreassen 2016, 118).

The subject is defined as being both knowledge-based and value-forming, and respect and tolerance are emphasized. Mutual tolerance across differences in religion and 'views on life' is explicitly identified as a 'necessity for peaceful

---

[6] The schools choose one religion in addition to Christianity, Islam, and the humanist lifestance (which in Norway is treated as being equivalent to belonging to a religious tradition).
[7] The role of Christianity in RE in Norway is much debated, although mainly at the primary and lower secondary level. In 2006, Norway was found by the European Court of Human Rights to be in violation of the European Convention of Human Rights (Protocol 1, Article 2) guaranteeing parents the right to decide on children's religious upbringing, by favouring Christianity without sufficient opt-out options.

co-existence in a multicultural and multi-religious society' (UDIR 2006, 1). The national curriculum states that religious, philosophical and ethical questions are 'important for each individual, and for society as a whole, both as the basis for who we are, and as a source of conflict' (ibid., 1). So, although the curricular aims of the subject are mainly focused on cognitive knowledge (ibid., 5), such as familiarity with holy texts, doctrines of faith, history, and traditions, the relevance of religion to contemporary Norwegian society is given as one of the main reasons in regard to the purpose of Religion and Ethics.

13.1.2 Sweden

Similarly to the Norwegian case, Swedish RE is a mandatory, non-confessional, integrative subject. The subject, *Religionskunskap,* is called Religion in the official English translation that is published by the Swedish National Agency for Education (Skolverket 2011a), and it has four broad themes as its framework. The first is 'Christianity, other religions and worldviews', in which the so-called 'world religions' are taught in terms of historical events and contemporary expressions, both nationally and globally. The second theme is 'views on gods and humanity', which focuses on the huge variety in doctrines and practices, both between and within religions, with a particular focus on gender, socio-economic factors, ethnicity, and sexuality. Third is 'religion and science', which delves into contemporary debates on the relations between the religious and scientific worldviews. Finally, there is 'ethical theories and models', which includes both secular normative ethics and ethical arguments that are based in the various religious traditions.

Just as in the Norwegian case, Sweden's Religion subject is explicitly based in the academic discipline of religious studies, which clearly separates it from its roots as a subject that was meant to teach about the national evangelical Lutheran church. Although the syllabus of the subject does not contain any explicit references to tolerance or multiculturalism, these arguments are clearly present in the national curriculum, which stresses that the school teaches respect and compassion, especially in relation to the internationalization of Swedish society (Skolverket 2011b).

13.2 The Two Cases

13.2.1 The Norwegian Case

The Norwegian part of this project is a case study with fieldwork conducted throughout the school year of 2015–2016.[8] The fieldwork was carried out in an upper secondary school in the Eastern part of Norway. With a little less than 1,000 students, it is a fairly large school by Norwegian standards. The school offers several programs and in 2015 had about 10 classes of around 30 students each, in all three years. Between 15 percent and 25 percent of the students in each class have a foreign background. Starting in September 2015, six RE teachers were interviewed and their teaching observed in eight different Religion and Ethics classes. Although the use of media materials was the primary research focus of the Norwegian study, the researchers also had individual research questions.[9] Fifty sessions were observed in total.

13.2.2 The Swedish Case

The Swedish case study was conducted within the broader framework of the *Teaching Religion in Late Modern Sweden* project,[10] in which Broberg is engaged as a PhD student. The project involves about 20 schools, and in order to make a comparison with the Norwegian case as relevant as possible, the school that was most similar to the Norwegian school was selected as the Swedish case study.

The selected school is thus a public upper secondary school on the outskirts of Stockholm. The school has about 2,000 students and an above-average number of them have a foreign background[11] (Skolverket 2015). While the Norwegian school supplies the students with laptops,[12] the Swedish school supplies their students with tablets, which were brought to, and to some extent used, in the

---

[8] The field work was conducted by PhD candidate Audun Toft and Professor Liv Ingeborg Lied.
[9] Toft's primary focus was the use of media representations of Islam in the classroom. The main body of observational data is thus from lessons about Islam. In total, Toft observed 45 sessions; 34 of these were about Islam. Lied's focus was related to the use of popular media in RE, and between November 2015 and March 2016 she observed five sessions.
[10] The Swedish research team consisted of Associate Professor Anders Sjöborg, Lecturer Malin Löfstedt, PhD candidate Maximilian Broberg, and master's student Johan Dynewall, all situated at the Faculty of Theology, Uppsala University.
[11] 33% compared to the national average of 25%.
[12] See Chapter 14.

majority of the lessons observed. Four Religion teachers and a total of 18 lessons were observed at the school during the school year 2015–2016.

13.2.3 Observations and Interviews

The main body of data was gathered by direct observation, with the researchers present in the classroom, most often sitting in the back row among the students. Data gathering were carried out by taking hand-written field notes, with no audio or video material being recorded. The students were informed about the project before the observation started. Outside the lessons, the researchers also followed the teachers during breaks and to meetings with the RE team. The data thus includes field notes from conversations and observations with RE teachers, and others, gathered in informal settings.[13] The teachers were interviewed using a semi-structured interview guide. These interviews were conducted later, after observations had started, so as to include questions about specific observations. The interviews were between 45 and 75 minutes in length. As the Norwegian and Swedish interview guides were different, due to their different aims, the Swedish study included email interviews based on the Norwegian interview guides to make for easier comparison.

13.3 Findings Across Cases

Regardless of the national differences, the material collected in both case studies are, to a great extent, comparable, and in several aspects they are strikingly similar. Though comparing cases from different countries has its problems (Bråten 2013), the similarities in media use are worth exploring in more detail.

In both the Norwegian and the Swedish cases we observed that different media consistently formed an integrated part of various classroom practices. Both schools make extensive use of media technology and media platforms. However, the Norwegian students made much more use of their laptops than the Swedish students did of their tablets, which resulted in different media practices. The profound impact that the use of laptops had in the Norwegian case will be discussed further in Chapter 14.

---

[13] This aspect of the fieldwork is more prominent in the Norwegian study, but to some extent it is also present in the Swedish study, particularly in the form of informal conversations before and after observations and interviews.

However, media materials and media discourses were used very similarly across the cases. In both of the schools we observed active and extensive media use in the practice of teaching and learning about religion. We will focus on two aspects of this: 1) how media materials are being used as pedagogical artefacts[14], and 2) how events, debates, and discourses in the news media influence the choice of the topics that are addressed and discussed in the RE lessons. Two examples from our observations will illustrate these aspects:

13.3.1 Observation 1 (Norway) – Anne Lise's Class, 2 November 2015 – Media Materials as Pedagogical Artefacts

Anne Lise[15] lets the students into the classroom. It takes some time for the class to come to order. Anne Lise turns her computer on and says, 'We are still on Islam. Today we will start with a song. Everyone grab one of these.' She passes Xeroxed copies of the song's lyrics to the students. The song is 'Tusen tegninger' (A thousand drawings) by the rap duo Karpe Diem.[16] As the students recognize this they cheer, and several of them express how much they like the song. Anne Lise tries to catch everyone's attention as she starts playing a YouTube clip of the music video. 'Just put away your PCs,' she says, 'Everyone! Put the PCs away.'

Once the clip starts, the students settle down and concentrate on the song. Several of them sing along. As the song fades out, the class is silent and Anne Lise tells everyone to turn the page of lyrics over. 'There are some questions written on the back. So use the lyrics to underline every reference you find to religion. Discuss the rest of the questions in groups. Spend a couple of minutes before we discuss it together.'

Here, we can see how the RE lesson was structured around a music video. The video is employed as a source with which to show what it is like to be a Muslim with an immigrant background in Norway, and it is transformed into a pedagogical artefact on which further questions and discussions are based. Such

---

14 By 'pedagogical artefact' we here mean tools used for educational purposes to amplify pedagogical activities in the classroom, see Chapter 14.
15 All names are changed to provide informant anonymity.
16 The artists behind the duo Karpe Diem are both born in Norway, with immigrant parents. Magdi is Muslim (his mother is from Norway and his father emigrated from Egypt); Chirac is Hindu and has parents of Indian origin. The song 'Tusen tegninger' is based on Magdi's experiences.

media use in education is nothing new, but the extent to which media materials are brought into, and made part of, the pedagogical practice is striking. This sort of media use is prominent in our observations. Articles and op-eds from newspapers, feature films, documentaries, TV series, talk shows, debates, video clips of stand-up comedy, as well as news broadcasts, both from web papers and from public service broadcasting, are only some of the many examples of media materials observed that are used as pedagogical artefacts in RE lessons.

13.3.2 Observation 2 (Sweden) – Anna's Class, 25 April 2016 – Media Discourses Set the Agenda

This is the second lesson about Islam and, after a brief discussion about what the students can remember from the previous lesson, the teacher brings up a Power Point about the early history of Islam and starts to lecture about the life of Muhammad. The first 20 minutes of this lesson are spent on this. Anna finishes the lecture and states:

> We won't linger too long on history, but it tells us something about the role of Islam in the world. What is often forgotten when writing history in the Western world is how much of our culture that can be traced to Islam and to this time. Before we move on, if you've read the newspapers or watched the news this last week, you'll have seen that several things related to Islam and The Green Party have happened.[17]

A student says, 'Khan wouldn't shake hands.' Anna replies, 'Exactly, pretty inflated in the media. The Green Party says that men and women should shake hands, and the prime minister says, "You ought to shake hands with both men and women." My question is this: is this self-evident?' One student immediately exclaims, 'This is just the West crying about people not falling into line.'

This was followed by a long debate that took up the remaining 40 minutes of the lesson. The students brought up many different angles: the potential tension between freedom of religion and the rights of women; whether a representative of a political party can be religious; if gendered ways of greeting are necessarily a bad thing, and much more.

Approaching the end of the lesson, Anna says: 'Could it be that this is blown out of proportion by the media?' Most of the students agree that perhaps this is

---

17 This refers to the so called 'handshake affair, when a Swedish politician refrained from shaking hands with a female reporter as a result of his Islamic faith. The incident received extensive media coverage, culminating in the politician's resignation. See Chapter 4 for further details.

not really that big a question after all, as most politicians shake hands, and the fact that one individual refuses is not at all a big deal.

In this example, a recent event that was heavily covered and debated in the Swedish news media was brought up by the teacher, and it was used as starting point for classroom discussion. The ensuing debate touches upon several issues concerning the role of religion in contemporary society, and a wide range of viewpoints are expressed by the students. Still, the media event remains the main point of reference throughout the lesson, setting the premises of the discussion.

Similar observations can be found in other classes. Events, debates, and discourses covered in the news media are frequently brought into the classroom, both by the teachers and the students. In several instances, these are also made to be the main focus of whole lessons. Some other examples from our observations were the terror attacks in Paris (November 2015), a newspaper debate about apostasy, the conditions for EU immigrants and refugees in Sweden, a newspaper series about sharia in Norway, and concerns about the veiling of women, a topic of recurring media coverage that inspired several different class discussions.

As these examples show, media, in various forms, play an important role in the RE lessons observed. One of the things that struck both teams of researchers as worth noting was the amount of time spent on media materials and on discussing recent events and debates that had been represented through the media. This frequently displaced the topics and content from the textbook and the curriculum. Moreover, these media representations of religion often influenced and conditioned the ways both the teachers and students engaged with topics of religion in the first place. We would like to explore the interplay between media, be it news media, entertainment, or social media, and the practice of teaching religion in more detail.

13.3.3 Showing the Relevance of Religion

When asked why she had decided to devote a 2.5-hour RE session (17 November 2015) to address the Paris terror attacks (13 November 2015) with a basis in a documentary about radicalization,[18] Charlotte said: 'I realize ... that I take time away from other topics. But what gives the whole subject legitimacy is that this is real. It's around us.' Here, she expresses one of the major concerns that are voiced by both the Norwegian and the Swedish teachers: namely, the

---

18 *Jihad: A Story of The Others* by Deeyah Khan (2015).

question about what gives RE legitimacy as a school subject in the first place. One of the main arguments in favour of RE is that knowledge about religious and non-religious worldviews is a prerequisite for a well-functioning multicultural and multireligious society.[19] The main reason given for learning about religion is thus instrumental; its importance is to be found in its relevance to contemporary society in Norway and Sweden respectively.

The importance of showing the relevance of religion is made even more urgent by what the teachers perceive to be the students' lack of experience with religion. The majority of the Norwegian and Swedish students are described by the teachers as non-religious, and they struggle to see why religious education concerns them.[20] Showing why the content of RE is relevant thus becomes one of the major challenges that the teachers face. It is interesting to see that the teachers, independently of each other, relate relevance directly to media coverage. Consider the following example, from an interview with one of the Norwegian teachers:

> Interviewer: Do you use various media material?
>
> Guro: I try to do that. And that is one of the challenges with religious education. It's to show that this is actually relevant and *aktuelt*[21] for our society today. Not just something that is historical. ... And therefore I think that religious education can have that function, to encounter things they are interested in, and that they see around them and in the media.

The same views are expressed by most of the teachers interviewed. It is through media that the relevance of religion can be shown. Media materials are needed to give access to 'what goes on around us', to 'what is real', to 'the world around us', and similar expressions that were used by the teachers. Not only are the media the primary source of information about what happens in society, but media materials, in the form of products produced by media professionals, are especially well suited for this task. Anna describes the advantages of showing interviews in class: 'I can't just stand there and tell them about everything. ... When you see someone saying it, it becomes a little more real.' The teachers expressed a strong dependence on media materials, ones produced by and for the mass media, when teaching about religion. Reality is primarily seen as being ac-

---

19 Explicitly stated in the Norwegian curriculum (UDIR 2006, 1).
20 Several studies confirm that religion seems to be of little importance to a majority of Scandinavian youths (Lövheim and Bromander 2012; Lippe 2008), although there are regional differences.
21 The Scandinavian word *aktuelt* is difficult to translate, but is the word mostly used in this context. *Aktuelt* implies that something is at once important, relevant, and current.

cessible through the media, resulting in media materials being viewed, and used, as necessary components of RE. Media materials thus become an integral, and indispensable, part of the pedagogical practice.

13.3.4 Facts vs. Reality

The expressed importance of constantly having to legitimize the relevance of the subject by using media materials points to what seems to be a perceived tension within the subject itself. This is the tension between what is seen to be the intention of RE, and the actual content of the subject, as specified in the learning outcomes of the curriculum. Throughout the interviews, the teachers made sharp distinctions between the content of the subject, 'the facts', and the world around us, 'reality'.[22] This distinction is also frequently communicated to the students during lessons, often through phrases like 'we need to go through the facts before we can talk about the things you hear about'. There is a strong focus on knowledge in the RE curricula in both Norway and Sweden. In both cases, we observed that the curricular aims, centred on knowledge, structured the lessons and were constantly communicated to the students.[23] The facts are also what the students will eventually be evaluated and graded on. The teachers, throughout the interviews, stressed the importance of the facts and the subject-specific knowledge. However, a mention of facts is most often followed by contrasting them with reality, with reference to events or debates that are represented through the various media. This consistent pairing of, or complementary distinction between, facts and reality is worth exploring in more detail. Facts are presented as: 1) necessary, to gain an adequate understanding of reality (and also as the basis for grading the students), but they are also, 2) boring, or at least not seen to be as interesting or relevant in their own right. We can see this in a typical presentation in a lesson about Islam:

> We are going to spend all next week talking about Islamism, extremism, and political Islam, and all the things you read and hear about the IS and so on, but first we will have to go through some basics.' (Beatrice, observation, 19 April 2016)

---

[22] We created these categories based on the wording of the teachers, both in the classrooms and in the interviews. The terms vary, but a distinction between 'facts/knowledge/subject-specific/school stuff', on the one hand, and 'reality/society/surroundings/the world/current events and debates', on the other, is discernible throughout the material. We use the terms 'facts' and 'reality' as shorthand for these.

[23] In most of the lessons, the curricular aims for the day are written on the blackboard or are shown on a screen, and they are referred to frequently.

The same notion is voiced in several interviews, for example, by Christine, concerning how she usually structures her lessons on Islam:

> I try to avoid the 'facts-trap' i.e. that the whole session is centred on the general traits of the religions. ... When it comes to the lesson series on Islam we usually, after having talked our way through the general stage ('the facts-trap'), work our way towards lived religion. In this way we can delve into the questions that the students often find interesting. (Email interview, 19 May 2016)

Where the facts are necessary, but boring, 'reality' (represented through the media) is: a) interesting, but, b) superficial. The majority of the teachers emphasized that the students really want to talk about current events and debates that are related to contemporary society. The teachers have different views on whether students find RE an interesting subject, but they agree that it is the link to what is going on in society that makes it interesting and relevant.

> I think that the fact that the course focuses so much on what happens in the world and that it helps you understand what is going on in society, is one of the reasons why the students are so interested in the subject. Should you let the media control the lessons? Instinctively perhaps it feels like 'no' should be the answer, but, yes, I think so. If the school shouldn't help the students understand the reality they live in, then who should? (Christine, email interview, 19 May 2016)

Again, we see that the teachers report a dependence on media representations in order to adequately teach about religion at all. This is not an unconditional dependence; the teachers will choose which representations to use, and these will be re-mediated in the classroom according to the pedagogical aims of the lessons. Still, the media representations are seen as being necessary to legitimize the relevance of the subject, since the facts alone are not enough. This dependence is mutual, as the media are frequently seen as superficial, and even biased,[24] in their presentation of reality. The students need scholarly facts in order to understand the mediated reality. However, as we have seen, the facts are often hurried through, and most time is spent on various media representations.

13.3.5 Media Dynamics in RE

The strong media presence in the RE classroom has consequences for the way religion is being represented and talked about. Integrating media materials

---

[24] This is prominent when it comes to Islam. See Chapter 15 for a discussion on how perceived biased and negative media coverage of Islam impacts on the Norwegian lessons.

and discourses into the pedagogical practice brings various media dynamics into play (see Chapter 3). This does not mean that the media determine the way religion is being represented, but rather that media have been institutionalized in the practice of RE in such a way that the conditions for teaching and learning about religion are altered. Dynamics specific to the media become relevant in the interplay with the dynamics of RE.

One way in which media dynamics influence the RE lessons is in the choice of which topics should be addressed in class. The agenda-setting power of the media is well documented and much researched (McCombs 2014). Through media coverage, the public gains cues as to the salience of particular topics, and several studies attest to the correspondence between news coverage and public opinion (e.g. Scheufele and Tewksbury 2007, 11). This is also relevant to the RE lessons, where we observed a close correlation between media coverage and the topics covered in the lessons. Kari put it like this: 'To me the media control the lessons in the way that what it says, what I get in my newspaper, which has anything to do with what we are doing, I will use that.' However, the choice of topics cannot be said to be completely determined by the media. The teachers discern between reliable and non-reliable media sources,[25] and make judgements on the relevance and suitability of topics before using them in the lessons. Teachers thus show clear signs of having the ability to 'access, analyse, evaluate, and communicate' (Aufderhide 1993, quoted by Hobbs 1998, 16) media content in various forms. This kind of competency has been described as 'media literacy' (Hobbs 1998), and it is vital for teachers in their selection of material. Despite this, media coverage still seems to be one of the main criteria when choosing what to address in class. As we have seen, this is primarily because the media give access to reality, but, here, the media take on an ambivalent role for the teachers. The media function simultaneously as *sources* of information about current events and as *arenas* in which events can take place. The lines between these are blurred. The complex duality between media that are seen as reporting on stories because they are important, and stories being important because they are reported in the media, is quite noticeable in the observations. This conflation of reality and media coverage will, in many instances, also run deeper. Beatrice says:

> In a way I might prioritize Judaism, Christianity, and Islam. ... Because of what happens globally, it is so easy to connect to the situation in various countries. ... This thing about

---

[25] Most favour the public broadcasting services, as well as the established non-tabloid newspapers, like *Aftenposten* and *Dagens Nyheter*, as well as international news channels like the BBC.

Hinduism and Buddhism, it does not really feel like – it feels quite out of date right now. (Interview, 5 November 2015)

In this example, as in several others, media coverage is equated directly with what is going on in the world. Even though several teachers expressed that they know that the sort of stories being covered in the media depends on specific criteria, the access to the sides of reality that are not being covered in the media is limited,[26] and this has an impact on the way religion is being taught. The most obvious example, in both cases, is the way the Eastern religions are seen, and presented, as being less relevant than Islam, and, to some degree, Christianity.

In addition to the impact on *what* is being addressed in the lessons, the use of media materials also influences *how* topics are being represented. When, for instance, a debate about the veiling of women in Islam, staged and moderated by *Aftenposten*, becomes the object of several lessons,[27] then *Aftenposten* takes on the simultaneous roles of transmitter of opinions, editor, gatekeeper, and commentator, thus setting the premises for the debate. The media have performative agency, present framings, and employ genre-specific criteria for presentation, according to what sort of media materials are being used (see Chapter 3). Dynamics involved in the production of media materials for use in the mass media, such as the selection of content, framings, formatting, genre, narrative structures, etc., then become part of the constituent conditions of RE. One of the more obvious effects of this situation is that material concerning conflict becomes privileged over other material. Conflict is one of the more well-documented criteria for news-worthiness and coverage (e.g. Ihlen and Allern 2008), and our observations confirm a strong focus on conflict and controversies related to religion. This will be examined in more detail in Chapters 14 and 15.

13.4 Mediatized RE

Looking through the lenses of institutional mediatization theory, it is fair to describe the religious education that was observed as mediatized. By this, we mean that the use of media is not only an integral part of the normal practice of RE, but also that the teachers see media use as a necessary component of the subject. It may well be that this is also the case with other school subjects, but our material

---

[26] The teachers also use field trips and talk about bringing in guest speakers. However, this is time-consuming and impractical. The immediate availability of media representations is an important part of their influence in the classroom.
[27] Using Xeroxed copies of op-eds from the newspaper as pedagogical artefacts.

points to several factors that are particular to religion. The place of religion in school is contested and controversial, both in Norway and in Sweden. It is through its relevance to contemporary Scandinavian society that the subject is most often legitimized. The defined learning outcomes of the subject, with strong emphasis on knowledge about doctrines of faiths, traditions, rituals, texts, and history, are not seen as being well suited to addressing the contemporary context without supplements in the form of media representations.

As media materials and discourses become integrated into pedagogical practice, media dynamics become relevant to how teachers and students engage with the representations of religion. Ideally, the media materials and media discourses are supplemented and put into context by the facts and content of the curriculum, and vice versa. However, this demands a certain degree of media literacy on the part of the teacher in order to fulfil the role of RE as a nuanced and relevant site in which young people can learn about, discuss, and engage with religion.

Bibliography

Andreassen, Bengt-Ove. 2016. *Religionsdidaktikk. En Innføring.* [Didactics of religion. An introduction]. 2nd ed. Oslo: Universitetsforlaget.

Alberts, Wanda. 2007. *Integrative Religious Education in Europe: A Study-of-Religions Approach.* Berlin: De Gruyter.

Alberts, Wanda. 2010. "The Academic Study of Religions and Integrative Religious Education in Europe." *British Journal of Religious Education* 32 (3): 275–290

Bråten, Oddrun M. H. 2013. *Towards a Methodology for Comparative Studies in Religious Education.* Münster: Waxmann

Davis, Derek H., and Elena Miroshnikova, eds. 2012. *The Routledge International Handbook of Religious Education.* London: Routledge

Ferrari, Silvio. 2014. "Teaching Religion in the European Union: A Legal Overview." In *Religious Education and the Challenge of Pluralism,* edited by Adam B. Seligman, 25–44. New York: Oxford University Press.

Hjarvard, Stig. 2008. "The Mediatization of Religion: A Theory of the Media as Agents of Religious Change." *Northern Lights: Film & Media Studies Yearbook* 6 (1): 9–26.

Hjarvard, Stig. 2013. *The Mediatization of Culture and Society.* London and New York: Routledge.

Hobbs, Renée. 1998. "The Seven Great Debates in the Media Literacy Movement." *Journal of Communication* 48 (1): 16–32.

Ihlen, Øyvind and Sigurd Allern. 2008. "This is the issue: Framing contests, public relations and media coverage." In *Communicating Politics: Political Communication in the Nordic Countries,* edited by Jesper Strömbäck, Mark Ørsten and Toril Aalberg, 233–248. Göteborg: Nordicom.

Jackson, Robert. 2014. *Signposts: Policy and Practice for Teaching about Religions and Non-Religious World Views in Intercultural Education*. Strasbourg: Council of Europe Publishing.

Kuyk, Elza, Roger Jensen, David Lankshear, Elizabeth Löh Manna, and Peter Schreiner, eds. 2007. *Religious Education in Europe: Situations and Current Trends in Schools*. Oslo: IKO

Lippe, Marie von der. 2008. "To Believe or Not To Believe: Young People's Perceptions and Experiences of Religion and Religious Education In Norway." In *Encountering Religious Pluralism in School and Society: A Qualitative Study of Teenage Perspectives in Europe*, edited by Thorsten Knauth, Dan-Paul Jozsa, Gerdien Bertram-Troost, and Julia Ipgrave, 149–171. Münster: Waxmann.

Loobuyck, Patrick, and Leni Franken. 2014. "Conclusion." In *Religious Education in a Plural, Secularized Society: A Paradigm Shift*, edited by Leni Franken and Patrick Loobuyck, 169–176. Münster: Waxmann.

Lövheim, Mia, and Jonas Bromander. 2012. *Religion som resurs? – Existentiella frågor och värderingar i unga svenskars liv*. [Religion as resource? Existential issues and values in the lives of Swedish youth]. Skellefteå: Artos Norma Bokförlag.

Lundby, Knut, and Ann Kristin Gresaker. 2015. "Religion i mediene – omstridt og oversett?" [Religions in the media – contested and ignored?]. In *Religionens tilbakekomst i offentligheten? Religion, politikk, medier, stat og sivilsamfunn i Norge siden 1980-tallet* [The return of religion in the public sphere?], edited by Inger Furseth, 69–104. Oslo: Universitetsforlaget.

McCombs, Maxwell. 2014. *Setting the Agenda: The Mass Media and Public Opinion*. Cambridge: Polity Press.

Scheufele, Dietram A. and David Tewksbury. 2007. "Framing, Agenda Setting, and Priming: The Evolution of Three Media Effects Models." *Journal of Communication* 57 (1): 9–20.

Schreiner, Peter. 2014. "Situation and Current Developments of Religious Education in Europe." In *Religious Education in a Plural, Secularized Society: A Paradigm Shift*, edited by Leni Franken and Patrick Loobuyck, 17–34. Münster: Waxmann.

Schrott, Andrea. 2009. "Dimensions: Catch-all Label or Technical Term." In *Mediatization: Concepts, Changes, Consequences*, edited by Knut Lundby, 41–61. New York: Peter Lang.

Skolverket. 2011a. Subject – Religion [LGY11]. Accessed 2 June 2017. https://www.skolverket.se/polopoly_fs/1.209323!/Religion.pdf.

Skolverket. 2011b. Curricula for Upper Secondary School [LGY11]. Stockholm: Skolverket

Skolverket. 2015. Upper Secondary School – Student Statistics: National. Accessed 21 April 2016. http://siris.skolverket.se/reports/rwservlet?cmdkey=common&notgeo=&report=gyelever_lgy11&p_ar=2015&p_lan_kod=&p_kommunkod=&p_skolkod=&p_inriktning=0

Utdanningsdirektoratet (UDIR). 2006. Læreplan i Religion og Etikk. [National curriculum of Religion and Ethics]. Accessed 9 Aug 2017. https://www.udir.no/kl06/REL1-01.

Wiborg, Susanne. 2009. *Education and Social Integration: Comprehensive Schooling in Europe*. New York: Palgrave Macmillan.

Liv Ingeborg Lied, Audun Toft

Chapter 14
'Let me Entertain You': Media Dynamics in Public Schools

Abstract: Today, the use of media technology, platforms, materials, and discourses is often integrated into the classroom practices of Scandinavian schools. Reporting from a case study of religious education (RE) in a Norwegian upper secondary school, this chapter explores how a media-saturated classroom intensifies and broadens already established dynamics of academic boredom. Media materials primarily chosen for their entertaining and attention-grabbing qualities make up a substantive part of the observed RE lessons. Focusing on conflicts and controversies around religion, these media materials are used to grab and keep the attention of the students, in competition with a multitude of options provided by laptops with Internet access. In the observed classrooms, this use of conflict and entertainment-oriented media materials resulted in the reproduction and reinforcement of stereotypical and exotic representations of religion.

Keywords: media-saturation, representations of religion, academic boredom, religious stereotypes

Kari[1] enters the classroom, carrying a box containing school editions of the New Testament under one arm and her computer under the other. The students are talking quietly to each other, some gathering around a laptop screen, others scrolling through their Instagram or Facebook newsfeeds. As the session is about to start, Kari notes the expected learning outcome of the day on the blackboard: 'Acquire knowledge about the Bible's organization, contents, origins, and use.'[2] The students are still talking to each other and many of them continue to be immersed in their online activities. 'We need to concentrate on today's task,' Kari says. 'Today the Bible is our topic, so I hope you are using your laptops for taking notes, and then after that you can put down the screens. ... I have prepared a Kahoot.[3] We are going to interpret a text,[4] and I want us to talk a little about the ongoing debate in the

---

1 All the names of the informants have been changed.
2 Referring to the competence aim 'Interpret some important texts from the Bible and Christian tradition' in the official curriculum (UDIR 2006). The Norwegian curriculum specifies learning outcome through specific 'competence aims', presented as a bullet-pointed list of learning outcomes. We will use this term, in accordance with the official English translation of the curriculum.
3 Kahoot is a game-based, online learning platform.
4 Note the direct reference to the mentioned competence aim.

OpenAccess. © 2018, Liv Ingeborg Lied, Audun Toft. [CC BY-NC-ND] This work is licensed under the Creative Commons Attribution-Non Commerical-NoDerivs 4.0 License. https://doi.org/10.1515/9783110502060-019

media about gay rights.' One of the students raises his hand, eagerly, 'Are we going to watch a film?' 'No,' Kari replies, 'I know that three hour sessions are rough,[5] but it is hard to find something that fits. I considered using *På tro og Are*, but I did not find it any good. So, no film. But, we are going to discuss homosexuality, and I hope that is a bit interesting?' (Observation in Kari's classroom, 28 January 2016)

This snapshot from a religious education (RE) [6] session in a Norwegian upper secondary school illustrates a very common classroom situation at this school, pointing to some of the challenges that teachers, such as Kari, are up against on an everyday basis. It also provides a preliminary indication of the place of media in a contemporary classroom, and the functions of various media materials in educational activities.

One of the main hypotheses of the mediatization theory, which is described in the first part of this volume (see Chapter 3), is that the media will come to shape and mould interaction in other social domains, fields, or institutions, and will increasingly become an intrinsic part of these other societal fields (e.g. Schrott 2009; Hjarvard 2013). Inspired by – and continuing the discussion of – the mediatization theory, this essay will discuss the potential influence of various media on areas of teaching and learning about religion in RE lessons in selected classroom settings. The essay will discuss some of the ways in which media may condition engagement with religion in Norwegian public school settings. We explore how profoundly media-saturated classroom environments may influence teachers' didactic choices and professional planning for RE lessons, pointing out some of the dynamics that drive their choices, and discussing the outcome of their strategies in the ongoing representation of religion in classroom settings.

The essay reports from fieldwork conducted in a select upper secondary school in the Eastern part of Norway, in the period from September 2015 to March 2016. The fieldwork included six teachers and eight classes, and consisted of the observation of classroom practices as well as interviews with teachers. Fifty RE sessions were observed during this period. The researchers were seated in the back row, allowing for the observation of both teachers' practices and students' simultaneous (online media) activity.[7] As this essay reports from a fieldwork in a single school setting, we make no claims for generalizability. Rather,

---

[5] The Norwegian term used is *seigt*, indicating a long duration in a negative way.
[6] The Norwegian name of the school subject is *Religion og etikk* (Religion and ethics). See Toft and Broberg's essay (Chapter 13) for more information.
[7] See Toft and Broberg (Chapter 13) for a full description of the fieldwork. The current essay draws on the data from both Toft's and Lied's observations.

this is a case study, and as such our aim is to point to some key findings that may subsequently be of interest and relevance to the larger field.

14.1 A Media-Saturated Classroom

Our first, major impression from the classroom observation was the constant, and sometimes massive, media presence. 'Media presence', then, broadly conceived,[8] indicates the simultaneous presence in the classroom of:
- *media technology*, that is, materialized media artefacts and gadgets, such as laptops and cell phones, but also other audio visual equipment that is present in the classroom;
- *media platforms*, that is, online portals that provide access to various categories of media, based on their purpose or function, such as news and entertainment media, as well as social/networked media;
- *media materials*, that is, media products on paper or on screen, mainly, but not exclusively, produced by media professionals and broadcast in the mass media;
- *media discourses*, that is, media language, genres, and frames that shape the way a topic is being talked about; as well as the selection mechanisms that decide the topics that are, in fact, talked about.

First, media technology, and laptops in particular,[9] made up an important part of the physical infrastructure of the classrooms observed. The teachers and students all had laptops. A high degree of student digital literacy is an explicit aim of the official Norwegian curriculum,[10] and many Norwegian municipalities and counties have equipped their student populations with laptops as part of fulfilling this goal. In the classrooms observed, the laptops were a vital part of the 'classroom-scape', becoming part of its spatiality and tangible materiality

---

[8] We find it relevant to make distinctions between different forms of media. Much of the literature on digital media and ICT in education conflates different kinds of educational technology thus creating methodological and conceptual problems (Livingstone 2012, 5).
[9] The use of cell phones differed from the use of computers. Students brought out their personal cell phones mostly in the breaks. Indeed, picking up the cell phone and the charger functioned as one of the main indicators of the break. We observed few cell phones in use during the lessons. In these few instances, the act of handling it could be understood as a specific act of resistance, being an obvious act of not paying attention.
[10] The curriculum defines digital competency as one of the five basic skills all students need across subjects alongside reading, writing, oral competency, and calculation. These skills are specified as part of the curriculum of every subject (UDIR 2006).

in the same way as the desks and chairs. The students' laptops were situated in front of them and were thus between the students and the teacher, often with the screen up. They were frequently in use during the lessons and during breaks, as part of various classroom practices.

The teachers approached the use of laptops differently, but they all tried to limit the students' use of them. The physically present laptops were a frequently recurring topic in the interaction among teachers and students. The teachers were constantly requesting that the students turn them off, or put down the screens during the time set apart for instruction, or reminding them to use the laptop only for the purposes for which they were intended in the teaching context. In fact, the laptops occur as a primary topic of meta-communication in *all* the observed, regular, classroom sessions. However, the teachers' request was never completely met by all of the students in any of the sessions. This constant material presence of the laptops on the students' desks, and the ways in which they attract student attention, create a classroom situation that influences the teachers' planning of educational activities.

Second, media were also present in the classroom in the shape of online media platforms, which were engaged with by the students during the lessons. Some of this activity was teacher-initiated and part of the planned educational practice. The students consulted Wikipedia, SNL,[11] the homepages of various religious organizations, and the textbook's online resources, which were available on the webpages of the publisher. However, from our location at the back of the classroom, it was evident that the vast majority of laptop use among the students during teaching hours involved media platforms that were foreign or irrelevant to the topic of teaching.[12] The students checked their email and visited various social media platforms, scrolling through their news feeds, or chatting. At times, their social media presence could be described as massive. Some students visited the major news portals, whereas others were engaging with sports or fashion sites, film portals, and gaming hubs. The large majority of students would quickly, although regularly and sometimes with high frequency, check updates, but otherwise follow the teaching. Occasionally, we observed online interaction between students in the same classroom. On some particular occasions, larger groups of students were interacting and simultaneously engaging in the same online activities, in effect creating an alternative collective 'reality' in the classroom. A small minority of students would spend the entire session streaming a

---

[11] *Store Norske Leksikon* (snl.no), the major online Norwegian encyclopedia.
[12] To protect the students' privacy, we chose not to present student online activity in detail. We provide generic descriptions of platforms, genres, and activities only.

film, or constantly gaming. Furthermore, it was evident that the students' laptop use increased during the course of the session. As the session approached its end, a large percentage of the students were online. In other words, the simultaneous engagement with a broad variety of media portals was a marked and persistent practice among the students. In some classes, and in some parts of the sessions, these practices were dominant in the group of students.[13]

Third, media materials produced by media professionals and distributed through the mass media, such as national newspapers and broadcasters, were frequently brought into the classroom. Teachers used a wide range of media materials among their pedagogical artefacts during teaching and instruction, and, on some occasions, media materials constituted the main pedagogical artefact in a given session.[14] Teachers would, for instance, bring Xeroxed copies of newspaper articles, and show documentaries and news clips on the screen, particularly from established national broadcasters, such as NRK[15]. Their use of media materials was not limited to news media sources, though. They would bring in clips from films and music videos, as well as from talk shows. Teachers also applied materials from non-media professionals, showing clips from YouTube and from blogs. Students would bring in a similar spread of media materials, as part of their home assignments or as an integral part of the work taking place in the classroom context. This was done in both smaller groups and in the plenary.

Fourth, and finally, media discourses, which are defined above as media language, genres, and frames that influence the choice of topics and shape the way a topic is being talked about were also clearly observable in the classroom set-

---

[13] Norwegian upper secondary schools regulate students' use of computers and their Internet access in classroom settings differently. The school we attended had a relatively liberal approach, both in regard to the use of computers and to online presence. However, it should be noted that the fieldwork was done at a time when the school's system for blocking Internet access malfunctioned. Whereas the teachers would normally be able to control, at least in part, the students' Internet access, the teachers had no such tools in this period.

[14] The term 'pedagogical artefacts' is used here to describe tools that are used for educational purposes to amplify pedagogical activities in the classroom. Such artefacts may serve as the main content of the instruction in their own right; they may serve as an example of a broader phenomenon the teacher wishes to highlight; or the artefact may function primarily as a pedagogical trigger, used to attract interest and introduce another activity.

[15] The Norwegian state-owned public service media company Norsk rikskringkasting (Norwegian Broadcasting Corporation).

tings. Although this was an important part of the media presence in the classroom, this aspect will not be discussed further in this essay.[16]

14.2 Media as a Challenge: Media-Saturation and Boredom Coping Strategies

Our first main observation is the massiveness of media presence in the classrooms. Media were engaged in the form of materially present technological artefacts, in students' parallel presence on social and popular media platforms, as pedagogical artefacts and sources of information, as references in language and bodily expressions, as well as in terms of contested social practices and artefacts that were manifest both in students' actions and in the teachers' metacommunication about computer use. In sum, we were witnessing a truly 'media-saturated' classroom.[17]

As the above outline shows, students' media engagement in the classroom is multifaceted. However, a substantive part of the student media practices that were observed can fruitfully be described as the expressive component of academic boredom, or as boredom coping strategies.[18] Engagement with online media that is irrelevant to the topic of the teaching session serves as a way of leaving the situation, and it displays a clear correlation with procrastination. As pointed out in a number of reports,[19] a high percentage of students cross-culturally will, for various reasons and at any given time, experience and express boredom.[20] As such, academic boredom is part and parcel of academic culture.

Academic boredom is not a novelty, for sure.[21] However, with the introduction of personal laptops in the classroom, and with no limits to online access, the menu of available boredom coping strategies becomes rich and varied. A

---

[16] See Chapter 15 on the use of media materials in the lessons about Islam for a more detailed discussion.
[17] The term media-saturation was used about societies where (mass) media have come to suffuse every part of life (e.g. Ortner 1998). Today, it is widely used to indicate both the way media are integrated across societal spheres and of the presence of a plethora of media competing for the attention of the audience (e.g. Sherry 2002).
[18] See the model developed by Pekrun (2006) and Pekrun et al. (2010). On academic emotions and boredom studies, see further, Goetz et al. (2014); Mann and Robinson (2009).
[19] See Dale (1997, 154); Mann and Robinson (2009).
[20] According to Pekrun et al. (2010) academic boredom consists of five factors: affective, cognitive, expressive, motivational, and physiological.
[21] It is likely, rather, that as long as there have been schools students have been bored.

whole world of online activities is constantly at the students' fingertips, and the laptop screens are physically located between the students and the teachers. In this way, the laptops become an extension of the students' individually tailored, alternative space. Our observations consistently suggest that the bar for paying attention to the teachers' planned educational activities is high, particularly over time and at the end of teaching sessions. Furthermore, the parallel and simultaneous activity pattern seemed habitual in the student group, and had already developed into an observable classroom practice. In this way, the media, broadly conceived, play an important role in shaping the conditions of classroom practices and interactions.

14.3 Entertainment and Controversies Over Religion: Teachers' Didactic Choices

Against this general backdrop of media-saturated classroom environments, and continuing the discussion of the potential media dynamics that are at work in Norwegian classrooms, a closer look at the didactic choices of the teachers in RE lessons is warranted. As pointed out in the description, above, media materials were brought into the classroom by teachers as well as by students. The teachers' selection and application of media materials as pedagogical artefacts are interesting, both because these are the situations where the use of media materials are both planned for and are explicitly integrated into the educational activity, and because this use of media materials may provide key information about the ways in which teachers deal with the challenges of the media-saturated classroom.

The RE sessions observed included the use of various types of media materials as pedagogical artefacts. In the following, we will present two examples that represent broader trends in the material. On several occasions we observed that the teachers tended to privilege media materials that were either entertaining or represented controversies about religion, and that these materials, which were chosen due to their entertaining or attention grabbing qualities, were transformed into instructional content.

På tro og Are

In the brief snapshot from Kari's classroom, which was presented in the introduction, we hear that Kari had considered using *På tro og Are* in her teaching session. Kari is certainly not alone. The Norwegian episodic show *På tro og Are* was one of the most popular and steadily recurring media references in the RE classroom settings that were observed.[22] This show, which was produced for NRK, premièred in 2010 and has been aired several times. The show can be described as a documentary series about religion, and is also labelled 'entertainment' and 'life style' on NRK's webpage. *På tro og Are* features a well-known Norwegian comedian and radio host, Are Sende Osen, who openly self-identifies as an atheist and sceptic, but is most often respectful of, and open to, the lives and traditions of religious others. In the first season, Sende Osen spends a week with a family from each of the main religious traditions present in Norway.[23] The interviews with the teachers confirm that this show is frequently used as a resource in the RE sessions. All of the teachers reported having used the show, and that they would continue using it. The episodes about Islam and Buddhism were by far the most used, but also the episode on Judaism was mentioned. *På tro og Are* was also referred to by the students in classroom contexts. We will describe observations from two sessions where the episode about Islam was used.

Erik's RE session (5 February 2016) was designed to cover Islam, with a focus on its main characteristics and various denominations. The very moment Erik enters the classroom he says, 'Prepare to watch an episode of *På tro og Are!*' The students cheer and start imitating Sende Osen, his particular dialect and well-known gestures. The students had already watched the episode on Islam several times, they were generally familiar with this show, and, judging by their reaction, it is evident that they had enjoyed it. The showing of the episode was postponed by some initial technological challenges, but the students calmed down as soon as the episode started playing and it generally had their full attention.

The episode about Islam is summarized like this on nrk.no:

> Muslims are the new enemy of the Western world. Atheist and sceptic Are Sende Osen will spend one week with the Muslim family Selahi in Oslo, trying to understand why. What are their beliefs, and do they want Norway to follow Islamic law? And what happens when Are attempts to fast during Ramadan?[24]

This description captures the main features of the episode, features that are probably also among the reasons for its success. The episode takes widely shared stereotypes about Muslims as both its starting point and structuring grid, and yet

---

22 The title *På tro og Are* plays on the Norwegian idiom *på tro og ære* (on [my] faith and honor), as well the name of the main character, Are Sende Osen. Two seasons have been produced; a third is in production (2017).
23 i.e. Islam, Buddhism, Mormonism, Christianity, Judaism, and Sikhism.
24 Our translation.

the meeting between Are and the Selahi family is portrayed as an honest, open-minded and warm-hearted meeting with lay practitioners of Islam. The focus on everyday life and all its trivialities, to which the average Norwegian viewer can relate, is intermingled with facts and information, many of which reflect the assumed perceptions of the Norwegian audience about Islam as a potential threat. The main focus is on Sende Osen, however, who with his characteristic pose, pitch, and pointed comments, makes the series obviously entertaining.

The first 45 minutes of Erik's class were spent on showing the episode. After the first break, Erik moves on to the other main focus of the session, the denominations of Islam. During this second sitting,[25] in a moment of meta-communication, he tells the class, 'And then there is something about "key features" – and that is why we watched *På tro og Are*.' The subtext of this mention of 'key features' is a particular, explicitly defined competence aim of the official Norwegian curriculum: 'elaborate on key features in the religion [Islam].' Teachers in Norwegian schools have (ideally) to cover all of these competence aims, and often plan their teaching to make sure that they have them covered. In Erik's meta-reflection he tells the students, us, and himself, that this goal has now been met. In this case, the teaching of the key features of Islam has been covered by the students watching the episode of *På tro og Are* about Islam.

After the session, Erik tells us that he had planned for a brief discussion of the episode, but due to the initial technological challenges he could not find time for it. In other words, he did not plan for the episode to be the only pedagogical artefact and the only means to meet the competence aim, but, as happens frequently in classrooms, unplanned events occur, and instead of dropping other parts of the planned session, Erik skipped the discussion, letting *På tro og Are* speak for itself. Consequently, the episode on Islam became the main pedagogical artefact and the only content of instruction on this particular aim, without introduction or a concluding discussion.

Towards the end of a three sitting RE session (5 November 2015), which was mainly devoted to Sharia and the ethics of Islam, Anne Lise used the same episode about Islam. As the students finish their mandatory activities, Anne Lise says, 'So, are you ready for *På tro og Are?*' The students cheer. Anne Lise looks at her watch saying, 'It looks like we won't have any time left for discussion, so take some notes.' The class spends the next hour watching the episode. As the showing comes to an end, only two minutes remains and Anne Lise dismisses the class. In this case, *På tro og Are* is used explicitly for its entertaining qualities and as a reward at the end of a long session. The episode was not put in

---

25 One sitting is 45 minutes, marked off by a break, usually 15 minutes.

connection with the previous theme of the lesson and had no apparent pedagogical value, although Anne Lise encouraged the students to take some notes during the episode, indicating that she was aware of this.

14.4 Controversy at Christmas

Another tendency observed in the classrooms is that the teachers tend to select media materials that focus on controversies about religion. A closer look at Charlotte's session on humanist life stances may serve as an example. At the end of her session (1 March 2016), Charlotte brings up a debate that played out in the Norwegian media in 2012 about the supposed 'de-Christianization' of the traditional and much loved hymn 'Fairest Lord Jesus' ('Deilig er jorden').

Charlotte puts the web page 'Avkristner "Deilig er jorden"'[26] up on the screen. This NRK-produced multimedia web page, dated 17 December 2012, contains news clips (video and audio) originally aired on *Dagsrevyen* and on *Kulturnytt*, as well as a presentation of the case. According to the news report, the Norwegian Humanist Association (Human-Etisk Forbund) had recently published a new version of the hymn, and NRK asked the editor in chief of the conservative Christian newspaper *Dagen*, Vebjørn Selbekk, who is well known to the Norwegian public, about his reaction to it. As might be expected, Selbekk condemned the de-Christianized version of the hymn. The driving force of the clip is the alleged conflict between atheists and believers, between tradition and 'rewriting', focusing on the hymn.

Charlotte introduces the web page, referring to the longstanding conflict between the Norwegian Humanist Association and the Church of Norway in the public sphere. She reads the text out loud, scrolling down and displaying the text on the projector, interrupted only by an instruction to the students to put down the computer screens if they are not using the laptop to take notes. She then shows them the video clip, which instantly catches the attention of all the students, before she moves on to YouTube to let the students hear a recording of the original version of the hymn. As the music fades out, she engages the students in discussion until the bell rings five minutes later.

---

26 Tone Staude, "Avkristner "Deilig er jorden"," *NRK*, 12 Dec 2012, accessed 27 Sept 2017, https://www.nrk.no/kultur/avkristner-_deilig-er-jorden_-1.10843699

14.5 'The Fight Against Everyday Boredom': Media as Part of the Solution

The descriptions above illustrate two broader tendencies in the teachers' use of media materials in the classrooms observed: the teachers tend to privilege: a) entertaining materials, and b) materials representing controversies about religion. Complemented by the glimpse into Kari's lesson in the introduction, we can see that entertaining and conflict-focused media materials are used by the teachers to cater for some of the same needs in the classroom. Although Kari did not fulfil the wishes of the student who was hoping to watch a film, she offered him something in return: a class discussion of the ongoing debate about gay rights among Christian groups, aided by selected articles from the two major Norwegian Christian newspapers, *Vårt Land* and *Dagen*, as well as a blog post. In other words, instead of a film, she offered him a media-based discussion of a conflict that runs deep among Norwegian Christians. Although they represent different media genres, these newspaper articles and blogposts are applied in a similar way to films: they are both effective means of catching and keeping the attention of the students.

From this example we can see that the teachers *plan* for students' boredom. They are very well aware of the challenge of academic boredom in the classroom, and their didactic deliberations and choices of pedagogical artefacts are affected by this challenge. They plan for a variety of activities in the classroom,[27] they plan for different activities at different points in the sessions, and they bring in pedagogical artefacts that they find fit to aid the teaching at the various stages of students' classroom activities. In other words, in the above description of the classrooms observed, we point out how media-saturation represents a challenge to teachers in the fight against student boredom and its manifest expressions in the classroom. The massive media presence makes the already well-known challenge of boredom all the more acute, with a multitude of alternatives available to the students through their laptops. In this way, the conditions for teaching in the media-saturated classroom resemble the conditions of the larger media-saturated society (Sherry 2002), for which media materials are produced in the first place. These are also the conditions for which certain media materials, particularly entertaining and conflict-oriented ones, are especially well suited. As the media-saturation represents a challenge, these media materials also become

---

[27] In accordance with the demands of the official curriculum and the standards of good teaching practice.

part of the solution. Our observations confirm that film clips, documentaries, and series such as *På tro og Are*, are among the few pedagogical artefacts that successfully gain the students' attention and are able to keep it over time.

This does not mean that just any entertaining or conflict-centred media materials can be used as pedagogical artefacts. Media materials are used as part of a didactic plan and are re-mediated into the classroom according to the aims and topics of the lessons, complemented by, for instance, textbooks, lectures, discussions, and other pedagogical tools that are available for the teachers. Mostly, the media materials are thus resources that are used critically by professional teachers as part of a larger didactical plan. Still, what we have observed is that the way media materials are included in the pedagogical practice influence and, in some ways, shape, the way that religion is being represented.

The transformation of media materials produced by media professionals, according to various institutional and genre-specific criteria, into pedagogical artefacts carries some wider implications. In our observations, we saw that the entertaining properties of media materials often gained priority over the academic content. Ideally, it should be possible to find media materials that satisfy both these criteria, but when weighed against each other, the attention grabbing properties are frequently given the most weight. The teachers are aware of this dilemma, and the use of the show *På tro og Are* illustrates this. During the interviews, and in several conversations with the teachers, we discussed the use of this show as part of the lessons. All of the teachers used episodes from *På tro og Are* from time to time, and the main reason given was that it was funny, entertaining, and drew the students' attention. However, they all had some misgivings about the academic value of the show. When they still chose to use it, their solution was to spend time afterwards to discuss and nuance the show. As the earlier examples show, this part often has to give way to unforseen occurences in the course of a hectic school day. However, even when there was room for discussion, it was the show that set the premises for what was being talked about. Media materials, chosen primarily for their suitability to catch and keep the students' attention, not only became part of the lessons, but were, in many instances, the main pedagogical artefacts of the lesson.[28] This leads us to the question of how this can influence the way religion is being represented in the classroom.

---

[28] We have several observations of media materials being used as the primary pedagogical artefact, setting the premises for classroom discussions. Examples include documentaries, feature films, and music videos.

14.6 The Representation of Religion

The wide range of media materials that are used in the lessons observed makes it difficult to isolate all the specific and different media dynamics that influence the ways in which the teachers and the students engage with religion. Still, we can point to some similarities across the observations which seem to be the result of the particular didactic choices made by the teachers when choosing media materials that deal with religion, and which then have consequences for the way religion is being represented.

The first consequence of these didactic choices is that contested issues pertaining to the religions in question tend to be brought up in teaching, and such contested issues may get a disproportionate share of the attention in the classroom. Not only are controversial issues actively sought by the teachers for their attention grabbing properties, but conflict, polarization and controversy are also key initial features of media-produced materials. Conflict has long been identified as one of the primary criteria for news media coverage (e.g. Ihlen and Allern 2008), but also as a narrative device in other media productions. A focus on conflict and controversies is also well documented in relation to the Norwegian media coverage of religion (Døving and Kraft 2013; Lundby and Gresaker 2015). The controversies may thus come to be perceived as key traits of the religious tradition and its practitioners. Conservative Norwegian Christians are, for instance, represented in the classroom by their views on gay rights and their reactions against the rewriting of a traditional Christmas hymn. Other sides to their religiosity, their other opinions, or their generally peaceful everyday coexistence with people of other convictions in Norwegian society, will seldom get the same attention.

A second consequence is that exotic and unexpected traits of religious practices, and features of religious traditions that either appeal to the emotions, or are conceived as being irrational to the Norwegian mind, may be increasingly accentuated. These traits of religious practices are commonly seen in media productions about religion. The consequence may be that media stereotypes of religions, which are designed to entertain a Norwegian audience, are brought into the classroom context and recirculated as teachable facts. This also agrees with studies of media coverage of religion that point to the way stereotypes, and exotic and controversial themes, are being repeated and reproduced in various media (Poole 2002). As in the case of the episode of *På tro og Are* about Islam, that is discussed above, it is often aspects of the religious diet and dress that typically gain attention, as do prohibitions and regulations that seem foreign or out of place to the larger society. Even the overarching frame of the show, where Are, as a professed atheist, sets out to explore religion as something that he finds strange and even threatening, accentuates this.

14.7 Mediatization

In this essay we have focused on two interrelated ways in which media are present in, and condition, the teaching and learning about religion in the classrooms. In the first part of the essay we showed how the classrooms observed were characterized by a profound and multivalent media-saturation. In the second part we discussed the teachers' choice of media materials as pedagogical artefacts, displaying a privileging of media materials that either entertain or focus on controversies about religion. The dynamics of academic boredom coping strategies that are described, on the one hand, and teachers' didactic choices in the fight against (perceived) student boredom on the other, have suggested that media-saturation in the classroom is an important reason why teachers privilege media materials that are entertaining or that focus on controversies about religion.

The theoretical perspective of mediatization is useful as a heuristic device through which to explore the role of the various media in the RE sessions that were observed. If we loosely define mediatization as the way in which institutions and societal spheres come to depend on institutional practices of the media (Hjarvard 2013), then this is relevant to understanding the lessons observed. The integration of a multitude of media in the day-to-day practice of the school impacts on the learning and teaching about religion,[29] offering challenges, but also solutions, through the use of media materials, which may in turn come to influence the representation of religion in the classroom. At the same time, this should not be understood as the introduction of radically new or different practices – boredom coping strategies existed long before the classroom became media-saturated. Rather, the media presence serves to mould practices that are already well established in schools, but also to intensify and broaden them, and so further conditioning and transforming the teaching practices. The introduction of near endless opportunities for entertainment, through laptops with Internet access, makes the classroom a setting in which the teachers need to fight for the students' attention in qualitative new ways.

---

[29] Presumably this is not confined only to religion. However, our material is limited to RE sessions.

More research is needed into the specific ways in which media materials can shape the representation of religion. We have briefly described how media materials that are chosen for their entertaining qualities can eventually reproduce stereotypical and exotic representations of religion; however, this is a field that warrants further study.

Bibliography

Dale, Erling Lars (ed.) 1997. *Etikk for pedagogisk profesjonalitet.* [Ethics for pedagogical professionalism]. Oslo: Cappelen Akademiske Forlag.

Døving, Cora Alexa, and Siv Ellen Kraft. 2013. *Religion i pressen.* [Religion in the press]. Oslo: Universitetsforlaget.

Goetz, Thomas, Anne C. Frenzel, Nathan C. Hall, Ulrike E. Nett, Reinhard Pekrun, and Anastasiya A. Lipnevich. 2014. "Types of Boredom: An Experience Sampling Approach." *Motivation and Emotion* 38 (3): 401–419.

Ihlen, Øyvind and Sigurd Allern. 2008. "This is the issue: Framing contests, public relations and media coverage." In *Communicating Politics: Political Communication in the Nordic Countries*, edited by Jesper Strömbäck, Mark Ørsten and Toril Aalberg, 233–248. Göteborg: Nordicom.

Hjarvard, Stig. 2013. *The Mediatization of Culture and Society.* London: Routledge.

Livingstone, Sonia. 2012. "Critical Reflections on the Prospects for ICT in Education." *Oxford Review of Education* 38 (1): 9–24.

Lundby, Knut, and Gresaker, Ann Kristin. 2015. "Religion i mediene – omstridt og oversett?" [Religions in the media – contested and ignored?]. In *Religionens tilbakekomst i offentligheten? Religion, politikk, medier, stat og sivilsamfunn i Norge siden 1980-tallet* [The return of religion in the public sphere?], edited by Inger Furseth, 69–104. Oslo: Universitetsforlaget.

Mann, Sandi, and Andrew Robinson. 2009. "Boredom in the Lecture Theatre: An Investigation into the Contributors, Moderators and Outcomes of Boredom Amongst University Students." *British Educational Research Journal* 35 (2): 243–258.

Ortner, Sherry B. 1998. "Generation X: Anthropology in a Media-Saturated World." *Cultural Anthropology* 13 (3): 414–440

Pekrun, Reinhard. 2006. "The Control-Value Theory of Achievement Emotions: Assumptions, Corollaries, and Implications for Educational Research and Practice." *Educational Psychology Review* 18 (4): 315–341.

Pekrun, Reinhard, Thomas Goetz, Lia, M. Daniels, Robert, H. Stupnisky, and Raymond P. Perry. 2010. "Boredom in Achievement Settings: Exploring Control-Value Antecedents and Performance Outcomes of a Neglected Emotion." *Journal of Educational Psychology* 102 (3): 531–549.

Poole, Elizabeth. 2002. *Reporting Islam: The Media and Representation of Muslims in Britain.* London: I.B. Tauris

Schrott, Andrea. 2009. "Dimensions: Catch-All Label or Technical Term." In *Mediatization: Concept, Changes, Consequences*, edited by Knut Lundby, 41–61. New York: Peter Lang.

Sherry, John L. 2002. "Media Saturation and Entertainment–Education." *Communication Theory* 12 (2): 206–224.
Utdanningsdirektoratet (UDIR) 2006. *Læreplan i Religion og Etikk*. [National curriculum of Religion and Ethics]. Accessed 9 Aug 2017. https://www.udir.no/kl06/REL1-01.

Audun Toft
Chapter 15
Inescapable News Coverage: Media Influence on Lessons About Islam

Abstract: For a long time, stories about terrorism, conflicts, and controversies, which are in various ways put in connection with Islam and Muslims, have been a prominent part of Norwegian news coverage. Based on a case study of a Norwegian secondary school, the current chapter deals with the ways in which the news coverage, and themes, events, and discourses contained in it, come to be included in religious education about Islam. Using the concepts of prototypes and cognitive frames, it is argued that the news coverage establishes and maintains certain associations and narratives connected to Islam. Due to the frequent and substantial use of media materials in RE classrooms, influencing the ways Islam is represented and talked about in the classroom, the same problematic issues are thematized over and over again in similar ways across the observed classes. By constantly addressing the news coverage with the intention of nuancing and correcting problematic representations of Islam, the result may in some instances be to reinforce and confirm the association of Islam with terrorism, conflict, and controversy established by the media.

Keywords: religious education, Islam, frames, news coverage, terrorism

15.1 Introduction

Anne Lise[1] is an experienced religious education teacher. Still, she is uncertain about how to teach about Islam. The question is how, and if, she should relate her lessons about Islam to terrorism and conflict. It is not really a part of the curriculum, and yet it seems relevant, especially with the constant coverage in the news media. 'Conflict and Islam, that's the elephant in the room,' she tells me. 'That's what all the students think about when they hear the word "Islam", but they are reluctant to say it.' This year, as she has done in previous years, she thus introduces the topic of Islam by going through several news pieces about terrorism and radical Islamism. In this way, she hopes to break the ice so that they can discuss it and can confront any prejudices about Islam and Muslims that the students may have from their exposure to the news media.

---

1 All names of informants are changed.

OpenAccess. © 2018, Audun Toft. This work is licensed under the Creative Commons Attribution-Non Commerical-NoDerivs 4.0 License. https://doi.org/10.1515/9783110502060-020

After the class had their last lesson about Islam, she showed me an evaluation note from one of the Muslim students. The note said: 'I think there has been too much focus on radicalization and extreme Islam. Islam is so big and contains so many exciting things. Where is all this?' 'This was what I was trying to avoid,' Anne Lise said. 'I tried to show them that Islam is not just about the things they learn from the media, but yet, that's the impression they're left with.'

The scene above illustrates one of the dilemmas that religious education (RE) teachers in upper secondary school face when teaching about Islam. Should they focus mainly on the curricular goals of the subject, or should they spend time on the many controversial issues that feature in the news media where conflict and terror are recurring themes? This chapter explores some of the ways the perceived massive and conflict-oriented news coverage of Islam both influences, and becomes part of, the pedagogic practices of RE lessons.

The material is approached using a mediatization perspective. Mediatization theory (Hjarvard 2013) gives a framework through which to understand media influence without positing a direct and determinant effect of the media on audiences' behaviour and opinions (see Chapter 3). Rather, the influence of the media comes from the ways in which various media become integrated into the practices of other societal institutions, thus altering and conditioning the said practices (Thorbjørnsrud, Figenschou, and Ihlen 2014). Chapters 13 and 14 discuss how media technology, platforms, and materials[2] form an integral part of the RE lessons observed, and how this impacts on the engagement with, and representation of, religion in the classroom.

This chapter will focus on the lessons about one specific religion, Islam. RE lessons about Islam offer an interesting case for exploring media influence. In most instances such an influence may be subtle and difficult to observe and isolate. However, in relation to Islam, the influence of the media on the pedagogical practice is explicit. All the teachers[3] in the case study on which this chapter reports are aware of, and admit to, being strongly influenced by the media when teaching about Islam. The observations show that media discourses, as well as events, debates, and topics that are covered in various news media, play a prominent role in lessons about Islam. All the teachers chose to address controversial issues like terrorism and extreme Islamism in their lessons, making the lessons about Islam very different from their lessons on other religions. Several lessons, in most of the classes I observed (see Chapter 13), were spent talking about how

---

2 See Chapter 14 for a description of the multifaceted aspects of media-presence in the classroom.
3 And many students too.

Islam appears in the news, with the explicit aim of nuancing and correcting what was perceived to be a negative and one-sided representation.

This chapter addresses the following research questions:
1. How do the teachers relate to the news coverage of Islam, and how does it influence the pedagogical choices that they make when planning and executing lessons about Islam?
2. In what ways can the news coverage of Islam be said to condition and influence the ways in which Islam is being represented, discussed, and talked about in the classroom?

This approach presupposes two levels of possible influence:
a) Indirect level: where the teachers take their perception of media influence into account when planning the lessons, and
b) Direct level: through the ways teachers and students engage with questions about Islam in the classroom.

Using the concepts of prototypes and cognitive frames, I will argue that a too linear and straight-forward understanding, among the teachers, of the effects of the news coverage on the students may in some instances lead to the reinforcement and confirmation of the very notion that is seen to be problematic – namely, the association of Islam with terrorism, conflicts, and controversies.

The empirical data for this chapter were gathered as part of a case study of an upper secondary school in the Eastern part of Norway. The study included the direct observation of a total of 50 RE sessions in eight classes, interviews with six RE teachers, as well as observations from, and notes taken during, informal conversations and meetings with the teachers. The fieldwork was conducted during the school year 2015–2016, with the majority of observations being conducted between October 2015 and March 2016. The observations were recorded as handwritten field notes. No audio/video recordings were made.[4] As detailed in Chapter 13, RE in Norway is organized as a mandatory non-confessional subject that is aimed at all students, regardless of their religious/non-religious background. The subject is called 'Religion and Ethics' in upper secondary schools, and is described as being both knowledge-based and value-forming. It has the explicit aim of promoting tolerance across religious, philosophical and ethical boundaries (UDIR 2006).

---

4 See Chapter 3 for a more detailed description of the data material and methodological considerations.

15.2 The Conditions for Teaching About Islam

As mentioned above, the lessons about Islam that were observed differed strongly from the lessons about the other religions and worldviews. When teaching about Islam, controversies, conflicts, and potentially problematic sides of the religion were given significantly more attention than is specified by the learning outcomes of the curriculum.[5] The notion that Islam is a controversial religion was explicitly communicated to the students, as in this example of Kari introducing Islam:[6]

> We will start with some brainstorming about what you associate with Islam. Because Islam is a controversial religion. It is a religion that is talked and written about a lot. I hope you dare to say what you are thinking. (Kari's lesson 5 November 2015)

In all the classes observed, terrorism and extremism were the main topic of several of the lessons. Much time was also devoted to controversial issues, like the veiling of women, the death penalty for homosexuality, infidelity or apostasy, religion as a problem for integration, the radicalization of youth, forced marriage, and the oppression of women, to name just a few. These topics were regularly thematized as part of the planned lessons, and were most often legitimized[7] by referring to the news media as a way of showing their relevance. However, as often as not, the same themes surfaced during the course of lessons devoted to other topics, even when this was not planned. I will return to this latter point, but first we will examine how the teachers relate to the news coverage of Islam, and why the teachers find it necessary to include problematic issues that are covered in the news media when planning and executing their lessons.

As the introductory description of Anne Lise's dilemma illustrates, the teachers are aware of, and constantly evaluate, the role given to conflict and controversy in lessons about Islam. They are all in agreement on one thing. the premises for teaching about Islam are very different from those of other religions and worldviews. The difference is ascribed to the role of the news media, and the ways in which stories about Islam are being covered and presented. Charlotte says:

---

5 The curricular learning outcomes for Islam are identical to those for Buddhism. The differences in how the two religions are approached are thus interesting.
6 In seven of the eight observed classes, Islam was introduced with explicit references to controversial issues from the news.
7 In most classes, the teachers found it necessary to provide an explanation of why various controversies were thematized.

The media determine the focus, totally, at least when it comes to Islam. Less so when it comes to Christianity, in my experience ... but in Islam the media influence the lessons one hundred percent. ... And when it comes to Islam, the students let themselves be moulded by the media to an unbelievable degree.

Although the other teachers are somewhat less categorical, they all agree that when teaching about Islam, news coverage is a factor that they have to take into consideration. The basic claim underlying the teachers' perceived need to treat Islam differently from the other topics is that the news media are the most influential sources for the students' knowledge about, and views on, Islam and Muslims. These conditions are not there in relation to other religions or topics in the subject, at least not to any comparable degree. This thus creates a unique situation in which the teachers experience all the students having at least some knowledge of Islam as it is represented through the news media. As Anne Lise put it: 'I know that when students think about Islam, they think about what appears in the media.' According to the teachers, the students are influenced by *the amount of coverage*, providing a steady influx of focus on Islam, but also the content of the coverage plays a role, being mainly *centred on conflict and controversies*. The knowledge the students have of Islam and Muslims is thus seen as problematic, and this needs to be addressed in the lessons.

15.3 Constant Coverage

The teachers claim that all the students are familiar with the media representations of Islam due to the sheer quantity of stories that are related to Islam in the news media.

> Interviewer: Do they refer to news media?
>
> Hanne: Yes, sometimes they do. When you talk about Islam, it is impossible to avoid all the news pieces about IS,[8] or The Ummah of the Prophet,[9] or Mullah Krekar.[10] *It is inescapable.*
>
> (Interview with Hanne, my emphasis.)

---

[8] Islamic State (IS) is the name that is most used in the Norwegian news media, but ISIS and ISIL are also used.
[9] Norwegian radical Islamist group (Bangstad 2014, 65–69)
[10] Najmuddin Faraj Ahmad aka Mullah Krekar is a well-known radical Islamist in Norway (Bangstad 2014, 63–65).

Several studies show that coverage of news stories relating to Islam has greatly increased in the last two decades (Niemelä and Christensen 2013, 14; Lundby and Gresaker 2015, 80). Even though religion, it must be said, is a marginal topic in the news (Lundby and Gresaker 2015), cases related to Islam seem to be over-represented in the Norwegian news media, if compared to the size of the Muslim population.[11] This coverage seems to be constantly high (relative to other news pieces on religion), even in years that have no major events connected to Islam (IMDI 2010).

The teachers perceive, and describe, the coverage of Islam as being constant and intense. The news coverage of Islam is something encountered on a daily basis, as part of normal everyday life. This is frequently communicated in both the interviews and the lessons observed, for example, when Guro asks her students about what image from the media they meet on an everyday basis, or the students in a lesson talk about the effects of hearing about Islam 'all the time'. News coverage related to Islam is thus seen as being part of the everyday background, something that the students encounter, and are exposed to, regularly.

This steady coverage is punctuated by short periods when there is massive coverage of terror attacks tied to radical Islamism.[12] When these events occur, the teachers tell me, the students are both interested and active in acquiring information. In these periods they follow the news more closely. The episodes mentioned explicitly in the interviews are the *Charlie Hebdo* attack in Paris in January 2015 and the Bataclan attacks in Paris in November 2015.[13] I asked Kari if she thought the students were interested in the news.

> Normally it varies. Now[14] they're really interested, but I have often thought that they are not really that interested. But it's obvious now. And in January, with those murders in Paris. They were interested then.

---

[11] Statistics on religion are complex. Of a population of 5 million people, the Muslim population is somewhere between roughly 100,000 (based on membership in Muslim faith organizations) and 200,000 (based purely on the majority religion in their countries of origin; Sultan 2012).

[12] I use the term radical Islamism/Islamist throughout this chapter, as these are the most common terms used, both in the classroom and in the Norwegian news media, to describe violent and extremist forms of Islamism. This use is not meant to suggest that radical Islamism necessarily entails endorsing violence.

[13] This event happened during the fieldwork; two of the interviews were conducted after the attack.

[14] Immediately after the November Paris attacks.

This interplay between a constant background of news stories about Islam, and the massive and recurring coverage of violent events thus ensures, again according to the teachers, that news media representations of Islam are well known among the students, to the point that this is all they know and think about when it comes to Islam.

15.4 Conflict-Centred Coverage

The coverage of Islam in the press has been quite well researched. So it is possible to get a clear picture both of the coverage now and also of the ways in which coverage has developed over time (e.g. Said 1981; Poole 2002; Døving and Kraft 2013). In many ways, the Norwegian coverage of Islam is becoming more nuanced. More voices are being heard and journalists are steadily improving their knowledge and understanding of the complexities of a world religion like Islam (Døving and Kraft 2013). The most basic underlying premise for coverage, however, still seems to be conflict in one form or another. Conflict is the main criterion when it comes to the choice of what stories should be covered (Lundby and Gresaker 2015), the framing of the stories (Bangstad 2011; Andersson et al. 2012), and even as an editorial criterion for what voices are being let into the debates through op-eds and the like (Lunde 2013).

In her seminal work on newspaper coverage of British Muslims in the late 1990s, Poole uses the notion of 'news framework' to analyse how portrayals of British Muslims are limited to a few recurring topics, which are then seen as being related (2002, 55). By looking at the main and secondary topics in the articles, as well as which topics were referred to in the articles, she identified a 'clustering of topics that connote several dominant symbolized meanings' (83). These are mostly negative and connected to the question of whether Muslim immigrants are a threat to various aspects of the British society (2002, 83–84). Døving and Kraft show how this is also the case for Norwegian news coverage of Islam. A set of different topics are repeatedly presented together and are made part of the same framework in a way that makes them seem relevant to each other[15] (2013, 147–148). Even though the coverage of Islam seems to have become more nuanced, old patterns and representations are being repeated and reproduced. One of these is of the Muslim fundamentalist who perpetrates

---

15 The example used is how a discussion about whether a hijab may be worn as part of a police uniform may include themes like homosexuality, terrorism, and the power of Imams, without the relevance of these themes being questioned (Døving and Kraft 2013, 148).

acts of terrorism because of his faith (Poole 2002). The linkage of Islam to extremism, radicalization, and terror has been established in news coverage of Islam for a long time (Altheide 2007; Lundby and Thorbjørnsrud 2012, 99), and also well before 9/11 in 2001 (Lueg 1995). Representing faith as the main motivation for terror links international terrorism to potential terror in European countries due to immigration (Poole 2002, 70–71).

In 2015, the period in which most of the observations were conducted, the Norwegian news media paid a lot of attention to the conflict in Syria, both in itself and as the background for other stories. The refugee crisis resulting from the war didn't just affect the adjacent countries, but also led to a large increase in the number of refugees arriving in Europe. The hazardous routes taken by the refugees, the response by European countries, and questions about integration and multiculturalism, made headlines throughout the year. The Islamist organization, IS, was also covered extensively. The establishment of a self-proclaimed Islamic Caliphate in Syria and Iraq attracted attention, especially as IS attracted foreign warriors from around the world. Their harsh laws, brutal treatment of prisoners and civilians, as well as their skills in advertising themselves through various forms of digital media, made them the symbol of extremist Islamism worldwide. The link between IS, the recruitment of European foreign warriors to Syria, and the threat of terror from refugees, or at least from people masquerading as refugees, was also a recurring theme in the Norwegian news coverage.[16] The Norwegian Islamist group The Ummah of the Prophet, gained much attention in this regard for supporting terrorist attacks, warning against attacks on Norwegian soil, and its involvement in the recruitment of foreign warriors to Syria (Bangstad 2014, 66).

The major concern, shared by all the teachers, is that the students have prejudices and negative sentiments towards Muslims. The teachers go far in assuming that the constant and conflict-centred media coverage shapes the way the students think about Islam and Muslims.

> Guro: I think it's important to challenge prejudices and established images, and do something about them.
>
> Interviewer: Do you experience there being prejudices there [with the students]?
>
> Guro: A lot! A lot, a lot, a lot.

---

[16] With the most explicit example perhaps being the Islam critical organization, Human Rights Service, which published an article saying that if Norway accepts 10,000 refugees, as many as 8,000 of them may be IS sympathizers (https://www.rights.no/2015/06/minst-8-000-is-sympatisorer-hentes-til-norge/; Accessed 6 April 2017).

As shown in Chapter 13, creating tolerance and understanding across religious boundaries is one of the main formulated goals for the subject 'Religion and Ethics'. The teachers therefore emphasize that the prevention and countering of prejudices is an important part of the pedagogical mandate of RE in the first place. These teachers use words like 'unavoidable', 'unnatural to omit', and 'necessary' to describe why they need to address the issues covered in the news media. The underlying premise is that the association of Islam with terrorism, conflict, and controversy is already firmly established among the students, and this needs to be addressed, corrected, and nuanced, or the result will be that prejudices and a negative view of Islam and Muslims prevail.

15.5 Islam in the Classroom: Prototypes and Cognitive Frames

Anne Lise: OK, we'll start on Islam. What do you think about when I say Islam?

Boy: Allah!

Anne Lise: Can you all come to the blackboard and write what you think about when I say Islam?

Some students stand up, most stay at their desks by their laptops.

There is a lot of unrest. As some write, others make jokes. A boy shouts, 'Allahu Akbar!' This evokes laughter from most of the class. Two boys talk quietly about the Islamic state and terrorism. I overhear another conversation between three students, about terrorism.

After a minute or so the students have written a list of words on the blackboard: Allah, mosque, IS, Shia and Sunni, kaba, Id, Eid Mubarak, hijab, The five pillars, and Ramadan.

A group of students discuss with the boy that wrote 'IS'.

Boy: Are you sick?

Boy: It is the first thing I think about when I hear Islam.

Boy: And you call us racist when we joke about it?

Anne Lise brings the class to order again.

Anne Lise: These are the things you think about? How about the things portrayed in the media?

Boy: It's propaganda.

Boy: Media portrays Islam as ... crazy people.

One boy says quietly to another: 'Are you allowed to say that?' He replies: 'Well, it's true.'

Anne Lise: How does this affect you?

Boy: Well it affects the way we see them, as dangerous people.

Girl: They focus on the terrorist part of Islam, the terrorist groups, and that's all we get to see. So it all becomes very negative.

Anne Lise: Are you able to separate facts about Islam from the image created by the media? There are a lot of prejudices created about the religion of Islam, aren't there? We will watch a clip from YouTube.

Boy: [*Interrupts*] After the 22nd of July, several people though …

Boy: Several Muslim people were beaten up.

Boy: So the first impression was that it was terror from Muslims.

(Anne Lise's lesson, 22 September 2015)

This episode, among several similar observations, shows support for the teachers' claims that terrorism is what the students think about when they hear the word Islam. The change in the class was sudden. At the start of the lesson they talked about dates for tests and holidays. However, immediately after Anne Lise introduced Islam, the mentions of terrorism surfaced. These were mainly jokey and within small groups, and were not addressed to the class as a whole, but they were loud enough for everybody to notice.

Two more things are worth noting. The first is that although terrorism was a theme among the students, this was in no way the only thing they thought about when they heard the word Islam. Several relevant terms were written on the blackboard, and the one item tied to terrorism (IS) was challenged internally by the students. The second point is that, at least in the full class discussion, most of the students show that they have a strong awareness of how the news media cover Islam. In fact, a lot of the students subscribe to the same view as the teachers. They hold that the media create prejudices and that the information you get from the media is one-sided at best. Most of the time, the students, with some exceptions, argued against the notion that terror and conflict were important aspects of Islam. The lack of negative claims and sentiments about Islam and Muslims was striking across all the classes,[17] and a large variety of discourses and opinions were heard.

These observations suggest that the influence of the news media is complex. There is little support for describing the influence as a one-way effect that deter-

---

[17] Of course, this does not mean that they necessarily don't hold those views. They may be afraid to voice them, as the students are getting grades in the subject, and/or they may not want to appear to be prejudiced. They may be too 'politically correct' to voice their views, as Erik put it in one interview. Still, most students express opinions that challenge any such negative sentiments.

mines the students' views on Islam and Muslims. As early as 1972, McCombs and Shaw problematized the power of the mass media to shape the way people think, arguing instead that the media's ability to mentally order and organize our world for us is perhaps the most important media influence. They quoted Bernard Cohen's assertion that the press 'may not be successful ... in telling people what to think, but it is stunningly successful in telling its readers what to think *about*', (Cohen 1963, quoted in McCombs and Shaw 1972, 177).

I propose to understand the observations through the two related concepts of prototypes and cognitive frames. I claim that the most important influence of the media coverage of Islam consists of:
a) Establishing and constantly reinforcing the association of the terms 'Muslim' and 'Islam' with extremism and terrorism, and
b) Establishing and maintaining cognitive frames which give us access to set ways of interpreting reality, but with room for conflicting views and discourses.

Using these two concepts provides us with a way to understand the classroom interaction, without having to make too far-reaching assumptions about what the students actually think, while still being able to account for the strong association that has been observed between Islam and terrorism, conflict, and controversies.

15.5.1 Prototypes

> There is a tendency, rooted in our usual forms of expression, to think that the man who has learnt to understand a general term, say, the term 'leaf', has thereby come to possess a kind of general picture of a leaf, as opposed to pictures of particular leaves. (Wittgenstein undated, 30)

In his attempt to clarify what he saw as philosophical confusions, Wittgenstein made the observation that we don't think in concepts that encompass all the essential properties of the term. This doesn't mean that we're not able to formulate common properties, but that the way we think about them is not in the form of general images. Rather, we tend to think by way of prototypes, where particular images come to mind when we think of a term, even though we know that the term often includes a lot of different varieties. Gullestad shows how prototypes played an important part in the Norwegian debates about immigration in the late 1990s. The example she used was how the prototypes for immigrants in Oslo at that time was 'Muslim' and 'Pakistani', even though this was not included in any lexical definition of the word immigrant. Gullestad claims this enabled debaters to talk about immigrants in general, while it was obvious to anyone listening that they meant only a small and particular group of immigrants (2002, 89–90).

Several Muslim students said they felt that the image of the extremist/Muslim was present among all the other students. Furthermore, they seldom had alternative images of what the Muslim students called 'ordinary Muslims'. This didn't mean that their classmates equated 'Muslims' with 'extremists', but that the extremist/Muslim image was established as the first thing that sprang to mind.[18] This concurs with the teachers' descriptions, that when students hear the word Islam, they think about what's in the media (i.e. terror and conflict).

The strength of using the concept of prototypes in relation to this material is that it allows us to distinguish between a prototype and an opinion. Perhaps terrorism is the first thing most of the students think of when they hear the word 'Islam',[19] but this does not necessarily correlate with their opinions about Muslims. However, the prototype of the extremist/terrorist also seems to be connected to a wider range of concepts that are related to the threat of radical Islamism, both globally and locally.[20] To account for this, I turn to the concepts of framing and cognitive frames.

15.5.2 Framing and Cognitive Frames

In media and communication studies, the concept of framing was developed as a tool for understanding media influence. According to Entman, frame analysis is helpful in examining the influence exerted by the 'transfer (or communication) of information from one location – such as a speech, utterance, news report, or novel – to that [human] consciousness' (1993, 51–52). Framing is to 'select some aspects of a perceived reality and make them more salient in a communicative text, in such a way as to promote a particular problem definition, moral evaluation, and/or treatment recommendation for the item described' (ibid., 52). The theory of framing relies on the ways in which we make sense of the world

---

[18] This is discussed in a Norwegian article about the Muslim students' views on RE about Islam (Toft, 2017).
[19] It even seems plausible that the teachers do the same.
[20] For example, how the mention of IS was often followed by reference to terror in Europe, to fundamentalist interpretations of the Koran, to the oppression of women, or to immigration or refugees. Just as often, it was the other way around: a discussion of immigrants, gender roles, or the Koran might suddenly include mention of IS or the Taliban.

through cognitive frames, an insight that has been developed across a range of disciplines and fields. Fillmore, a linguist, gives this example:

> Here is an example of a cognitive frame. There is in English, and presumably in every language spoken by people with a money economy, a semantic domain connected with what we might call the commercial event. The frame for such an event has the form of a scenario containing roles that we can identify as the buyer, the seller, the goods, and the money. ... Any one of the many words in our language that relate to this frame is capable of activating the whole frame. Thus, the whole commercial event scenario is available or 'activated' in the mind of anybody who comes across or understands any of the words 'buy', 'sell', 'pay', 'cost', 'spend', 'charge', etc., even though each of these highlights or foregrounds only one small section of the frame. (Fillmore 1976, 25)

Frames can be said to be cognitive toolkits, or symbolic–interpretative constructs, the main idea being that humans order experiences by relating them to already known patterns (Triandafyllidou and Fotiou 1998). As Fillmore puts it, framing is 'the appeal, in perceiving, thinking, and communicating, to structured ways of interpreting experiences' (1976, 20). We do not go around with every bit of information we possess in the foreground of our consciousness, but we make use of associations, schemata, and frames to understand and interpret what's going on around us (Goffmann 1973).

According to Entman, this is also the case in conversations, and even in thinking (1993). Frames are activated by coming across words that form part of the frame, and a frame often has a set of central concepts that will activate the frame for the listener. Frames can be individual, and different people can use a wide variety of frames (Scheufele 1999), but there are often a stock of commonly invoked frames in social groupings, the *culture*, an empirically demonstrable set of common frames that are exhibited in the discourse and thinking of most of the people in a social grouping (Entman 1993, 53).

Using the concept of cognitive frames provides us with a way to understand how different themes and words are being grouped together in ways that make them relevant to each other. Perhaps more importantly, the activation and application of a frame does not necessarily determine the discourses or opinions of the people using them.

15.5.3 The 'Radical Islamist' Frame

I propose that the 'radical Islamist' (RI) frame[21] is such a commonly invoked frame, established by the news media as the dominant source of information about events around the world, but, more importantly, maintained and reinforced by a constant reactivation of the frame on a (more or less) daily basis. The frame revolves around the radical Islamist, a person or group, who wants to establish a state under Islamic rule that is guided by the Sharia and is modelled on the Caliphate of the first generations after Muhammad. The radical Islamist is prepared to use violence, and sees terrorism as part of the Jihad, the holy war against the unbelievers (most often the West), and is willing to die as a martyr. The radical Islamist is a threat to Europe (and Norway), as we already have a Muslim population among which some, or many, may be radical Islamists, or may potentially be recruited by charismatic mosque leaders or extremist groups, either globally or locally, and as refugees from Muslim areas, some may sympathize with the Islamists, and some may be sent here under cover. I do not argue that other frames are not in play, but the RI frame provides a comprehensive way of interpreting and making sense of the ways in which different topics and terms were clustered and brought up in the classroom.

15.6 The Prototype and the Radical Islamist Frame in Play

As seen in the above select examples, and as several other observations confirm, the mention of Islam seems to raise the prototype of the terrorist immediately in the classroom, resulting in different discussions within the radical Islamist (RI) frame. For example, the cry of '*Allahu Akbar*' was jokingly uttered by a student, who was imitating the stereotypical terrorist, just as talk of suicide bombs and the hijacking of planes occurred often, and discussion, and mentions of IS took place in most of the classes observed. Even more striking was the way that class discussions about very different topics soon begin to follow the same patterns and to include similar references and themes. I will give one example in which the teacher activates the RI frame, whereupon this impacts upon the lesson's content.

---

21 Constructed here as a heuristic device to account for patterns observed in the data.

Kari starts a brainstorming session to find out what the class associates with Islam. The class responds with 'the Koran', 'Allah', 'the five pillars', 'Shia and Sunni', 'mosque', and 'Muhammad'. As they suggest words, Kari writes them on the blackboard. They move quickly through the words until a boy says 'sharia'.

Kari: Yes, what is sharia?

Boy: Isn't that rules?

Kari wipes away some of the words, rearranging the space around 'sharia'.

Kari: I need more space if we are to write more about sharia.

Boy: I thought it was a court of law.

Kari: I think you wanted to say more?

Boy: Haram.

Girl: And halal.

Kari: But sharia? What is that? Someone asked about it, but it sort of stopped there.

Noora, one of the Muslim girls, starts talking about the sources of sharia and the Four Schools of Law. After a short while, Kari takes over.

Kari: And there is a lot of discussion about whether to use it or not.

Boy: Use where?

Kari: There are some countries that use it, and some of the laws are a bit …

She hesitates, and flips through the textbook.

Kari: We can turn to page 156 in the textbook.

This page is about Islamism and the question of whether a society should be based on Islamic law and sharia.

Kari: So Islamists want to spread sharia in society, that society should be based on sharia. And then there's the hudud punishments, they have drawn a lot of attention. They are detailed on the next page. 'That theft shall be punished by the amputation of the hand.'

The students are shocked by this, and soon the discussion turns to how Muslims in Norway relate to the hudud punishments and to Norwegian laws and values. Most of the class agrees that it does not represent a danger to Norwegian society, as Norwegian Muslims don't generally want sharia rule in Norway.

(Kari's lesson 5 November 2015)

This example illustrates a typical pattern that was observed across classes. A central concept of Islam – in this case, sharia – comes up. For Kari, this activates the RI frame and consequently also the concern for what the students might think about what she sees as a potentially controversial issue. As the class carries on with the brainstorming, Kari finds it important to halt and expand on this, and it doesn't take long before the topics are the hudud-punishments and radical Islamists. Similar situations occurred in both Anne Lise's and Hanne's classes. In Anne Lise's case, her lesson about the ethics of Islam turned into a discussion about the hudud punishments in less than five minutes. Hanne saw the need to include a long session on the hudud punishments, with reference to IS, in her lessons on different voices in the Norwegian media debates. The same pattern was observed in lessons about gender and gender roles, an important curricular aim in relation to all religions. In all eight classes observed, the discussions included references to Saudi Arabia and Iran, the Taliban and IS, as well as the question of whether Norwegian Muslims oppressed women because of their interpretations of the Koran.

This sweeping use of examples may give the impression that all of the lessons about Islam were about radical Islamism and terror. I have to stress that this was not the case at all. Although this was something that was often the theme of lessons, most focused on other aspects of Islam. However, one of the points illustrated is how easy any topic could almost seamlessly include elements from the RI frame.[22]

In the example, above, we can also see how different frames can be applied and contested. The central question is not 'What is sharia?' rather, it is 'What do we, in this context, see sharia as an example of?' There are, at least, three different interpretations in play in this example:
1) The object of the lesson is brainstorming about central terms related to Islam. Sharia is one of several such terms. (Most of the students)
2) The object is defining sharia as a concept and its sources. (Noora)
3) The object is the debate about the implementation of sharia-based laws. (Kari)

Once the object of the lesson is settled by Kari, the RI frame is activated for most of the students, turning the debate into one mainly about Islamism.

15.7 Media Influence

Returning to the question of media influence, there seem to be reasons for saying that there is a significant influence of the news media on the lessons about Islam. However, this influence is multifaceted. The most obvious influence of

---

[22] Most of these transitions felt natural and relevant in the classroom situation, as they did to me as an observer.

the news media on RE about Islam in the material observed is the way the teachers take the media coverage into account when planning their lessons, and this is manifested in altered pedagogical practices. This influence is dynamic and complex, though. The teachers actively choose how to relate to the news media in the classroom, remediating, nuancing, and, on several occasions, challenging and negating the content, claims, and views expressed in various media. We thus do not see a situation where the news media determine the way Islam is being represented in the classroom; rather, we see teachers consciously planning their lessons with a basis in pedagogical reasons that agree with the aims and mandate of RE to counter possible negative sentiments and prejudices towards Islam and Muslims created by the media coverage. This revolves around their assumption that all students associate Islam with terrorism, a notion that seems plausible, based on the observations in this study. We do not, however, find support for the assumption that the majority of the students have strong prejudices, and that their opinions are determined by the news media. Rather we see a large range of claims, discourses and opinions about Islam and Muslims, many of them in opposition to the perceived negative media coverage.

I have argued that the way the news media establish and maintain frames influences the classroom in several ways. Even though the media are currently becoming more nuanced in their coverage and make room for a wider range of voices in relation to Islam, established patterns and clusterings of topics are still repeated and reproduced. Maintained by a continuous stream of low key coverage of different stories put into this frame, this seems to influence the classroom scene. Everyone is familiar with the frame and thus the teachers' need to address this is warranted.

However, this also means that constantly thematizing terrorism and radical Islamism in the lessons about Islam strengthens the perceived relevance of the frame, as well as the terrorist prototype, even when explicitly saying that Islam and terrorism aren't closely connected. Lakoff, in a book aimed at liberal politicians in the US, offers an important insight for those wishing to influence the opinions of others. Words are defined relatively to frames. 'When we negate a frame, we evoke the frame. ... When you are arguing against the other side, do not use their language. Their language picks out a frame – and it won't be the frame you want' (Lakoff 2014, 19). Even though the intention behind talking about how media coverage of Islam is centred on conflict and terrorism is to show that this is not a fair representation of Islam, the result is to confirm that this is the most relevant and important thing to discuss when learning about Islam. In this regard it seems that the RE lessons about Islam actually work in synergy with the news media. In some cases, the school even strengthens the frame, by making aspects of it an important part of the pedagogical practice.

Bibliography

Altheide, David L. 2007. "The mass media and terrorism." *Discourse & Communication* 1 (3), 287–308.
Andersson, Mette, Christine M. Jacobsen, Jon Rogstad, and Viggo Vestel. 2012. *Kritiske hendelser – nye stemmer: Politisk engasjement og transnasjonal orientering i det nye Norge.* [Critical events – new voices: political engagement and transnational orientation in the new Norway]. Oslo: Universitetsforlaget.
Bangstad, Sindre. 2011. "The morality police are coming! Muslims in Norway's media discourses." *Anthropology Today*, 27 (5): 3–7.
Bangstad, Sindre. 2014. *Anders Breivik and the Rise of Islamophobia.* London: Zed.
Døving, Cora Alexa, and Siv Ellen Kraft. 2013. *Religion i pressen.* [Religion in the press]. Oslo: Universitetsforlaget.
Entman, Robert M. 1993. "Framing: Toward Clarification of a Fractured Paradigm." *Journal of Communication* 43 (4): 51–58.
Fillmore, Charles J. 1976. "Frame Semantics and the Nature of language." *Annals of the New York Academy* 280: 20–32.
Furseth, Inger. 2015. *Religionens tilbakekomst i offentligheten?: Religion, politikk, medier, stat og sivilsamfunn i Norge siden 1980-tallet.* [The return of religion in the public sphere?]. Oslo: Universitetsforlaget.
Goffman, Erving. 1974. *Frame Analysis: An Essay on the Organization of Experience.* New York: Harper & Row.
Gullestad, Marianne. 2002. *Det norske sett med nye øyne: kritisk analyse av norsk innvandringsdebatt.* [The Norwegian reconceptualized]. Oslo: Universitetsforlaget.
Hjarvard, Stig. 2008. *The Mediatization of Religion.* Bristol: Intellect.
Hjarvard, Stig. 2013. *The Mediatization of Society and Culture.* New York: Routledge.
IMDI 2010. *Innvandrere i norske medier: Medieskapt islamfrykt og usynlig hverdagsliv.* [Immigrants in Norwegian media]. Årsrapport 2009. Oslo: IMDI.
Lakoff, George. 2014. *The All New Don't Think of an Elephant!: Know Your Values and Frame The Debate.* White River Junction, VT: Chelsea Green Publishing.
Lundby, Knut, ed. 2009. *Mediatization: Concept, Changes, Consequences.* New York: Peter Lang.
Lundby, Knut, ed. 2014. *Mediatization of Communication.* Handbooks of Communication Science, 21. Berlin: De Gruyter Mouton.
Lundby, Knut, and Ann Kristin Gresaker. 2015. "Religion i mediene – omstridt og oversett?" [Religions in the media – contested and ignored?] In *Religionens tilbakekomst i offentligheten?: Religion, politikk, medier, stat og sivilsamfunn i Norge siden 1980-tallet* [The return of religion in the public sphere?], edited by Inger Furseth, 69–104. Oslo: Universitetsforlaget.
Lundby, Knut, and Kjersti Thorbjørnsrud. 2012. "Mediatization of Controversy: When the Security Police Went on Facebook." In *Mediatization and Religion: Nordic Perspectives*, edited by Stig Hjarvard and Mia Lövheim, 95–108. Gothenburg: Nordicom.

Lunde, Anders F. 2013. "– Det er opp til muslimene. Redaksjonelle ledere om islam i den norske offentligheten." [– It is up to the Muslims]. Master's thesis. University of Oslo.

Lueg, Andrea. 1995. "The Perceptions of Islam in Western debate." In *The Next Threat: Western Perceptions of Islam*, edited by Jochen Hippler and Andrea Lueg, 7–32. London: Pluto Press.

McCombs, Maxwell and Donald Shaw. 1972. "The Agenda-Setting Function of Mass Media." *Public Opinion Quarterly* 36 (2): 176–187.

Niemelä, Kati, and Henrik Reintoft Christensen. 2013. "Religion in Newspapers in The Nordic Countries in 1988–2008." *Nordic Journal of Religion and Society* 26 (1): 5–24.

Poole, Elizabeth. 2002. *Reporting Islam: Media Representations of British Muslims*. London: I. B. Tauris.

Said, Edward W. 1981. *Covering Islam: How the Media and the Experts Determine How We See the Rest of the World*. London: Routledge & Kegan Paul.

Scheufele, D. A. 1999. "Framing as a Theory of Media Effects." *Journal of Communication* 49 (1): 103–122.

Sultan, Shoaib. 2012. "Medlemskap i norske moskeer." [Membership in Norwegian mosques]. In *Religionsstatistikk og medlemsforståelse* [Statistics of religion and understanding of membership], edited by Ingunn Folkestad Breistein and Ida Marie Høeg. Trondheim: Akademika.

Thorbjornsrud, Kjersti, Tine Ustad Figenschou, and Øyvind Ihlen. (2014). "Mediatization of Public Bureaucracies." In *Mediatization of Communication*, edited by Knut Lundby, 402–422. Handbooks of Communication Science, 21. Berlin: De Gruyter Mouton.

Toft, Audun. 2017. "Islam i klasserommet. Unge muslimers opplevelse av undervisning om islam." [Islam in the classroom. Young Muslims' experiences with education about Islam]. In *Ungdom og Religion*, edited by Ida Marie Høeg, 33–50. Oslo: Universitetsforlaget.

Triandafyllidou, Anna, and Anastasios Fotiou. 1998. "Sustainability and Modernity in the European Union: A Frame Theory Approach to Policy-Making." *Sociological Research Online* 3 (1).

Utdanningsdirektoratet (UDIR). 2006. Læreplan i Religion og Etikk. [National curriculum of Religion and Ethics]. Accessed 9 Aug 2017. https://www.udir.no/kl06/REL1-01

Wittgenstein, Ludwig. n.d., ca. 1934. *Blue Book*. Rose Rand Papers, 1903–1981. Archives of Scientific Philosophy, Special Collections Department, University of Pittsburgh. http://digital.library.pitt.edu/u/ulsmanuscripts/pdf/31735061817932.pdf

Part III: **Crosscurrents**

Mona Abdel-Fadil, Louise Lund Liebmann
Chapter 16
Gender, Diversity and Mediatized Conflicts of Religion: Lessons from Scandinavian Case Studies

Abstract: Drawing on empirical data from the Scandinavian project Engaging with Conflicts in Mediatized Religious Environments (CoMRel), this chapter analyses the findings from case-studies in: classrooms, online communities, public service media (PSM) production rooms, local news outlets, and interreligious dialogue initiatives. Gender and ethno-religious diversity receive particular analytical attention. We discuss the multiple ways in which various social actors in Scandinavia engage with mediatized conflicts about religion, and the ways in which dominant media frames are replicated, contested, and nuanced. A main finding is that mediatized conflicts about religion are symptomatically entangled in a dichotomy between good or bad religion, and that social actors in the diverse settings are often cast in the role of 'the ideal citizen' or 'the religious other'. Despite attempts at going beyond enmeshed discourses of immigration and othering, and a general awareness of the dominant media frame 'Islam as a bad religion', the frame proves difficult to overcome.

Keywords: gender dimensions, ethno-religious diversity, mediatized conflicts, media frames, securitization of Islam, Scandinavia, emblematic religion, othering

16.1 Mediatized Conflicts

In *Contested Religion: The Media Dynamics of Cultural Conflicts in Scandinavia*, we examine how media condition public engagement with contested issues about religion in a variety of social settings in Scandinavia. Our case studies in Norway, Sweden, and Denmark are founded on conceptually driven comparisons. The strength of our research is that we approach the case studies with a range of epistemological backgrounds and methodological tools and across a variety of social settings, yet are interested in overlapping questions and conceptualizations of media, religion, and conflict. Our methods include a quantitative survey, participant observation, qualitative interviews, focus group interviews, analysis of media content, multi-sited fieldworks, and an online ethnography.

Our unique and rich data are collected from various media-saturated environments in Scandinavia, such as classrooms, online communities, public service media (PSM) production rooms, local news outlets, and interreligious dialogue initiatives. Drawing on the entire body of case studies, in this chapter we ask the following: In what way and to what extent are media implicated in conflicts about religion in Scandinavia? This chapter moves across the different case studies in the book. We discuss and analyse the findings of the previous chapters, and highlight the commonalities and crosscurrents that we find across the empirical cases. We delimit our discussion to the ways in which the intersection of gender, diversity, and media frames of religion play out across the case studies described in previous chapters. In particular, this chapter reflects on how gender dimensions and the management of diversity are implicated in mediatized conflicts in the various studies. The chapter also reflects upon the theories of mediatization of religion and the mediatized conflicts outlined in the first part of the book (see Chapters 3 and 4). The further development and revision of the mediatization theory based on our case studies will nonetheless be dealt with in more detail in Chapter 17.

By management of diversity, we refer to the social practices of addressing, supporting and framing ethnic and/or religious minorities. We delimit our discussion of the management of diversity to the empirical findings from our cases (Chapters 5–15). The interrelation between media, culture, social life, and politics, is one of mutual influence and thus important to analyze (Hepp, Hjarvard and Lundby 2015; Eskjær, Hjarvard and Mortensen 2015). Put simply, media, shape culture, social life and politics – and vice versa – as media brings about dual functions, reflecting and shaping issues occurring within these three domains. A fundamental theoretical premise across the case studies is that frames direct our perception, thought, and action during social and media events (Goffman 1986, 10–11) for which reason control and distribution of frames is a prime concern in the operation and analysis of management. What emerges is a highly mobile manner of directing collective conduct, which traverses and correlates social spaces with frame spaces (Jacobsen 2016, 30). Framing processes involve processes of selection and salience and tend to promote problem definitions, causal interpretation, moral evaluation, and treatment recommendation for the people and incidents described (Entman 1993, 52, See Chapters 11, 15). In other words, media frames, framing and frameworks illustrate how communicative 'texts' exercise power (ibid.) and, thus, framing processes inadvertently bring about implicit forms of governance that may be analytically excavated.

Frames are more salient when certain aspects of the frame resonate with an individual's cognitive schema or themes already established in public discourse, such as 'Islam = bad religion'. According to Ettema (2005, 133), the success of a frame relies on the ability of a frame to 'strike a responsive chord' and 'draw upon a cultural repertoire of themes and stories'. Still, in our case studies, we also find that dominant frames do not go uncontested in the various social settings we study, although some counter-frames are less successfully crafted than others (see Chapters 8 and 11), or receive less consideration than the dominant frames (see Chapter 6). At times, the salience and appeal of certain frames lead to a disproportionate amount of attention to a news story such as in the case of 'the Swedish handshake' (see Chapter 13).

In this chapter, we explore the interplay between media, religion, and conflict across a range of social settings, and take into consideration that media audiences are not simply uncritical recipients of media frames. Audiences engage with and contest media stories and events, but are nonetheless affected by dominant media frames. We have looked into the multiple ways in which social actors in Scandinavia engage with conflict and dominant media frames – ways that include contesting media frames, as well as replicating and nuancing them.[1] In the World Values Survey, Scandinavia counts as the most secular corner of the world. The levels of personal religious practice and religious self-identification are low. However, the majority of the population in all three countries are members of the national Lutheran Church. For most members, the affiliation to the church is more of a cultural belonging than matter of personal belief (see Chapters 2, 4, 6, and 10; Marzouki et al. 2016). While, there is a broad historical Protestant Christian tradition in Scandinavia (see in particular Chapters 1 and 2), today, this region comprises a greater diversity of religious and secular worldviews. While there are commendable attempts at ensuring a broader and unbiased representation of religious and ethnic minorities in Scandinavian media, minorities are often under-represented or stereotypically portrayed in the media at large (Axner 2016, 2015; Jørndrup 2017; Figenschou and Beyer 2014). The chapters in this book on 'contesting religion' focuses precisely on controversies and mediatized conflicts about religion that arise with diversity.

16.2 Managing Diversity

Religious and ethnic diversity can be managed in a variety of ways. Interestingly, all the empirical findings from our case studies and survey demonstrate that in a Scandinavian context, Islam is repeatedly pitted against either

---

[1] On framing, see Chapter 3 and Chapter 7.

Christianity or secularism – rendering other belief systems close to irrelevant. As previous chapters have elucidated, contestations of religion are enmeshed in discourses about immigration and othering, and majority and minority population relations (see Chapters 6–15). Here, we reflect on how religious diversity is managed in a variety of Scandinavian contexts, based on the empirical findings presented in the previous chapters. While our analysis across the Scandinavia case studies focuses primarily on how issues of framing, gender, and diversity are managed with regards to primarily Islam and Christianity, we are in no way suggesting that there are no other important belief systems or minority religions in the region. Nor is our purpose to make a normative claim about what ethno-religious diversity essentially entails. Instead, we reflect on the multitude of empirical ways (See Chapters 1–15) in which mediatized contestations of religion play out in present-day Scandinavia. The omnipresence of 'dominant negative media frames' is palpable in our study. Such frames depict Islam as an authoritarian, oppressive, and violent religion, which clashes with so-called 'Scandinavian values'. Dominant frames are remediated in a variety of Scandinavian social settings (see Chapters 6–15), and shape the ways in which diversity is managed in everyday social interactions.

A striking similarity across many of the case studies is the manner in which dealing with the dominant media frames about Islam head-on is considered a necessary – and perhaps somewhat courageous – act of facing 'the elephant in the room'. 'Conflict and Islam, that's the elephant in the room,' says a secondary school teacher (Chapter 15), when describing how she feels obliged to talk about the negative media frames about Islam. Yet, by repeatedly referring to news coverage with the purpose of countering dominant frames about Islam, teachers may unintentionally serve to reinforce and confirm the association of Islam with controversy. We argue that despite a general awareness of dominant media frames, they nonetheless seem difficult to overcome. Indeed, the dominant images of Muslims and Islam are continuously reproduced, remediated, or renegotiated in *all* of the Scandinavian settings we have studied.

This dilemma is partially addressed by some of the social actors we study, for instance by the teachers and PSM producers in Chapters 7, 13, 14, and 15, which suggests that teachers and PSM producers believe they cannot ignore the dominant negative frames, yet at the same time they struggle with *how* to talk about their content in a manner that neither offends religious minorities, nor contributes to giving such frames more momentum. Coupled with this self-awareness is the fear of cementing the idea that Islam is a 'bad religion'. Essentially, the teachers, PSM producers, social media users, and participants in inter-religious dialogues all face the same predicament. On the one hand, they feel compelled to interact with the dominant frames – without condoning them –

and on the on the other hand they are acutely aware of the fact that they may unintentionally come to reinforce the image of Islam as a 'bad religion' and Muslims as less than ideal citizens. For instance, in the interreligious dialogue meetings or religious education (RE) classes, by stating that Muslims are 'not just terrorists', one simultaneously reinforces the idea that many Muslims *are* indeed terrorists (Lakoff 2014, as discussed in Chapter 15; see also Chapter 11).

Across the case studies we see how social actors, even those who attempt to do otherwise, may get entrapped by stereotypical representations. In Chapter 11, Kinnvall and Nesbitt-Larking's (2011, 275) term 'banal securitization' is used as a signifier of the ways in which the securitization of Islam[2] affects the everyday lives of Scandinavian Muslims in highly tangible ways (see also Chapter 12). 'Banal securitization of Islam', as defined in Chapter 11, denotes everyday practices in which people and themes are categorized in stereotypical terms in response to macro-events with local ramifications. Thus, the banal securitization of Islam applies to the ways in which Muslims are perceived by scores of others in light of global media events. Teachers (Chapters 13–15), PSM producers (Chapters 7 and 8), as well as social media users (Chapters 6 and 9), irrespective of their own personal faith or inclination towards secularism or atheism, all contribute to the 'banal securitization' of religion.

Still, PSM producers, school teachers, participants in interreligious dialogue programmes – are all acutely aware of the risks of reinforcing negative stereotypes about Muslims and go to great pains to try to fashion counter-narratives about Islam. Members of the Danish PSM production team in Chapter 7 explicitly state that they feel cornered into a choice between the entrenched positions of being either an Islam basher or an Islam apologist, neither of which appeals to them. In their efforts to stay clear of both, the Danish PSM producers downplay the religious identity of their participants, which may well result in a depiction that transcends 'the religious other' ascribed representation (Nadim 2017). While, this strategy provides more nuanced representation of religious and ethnic minorities, it nonetheless demonstrates how Danish PSM producers are locked into a dialectic relationship with the dominant media frames that posit Islam as a 'bad religion'. PSM producers may inadvertently end up reinforcing the negative stereotypes about Muslims as well as the dominant media frames that posit Islam as a 'bad religion', For instance, Swedish PSM producers aim to present an alternative to the dominant negative media discourses by providing

---

[2] Jocelyne Cesari (2013) and others have coined the term 'securitization of Islam' for the rhetorical tropes, partly induced by the media, that depict Muslims in Western countries constitute as a threat to national security.

a platform for the equal representation of Christianity and Islam (Chapter 8). Nonetheless, they end up reinforcing dominant frames about Islam as a problematic religion to be associated with violence and extremism. Despite the producers' initial intent to provide a more nuanced representation of Islam, the programme *Människor och tro* (People and belief), ends up portraying Christianity as a 'good religion', which in turn is contrasted to Islam.[3]

Intriguingly, the lack of viable positions and the sense of entrapment is evident in many of the case studies. Even in the case of the *Yes to wearing the cross whenever and wherever I choose* (YWC) Facebook group, in which participants appear to have a wider spectrum of ideological positions, we find that ultimately one must choose being either for or against Islam – but also – for or against Christianity and religion in general, respectively (see Chapter 6; Abdel-Fadil 2017). When taking the case studies together, it seems that completely escaping the 'good vs. bad religion' dichotomy is close to impossible. Downplaying religion altogether may well be an attempt at overcoming this good vs. bad religion dialectic (see Chapter 7), but might not necessarily resolve all tensions.

16.3 Moulding the Ideal Citizen

The good vs. bad religion frames are circumvented by Danish PSM producers' attempt to portray minority citizens in a different light (Chapter 7). Yet, in our view, rendering religion invisible, plays into the moulding of an ideal minority citizen, particularly when the alternative is 'bad religion'. A similar dynamic is in play when the inclusion of more diverse voices is attempted in the various arenas (see Chapters 5–15). Religious and ethnic minorities experience greater access to the media, when cast as 'the ethnic/religious other' (Nadim 2017). As exemplified in the PSM case from Sweden minority voices have unequal access (see Chapters 8). More importantly, a rather narrow space for the idealized citizen with a minority religious background is carved out (Schinkel 2008; van Es 2016).

Meeting the ideal requires a particular vernacular and a specific vocabulary and conduct. In this sense, diversity is encouraged but only in specific and highly governed ways. Intriguingly, it seems that the projection of the ideal religious minority citizen shapes interactions in several of the settings, not least in the interreligious dialogues, classrooms, and everyday interactions both on- and off-

---

[3] See also Mahmood Mamdani's famous article 'Good Muslim, Bad Muslim: A Political Perspective on Culture and Terrorism' (2002). Here, Mamdani deconstructs cultural explanations of political results, such as the events of September 11, and (re)situates the terrorist events in a historical and political context.

line (See Chapters 6, 8, and 11–15). Still, there appears to be an implication that all citizens ought to hold similar views. We would argue that by sidestepping discussing religion (Chapter 7), Danish PSM producers showcase articulate, idealized, minority citizens, whose real or imagined religiosity, is downplayed in an attempt to overcome representations as the 'religious other' (Nadim 2017). Still, the idealized Scandinavian citizen can take the shape of a more explicitly religious persona, albeit in governed ways. In effect, the idealized citizen must choose between 'good religion' or 'no religion', in order to avoid being associated with 'bad religion'. Despite their attempts at diversifying the participants and speakers in their shows, the Scandinavian PSM programmes still provide uneven and unequal access to religious minorities (see Chapter 8), and those who participate in public debates and interreligious forums are stylized to fit a mould of an ideal citizen (see Chapters 7, 8, 11) who is knowledgeable, peaceful, articulate, and compassionate.

In Chapter 11, Gullestad's concept of 'prototypes' is referred to and in Chapter 4, the authors write about 'emblematic' renderings of religion. What we see across many of the case studies is what can be called 'emblematic prototypes', renderings that come to reproduce the symbolic, emblematic facets of religion while simultaneously replicating prototypes – or what Amin Maalouf (2012) refers to as 'essentialized identities'. For instance, a woman who wears the hijab is reduced to 'Muslim' or the piece of cloth she wears on her head, rendering her individuality and other facets of her identity entirely irrelevant. Thus, Scandinavian Muslims do not seem to be able to escape the ways in which mediatized frames of 'Islam' seep into their everyday lives. Yet, 'emblematic prototypes' also shape the everyday interactions of the conservative Christians and atheists in YWC where there is a strong symbolic attribution to either faith or non-faith.

Across the various cases, we find the construction of the ideal Scandinavian citizen, particularly as a mould for the Muslim but also for other citizens to conform to (Liebmann 2017). Interreligious forums offer a prime space for displaying the self as the peaceful, egalitarian, rational, civilized, tolerant, empathetic – and thus idealized – citizen. Although this might be most evident in terms of moulding the ideal Muslim participant, it also goes for the other citizens (see Chapter 11). When considering the case studies together we can detect traces of how all citizens are governed in a way that is aimed at transforming them into more idealized versions of themselves and their respective citizenships whether they identify as atheists, Christians, secularists, Muslims, etc. This way, we detect the ways in which media condition processes of what in a post-Foucauldian governance sense may be referred to as 'citizen formation' (Rose [1999] 2010) in relation to religion.

In Chapter 8, we see how, somewhat surprisingly, the Swedish police academy student Donna Eljammal, posing in uniform and a hijab, was met with mostly positive feedback in the online comments to the posting of her image. Her occupational commitment to Sweden is commemorated and Donna Eljammal is framed as a national symbol of how a young Muslim woman ideally should take part in, and contribute to, Swedish society. Thus, the mediated Donna Eljammal in this rendition, comes to represent the civic ideal for a Muslim woman in Sweden.

The Norwegian PSM show *Faten tar valget* (Faten makes her choice) follows the 22-year-old (non-fictional) Faten Al-Mahdi Hussaini, a Muslim hijabi woman while she makes up her mind about which political party to vote for in the Norwegian parliamentary elections of 2017. While Swedish Donna Eljammal was for the most part hailed, Norwegian Faten Al-Mahdi Hussaini received many hateful comments about both her and the hijab, including death threats.[4]

Considering this volume's aim of examining how various media condition public engagement with contested issues about religion, it is worth reflecting on why two seemingly similar incidents in Norway and Sweden may have spurred such different responses. *Faten Makes Her Choice* evidently stirs up negative emotions among what Michailidou and Trenz (2015) call 'enraged fans'. And in this context, insisting on the removal of a young Muslim woman's hijab to prove that she is wearing it of her own free will is considered a legitimate demand. The irony of intimidating and forcing a young woman to remove a hijab in order to demonstrate that her attire is voluntary is considerable. However, what complicates the picture somewhat is that in both Norway and Sweden a number of the positive public reactions to Faten Al-Mahdi Hussaini and Donna Eljammal, respectively, emphasized how it was the *individual* and her civic engagement, not her hijab or her religion, that came to the foreground. It would seem, then, that mediation of civic engagement and participation in the democracy as an ideal citizen holds the potential to overshadow the at times near obsessive focus on the hijab in other contexts. Thus, under particular circumstances, the individuality of a media player may trump her 'ascribed representation' of a religious or ethnic group or her being cast as an 'ethnic other' as has been found to be the case in recent studies (Nadim 2017, Midtbøen 2016).

To what extent can the different responses in Sweden and Norway be attributed to differences in the debate climate, timing, medium, or stratified audien-

---

4 Faten Al-Mahdi Hussaini since repeatedly addressed the vile comments in public videos and expressed her claim to both Norwegianess and the hijab – but also exposed her vulnerability and sadness about this turn of events.

ces? Contextual factors such as the timing of the Norwegian show just before the parliamentary elections in September 2017 may have amplified the conflict around Faten Al-Mahdi Hussaini, while the predominantly middle-aged, well-educated audience of *People and Belief*, on which Donna Eljammal appeared, may have subdued the level of conflict in Sweden. Yet, there seems to be more at play. In retrospect, the massive negative response to *Faten Makes Her Choice* was perhaps more about the context of the 'cross case' and the emblematic Christianity of identity it inspired than the hijab itself. As described more in detail in Chapter 6, the cross case was a controversy in 2013 over the Norwegian Broadcasting Corporation's (NRK) decision to bar one of its news anchors from wearing her cross pendant while hosting an NRK evening news programme.

The fact that in 2017 NRK received more than 5,000 complaints about *Faten Makes Her Choice* before the show had even been aired raises suspicions that this response was coordinated. The complainers accused NRK of a double standard: NRK was allowing one form of religious attire, the hijab, but not another, the cross, on their TV programmes. In other words, the engaged, and enraged, publics were in fact primarily critiquing the neutrality policy in the NRK cross case (see Chapter 6). By extension, Faten Al-Mahdi Hussaini and her hijab are understood as a threat to the cross and its visible presence. For conservative Christians and others who see Christianity mostly as a form of belonging, rather than believing, the NRK cross case comes to symbolize the deterioration of 'Christian values' on PSM while Faten Al-Mahdi Hussaini gets to flaunt her hijab. The conflation of the principle of neutrality for news bulletins with the less strict policy for hosts of all other types of programming has been an integral part of the cross controversy from the very start, as has the erroneous perception that the cross is banned but the hijab is not in PSM programming. Regardless, both Donna Eljammal and Faten Al-Mahdi Hussaini are fashioned into prototypes of 'Muslim women' imaginaries who either conform to 'the ideal citizen' or its antithesis.

More importantly for our purposes, the brief comparison between Donna Eljammal and Faten Al-Mahdi Hussaini's experiences aptly demonstrate how meditatized conflicts about religion can be amplified, transformed, and multiplied into new conflicts based on the perseverance of particular social actors. Moreover, it demonstrates how one side of a debate may succeed in getting a disproportionate amount of attention on one particular aspect.

In some of the case studies we see a co-dependant dialectic between Islam depicted as a 'bad religion' and Christianity portrayed as a 'good religion'. But we also see that within a religion, certain renderings are deemed more desirable than others, often in accordance with or as an extension of a conceptualization of an ideal citizen. Faten Al-Mahdi Hussaini's ideal citizenship was even condoned by the prime minister of Norway who, not insignificantly, chose to highlight how Faten Al-Mahdi Hussaini has contributed actively to anti-radicalization programmes.[5]

The sense that religion comes to be more about belonging than believing cuts across several of the case studies. We repeatedly see how media condition both the culturalization and securitization of religion (see Chapter 4), most notably with regards to Islam (see Chapters 8, and 11–15) and Christianity (see Chapters 6 and 10). Within this framework, the hijab becomes emblematically linked to Islam, and the cross becomes emblematically associated with Christianity and nationhood and we see several examples of how Islam is cast as a 'bad religion' and Christianity is cast as its opposite, a 'good religion'. However, in some instances, we observe that Christianity is being contested from within (see Chapters 6 and 10) where tensions between 'golden rule Christianity' and Christianity as identity clash. Yet, in some cases it is religion per se that is cast as the villain (see Chapter 6). This draws a web of components that the ideal citizen is expected to adhere to and promote.

16.4 'The Muslim Woman'

Despite being a trope across many of the book's chapters, none of the chapters is solely devoted to what has become the most prominent symbol of cultural and religious encounters, and subsequent societal tensions, in present-day Scandinavia: 'the Muslim woman'. Muslim women have during the last 20 years repeatedly been placed at the centre of public debates in Europe and would seem an obvious point of departure in a book that explores the media dynamics of cultural conflicts in Scandinavia. The fact that the contributions in *Contested Religion* do not dwell on this matter does not mean that gender dimensions are not an interrelated part of the various case studies.

The many public debates related to the female Muslim body, clothing, and lifestyle testify to the status of the notion of what is taken to be a highly religious and oppressed – primarily Muslim – woman symbolizing what many perceive as the restraining effect of religion. Tied in with this widespread imaginary is the dominant media frame (see Chapter 3). Mass media tend to frame Islam as a distinct threat to women's rights and gender equality, thus giving way to notions of Muslim women as emblematic of religiously motivated violence. However, an al-

---

[5] Espen Alnes and Hanna Huglen Revheim, "Solberg: – Faten fortener ikkje hetsen," *NRK*, 23 Aug 2017. https://www.nrk.no/kultur/solberg_-_-faten-fortener-ikkje-hetsen-1.13655103

ternative media frame is gradually emerging in part as a response to the dominant media frame and widespread stigmatization of young Muslims as threats to national security in Western societies. Especially public service media, as analysed in Chapters 7 and 8, employ alternative frames comprised of three strands: first, a frame consisting of young Muslim women as symbols of tolerance; second, a human-interest frame in which personalization, stories, ideal cases, and emotions are deployed in the dramaturgy of the media; and third, representations of 'ordinary Muslims' with an inherent focus on Islam as (everyday) lived culture.

The focus on ordinary Muslims is a tendency which has its equivalent in the focus on lived religion as a distinct field of study within academia, a research strand that has developed over the last three decades and affords attention to everyday religion as it is lived, and practised, by millions of people (see Dessing et al. 2013; McGuire 2008).[6] But how does this alternative and budding media frame impact the way gender and religion are approached in public service media? As seen in Chapter 7, in relation to Islam, gender may, on one hand, work as a trigger theme in relation to Islam that can easily activate tensions and conflicts. On the other hand, the chapter also demonstrates how conscious planning of debates – and drawing on available professional resources in public service media – may allow gender issues such as sexuality to be addressed in relation to religion in ways that create intense debates but at the same time allow new voices and marginalized arguments to be heard – at least in comparison with traditional news agendas on Islam. One aspect of this strategy is to downplay the explicit religious dimensions of gender issues and instead discuss them as generational and cultural issues.

The much-contested trope of 'the Muslim woman', particularly when adorned with the hijab, is, as mentioned earlier, depicted as posing a threat to the idealized citizen. The hijab becomes a highly visible and emblematic symbol of Islam, and is intrinsically tied to the negative mediatized framing of Islam as a source of conflict and gender-based oppression, leading to construing a woman's active choice to wear a hijab as 'false consciousness' and in consequence 'the oppressed Muslim woman' for whom concern is expressed, is simultaneously stripped of agency by her alleged saviours (Abdel-Fadil 2006; Abu-Lughod 2013).

The tensions surrounding the hijab surface in many of the case studies. For instance, in Chapter 12 the hijab is what makes the female converts 'visibly Mus-

---

6 Studies on lived religion tend to focus on laity, instead of clergy or elites; on practices rather than beliefs; on practices outside religious institutions rather than inside; and on individual agency and autonomy rather than on collectivities or traditions (Ammerman 2016).

lim' and their identity contentious in public space. This is in stark contrast to the Muslim male converts who are not as 'visibly' Muslim. Regardless of ethnicity, women who wear the hijab are not only detectable in public space, but in effect 'hypervisible', to use Gullestad's (2006) terminology. Hypervisibility implies a distinguishability that is inescapable and fraught with tensions, often coupled with a voice that is rendered irrelevant or not listened to, i.e. silencing diversity. As discussed in Chapter 12, Muslim women who successfully wield the image of a hijabi fashionista somehow evade some of the negative projections on the hijab, and inch closer to the ideal citizen; apparently (Muslim) women cannot be all that oppressed if they wear fashionable clothes and an eye-catching lipstick colour, this logic seems to suggest.

16.5 Gendered Interactions

Mediatization implies long-term transformations of social and cultural patterns in media-saturated societies and thus shapes social interactions. However, mediatization does not determine the outcome of the social and media dynamics (see Chapter 3). The ways in which religion sometimes allows for alternative ways of imagining gender does not necessarily overthrow the mediatization thesis but it does underline the complexity of the relationship between religion and media and questions who exactly sets the agenda for how we understand religion and gender (Lövheim 2013a; Sjö 2016, 137).

Chapters 11 and 12 share a focus on the responses by Scandinavian Muslims to the predominantly negative media frames and thus of Muslims' negotiations of belonging in a mediatized society. Hence, these two case studies inhabit representational challenges symptomatic to qualitative studies of this kind. When mobilizing interlocutors – informants – for a qualitative, humanistic, or social scientific study through institutions, organizations, and networks, researchers often wind up with predominantly male participants who thus come to represent various religious affiliations and organizations in a generic sense but with a tacit, gendered bias (Rayaprol 2016). For instance, the Swedish PSM producers inadvertently reinforce traditional forms of religious authority, by inviting chairpersons, imams, and professors, who, in most cases, were male (see Chapter 8). The over-representation of men when attempting to up minority media representation appears to be part of a general tendency in Scandinavia (Jørndrup 2017). Yet, as discussed in Chapter 2, there are several differences between the ways in which men and women relate to religion in general, and with regards to media practices. These differences follow a pattern established in previous studies: female respondents seem to be more supportive of the statement that all religions should be respected, while male respondents in general seem more critical of expressions of religion in public, especially Islam, and support critical coverage of Islam and Judaism in the media more than women do. Moreover, gender has the strongest significance in the survey analysis when it comes to respondents' willingness to discuss news on religious extremism with others; men are more likely to do so than women (see Chapter 2). Men are also more inclined to discuss religion and in particular religious extremism online. Within these topics, gender is more significant than for example religious self-identification and political position. Besides reflecting persistent gender roles and positions in the Scandinavian context, these gender differences remind us of how research must always be attentive to the way in which divergences between men and women (and other genders), respectively, tie in with how different genders come to grasp, approach, and interpret religion differently.

A number of studies suggest that there is a gendered dimension to the ways in which men and women engage with social media and online debates about sensitive topics like religion and politics (see Chapter 2, 6, 11; Lövheim 2013a, 2013b). Notably, women appear to be less active in online debates and our survey in Scandinavia supports this understanding in that more men state that they frequently discuss religion online. However, the online ethnography of the Facebook page *Yes to wearing the cross whenever and wherever I choose* (YWC) (see Chapter 6) points to the importance of the triangulation of methods. In YWC we find a handful of dedicated women with particularly high levels of activity that are unparalleled by male participants. This suggests that some women may in Miller et al.'s (2016, 178) terminology be both 'doing politics' more, and participating in more *active* ways than some of the men that statistically speaking are very active online. The frequency with which women and men report to participate in online debates reveals little about the level of engagement or the emotional labour involved. Future studies must strive to nuance our understandings of gendered online involvement in mediatized conflicts with all its invisibilities and complexities.

Correspondently, another gender issue of concern to these, and other, chapters is that of gendered agency. Since the 1980s, a focus on women as religious actors has gradually occurred in response to the predominant view that religious women are passive victims of religious ideologies. In both Chapters 11 and 12, the issues of belonging – and citizenship – can be connected to gender at the intersection of religion and nationality (Sauer 2016, 108). Birgit Sauer argues that a new concept of citizenship is constructed, negotiated and promoted in European countries through the hijab debates (ibid.). This perspective ties in with discussions of how debates on covered women in Europe should be interpreted in the light of an underlying and dominant frame of secular European progress (Woodhead 2009) and with the post-secular turn in humanistic and social scientific research (Gemzöe and Keinänen 2016, 3).

So, what did we learn? We learned that two main aspects are pivotal when reflecting on gender in respect to mediatization, media frames and ethno-religious conflicts in the respective case studies. The first is the representation of gender – understood both as the relative number of participants active in mass and social media, various organizations, and local civic settings, and as the way in which gender is portrayed and comes to be enacted in these arenas. The second aspect is gendered agency in relation to, and as part of, the representations in question. Especially women's religious agency outside a simple frame of oppressor–oppressed in the field of gender and religion (Gemzöe and Keinänen 2016, 8), continues to be of significance.

In important ways, the abovementioned dominant frames and embedded debates form the background of what has been labelled the post-secular turn in humanistic and social scientific research (Gemzöe and Keinänen 2016, 3). This turn involves a questioning of earlier theories based on the premise that religion would gradually (continue to) lose importance as a social force in Europe and in the rest of the world. The turn implies instead that new theoretical frameworks, such as the sub-frames mentioned above nuancing the role of religion and gender in media (and media in gender and religion), are necessary to comprehend what religion is and is coming to be in present-day societies and how religion is related to secularism. In this, the turn also involves revisiting gender dimensions in religion, and not least in Islam. This is a task for further studies on religion and the mediatization of religion.

16.6 The Dynamics of Mediatized Conflicts of Religion

Media production teams and editors make choices that may have far-reaching ramifications of which they are unaware. For instance, they may unintentionally influence and confirm male-dominated religious hierarchies of authority or grant unequal access to social actors in their attempts to manage, diversity. The gendered and unsteady management of diversity plays into the multiple ways in which mediatized conflicts about religion are enacted, by a spectrum of social actors, in a wide range of Scandinavian online and offline mediatized social settings (see Chapters 6–15). Across the case studies, we find that minorities are frequently 'ethnicified' and/or moulded into idealized forms of minority citizens (Nadim 2017, 230).

Tensions, controversies, and conflicts have become so integral to both media coverage and audience engagement that they increasingly come to represent normalcy. Many discussions about religion in everyday life are centred around mediatized conflicts, as evidenced in the various case studies in this book. We find that various Scandinavian publics engage and interact with mediatized conflicts about religion in ways that betray an attention economy – where conflict at times is the glue of a given news story.

A striking feature across many of the cases studies is the importance of entertainment and media events. We see for instance how the school teachers lean heavily on both popular culture media products and over-focus on controversies and media events linked to religion, in particular with regard to Islam, in their attempts to reel in the students' attention (see Chapters 13–15). Likewise, the choices PSM producers make play into the media dynamics of entertainment and conflict and may in turn attract or put off publics. We must not overlook the fact that dealing full-on with controversies can in itself be viewed as a form of entertainment as evidenced in the classrooms, as well as in PSM production rooms (see Chapters 7 and 8) and in the online debates we examine (see Chapter 6).

Mass media and social media co-construct and condition worldviews and social interactions, as illustrated throughout this volume (see Chapters 3–15). *Contested Religion: The Media Dynamics of Cultural Conflicts in Scandinavia* contributes to a refined understanding of mediatization of religion, through theoretical contributions on how mediatization is shaped through social interactions (Chapters 3, 4 and 17), and empirical cases demonstrating how a variety of social actors and media users engage with mediatized conflicts about religion (Chapters 5–15). In this chapter, we have provided an analysis of the interplay between media framings and the multitude of ways in which conflicts are enacted and religion is contested based on a range of Scandinavian case studies. We contend that our empirically-grounded analysis, of the gendered and unsteady management of diversity, in mediatized conflicts about religion, provides a platform from which to challenge and further develop the conceptualizations of mediatization of religion (see Chapter 17). Our analysis will, together with the entire volume, *Contested Religion: The Media Dynamics of Cultural Conflicts in Scandinavia*, hopefully inspire further in-depth studies on the complexity of contested religion in mediatized societies.

Bibliography

Abdel-Fadil, Mona. 2017. "Identity Politics in a Mediatized Religious Environment on Facebook: Yes to Wearing the Cross Whenever and Wherever I Choose." *Brill Journal of Religion in Europe* 10 (4): 457–486.

Abdel-Fadil, Mona. 2006. "'Hvis Gud ville at vi skulle bruke higab ville han skapt oss hårete som bjørnen' – Ulike perspektiver på hijab." ['If God wanted us to wear the higab he would have created us hairy like the bear' – Different perspectives on hijab]. *Babylon: Nordisk Tidskrift for Midtøstenstudier* 1.

Abu-Lughod, Lila. 2013. *Do Muslim Women Need Saving?* Cambridge, MA: Harvard University Press

Ammerman, Nancy. 2016. "Lived Religion as an Emerging Field: An Assessment of its Contours and Frontiers." *Nordic Journal of Religion and Society* 29 (2): 83–99.

Axner, Marta. 2016. Stuck in a Rut? Representation of Muslims in Swedish Media Still Stereotypical, *Religion: Going Public*. http://religiongoingpublic.com/archive/2016/stuck-in-a-rut-representation-of-muslims-in-swedish-media-still-stereotypical

Axner, Marta. 2015. Representationer, stereotyper och nyhetsvärdering. Centrum för forskning om religion och samhälle, Uppsala universitet.

Cesari, Jocelyne. 2013. *Why the West Fears Islam: An Exploration of Muslims in Liberal Democracies*. New York: Palgrave Macmillan.

Dessing, Nathal M., Nadia Jeldtoft, Jørgen S. Nielsen, and Linda Woodhead. 2013. *Everyday Lived Islam in Europe*. Farnham, UK: Ashgate.

Entman, Robert M. 1993. "Framing: Toward Clarification of a Fractured Paradigm". *Journal of Communicationm* 43 (4): 51–58.

Ettema, James S. 2005. "Crafting Cultural Resonance: Imaginative Power in Everyday Journalism." *Journalism* 6 (19): 131–152.

Figenschou, Tine. U., and Audun Beyer (2014). Elitene, minoritetene og mediene – Definisjonsmakt i norsk innvandringsdebatt. *Tidsskrift for samfunnsforskning* 55 (1): 24–51.

Gemzöe, Lena, and Marja-Liisa Keinänen. 2016. "Contemporary Encounters in Gender and Religion: Introduction." In *Contemporary Encounters in Gender and Religion: European Perspectives*, edited by Lena Gemzöe, Marja-Liisa Kainänen, and Avril Maddrell, 1–28. Cham, Switzerland: Palgrave Macmillan.

Goffman, Erving. 1986 [1974]. *Frame Analysis: An Essay on the Organization of Experience*. Boston: Northeastern University Press.

Gullestad, Marianne. 2006. *Plausible Prejudice: Everyday Experiences and Social Images of Nation, Culture, and Race*. Oslo: Universitetsforlaget.

Hepp, Andreas, Stig Hjarvard, and Knut Lundby. 2015. "Mediatization: Theorizing the Interplay Between Media, Culture, and Society". *Media, Culture & Society* 37 (2): 314–324.

Hjarvard, Stig. 2016. "Mediatization and the Changing Authority of Religion." *Media, Culture & Society* 38 (1): 8–17.

Hjarvard, Stig, Mette Mortensen, and Mikkel Fugl Eskjær. 2015. "Introduction. Three Dynamics of Mediatized Conflicts." In *The Dynamics of Mediatized Conflicts*, edited by Mikkel Fugl Eskjær, Stig Hjarvard and Mette Mortensen, 1–27. New York: Peter Lang.

Jacobsen, Casper. 2016. Multicultourism in Mexico's Magical Village Cuetzalan: Regenerating Mestizo Nation. Ph.D. thesis. University of Copenhagen, Faculty of Humanities.

Jørndrup, Hanne. 2017. *"Dem vi taler om": Etniske minoriteter i danske nyhedsmedier*, Foreningen Ansvarlig Presse.

Kinnvall, Catarina, and Paul Nesbitt-Larking. 2011. "Global Insecurity and Citizenship Strategies: Young Muslims in the West." *Distinktion: Journal of Social Theory* 12 (3): 271–290.

Lakoff, George. 2014. *The All New Don't Think of an Elephant!: Know Your Values and Frame The Debate*. White River Junction, VT: Chelsea Green Publishing.

Liebmann, Louise Lund. 2017. "Interfaith Dialogue in Christian Norway: The Enactment of Inclusive Religiosity as Civilized Behaviour." *Journal of Religion in Europe* 10 (3): 301–327.

Lövheim, Mia, ed. 2013a. *Media, Religion and Gender: Key Issues and New Challenges*. Oxon: Routledge.

———. 2013b. "New Media, Religion, and Gender: Young Swedish Female Bloggers." In *Religion Across Media. From Early Antiquity to Late Modernity*, edited by Knut Lundby, 153–168. New York: Peter Lang.

Maalouf, Amin. 2012. *In the Name of Identity: Violence and the Need to Belong*. Translated by Barbara Bray. New York: Arcade Publishing.

Mamdani, Mahmood. 2002. "Good Muslim, Bad Muslim: A Political Perspective on Culture and Terrorism." *American Anthropologist* 104 (3): 766–775.

Marzouki, Nadia, Duncan McDonnell, and Olivier Roy, eds. 2016. *Saving the People: How Populists Hijack Religion*. New York: Oxford University Press.

McGuire, Meredith. 2008. *Lived Religion: Faith and Practice in Everyday Life*. Oxford: Oxford University Press.

Michailidou, Asimina, and Hans-Jörg Trenz. 2015. "Mediatized Transnational Conflicts: Online Media and the Politicisation of the European Union in Times of Crisis." In *The Dynamics of Mediatized Conflicts*, edited by Mikkel Fugl Eskjær, Stig Hjarvard, and Mette Mortensen, 51–70. New York: Peter Lang.

Midtbøen, Arnfinn H. 2016. "The Making and Unmaking of Ethnic Boundaries in the Public Sphere: The Case of Norway" In *Ethnicities*. Online first. DOI: 10.1177/1468796816684149

Miller, Daniel, Elisabetta Costa, Nell Haynes, Tom McDonald, Nicolescu Razvan, Jolynna Sinanan, Juliano Spyer, Shriram Venkatraman, and Xinyuan Wang. 2016. *How the World Changed Social Media*. UCL Press. http://discovery.ucl.ac.uk/1474805/.

Nadim, Marjan. 2017. "Ascribed Representation: Ethnic and Religious Minorities in the Mediated Public Sphere." In *Boundary Struggles: Contestations of Free Speech in the Norwegian Public Sphere*, edited by Arnfinn H. Midtbøen, Kari Steen-Johnsen, and Kjersti Thorbjørnsrud, 229–56. Oslo: Cappelen Damm Akademisk.

Rayaprol, Aparna. 2016. "Feminist research: Redefining methodology in the social sciences". *Contributions to Indian Sociology* 50 (3): 368–388.

Rose, Nikolas. (1999) 2010. *Powers of Freedom: Reframing Political Thought*. Reprint, Cambridge: Cambridge University Press.

Sauer, Birgit. 2016. "Gender and Citizenship: Governing Muslim Body Covering in Europe." In *Contemporary Encounters in Gender and Religion: European Perspectives*, edited by Lena

Gemzöe, Marja-Liisa Kainänen, and Avril Maddrell, 105–130. Cham, Switzerland: Palgrave Macmillan.
Schinkel, Willem. 2008. "The Moralization of Citizenship in Dutch Integration Discourse." *Amsterdam Law Forum* 1: 15–26.
Sjö, Sofia. 2016. "Beyond Cinematic Stereotypes: Using Religion to Imagine Gender Differently." *Journal for Religion, Film and Media* 2 (2): 123–140.
van Es, Margaretha A. 2016. *Stereotypes and Self-Representations of Women with a Muslim Background: The Stigma of Being Oppressed.* Cham: Palgrave Macmillan.
Woodhead, Linda. 2009. "Old, New, and Emerging Paradigms in the Sociological Study of Religion." *Nordic Journal of Religion and Society* 22 (2): 103–121.

Knut Lundby
Chapter 17
Interaction Dynamics in the Mediatization of Religion Thesis

Abstract: In light of the preceding case studies, this chapter revisits the theories on the mediatization of religion and on mediatized conflicts that were outlined in the first part of the book. The focus is on the interplay between media representations of religious conflicts and the social interactions relating to the contentious issues. With a basis in general mediatization theory, it is argued that audience activity and other forms of civic participation must be seen to be an integral part of the mediatization processes.

Keywords: mediatization theory, mediatization of religion, interaction, audience activity, Scandinavia

How is contested religion transformed through media dynamics? This piece builds on and adds to the conclusions on gender and diversity in Chapter 16 by focusing a theoretical concern across the case studies. They have all been carried out against the backdrop of mediatization theory (see the Introduction and Chapters 3–4). It has been our ambition, to refine the theory on the mediatization of religion when it comes to the roles' regular media *users*, i.e., people play within the communication dynamic through their interpretations and interactions with representations in the media. Here, firstly, there is a section on the ways in which social interactions contribute to mediatization. Then (in 17.2) an exposé of the mediatized dynamics that are uncovered throughout the book follows. Thirdly, as mediatized expressions on religion do not necessarily have to lead to conflicts but may also help to handle and play down tensions, this is demonstrated through examples from our case studies. Finally, there are concluding notes on the ways in which the book contributes to the theory on the mediatization of religion.

17.1 Mediatization through Interactions

Mediatization implies long-term transformations of social and cultural patterns with the media as key actors in the fabric of society, although not necessarily as the causes of changes (Hjarvard 2013; Lundby 2014). 'Media' are technologies for and social vehicles of communication. In media-saturated societies the 'social construction of reality' (Berger and Luckmann 1966) has become the 'mediated construction of reality' (Couldry and Hepp 2017). Mediatization research tries to capture the interrelations between media changes, on one hand, and changes in other parts of culture and society, on the other. Whether they are termed 'mass media' or 'social media', they are increasingly digitized and integrated into global communication networks. Mediatization is driven by big companies and big data, as well as by individual media users and producers. Various actors are thus involved in the mediatization of religion, from 'above' as well as from 'below' (Lundby forthcoming 2018).

Here, the mediatization perspective is employed to analyse cultural conflicts over religion in Scandinavia. Denmark, Norway and Sweden are media-rich societies where mediatization theories certainly apply. In Scandinavia, technological media of some sort are embedded in almost all social institutions and everyday relations (see Chapter 1), including religion (Hjarvard and Lövheim 2012).

The general dynamics of mediatized conflicts are important in studying when we try to grasp the media influences on the tensions and contestations over religion, which is the task of this book. Danish scholars have proposed three dynamics of mediatized conflicts which have inspired our analyses (Hjarvard, Mortensen, and Eskjær 2015). They primarily aim at the news media, but they may also apply to both entertainment media and social media. The media may, first, *amplify* the event or phenomenon that is reported or commented upon. A second dynamic is the *framing* of content by the actors performing the media production. Third, the media may *co-structure* power relations in communication and practices in institutions and among people (see Chapter 3).

Here, the theorization on mediatization and on the dynamics of mediatized conflicts is directed towards a deeper understanding of the mediatization *of religion* in times of contestation (see Chapter 4). The particular theory on the mediatization of religion builds on a general understanding of mediatization processes.

We explore the *dynamics* of ongoing mediatization rather than the *outcomes* of the transformations. We are thus in line with the ambition behind the *Dynamics Of Mediatization* (Driessens et al. 2017) as well as with *The Dynamics of Mediatized Conflicts* (Eskjær, Hjarvard, and Mortensen 2015). These dynamics may be studied from *above*, through amplification, framing and co-structuring in the media production processes. They may also be seen from *below*, in the manner in which the amplification, framing and co-structuring is responded to by the media users, as both citizens and audiences.

Individuals have various forms of engagement with the media. While 'engagement' is a general term, 'participation' may point to democratic activity in bottom-up civic processes (Carpentier 2011a). Media users have new participatory opportunities with the greater repertoire of personal, networked media and digital multimodal tools of expression. As media user activity, the term 'participation' should primarily be applied to the media production of 'user-generated content.' This is an active form of audience activity (Carpentier 2011b). Audiences in the contemporary cross-media landscape (Carpentier, Schrøder, and Hallett 2014) are transformed, and thus, mediatized. Individual media users do not themselves make audiences, as audiences refer to collective formations of media users (Livingstone 2005, 2014). In today's fragmented media landscape, audiences may be made up of rather limited circles of participation and consumption relating to a shared content concern. The common social and cultural pattern of user activity or engagement are what make audiences.

The audience perspective has been surprisingly absent in mediatization studies (Lundby 2016). The focus has mostly been on 'media logic' and structuring frameworks in technology, organization and the symbolic horizons on the production side of communication. Kim Christian Schrøder (2017) has taken this to task, suggesting audience dynamics as co-constitutive of mediatization processes. To him, the 'audience dynamics' are part of the media dynamics in the mediatization processes (2017, 94, 97). He argues that audiences have an integral role as agents in the transformative communication processes. The structural power of media audiences must be included in mediatization theory.

Schrøder defines 'audiences' in digital, mediatized societies as 'the people who, in their capacity as social actors, are attending to, negotiating the meaning of, and sometimes participating in the multi-modal processes initiated or carried out by institutional media' (2017, 89). He sees 'any citizen activity that can be seen to derive from attention to or engagement with media' as audience activity, if it 'can be argued to exert a formative influence on media performance or content' (2017, 90). This is a wide definition of 'audiences'. Rather, I consider people's social interaction in 'citizen activity' that contests religion, whether this implies active participation, or more laid-back forms of engagement as crucial part of the definition of audiences.

Audience activity is *social interaction*, as is all citizen engagement. Audience activity includes the identity work in which people engage with media content in the processes of interpretation that are triggered by media consumption (Carpentier 2011b). Media consumption and participation in content creation are two forms of social interaction with the media. All smart phone users know how these two forms of social interaction overlap. Media consumption and contribution to media content both imply identity work, i.e., processes of *identification*. Identity work in relation to media content also always implies *interpretations* of the symbolic and narrative media material. These three 'i's:

interaction, identification and interpretation, form a triangle in audience activity, as in another citizen activity in mediatized settings. This also applies to contested religion in media dynamics. The mediatized engagement in cultural conflicts on religion include interactions, interpretations, and identifications.

People may influence mediatization processes though audience activity, i.e., when they constitute themselves as audiences. However, we start with the range of social roles in which people engage, as citizens, or act in society as 'Christians', 'Muslims', or whatever. Mediatization makes the media relevant to all kinds of social roles; and media practices become more or less integrated into the performance of most social roles. With mediatization, our different citizen roles are conditioned or co-structured by the omnipresence of media, and through activity in the various roles through which people contribute to further mediatization. This also applies to audience activity. Sometimes, people gather and act as audiences, but not always.

In this book, we understand religion as being a practice of mediation (Meyer and Moors 2006, 7), a form of social interaction within which meaning-making takes place (Lövheim 2011). In the preceding case studies, different media are intertwined with the three 'i's in classrooms, civic settings, and in the production and reception of public service programmes. We study public tensions and conflicts over religion in the interplay between representations in professional media production, on the one hand, and interactions, interpretations, and identifications in user activity, on the other.

In this book, we mostly cut short the interlinked chain of interactions, identifications and interpretations by focusing on the interactions. The interactions are conditioned by the institutional, mediatized structures against and within which they take place, but the interactions also influence the institutional frames and the ongoing mediatization processes.

Interaction patterns are inherent to mediatization theory. Stig Hjarvard presents the circle between the regular mediation processes, i.e., communicative interaction with technical media, which, over time, may result in transformations in mediatization. In the next round, the structural changes that are implied in mediatization set up new conditions for the ongoing mediation and interaction (Hjarvard 2018). The institutional approach to mediatization that Hjarvard explicates, observes interactions between institutions, between individuals and between citizens and institutions (Hjarvard 2013), thus, from 'above', as well as from 'below'. The social constructivist approach (Krotz and Hepp 2013; Couldry and Hepp 2013; Hepp 2013) observes mediatization through everyday interactions from 'below'. However, as argued by Schrøder (2017, 92–98), neither of these main approaches to mediatization include a perspective on the power of the audiences.

Analysing the transformations of religion from a gender perspective (Chapter 16; Lövheim 2016) opens the door between mediatization and patterns of social interaction. So do the various case studies in the book. Against this backdrop, I ask: How does mediatization work through the dynamics of amplification, framing, and co-structuring as interaction from both 'above' and 'below'?

17.2 Mediatized Dynamics in the Selected Settings

It's a claim from mediatization theory that the media shape and mould interaction in other social domains, fields, or institutions, and increasingly become an intrinsic part of these other societal fields (see Chapter 14; Hjarvard 2013). This occurs in the encounter between framing and representations from 'above', and of social interaction from 'below'. In this book, we explore this interplay in three different public spaces in Scandinavia: in public service media, in local civic settings, and in public schools. In each setting, we ask how religious expressions are thematized and enacted in the media (from 'above') and further articulated in social interaction (from 'below'). The thesis of mediatization cannot be evidenced through the cases studies, but they offer empirical material for further explorations of how the theory can be improved by this closer look at patterns of interaction.

17.2.1 Public Service Media

The public service media (PSM) in Scandinavia have a strong position among audiences if compared to most other countries (see Chapter 5). This implies that they are also in a strong position to amplify, frame and co-construct tensions over religion. However, the Scandinavian public broadcasting companies continuously have to adapt to ongoing mediatization by developing their services, in particular, those on digital platforms, in order to maintain audience attention and interaction. The PSM companies could do so by introducing new and contested voices in established as well as new programme formats. The Danish television documentary *Rebellion from the Ghetto* portrays minority voices that are framed by the producers to counter dominant negative images of contested issues among the audiences (see Chapter 7). The Swedish radio programme *People and Belief* deliberately introduces new Muslim voices in order to strive for better representation. This case demonstrates the dynamics of framing and performative agency in the internal interaction between producers within the radio company, and how they come to control the interaction with the listeners through asymmetrical relations in phone-in sessions. Despite intentions to contribute to a more nuanced public debate on the role of Islam in Sweden, the programmes' representations play into the dominant understandings and established relations between various groups in society. Despite the efforts by the producers, the programmes do not manage to challenge and change the existing co-structuring of power relations (see Chapters 8 and 16).

However, in general, the PSM companies, through their programming, exploit mediatization dynamics that co-structure the perceived conception of religion and of conflicts that are related to religion, among the audiences. Reactions from the audiences also help producers to adjust the framings of the programmes, as demonstrated in the case of *Rebellion from the Ghetto*. Being aware of the mediatized conditions of conflicts over religion, PSM companies in Scandinavia have the expertise and resources, through careful planning, to counter the entrenched positions in conflicts over religion, as the authors of Chapter 7 note.

The Facebook group following the radio magazine on *People and Belief* is more accessible to alternative voices than are the phone-ins, but there is little interaction across postings, and thus a limited counter influence on the framing that is undertaken by the producers (see Chapter 8). This is different in the Norwegian Facebook group *Yes to wearing the cross whenever and wherever I choose*, which was set up after the incident in which the Norwegian Broadcasting Corporation, NRK, would not allow a news anchor wear a cross pendant whilst reading the news. The careful analysis of this Facebook group, in Chapter 6, reveals a variety of attempts to frame the debate from 'below'. The interaction on this site mediatizes the debate by 'nationalizing Christianity and hijacking religion', as the title of the chapter phrases it. Despite the fact that there are more than 110,000 participants in the Facebook group, the amplification into the general public sphere of this intense interaction and audience activity from 'below' may be rather limited. However, triggered by public service programming, this study offers insight into a social media space in which people engage with each other over cultural conflicts that are related to religion, thus mediatizing a debate within the frames of the Facebook group.

17.2.2 Local Civic Settings

In local civic settings dominant media frames on religion and conflicts, mainly those relating to Islam and Muslims, form a backdrop for local interactions between various actors. These dominant frames are generally critical of the Muslim presence and of Islam as a religion; at least this seems to be the predominant perception amongst the Muslims who are interviewed in studies for this section of the book. One is the chapter on 'Media, Muslims, and Minority Tactics' in two Norwegian urban settings (Chapter 11). Another is the study of Danish converts to Islam in Greater Copenhagen (Chapter 12). These settings are characterized as being 'mediatized civic settings' to underline how various media transform the local context through the amplification of religious conflict, the negative framing of Islam and Muslims, and the media's co-construction of a critical social and communication space on contested religion (see Chapter 9). However, as we are reminded in Chapter 12, to 'properly understand the dynamics of mediatization in particular cases, media dynamics need to be rigorously contextualized by broader processes of historical and social change' (page 221).

There are initiatives to create 'counter publics' that are based in social media networks, telling other stories from, and on, the minorities in question. Such uses of social media do not seem to fit easily into the typology of the dynamics of mediatized conflicts (see Chapter 9). However, counter publics try to amplify alternative framings and to co-construct another communication space on contested religion. Whether dominant or alternative, the mediatized setting and contested understanding of religion is played out in social interaction, the dominant from 'above', and the alternative from 'below'. These moves from above and below meet in the particular setting being studied.

For those taking part from 'below', identifications with particular meanings or positions are always part of the social interaction. This comes through strongly in the study of the dual identity as both Muslim and Dane amongst converts in Copenhagen. In their interaction with the negative media frame, with ethnic Danes, and in their experience of Danish institutions, they are torn between their religious and national sense of belonging. Given all the negative attention they receive, they tend to give priority to their identities as Muslims. Their own interpretations of the conflicts are expressed in media engagement, in particular, in social media, which is more accessible to them than the mass media (Chapter 12). The tensions between these dual identities are thus played out in a mediatized setting.

The mediatized context also guides much of the minority-majority social interaction by young Muslims in the Norwegian cities (Chapter 11). Although they live in localities with a strong Muslim presence, they are the minority in local interactions relating to religion. They have to relate to the co-structuring of the local interaction that follows from the conflictual media representations of Islam and Muslims. Participation in local interreligious dialogue fora emerges as a minority strategy through which 'to cope with, counter-, and calibrate negative media portrayals, since these actions are ways of performing belonging to the Norwegian nation and conducting Norwegian citizenship' (Chapter 11, page 190).

During the period of this research, the Norwegian government has laid down a strict policy on refugees and asylum seekers, as noted in Chapter 10. The then Minister of Immigration took a tough line, backed up by decisive and rhetorically smart media representations. Her critical public comments on religion and immigration in mass and social media, with the coining of 'sticky tropes' such as 'immigrants are carried into Norway on a chair of gold' and the denouncing of the pro-immigration camp as a 'tyranny of good', served to amplify tensions and had repercussions in everyday interactions in Norway. The Minister and her communication advisor utilized the media dynamics of mediatized conflicts to the extent that her controversial comments were always in the spotlight. Both her staging of contentious issues in public debate and her frequent reinforcement of dominant media frames in regard to Islam are textbook examples of the amplification and co-structuring of mediatized conflicts.

Chapter 10 analyses some counter communication against these governmental media representations. This opposition appears in local Christian papers and in online publications in the 'bible belt' in Southern Norway. These outlets are 'religious media', one of the categories of mediatized religion alongside journalism on religion and the 'banal religion' in popular entertainment media (Hjarvard 2012). Of the three forms of mediatized religion, religious media are the ones that usually transform the religious material the least, according to media criteria. In the interaction with their in-group local audiences these religious media perform a kind of counter-mediatization against the mediatized representation and framing of the governmental policy by the Minister of Immigration. The local Christian media frame the issues differently and try to co-construct another communication space on immigration issues.

17.2.3 Public Schools

The studies in public schools are undertaken in upper secondary classes in Norway and Sweden, with field observations in classrooms during lessons on religion and ethics. The pupils come from a variety of religious backgrounds. At the outset, we knew that mediatization makes media texts into resources for social interaction, shapes the social environment and configures relationships and structures of power between institutions and between individuals. The field observations of the classroom interaction gives flesh on these bones.

The mediatization perspective appears to be highly relevant to the practice of Religious Education (RE). Media material provides references for the interactions and discussions, and they are brought into the classroom by the students as well as by the teachers. The mediatized coverage of religion and of conflicts related to religion, thus influence the interactions within the classroom in RE sessions (see Chapters 13, 14 and 15). As noted by the authors, when 'media materials and discourses become integrated into pedagogical practice, media dynamics become relevant to how teachers and students engage with the representations of religion' (Chapter 1, 240). Such an influence on the classroom practices is another example of the co-structuring of power relations.

Sitting at the back of the classroom, the researcher is able to see what's on the students' laptop screens during RE sessions. The concentration may be on entertainment and social media rather than on the topic of the lesson. The teacher fights to get attention. The 'song' title of the chapter is pertinent: 'Let Me Entertain You.' To cope with the students' boredom and to make the teaching relevant to their mediatized world, the teacher brings in a variety of media material. A lesson on basic elements in Islam boils down to the screening of an entertainment television programme on Islam. The availability of physical media and the wide use of media material make media dynamics an inherent part of classroom situations. The media representations and the media use extensively condition the engagement with religion in Norwegian public schools (see Chapter 14). The media co-construct the learning and teaching setting in religious education.

The framing of religion in the media which focuses on conflicts, makes it difficult to teach the basic structures of religions. This is demonstrated in Chapter 15. In lessons on Islam, the amplification into the teaching of news coverage that frames Islam through terrorism and conflict, co-constructs the classroom into a mediatized meeting-place. Despite teachers' intentions to nuance and correct the media representations of Islam, the outcome of the extensive media references may be to confirm the media depictions of Islam.

17.3 Playing Conflicts Up or Down

Amplification, framing and the co-construction of and over religion may also offer resources with which to handle tensions. Religious symbols, artefacts, and claims put forward in the media may also work to manage, soften, and nuance what is otherwise contested.

The Danish TV production *Rebellion from the Ghetto,* offers an example of how careful production planning has reduced conflicts around the Muslim presence – by downplaying the term 'religion' (Chapter 7). In Scandinavia, in recent years, social and cultural conflicts have easily tended to be labelled 'religious conflicts'. This, for example, occurs when immigration from countries with a Muslim-majority is linked to conflict and terrorism. However, a person coming from a country where Islam is strong does not need to be a practicing Muslim at all. He or she may even be fleeing religious domination by emigrating to secular Scandinavia.

In *Rebellion from the Ghetto* the producers portray the young minority participants in the documentary without labelling them as religious. The participants in the programme were allowed to step forward as persons with a wider repertoire of experiences. Instead of a focus on their religious beliefs the documentary took on issues like homosexuality and the freedom to choose your partner. This conscious producer strategy resonated in the interaction with the audiences. Minority actor's voices were heard in printed press and broadcast radio discussions. The proportion of minority voices was also high on the Facebook page of the documentary. The strategy to downplay 'religion' as a main marker seems to have encouraged minority voices to step forward and to avoid an aggressive debate. The authors conclude that the dynamics of mediatized conflict – amplification, framing and co-structuring – can 'be mobilized to support a more sensitive and nuanced debate about controversial issues (Chapter 7, 132). Satire may offer a similar contribution to counter the dominant negative framing on religion in news media, as seen in the Danish comedy show *Still Veiled*, with four Muslim minority actresses poking fun at Danish stereotypes and prejudices (Hjarvard and Rosenfeldt 2017).

On the other side, entertainment may also be used to play up conflicts or controversies that are related to religion, as pointed out towards the end of Chapter 16. This applies, for example, in classroom sessions in Religious Education (see Chapters 13 – 15) and in social media debates on public service programming (see Chapter 6). These are examples of mediatization, the transformation of social and cultural practices through social interaction by the use of various media in the said settings.

Whether conflicts are played up or down also depend on the structural frames. The study of participation in the Swedish radio programme *People and Belief* (Chapter 8) shows how the structure of operation conditions – and limits – the scope of interaction and diversity in the programme, particularly with regard to invited guests. Similar structural limitations are discussed in Chapter 9 which focuses on civic settings for social interaction over contested media representations. Mass media as well as social media co-construct and condition social interaction (see also Chapter 16).

17.4 Contributing to the Theory on the Mediatization of Religion

What do the case studies in this book teach us about the dynamics of the mediatization of religion from the perspective of social interaction and of audience activity in particular? As stated in Chapter 16, a main presupposition in our research is that media audiences actively engage with media stories and events, and are affected by dominant media frames. Nevertheless, they cannot be reduced to uncritical recipients. Our studies take a broader approach to social interaction with the media, as discussed above (in 17.1).

The theory of the mediatization of religion is presented in Chapters 3 and 4, in which further references are also given. In brief, the mediatization of religion concerns the dynamics within which religious expressions, practices and institutions are influenced, or re-shaped, through their involvement with various media in a media-saturated environment. We delimit ourselves to the public aspects of religion. The claim is that religion in public spaces, over time, is transformed in its interplay with the media (Lundby 2013, 2017). As stated in the Introduction, we are concerned with media producers, but more so with the roles that media users play through their interpretations and interactions with media representations – and with how these user patterns in turn work on religious practices and religious institutions. The mediatization of religion depends on the interplay between the particular form of media and the religious setting (Lövheim 2011). The various case studies in this research inform the understandings of the mediatization of religion from various viewpoints.

As we look for controversies and conflicts that are related to religion in mediatized public settings, we go beyond individual user experiences. We consider patterns of media use in collective formations, amongst the audiences, and through agency in various social roles. The aim to contribute to the theory on the mediatization of religion through patterns of user interaction thus represents an ambition to contribute to the theory from the perspective of audience activity, as well as from civic activity in engagement with media.

The interaction aspects of mediatization encompass more than audience activity, as indicated in Chapter 3 and in Section 17.1, above. Media institutions condition the social interaction and meaning making. Here, the question is, how do various patterns of audience and civic engagement mould the processes of the mediatization of religion? What do the case studies in the three selected settings tell us? The answers concern specific conflicts and controversies about religion, but that may inform the theory on the mediatization of religion in general.

First, the audiences and media uses in the researched public spaces are very diverse. People who relate to outlets from the selected public service media are the closest to being considered media audiences. In the public schools, the students in the classroom make a small-scale audience in their interaction with their teacher and with all the media material that is brought into the classroom. In the local civic setting, the media users may gather as small, local audiences, as when the grass-roots Christian communities relate to national policies through parish publications (Chapter 10), or when Muslim youth try to cope with the dominant negative media framings of Islam (Chapters 11 and 12).

These media users exert an influence on the conceptions of contested religion in their respective mediatized environments. The Muslim youth in the Norwegian urban context exert an indirectly formative influence on media performance or content, as with Zunair through a counter film project, or through involvement in dialogue work that may later be channelled into media representations (Chapter 11). The Muslim converts in Copenhagen, rather, exert their influence through their resistance to what are perceived to be the hostile media, and this may be picked up by news media and elaborated in social media (Chapter 12). The local Christians in the Norwegian 'bible belt' exert audience influence through their support for, and use of, the local publications that criticize national immigration policies (Chapter 10). In the classrooms in upper secondary schools the boredom or conflictual media discussions on Islam change the content of the teaching (Chapters 13–15, see also Chapter 16).

The three cases from public service media relate to three different countries, one focusing on radio, another on television, and a third on a Facebook group. The phone-in sessions and feedback through social media to the Swedish radio magazine *People and Belief* document the programme's audience activity. However, the structure of the phone-in sessions, with a gatekeeper host, made it difficult for listeners to react directly to the representations within the programme (Chapter 8). The producers of the Danish TV documentary *Rebellion from the Ghetto* managed to engage the audience through careful planning, letting the audience reactions inform the crafting of the programme (Chapter 7). The establishment of the Norwegian Facebook group *Yes to wearing the cross whenever and wherever I choose* was an audience reaction to incidents in public service news practices. Participants taking different positions in these ongoing debates influence the conception of these contested issues on religion and nationality (Chapter 6).

Second, in most cases the audience and civic activities played back on, and influenced, the institutions that framed the media material. The exception is the said Facebook group, which did not manage to change the broadcasting guidelines. However, even in this case, the interaction within the Facebook group shaped the conceptions of the contentious issues at play. In the Swedish PSM case, *People and Belief*, the audience activities had a limited influence on the representations in the programme due to the established production structures. The producers grasped the audience's sentiments, but they were trapped by the traditional ideals and formats of public service radio. Different production structures make it difficult to compare, but in the Danish programme *Rebellion from the Ghetto* such discrepancies were avoided by the careful planning of the ways in which audience voices should be included in the programme set-up. In the local settings, the audiences of young Muslims had a limited and indirect feedback to the media institutions that portrayed them but, as they lifted their voices, they could be heard. The readers of the local Christian publications, in contrast, had a direct influence of these online and offline outlets within their communities, but possibly had a limited influence on national policies. In the public schools, the audience activity among the students clearly influenced the representations of Islam and other issues in Religious Education. The media materials that were drawn into the classroom by the teachers, as well as by the pupils, did make the teaching about religion more conflictual and contentious than had originally been set in the curriculum.

Third, the above examples indicate that the theory on the mediatization of religion (and on mediatization theory in general) should encompass interactions, interpretations and identifications among the audiences as part of the theory. As Kim Schrøder puts it: 'audience dynamics should be seen as an integral part of the ongoing processes of building the media logics that govern the media institutions' encounter with other societal institutions in overall processes of mediatization'. Media logics have to include 'audience logics' (Schrøder 2017, 102). However, our case studies also demonstrate that an audience perspective alone does not capture the variations in mediatized influences from 'below'. We need a broader grasp on social interactions in audience activity, as well as in wider civic activity, the co-construction from below of power relations.

The media construct the ways in which contested religion becomes represented in the public realm. However, the representations are informed by the ways in which citizens interpret the religious dimensions of social conflicts. Together, the media institutions, the audience and civic activities have a considerable influence on how conflicts on religion are amplified and dramatized. The amplification, framing and co-structuring of the communication in mediatized conflicts on religion have to be studied from 'below', as well as from 'above'. The theory on the mediatization of religion must accommodate this interplay.

Acknowledgements

This chapter relies heavily on discussions with the co-authors of the book, in particular with Stig Hjarvard and Mia Lövheim. The two have commented on and helped to improve this chapter. The three of us have, through the years, exchanged ideas and writings on mediatization, in general and on the mediatization of religion in particular.

Bibliography

Berger, Peter L., and Thomas Luckmann. 1966. *The Social Construction of Reality. A Treatise in the Sociology of Knowledge*. New York: Anchor Books.

Carpentier, Nico. 2011a. *Media and Participation. A site of ideological-democratic struggle*. Bristol: Intellect.

Carpentier, Nico. 2011b. "New Configurations of the Audience? The Challenges of User-Generated Content for Audience Theory and Media Participation." In *The Handbook of Media Audiences*, edited by Virginia Nightingale, 190–212. Malden, MA: Blackwell Publishing.

Carpentier, Nico, Kim Christian Schrøder, and Lawrie Hallett, eds. 2014. *Audience Transformations. Shifting Audience Positions in Late Modernity*. Routledge Studies in European Communication Research and Education. New York: Routledge.

Couldry, Nick, and Andreas Hepp. 2013. "Conceptualizing Mediatization. Contexts, Traditions, Arguments." *Communication Theory* 23 (3): 191–202.

Couldry, Nick, and Andreas Hepp. 2017. *The Mediated Construction of Reality*. Cambridge: Polity.

Driessens, Olivier, Göran Bolin, Andreas Hepp, and Stig Hjarvard, eds. 2017. *Dynamics Of Mediatization. Institutional Change and Everyday Transformations in a Digital Age*. Basingtoke: Palgrave Macmillan.

Eskjær, Mikkel Fugl, Stig Hjarvard, and Mette Mortensen, eds. 2015. *The Dynamics of Mediatized Conflicts*. New York: Peter Lang.

Hepp, Andreas. 2013. *Cultures of Mediatization* Cambridge: Polity.

Hjarvard, Stig. 2012. "Three Forms of Mediatized Religion. Changing the Public Face of Religion." In *Mediatization and Religion. Nordic Perspectives*, edited by Stig Hjarvard and Mia Lövheim. Gothenburg: Nordicom.

Hjarvard, Stig. 2013. *The Mediatization of Culture and Society*. London: Routledge.

Hjarvard, Stig. 2018. "The Logics of the Media and the Mediatized Conditions of Social Interaction." In *Media Logic(s) Revisited. Modelling the Interplay between Media Institutions, Media Technology and Societal Change*, edited by Caja Thimm, Mario Anastasiadis and Jessica Einspänner-Pflock, 63–84. Basingtoke: Palgrave Macmillan.

Hjarvard, Stig, and Mia Lövheim, eds. 2012. *Mediatization and Religion. Nordic Perspectives.* Gothenburg: Nordicom.
Hjarvard, Stig, Mette Mortensen, and Mikkel Fugl Eskjær. 2015. "Introduction. Three Dynamics of Mediatized Conflicts." In *The Dynamics of Mediatized Conflicts*, edited by Mikkel Fugl Eskjær, Stig Hjarvard and Mette Mortensen, 1–27. New York: Peter Lang.
Hjarvard, Stig, and Mattias Pape Rosenfeldt. 2017. "Giving Satirical Voice to Religious Conflict. The Potentials of the Cultural Public Sphere." *Nordic Journal of Religion and Society* 30 (2): 136–152. DOI: 10.18261/issn.1890–7008–2017–02–03.
Krotz, Friedrich, and Andreas Hepp. 2013. "A Concretization of Mediatization: How Mediatization Works and why 'Mediatized Worlds' are a Helpful Concept for Empirical Mediatization Research." *Empedocles – European Journal for the Philosophy of Communication* 3 (2): 119–134.
Livingstone, Sonia. 2005. "Introduction." In *Audiences and Publics: When cultural engagement matters for the public sphere*, edited by Sonia Livingstone, 9–16. Bristol: Intellect.
Livingstone, Sonia. 2014. "Identifying the Interests of Digital Users as Audiences, Consumers, Workers and Publics." In *Media Technologies. Essays on Communication, Materiality, and Society*, edited by Tarleton Gillespie, Pablo J. Boczkowski and Kirsten A. Foot, 241–250. Cambridge, Mass.: The MIT Press.
Lundby, Knut. 2013. "Media and the Transformations of Religion." In *Religion Across Media. From Early Antiquity to Late Modernity*, edited by Knut Lundby. New York: Peter Lang.
Lundby, Knut, ed. 2014. *Mediatization of Communication.* Vol. 21, *Handbooks of Communication Science.* Berlin: de Gruyter Mouton.
Lundby, Knut. 2016. "Where are Audiences in Mediatization Research." 6th European Communication Conference, Prague, 9–12 November 2016.
Lundby, Knut. 2017. "Public Religion in Mediatized Transformations." In *Institutional Change in the Public Sphere. Views on the Nordic Model*, edited by Fredrik Engelstad, Håkon Larsen, Jon Rogstad and Kari Steen-Johnsen, 241–263. Warsaw/Berlin: De Gruyter Open. doi.org/10.1515/9783110546330–013
Lundby, Knut. Forthcoming 2018. "Media Formatting Religion and Conflict." In *Formatting Religion. Politics, Education, Media, and Human Rights*, edited by Marius Timmann Mjaaland. London: Routledge.
Lövheim, Mia. 2011. "Mediatisation of Religion: A Critical Appraisal." *Culture and Religion* 12 (2): 153–166.
Lövheim, Mia. 2016. "Mediatization: Analyzing Transformations of Religion from a Gender Perspective." *Media, Culture & Society* 38 (1): 18–27.
Meyer, Birgit, and Annelies Moors. 2006. "Introduction." In *Religion, Media, and the Public Sphere*, edited by Birgit Meyer and Annelies Moors, 1–25. Bloomington: Indiana University Press.
Schrøder, Kim Christian. 2017. "Towards the "Audiencization" of Mediatization Research? Audience Dynamics as Co-Constitutive of Mediatization Processes." In *Dynamics Of Mediatization. Institutional Change and Everyday Transformations in a Digital Age*, edited by Olivier Driessens, Göran Bolin, Andreas Hepp and Stig Hjarvard, 85–115. Basingtoke: Palgrave Macmillan.

Lynn Schofield Clark, Marie Gillespie
Chapter 18
Globalization and the Mediatization of Religion: From Scandinavia to the World

Abstract: Scholarship on mediatization has focused on the interactions between the institutions of the media and the realms of society that have been historically separate from those institutions, seeking to develop an empirical record that allows us to better understand the role of media in sociocultural change. The chapters in this book have sought to contribute to this field by asking: what role have the various media industries, platforms, and practices played in the unfolding of conflict, and, in turn, how have these dynamics shaped and continue to shape religion? And although mediatization research has now taken place all over the world, this book has provided a rich set of theoretically informed, empirical case studies on the role of media in exacerbating and/or assuaging conflicts around religion in contemporary Scandinavian societies, recognizing that northern Europe is the context in which much of the theoretical work on mediatization had its origins and has continued to develop. The purpose of this chapter, then, is to discuss the relevance of mediatization theory for scholars interested in the comparative analysis of the often turbulent relationship between media, religion, and conflict in national contexts outside of Scandinavia. In this chapter we examine three underlying points of connection between Scandinavian and other national contexts to explain the general salience of this book for scholars. First, we examine the significance of national myths and their relationship to an imagined homogenous community in public responses to immigration. Second, we explore processes of globalization: the worldwide realities of migration, and displacement, and the complex entanglements of religion with alterity in national contexts of secular governance. Finally, with reference specifically to current challenges to public service media, we argue that the book provides a valuable framework for further analyses of the changing ways in which media condition public engagement with religion, thus contributing to our understandings of the mediatization of religion.

Keywords: globalisation, conflict, religion, Scandinavia, national myths, mediatization of religion

18.1 Introduction

Researchers from around the world have long been interested in the relationship between communication technologies and sociocultural change. In recent decades, scholars in northern Europe have been especially productive in generating research in the tradition of *mediatization*, exploring the ways that communication media have shaped the conditions of societal institutions throughout various epochs in history. This book has curated a series of empirical studies that have focused on conflict, considering how communication media have mediated conflict and, in turn, shaped the ways in which religion has been represented, practiced, taught, and negotiated in the public spaces of Norway, Sweden, and Denmark. Given that the cases are set in Scandinavia, the purpose of this final chapter is to explore the specificity of this context, and to flesh out how the theory of mediatization of religion as explored in this book (see Chapters 3, 4 and 17) can contribute to scholarship on the role of media, conflict, and change *in other parts of the world*.

It is very tempting to romanticize Scandinavian cultures and there is fairly reliable evidence to substantiate particular idealized perceptions. Norwegians are the happiest people in the world, according to the UN's 2017 World Happiness Report. When US citizens are asked to describe what they think an ideal distribution of wealth would look like in the US, the picture that emerges looks a lot like Sweden (Norton and Ariely 2011). Norway regularly tops the lists of the wealthiest and the most naturally beautiful countries on earth (Miller 2014; Tasch 2016). Scandinavian welfare states and secular democracies are the envy of the world, with relatively high income equality, healthy labor unions that defend workers' rights, pluralist, coalition-based political systems, and relatively low unemployment rates (Mulvad and Stahl 2015). Scandinavians are perceived as healthy, happy, beautiful people who live in beautiful places; they seem 'practically perfect in every way', enthuses British journalist Michael Booth (Worrall 2015).

Scandinavians, as the studies here reveal, see themselves as individualistic and rational, secular and tolerant, and as supporters of democratic governments that earn trust by protecting the rights of all (see Chapters 1 and 2). For example, since 1766, Swedish law has granted public access to government documents unless they fall under special secrecy restrictions. It is the oldest piece of freedom of information legislation in the world (Eck and Fariss 2017). Robust public service media systems that promote pluralism and tolerance are understood as the bedrock of participatory social democracy, and Scandinavian public media generally appear to avoid the worst excesses of racism (see Chapter 5). Or so it looked until the autumn 2015 when seemingly uncharacteristic racialized resentment in Scandinavia was expressed in public and media forums at the number of new arrivals, mainly Syrian and Iraqi refugees and asylum seekers (Tanner 2016). Such sentiments are by no means unprecedented but they acquired an alarming intensity as racist and xenophobic sentiments were being more openly expressed and right-wing populist movements seemed to be gaining a greater foothold across Scandinavia.[1] The risible case of an anti-immigrant Norwegian group mistaking empty bus seats for Muslim women wearing burqas captured the absurd extremes of Islamophobic rhetoric.[2] Europe's migration crisis had reignited debates about immigration linked to controversies about religion that had been sparked a decade earlier by the publication of the Muhammad cartoons in the Danish *Jyllands-Posten*. Such discouraging and troubling responses challenged visions of Norway, Sweden, and Denmark as tolerant and welcoming societies, calling into question the very strength of the democratic institutions and egalitarian values upon which they pride themselves.

Media controversies that implicate religion as *a* or *the* source of conflict provide templates for understanding the mediatization of religion (see Chapters 3 and 4). As this book has noted, Hjarvard, Mortensen, and Eskjaer (2015) have described the role of conflict in mediatization processes (see Chapter 3) in relation to three dynamics. First, the media *amplify* an event or phenomenon by reporting on it in particular ways using specific templates. Second, the institutional logics and practices of media professionals play a role in *framing* the phenomenon. And third, the media *co-structure* power relations by providing the platforms for the staging and performance of conflicts.

The dominant media framing of the Muhammad cartoon controversy, for example, was that of a 'culture war' – a battle between Denmark's Christian heritage and a confrontation with Islam. The news media amplified Samuel Huntingdon's 'clash of civilizations' trope that was promulgated after the attacks of 11 September 2001 (Eine, Risto, and Phillips 2008). Public and media responses

---

[1] David Zucchino, "'I've Become a Racist': Migrant Wave Unleashes Danish Tensions Over Identity," *The New York Times*, 5 Sept 2016, accessed 25 Sept 2017, https://www.nytimes.com/2016/09/06/world/europe/denmark-migrants-refugees-racism.html;

Alberto Nardelli and George Arnett, "Why Are Anti-Immigration Parties So Strong in the Nordic States?" *The Guardian*, 19 June 2015, accessed 1 Sept 2017, https://www.theguardian.com/news/datablog/2015/jun/19/rightwing-anti-immigration-parties-nordic-countries-denmark-sweden-finland-norway

[2] Jon Henley, "Bus Seats Mistaken for Burqas by Members of Anti-Immigrant Group," *The Guardian*, 2 Aug 2017, accessed 1 Sept 2017, https://www.theguardian.com/world/2017/aug/02/bus-seats-mistaken-burqas-anti-immigrant-group-norwegian

to the 'refugee crisis' in Scandinavia, as elsewhere, similarly reproduced this kind of binaristic thinking, linking refugees with Islam and with terrorism, and creating an opposition between deserving and fake refugees (Chouliaraki, Georgiou, and Zaborowski 2017). Some media reports then suggested that terrorists and rapists were hiding amidst the new arrivals, provoking spirals of public fear and social insecurity (Gillespie et al. 2016). Social media platforms then served as primary locations where conflicts over these understandings played out, with various groups and individuals striving to reinforce or reframe dominant assumptions.

Processes of mediatization, like those of urbanization and globalization, have their roots in the rise of institutionalization, as autonomous industries, structures, and organizations began to coalesce in the realms of religion, education, science, politics, and trade. It was during the late modern period that media began to emerge as a series of semi-autonomous industries and related practices that were then integrated into "the very fabric of human interaction (Hjarvard 2012, 30). Studies of mediatization have explored how particular domains of society that have become institutionalized – politics, religion, education, trade, for example – and the various sociocultural aspects of that domain – including a domain's organizations, norms, and practices – have been potentially affected by the media. Mediatization studies, then, are especially interested in teasing out how the institutional, technological, or cultural aspects of how one or more of these domains have changed within a broad timescale.

In this book, religion has been viewed as 'a practice of mediation and a form of social interaction within which meaning-making takes place' (Lövheim 2011). Religion is an institution in that religion refers to both individual and collective practices and the organizational settings through which some of those practices are codified and passed down through generations. The claim of the book overall, then, is that religion as a societal domain, including especially its form in public spaces, is transformed over time in tandem with the societal domain of the media. And a focus on the mediatization of religion brings attention to how overall changes, of which media are a part, contribute to new forms of action and interaction and give shape to how we think of humanity and our place in the world. Thus the authors of this book argue that processes of mediatization give rise to how humans understand their relationships with one another and with those very domains (Clark 2011).

Processes of othering, of structuring social identities and differences are inherent in the mediatization of religion. Ritualistic representations of Islam as a primary cause of cultural conflict are now so deeply embedded in European and North American public and media imaginaries that they are very difficult to dislodge. Such media templates have done little to advance public understanding of either religion or conflict, but they are vital to the cyclical reproduction of insecurity (Gillespie and O'Loughlin 2017).

The studies in this book show that many so-called 'religious conflicts' have less to do with religion or culture than with endemic processes of globalization: new nationalisms, failed states, militarism, migration flows, economic interdependence, ecological degradation. Poverty, inequality, and oppression are the principal driving forces of societal conflicts that implicate religion or mobilize it for political purposes. As a consequence, it is important to reframe investigations of 'religious conflicts' in the wider context of globalization processes. In our own work as ethnographers, we have advocated a mixed method approach to the study of these sociocultural conflicts, foregrounding the empirical analysis of historical documents and lived experiences within specific domains so as to shed light on the contours of these changes while also resisting a presentism that might overemphasize newness at the expense of continuity. We believe that this is an important first step towards offering more nuanced analyses of the various ways in which religion is imagined, constructed, and implicated in conflict.

In examining mediatized controversies that implicate and mobilize religion, the studies in this book enable us identify the various textual politics at work in depictions of conflict, including forms of orientalising and demonizing, denigration and idealization, and sublimation and displacement. Rather than presuming the meanings ascribed to religion, it becomes possible to see when, how, and where religion emerges as a controversial issue, as a cause of conflict, or indeed as a means of conflict resolution. In this way, the book offers a prism through which further analyses and comparative case studies can develop. But the key question for scholars unfamiliar with Scandinavian national contexts remains: How might we tease out from these Scandinavian studies the wider implications for the ways in which we research the role of media in producing and reproducing 'religious controversies', as well as conditioning public engagement with religious conflict in other parts of the world? To answer this question we argue that not only do we need a global and a comparative perspective, but also an historical approach to situate practices of othering in myths of national origin and to explicate how media are linked to processes of socio-cultural change over the longue durée.

18.2 Ancient and Modern Myths of Nationhood

This book explores the particularities of Scandinavian countries but what is perhaps most interesting and surprising for the non-Scandinavian reader is not how different Scandinavians are when it comes to questions of the relations between religion, nation, and ethnicity, but how *similar* they are to many other places in the world in the ways that broad historical processes shape contemporary conflicts. Like most European countries, they experienced nationalist fervor and anti-Semitism before World War II. They also have complex intertwined histories of colonialism, with Greenland first being ruled by Norway and then Denmark, and then later the Swedish Gold Coast being taken over by Denmark (and the Dutch). And they, too, have seen a growth in right-wing populist nationalism, not unlike recent similar developments in France, Germany, and Switzerland, as well as in the US and UK.

Scandinavian countries, moreover, share with other liberal secular democracies around the world a certain idealism about how citizens can and should work together for the public good via democratic decision-making, and in so doing sustain a common national identity. This idealism can be characterized as based on a unifying societal *myth*, following the work of Roger Silverstone who, in turn, drew upon anthropological concepts and theories of religion, in particular those of Clifford Geertz and Mircea Eliade. Silverstone argues that myths are not logical or rational but they hold often-inexplicable, emotionally satisfying deep meanings for collectivities (Silverstone 2006). This is not just true of ancient myths but also holds for television and film. Despite their reliance upon recognizable genres and narratives, media myths are not static. Ancient myths and contemporary media narratives have two important and complementary dimensions, Silverstone argues: they are *collective* and *constraining*. They are collective in the sense that the narratives must elicit some degree of consensus and acceptance, and hence reinforce the values and viewpoints that are most central – to at least a large segment of a community at any one moment. Myths are also constraining because, in the requirement to resonate with expectations, mythical codes tend to reinforce hierarchies of actually existing social relationships. Cultural contexts of production constrain expectations and shape the reception of myths.

To us as scholars based in the US and UK, Scandinavian myths of the origins of democratic governance appear to have strong echoes with American and British national narratives. They involve stories about, for example, the rise of democracy out of various workers' movements that resulted in conflict that ultimately challenged monarchical sovereignty and brought about more representative forms of governance. There are also stories about how contemporary structures of governance arise out of a primordial national identity rooted in the mists of time bearing essential defining traits and values. Such myths of national identity encapsulate a common historical trajectory and destiny: in particular the shift from monarchy to self-governance and from ethno-cultural homogeneity to diversity. Myths of the origins of democratic governance rooted in cultural homogeneity are deeply entwined in the flourishing of contemporary anti-immigrant populist movements and their visions of society – an important part of 'the context' to be factored in when explaining how public responses to migrant religion and socio-political conflict evolve.

National myths of cultural and religious homogeneity are especially perverse in the US context. In excluding North American Indians, the national story wraps the earliest waves of settler migration into a myth of manifest destiny, denying the realities of extermination, ethnocide, and exploitation. The point here is that while the style in which the 'imagined community' of the nation is conceived is unique (Anderson 1983), national myths and rituals that are represented and performed via media function in similar ways across societies – to include and exclude, to draw boundaries between those who belong and outsiders. By investigating how mediatized national myths operate in Scandinavian countries, this book brings to light how their collective and constraining features can be compared with other contexts. This can help other scholars arrive at a better understanding of how mediatized unifying myths of origin, by their very nature, position migrants' cultures and religions as disruptive and other, and how they work to reproduce a particularistic national sense of belonging and identity. But we can only get so far with this historical perspective. We must also situate current debates about cultural conflicts, migrant religions, and public controversies in the wider contexts of the forces driving globalization and forcing migration.

18.3 Shared Worldwide Realities of Migration and Forced Displacement

This book was researched and written in the context of the greatest period of forced displacement in recorded history. The UN Refugee Agency's (UNHCR) Global Trends Report found that in 2015, 65.3 million people, or one person in every 113 globally, were displaced from their homes due to war and persecution. Children made up 51 percent of the world's refugees. The number of recent, internally displaced people and refugees fleeing their countries was four times higher than it was in 2014. These migrations are directly related to longstanding and ongoing political conflicts in Iraq; others, such as those in Somalia and Afghanistan, have lasted more than three and four decades respectively, while the war in Syria is in its seventh year as we write. Seemingly intractable conflicts have been occurring more frequently, yet the rate of effective solutions and resolutions of conflicts is slowing down (Edwards 2016) or is even a total failure as with Syria.

Around the world, successive conflicts and the resulting tumult have shaped patterns of migration, displacement and diaspora formations, as have natural and environmental disasters, and dreams of better economic opportunity. Today, London is home to the most ethnically diverse population in the world, largely as a result of migration from former UK colonies in the post-World War II period. The US and Russia have the second and third largest numbers of foreign-born residents, with the journey from Mexico to the US being the most frequent migrant journey in the world. The countries with the highest shares of foreign-born workers are the United Arab Emirates, Qatar, Kuwait, and Bahrain – all of which are rich in resources especially compared with their neighboring countries (Inkpen 2014).

Nation-states throughout the world have long experienced migration and demographic shifts as a result of invasions, slavery, human trafficking, disasters, and labor opportunities. The 16th century saw notable changes in the US, the UK, and central European countries' populations due to heightened trade and a desire to escape persecution. Changes to the populations in Brazil, Russia, India, and China began occurring later, dating back to the 19th century in response to the labor demands that arose with the abolition of slavery. The late 19th and 20th centuries saw the development of immigration laws and border policies and practices that triggered a net emigration of educated workers from China, India, the Middle East, and many Asian countries to former colonizing countries. Some countries, like Portugal, have changed more recently from countries of net emigration to net immigration due to a strengthening economy and the end of right-wing authoritarian regimes.

Throughout these shifts, like many countries in central and southern Europe, Sweden, Norway, and Denmark maintained largely stable populations, although these countries experienced significant outward migration from the mid 19th until the early part of the 20th century due to economic pressures. These trends began to change following the Second World War. Now with the strengthened economies of Scandinavian societies, they have become very attractive sites for migrants, and for Iraqi, Afghan and Syrian refugees in particular (Tanner 2016).

The war in Syria has been devastating. In 2016, from an estimated pre-war population of 22 million, the UNHCR Global Trends report identified 13.5 million Syrians requiring humanitarian assistance, of which more than 6 million are internally displaced within Syria, and around 5 million are refugees outside of Syria. In 2018 as this book goes to press the figures reported by the UNHCR are even higher: 6.5 million displaced within Syria, 5.6 million refugees have fled and 3 million are in neighbouring countries. An inestimable 884.000 asylum claims in total.³ The countries that have taken the highest number of Syrians are Turkey, Jordan, and Lebanon. Conflicts in Yemen, Somalia, South Sudan, and the Central African Republic are resulting in refugees in Chad, Nauru, Mauritania, Kenya, and Djibouti. The fact is that we are living through a time of displacement of unprecedented scale and scope, and its consequence is the shared global reality of complex migratory flows, and will be for a long time to come.

One key difference between the countries in Scandinavia and other countries is that, as noted in this book's first chapter, Scandinavian countries are relatively small in population size. As a result, demographic shifts following recent immigration have been felt more intensely. Size matters. This is reflected in a common media framing of immigration controversies – the numbers game. A great deal of media debate revolves around two dominant public perceptions: first, that there are just too many of 'them' coming and second, that 'the welfare state' simply does not have the resources to cater for 'them' and for 'us', and 'we' will be the losers. These fearful representations and perceptions combine with an already potent, intense social anxiety around accelerated social change caused by complex external and internal factors. This (re)produces a toxic mix of public unease that becomes fixated on immigration as the main cause of all social ills. Social insecurity becomes indissolubly tied to fears about immigration, calling into question Scandinavian self-identification as welcoming and tolerant. Competition over scarce resources can very quickly topple myths of tolerance. These mediatized chain reactions have historical and comparative precursors and precedents and are common in many countries. Understanding these common threads between nations as well as their differences is very important.

It should be noted that Sweden has taken in more asylum seekers and refugees in the last two years than any other European nation (relative to its size), including Germany, and Sweden's provision for refugees is widely regarded among European refugee support groups as exemplary. But for others, Sweden, though a 'humanitarian superpower', has become a textbook case of how not to tackle immigration – taking too many asylum seekers in and not managing their integration well.⁴ One of the very compelling and most valuable aspects of this book is the ways in which it highlights differences among Scandinavian countries, offering rich opportunities for comparisons at the cross-national level not just from case studies but from survey data. Another valuable aspect is

---

3 UNHCR, "Syria Emergency," accessed 1 Sept 2017, http://www.unhcr.org/uk/syria-emergency.html
4 Tove Lifvendahl, "How Sweden Became an Example of How Not to Handle Immigration," *The Spectator*, 3 Sept 2016, accessed 25 Sept 2017, https://www.spectator.co.uk/2016/09/how-sweden-became-an-example-of-how-not-to-handle-immigration/

the recognition that there are contexts that still hold greater trust in societal institutions than is the case in the US, UK, and elsewhere in the world (Gray 2016). Will current conflicts and controversies, as they are amplified, framed, and played out in commercial social media spaces, contribute to a rejuvenated sense of trust in societal institutions, or in an undermining of that trust? Only time will tell. Finally, this book is telling in that it reveals a tendency to view recent religious controversies through the lens of 'culture wars' that position religion in opposition to the secular and as a source of conflict rather than of collaboration.

18.4 Contesting the lens of 'Culture Wars'

Although about half of the Scandinavians in the 2015 CoMRel survey regard Islam as a threat to their national culture, a majority do not support hostility towards foreigners (Chapter 2). This suggests a greater fear of religious than of national differences. The book shows that the struggle between secularized versions of religion and traditional, conservative and fundamentalist versions of religion is understood in quite specific terms – primarily as a struggle between Christian heritage and militarized Islam. Such a predominant 'culture war' lens of a Christian 'us' and a militant Muslim 'them' is deeply contested and disputed, but remains compelling for some and difficult to dislodge (Hunter 1992; Fiorina 2010). Dogmatic beliefs about the incompatibility of Islam with Christian Scandinavian society are often closely tied to myths of origin and of the nation, as described above, that portray a transition from harmonious homogeneity to intrusive diversity.

There is little doubt about the realities of Islamist terrorism – or indeed about other religious fundamentalisms that are rooted similarly in complex historical political and economic relationships. But in recent years Islamist-inspired attacks by different groups have received much greater media prominence and the mediatization of these events conforms to certain patterns that condition and shape public responses and can reinforce the 'us' vs. 'them' frame. Reports on attacks include those on Paris (2015 and 2017), on Beirut (2015 and 2017), and on the Kandahar airport in Afghanistan (2015), the attacks against the Sehwan worshippers in Pakistan (2017), the Palm Sunday attacks on Christian churches in Tanta and Alexandria, Egypt (2017), and Boko Haram attacks in northern Nigeria (2015). The US and UK have also experienced attacks, in London (2005, 53 killed and more than 700 injured) and Westminster (2017), as well as an earlier attack on the Israeli embassy in London in 1994. The US attack in San Bernardino (2015) followed the attacks on New York City and Washington, DC, in 2001 in which nearly 3,000 were killed and 6,000 injured. This was when the frame of 'culture war' first came into focus for US citizens, centered on the question of the relationship between Islam and terrorist violence. In 2017, the seven-country immigration ban Trump imposed brought conflicting approaches to migration to the forefront of media and public debate once again.

What is often overlooked is the way that ritualistic media *responses* to these attacks provoke and exacerbate social insecurity, and bring about grave consequences for those seeking asylum and reunification with families already in the UK or US who have no connection with terrorism or terrorist acts. And violent conflict, of course, is not confined to those affiliated with Islamist organizations. Some strains of Buddhism have become militant, for example in Myanmar where the current torture and expulsion of Rohingya Muslims continues to shock the world. The 2011 killing of 77 people in Norway was carried out by a right-wing extremist claiming affiliation with Christianity, and the US has seen a rise in similar terrorist acts carried out by extremists with Christian affiliations (ADL 2017).

Islam, like all religions, is both a set of principles and practices with cultural precepts, but legacy news media sources have tended to portray Islam as homogeneous, one dimensional and inherently violent. But this is misguided, as religious wars of the medieval period that sought to reclaim Muslim-dominated lands for the Latin church serve as a reminder that religions are never inherently violent or non-violent; such characterizations are too simplistic and unhelpful. By calling the 'culture wars' framework into question, this book moves the discussion forward – reframing current conflicts as in large part due to struggles over material resources that have resulted from centuries of exploitation in certain parts of the world for the benefit of those living other parts of the world.

Scandinavian nations see themselves as largely secular despite the lengthy tradition of Lutheran state religion. This may be due to the fact that over time, paradoxically, religion itself has undergone a process of secularization. The notion of the secular in any case is itself very slippery (see Chapter 4). Nevertheless the very concept of secular democracy sets the tone and the conditions in which the publicness – the visibility and audibility – of religion can be expressed. In Scandinavia, even Christianity, if practiced 'too fervently', can be perceived as just as much a threat to national identity as the zealous practice of Judaism or Islam (see Chapters 6–8).

The notion of secular Scandinavia may well be misleading and need to be challenged. The book shows how some citizens contest claims about a transition in Scandinavian society from Christian Lutheran values and traditions towards secularism. Such a recognition draws attention to the fact that the notion of the secular only derives its meanings by its association with the Christian religion and the sacred. The media play with the scared–secular distinction in ways that defy easy categorization (Knott, Poole, and Taira 2013). This is something we need to grapple with in understanding the mediatization of religion around the world and its role in effecting socio-cultural change. While the book privileges the concept of mediatization and its potential role in precipitating socio-cultural change, we must keep in perspective that media – especially public service media – are undergoing profound challenges and transformations, as well.

18.5 Media as Sites of Contestation in Democratic Governance

In the Scandinavian context, the concept of public service media refers mainly to legacy news media, as these organizations are charged with reflecting and shaping public opinion (see Chapter 5). By public service media, we mean mainly broadcasting and online media funded by the state rather than the press and other publications which are mainly funded privately. Public service media are seen to play an important role in both sparking and managing public debate about religion (through framing, as mentioned in Chapter 9). Because public service media are expected to reflect widely held views of tolerance, they also are understood to shape the ways that controversies around religion are represented and negotiated in reception processes and social interaction. In this book public service media are seen as playing a catalytic role in exacerbating as well as assuaging conflict. They are deemed to have a social responsibility to contain and productively manage conflict (see Chapter 5). Religious publications are viewed as somewhat apart from this mandate, and reflect alternative perspectives (see Chapter 10). However, the media thrive on controversy and conflict in order to attract and maintain audiences and, in their predisposition to dramatize and even sensationalize events, they reinforce the semantic and symbolic connections between religion and controversy. So we argue that there is a structural conflict in public service media – on the one hand to promote tolerance and multiculturalism, and on the other to secure audiences' attention via conflict and controversy. The same may be said for how teachers try to arrest the attention of their pupils by focusing on conflict and controversy (see Chapter 14).

But the news media, too, have themselves become a hotly contested topic as allegations of 'fake news' and post-truth media abound. Scandinavian countries are no exception in having witnessed a massive decline in audience share for public service media as Facebook, Google, Amazon, Netflix, and other services divert audiences' attention. Media, like migration, are increasingly best understood as part of processes of globalisation. What happens elsewhere in the world is immediately transmitted and circulated, with social media users often breaking news well before broadcast and print media. Moreover, when people migrate, they carry media preferences with them. The emergence of diaspora communications and media, the challenges of social media, and the potency of global media corporations and instantaneous and perpetual digital connectivity profoundly alter the centrality of public service media in any one nation-state and public service media's ability to condition public responses to controversies.

In February 2017, for instance, when Donald Trump defended his ban on travel from seven Muslim-majority countries by claiming that Sweden had suffered Islamist terrorist attacks the night before, this baffled Swedish audiences who had experienced no such thing. The statement was one of hundreds of falsehoods uttered by the US president, many of which had their origins in the commercial and highly partisan US news organization Fox News (Tronarp and Sundholm 2017; Eck and Fariss 2017). But the falsehood was also clearly intended to construct a boundary between 'us' (those of us who are victims or prospective victims of terrorist attacks) and 'them' (those who are imagined as perpetrators or supporters of such acts). It touched upon the myth of the nation and the 'other' as it circulated through memes, tweets, image macros, and other forms of social media. In much of the theorizing about media, news media have been understood as institutions that orchestrate relations between various societal actors and institutions in a democracy through established professional ethics, but when that role is jeopardized, it makes citizens wonder who they can trust. Politicians and media are among the least trusted professionals (Skinner & Clemence 2017).

The book offers important insights into the multifarious intersections of social media and public service media, including why users may or may not want to share and/or discuss matters of religion in online spaces (Chapter 12), and how they discuss matters of religion in public debate (Chapter 10) and in schools and their online portals (Chapters 13–15). Social norms about which kinds of speech acts are permissible in public spaces emerge as factors of great interest. Who is allowed to speak about what is a persistent topic of debate too among public media producers charged with attracting huge audiences while also fostering greater awareness and tolerance (see Chapter 5). The case studies in this book open the door to considering the many ways in which the theories of mediatization have been rooted in a 'legacy media' and a public service media model that has been surpassed by social media. Indeed mediatization theorists these days, e.g. Stig Hjarvard, are very much concerned with analysing social media.

While this book was being finalized, a song denouncing UK Prime Minister Theresa May as a 'liar' climbed the charts of Amazon UK's downloads despite receiving no mainstream radio airplay due to impartiality guidelines (Weaver 2017). Such examples cause us to wonder whether our very concepts rooted in legacy media need fundamental revision in light of social media. Mediatization theorists have been grappling with how best to understand and research social media and the ways in which these platforms have created new centers of power that have unforeseen and unforeseeable implications for the exacerbation of social and political conflicts. Social media both empower civil society and enrich corporate actors like Facebook who are increasingly garnering the kind of editorial authority once ascribed to institutional media. This book offers important insights into how these dynamics play out in contemporary controversies about religion and conflict. The implication of the book is that we need to protect public service media more than ever in the face of the onslaught of social media and their partisan echo chambers, and the steady erosion of public media systems that can provoke national conversations and therefore approximate the ideals of a public sphere of democratic communication.

18.6 Conclusion

This chapter has focused on why scholars outside the Scandinavian context might find in this volume many points of connection worthy of further dialogue and exploration. First, we noted that all modern nations produce foundational myths of origin and destiny even if the style in which they are imagined is very different. Myths of the birth of democratic governance in Norway, Sweden, and Denmark has striking parallels with those of the US and UK. While the book underscores differences between Scandinavian countries, such parallels provide rich comparative material on which to build.

Second, we argued that like in Scandinavia, many countries around the world are experiencing the effects of globalization, migration, and displacement. Such experiences represent a shift from out- to in-migration in Scandinavian countries, offering a distinctive vantage point from which to compare countries. All over the world states are grappling with migration, changing populations and cultural and religious change. It is vital to understand how our interwoven histories also present us with moral responsibilities in situations of humanitarian need. Sweden presents a good case in point to compare with other European nations in terms of how they have responded to the current 'migration crisis' and to ensuing socio-cultural change.

Third, we argued that many nations around the world are struggling to deal with the tensions that arise between a commitment to secular governance and the realities of living in a world in which religion remains a vital social force.

Its resurgence and renewed public visibility underscore the fact that modern nations are shaped by their own particular religious histories and that viewing conflicts through the lens of culture wars is divisive.

To the extent that this book considers the evolving role of media in democratic governance, and the specific contours of religion and religious conflicts within that governance, it provides a means of exploring the particular conditions under which mediatized conflicts might produce worse or better outcomes for peaceful multicultural co-existence. In exploring the role of media in how conflicts are constructed, constituted, and reproduced in Scandinavia, the book also provides a framework for scholars elsewhere who similarly want to understand, and respond to, the cyclical and ritual, systemic and changing role of the media in relation to the state and other political and social institutions. In so doing it affords a deeper understanding of the specific nature of and particular conditions under which mediatized conflicts that implicate religion might get *worse* or get *better* over time.

Bibliography

ADL (Anti-Defamation League). 2017. *A Dark and Constant Rage: 25 Years of Right Wing Terrorism in the United States*. New York: ADL. https://www.adl.org/sites/default/files/documents/CR_5154_25YRS%20RightWing%20Terrorism_V5.pdf

Anderson, Benedict. 1983. *Imagined Communities: Reflections on the Origin and Spread of Nationalism*. London: Verso.

Chouliaraki, Lilie, Myria Georgiou, and Rafal Zaborowski. 2017. "The European 'Migration Crisis' and The Media: A Cross-European Press Content Analysis." Project report, Department of Media and Communications, London School of Economics and Political Science. Accessed 25 Sept 2017. http://www.lse.ac.uk/media@lse/research/Media-and-Migration/Migration-and-media-report-FINAL-June17.pdf

Eck, Kristine, and Christopher J. Fariss. 2017. "No, Sweden Isn't Hiding an Immigrant Crime Problem. This Is The Real Story." *Washington Post*, 24 Feb. Accessed 3 June 2017. https://www.washingtonpost.com/news/monkey-cage/wp/2017/02/24/no-sweden-isnt-hiding-an-immigrant-crime-problem-this-is-the-real-story/?utm_term=.2943fc294e63

Edwards, Adrian. 2016. *Global Forced Displacement Hits Record High*. UN Refugee Agency, 20 June. Accessed 22 April 2017. http://www.unhcr.org/news/latest/2016/6/5763b65a4/global-forced-displacement-hits-record-high.html.

Eide, Elisabeth, Risto Kunelius, and Angela Phillips, eds. 2008. *Transnational Media Events: The Mohammed Cartoons and the Imagined Clash of Civilizations*. Gothenburg: Nordicom

Fiorina, Morris. 2010. *Culture War? The Myth of a Polarized America*, 3rd ed. Boston: Longman.

Gillespie, Marie, and Ben O'Loughlin. 2017. "The Media-Security Nexus: Researching Ritualised Cycles of Insecurity." In *Routledge Handbook of Media, Conflict and Security*, edited by Piers Robinson, Philip Seib, and Romy Frohlich, 51–67. New York: Routledge.

Gillespie, M., Ampofo, L., Cheesman, M., Faith, B., Iliadou, E., Issa, A., Osseiran, S., Skleparis, D., *Mapping Refugee Media Journeys: Smartphones and Social Media Networks*. Milton Keynes: Open University. http://www.open.ac.uk/ccig/sites/www.open.ac.uk.ccig/files/Mapping%20Refugee%20Media%20Journeys%2016%20May%20FIN%20MG_0.pdf

Gray, Alex. 2016, December 21. "Do you trust other people? Don't worry, most people don't trust you either." World Economic Forum. Available: https://www.weforum.org/agenda/2016/12/if-you-live-in-a-nordic-country-then-you-probably-trust-others-a-mediterranean-country-forget-it/

Hunter, James Davison. 1992. *Culture Wars: The Struggle to Control the Family, Art, Education, Law, and Politics in America*. New York: Basic Books.

Inkpen, Christopher. 2014. "Seven Facts About World Migration." *FactTank: News in the Numbers*, 2 Sept. Pew Research Center. Accessed 3 June 2017. http://www.pewresearch.org/fact-tank/2014/09/02/7-facts-about-world-migration/.

Knott, Kim, Elizabeth Poole, and Teemu Taira. 2013. *Media Portrayals of Religion and the Secular Sacred: Representation and Change*. London: Routledge.

Marglin, Jessica. 2015. "ISIS vs. Islam." *Huffington Post*, 23 Nov. http://www.huffingtonpost.com/jessica-marglin/isis-vs-islam_b_8613826.html

Miller, Lisa. 2014. "25 Reasons Why Norway is the Greatest Place on Earth." *Huffington Post*, 7 Jan. http://www.huffingtonpost.com/2014/12/31/norway-greatest-place-on-earth_n_4550413.html

Mulvad, Andreas Møller, and Rune Møller Stahl. 2015. "What Makes Scandinavia Different?" *Jacobin*, 4 Aug. https://www.jacobinmag.com/2015/08/national-review-williamson-bernie-sanders-sweden/

Norton, Michael I., and Dan Ariely. 2011. "Building a Better America – One Wealth Quintile at a Time." *Perspectives on Psychological Science* 6 (1): 9–12.

Olesen, Thomas. 2016. "Malala and the Politics of Global Iconicity." *The British Journal of Sociology* 67 (2): 307–327.

Silverstone, Roger. 2006. *Media and Morality: On the Rise of the Mediapolis*. Cambridge: Polity Press.

Skinner, Gideon and Michael Clemence. 2017, November 29. "Politicians remain the least trusted profession in Britain." IPSOS MORI Game Changers. Available: https://www.ipsos.com/ipsos-mori/en-uk/politicians-remain-least-trusted-profession-britain

Tanner, Arno. 2016. "Overwhelmed by Refugee Flows, Scandinavia Tempers its Warm Welcome." Migration Policy Institute, 10 Feb. http://www.migrationpolicy.org/article/overwhelmed-refugee-flows-scandinavia-tempers-its-warm-welcome

Tasch, Barbara. 2016. "The 25 Richest Countries, Ranked." *Business Insider*, 31 March. Accessed 3 July 2017. http://www.businessinsider.com/the-richest-countries-in-the-world-2016-3.

Tronarp, Gustaf, and Magnus Sundholm. 2017. "After Trump's 'Last Night in Sweden': Here are the Errors in Fox News' Report on Swedish Immigration." *Aftonbladet*, 19 Feb. Accessed 1 June 2017. http://www.aftonbladet.se/nyheter/a/g26Lk/after-trumps-last-night-in-sweden-here-are-the-errors-in-fox-news.

Weaver, Matthew. 2017. "'She's a liar, liar': Anti-Theresa May Song Heads to Top of Charts." *The Guardian*, 31 May. Accessed 1 June 2017. https://www.theguardian.com/politics/2017/may/31/liar-liar-anti-theresa-may-song-heads-to-top-of-charts.

Worrall, Simon. 2015. "True or False: Scandinavians are Practically Perfect in Every Way." *National Geographic,* 25 Feb. Accessed 3 July 2017. http://news.nationalgeographic.com/news/2015/02/150225-scandinavia-finland-norway-sweden-denmark-culture-ngbooktalk/.

Birgit Meyer
Afterword: Media Dynamics of Religious Diversity

Abstract: In this afterword I reflect on the development of the concept of mediatization in light of increasing diversity and contestations of religion and sketch some directions for further research on the dynamics of co-existence across religious and other differences.

Keywords: mediatization, media dynamics, religious diversity, co-existence

Focusing on contestations around the public presence and representation of religion in the increasingly diverse and at the same time strongly secularized societies of Denmark, Norway, and Sweden, the starting point of this volume is the hypothesis that 'public practices and expressions of religion are transformed through their interplay with various media' (Introduction, 6). In so doing, it builds upon the debate around the mediatization of religion (and society) in which many of the contributors participated over the past decade. Obviously these debates generated a productive and convivial scholarly discursive community that proved to be able, under the competent and generous guidance of Knut Lundby, to pull off a joint interactive research project across countries and disciplines. Responding to the Research Council of Norway's call to study processes of social change from the angle of ideas and communication practices, this volume identifies the media–religion–society nexus as a privileged entry point into the dynamics of the co-existence of actors with increasingly diverse religious backgrounds and different attitudes towards religion in modern European societies.

Importantly, as the volume shows (see especially Chapter 4), understanding current transformations and contestations depends on a clear grasp of how past modes of organizing and representing the role and place of religion in society have repercussions on current representations of and attitudes towards religious diversity, especially with regard to Islam. The three Scandinavian societies have in common characteristics – such as the longstanding dominance of the Lutheran state church, strong traditions of welfare and egalitarian values, and a widely shared secular attitude – that resonate in the ways in which diversity is addressed on the levels of politics, policy, and everyday life. The volume offers not only a well-integrated comparative study of the complex, transforming relations between media, religion, and society in times of high diversity in Scandinavia that can serve for further comparison with other regions in Europe. It also provides a stimulating conceptual intervention that seeks to reflect on and push further the theory of mediatization in light of the current challenges with regard to transformations related to diversity as they occur in the contexts of public service media, local civic settings, and schools.

The Mediatization of Religion

The rise of the notion of mediatization and the debates fuelled by it would deserve a study of its own. My concern here is more modest. In my understanding, scholars such as Lundby, Stig Hjarvard, and Mia Lövheim launched the theory of the mediatization of religion as an intervention into debates about religion and modernity in the social sciences. Arguing against a simplistic understanding of secularization as the disappearance of religion, in a foundational piece Hjarvard called attention to the process 'through which core elements of a social and cultural activity (for example, politics, teaching, religion and so on) assume media form' (2008, 13). The various subsystems into which modern Scandinavian societies were differentiated were subsumed under the logic of the media. This implied that the authority with regard to the public representation of religion rested no longer within the Lutheran (state) churches; instead the church, as the prime religious institution, became subject to modes of framing and reporting employed in the mass media. Tellingly, Hjarvard paid most attention to the process of mass media taking over functions that had so far been accommodated by the Christian churches, and to the rise of 'banal religion' as a secular functional surrogate for Christian belief. The central argument, as Hjarvard put it in another important piece, was that 'the media have taken over many of *the cultural and social functions of the institutional religions* and provide spiritual guidance, moral orientation, ritual passages and a sense of community and belonging' (2011, 119, emphasis added). This argument made a lot of sense with regard to Christianity as a major exponent of institutional religion in the Nordic countries. Mediatization theory clearly owes its initial explanatory strength to offering an alternative perspective on the decline of belief, church attendance, and church membership by calling for seeing these changes through the lens of the media rather than the lens of religion. But what about other 'institutional religions' associated with migrants and refugees, in particular Islam? In the initial articulations of mediatization theory, even though issues such as the conflicts around the Muhammad cartoons were mentioned, religious diversity was not yet addressed conceptually. How suitable is this theory, albeit in its initial articulation, for understanding the stakes in current contestations about religious diversity in today's highly differentiated media environments? How, in other words, to move from what one could call 'Mediatization.1' to a follow-up version, 'Mediatization.2' – taking into account the diversification of the media (especially regarding the rise of social media) and the plurality and pluriformity of the religious field?

I read this volume and the research on which it is based as a double-sided project. It not only assesses and showcases the merits of a media perspective for the analysis of concrete instances of contestations around religion, but also seeks to further develop mediatization theory so as to accommodate the current dynamics of diversity. The introductory chapters convey a broad (and soft) understanding of the mediatization of religion. Useful distinctions are made between forms of mediatized religion – '"religious" media that are controlled by religious organizations; journalism on religion, as represented by the secular press, and "banal religion"' (Introduction, 6) – and types of media dynamics – 'amplification', 'framing and performative agency', and 'co-structuring' (see Chapter 3). The fact that many contributions fruitfully work with these sets of categories – foregrounding in particular the amplification and framing undertaken by journalism on Islam – testifies to their heuristic value for analysing how media intervene in and shape the ways in which diversity is experienced and debated. In their concluding reflection, Mona Abdel-Fadil and Louise Liebmann (in Chapter 16) and Lundby (in Chapter 17) stress that the goal of the volume is not to assess whether the thesis of mediatization can be evidenced through the various empirical case studies. And yet, these studies offer intriguing insights that could to be taken up for further theoretical reflection. What I find particularly intriguing is that institutionalized religions as Christianity and Islam appear to be subject to fundamentally different mediatizations. Many of the case studies spotlight how dominant media frames repeatedly offer representations of Islam as a 'bad religion' which is implicitly contrasted with Christianity as a 'good religion'. In my reading, the case studies propose that a conceptual shift is needed from the framework of the mediatization of religion towards the media dynamics of religious diversity.

Another remarkable finding of these case studies is the fact that the reporting about Islam in relation to various contested events tends to fall back on an old and resilient notion of religion as shaped by Lutheran Christianity that, as pointed out by Lövheim and Liv Ingeborg Lied, 'has acted as a model for the ways in which Scandinavians perceive religion in general, and also its place in society' (Chapter 4, 66). As a consequence, Islam and other religions associated with migrants and refugees are apprehended in relation to the normative ideal of Lutheran Christianity, rather than on their own terms. That this is the case on the level of public debate should, of course, not imply that this normative ideal should guide our scholarly analysis. As Lövheim and Lied point out, 'a more nuanced grasp of contemporary religion and its complexities' (Chapter 4, 71) is needed. At stake is the relation between media, religion, and secularity. Secularity 'produces' a particular modern form of religion (e. g. Asad 2003), which serves as the normative backdrop against which the various religious manifestations in diverse societies are evaluated but into which they do not necessarily fit. Exactly for this reason, any analysis of contestations about religion and differences between religions needs to reflect thoroughly on the genealogy of the prime notion of religion mobilized in these contestations, as Lövheim and Lied also point out. The point here is that the resilience of a Protestant model of religion in a secular setting, which forms the implicit subtext of dominant media frames, has repercussions for the ways in which Islam is mediatized. This does not seem to be analogous to the mediatization of Christianity. Rather than mixing Islamic forms into a cocktail of 'banal' religion for public use, Islam is primarily reported about against the backdrop of an understanding of a normative Christian ideal from which it deviates. The mediatization of Islam in public journalism in mass media tends to yield a stereotype framing of Islam as being problematic. It does not lend itself easily to being 'banalized', as the frequent contestations about the representation of Muslims and signs referring to Islam show. Media clearly have the power to shape and control the terms of public debate (as the idea of co-structuring suggests), but they do so by echoing a particular configuration of the relation between state and religion as it existed prior to the onset of the mediatization of Christianity. As a follow-up to this research project, it would be interesting to undertake a systematic comparison of the mediatization of Christianity and the mediatization of Islam, and other religious traditions. In this context, it would also be important to pursue further the differences with regard to dynamics of mediatization in dominant mass media and social media in relation to Christianity and Islam (as pointed out by David Herbert in Chapter 9)

In sum, placing this volume in the history of the study of mediatization in the Nordic network, it seems to me that mediatized religion no longer primarily features as a symptom of secularization in the sense of taking over cultural and social functions formerly provided by the church. Mediatization, as the case studies spotlight, (re)produces above all the dominant normative frame into which old and new religions have to fit in a secular society. The implications of this shift, which is documented in many of the case studies, still await being spelled out in full on the conceptual level of 'Mediatization.2'.

Studying Diversity

Conducting research on the relation between religion and media myself, over the past decade I have engaged in stimulating conversations with the scholarly community that produced this volume. Notwithstanding certain reservations with regard to the scope of the theory of mediatization (Meyer 2013), I appreciate the intellectual energy that is unleashed in the search for patterns in the transforming relations between media, religion, and society. As the rich case studies show, both media and religion are umbrella terms that encompass highly diverse phenomena and need to be unpacked. While the term media refers to different kinds of mass media and social media, the term religion points to a pluralistic environment in which practitioners of various religious traditions – most prominently Lutheran Christianity and Islam – co-exist with New Age spiritualists, staunch atheists, and people who emphasize the civilizational value of Christianity. The volume convincingly points at the crucial role played by media in influencing current contestations around newly visible and relatively unfamiliar manifestations of religion. The case studies, though focusing on Scandinavia, certainly speak to the dynamics of diversity as it plays out in, for instance, Germany and the Netherlands. I very much applaud the focus on neighbourhoods and schools as concrete sites in which people with different ethnic, cultural, and religious backgrounds co-exist and live and struggle with each other. I am much intrigued by the point raised by Herbert that 'more diverse neighbourhoods, with an established history of migration and with many immigrants from different backgrounds, seem to work in favour of civic integration', because in these settings binary categories of 'us' and 'them', though reiterated on the level of mass media, do not hold (Chapter 9, 166–167). In my view, more comparative research, on a European level, is needed to explore the dynamics of such microfields in which difference is articulated, contested, accommodated, and maybe even overcome or relativized.

Another intriguing issue concerns the 'nationalization' of Christianity which, as pointed out by Abdel-Fadil in Chapter 6, is mobilized in an exclusivist manner that emphasizes the importance of Christian symbols, such as the cross, as expressions of a core national identity threatened by diversity. This resonates with a broader post-secular re-apprehension of Christianity as cultural heritage. This stance is also articulated in public debates about how to preserve the material remains of 'unchurching', such as abandoned church buildings, sacred places, and (holy) objects (Knott, Krech and Meyer 2016). Even people with a secular mindset are hesitant to simply do away with these traces of the Christian past.

Understanding the dynamics of diversity and the modalities of co-existence is the prime challenge we face as scholars in the social and cultural sciences at this moment. To advance our understanding, I suggest to forge connections between scholars of mediatization of religion and scholars working on 'superdiversity' and 'new diversities' (e.g. Vertovec 2015) and the 'culturalization of citizenship' (e.g. Duyvendak, Geschiere, Tonkens 2016). In September 2016 I started the collaborative research project *Religious Matters in an Entangled World* (www.religiousmatters.nl), which approaches contestations arising about religion by focusing on concrete religious items such as buildings, images, objects, food, bodies, and texts. Of course, the items may be analysed as religious media in a framework of mediation so as to assess their value within a particular religious grouping, but at the same time they certainly are subject to constant mediatization. As prime operators in shaping publics and making communities, media are key to framing commotions around the material presence of religion into contested matters in broader society. The volume offers much food for thought and I will certainly follow the work of my Scandinavian colleagues with keen interest and look forward to future conversation and collaboration.

Bibliography

Asad, Talal. 2003. *Formations of the Secular: Christianity, Islam, Modernity.* Stanford: Stanford University Press.

Duyvendak, Jan-Willem, Geschiere, Peter, and Eveline Tonkens, eds. 2016. *The Culturalization of Citizenship. Belongong and Polarization in a Globalizing World.* London: Palgrave Macmillan.

Hjarvard, Stig. 2008. "The Mediatization of Religion: A Theory of the Media as Agents of Religious Change." *Northern Lights* 6 (1): 9–26.

Hjarvard, Stig. 2011. "The Mediatisation of Religion: Theorising Religion, Media and Social Change." *Culture and Religion* 12(2): 119–135.

Knott, Kim, Volkhardt Krech, and Birgit Meyer, eds. 2016. Iconic Religion in Urban Space. Special Issue of *Material Religion* 12 (2).

Meyer, Birgit. 2013. "Material Mediations and Religious Practices of World-making." In *Religion Across Media: From Early Antiquity to Late Modernity*, edited by Knut Lundby, 1–19. New York: Peter Lang.

Vertovec, Steven, ed. 2015. *Diversities Old and New: Migration and Socio-Spatial Patterns in New York, Singapore and Johannesburg.* London: Palgrave Macmillan.

Haakon H. Jernsletten
Appendix: Regression Analyses to Chapter 2

The Appendix presents the detailed results of the regression analyses described in Chapter 2 on Attitudes: Tendencies and Variations. Table A.1 describes the variables included in the regression analyses, while Table A.2 and A.3 show the results of the regression analyses. All the regression models were estimated in STATA 14.2.[1]

---

[1] For ease of interpretation and comparison, the variables age, religious self-identification, and political orientation (GAL/TAN) have been recoded from scales into dichotomous variables. As such, the results may differ from an analysis when these variables are used as continuous scales. However, preliminary tests do not give reason to suspect such differences.

Table A.1 Variables included in the regression analyses.

Variable description	Values
Dependent variables	
Islam represents a threat to Danish/Norwegian/Swedish culture	(1) Fully or partly disagree, (2) Neither Nor, (3) Fully or partly agree[2]
Xenophobic attitudes should be tolerated	
Mockery of religion should be tolerated	
How often do you discuss news about religious extremism with others?	(0) Monthly, more seldom or never, (1) Daily or weekly[3]
Have you during the last 12 months discussed news on religious extremism with others through comments or discussion online?	(0) No, (1) Yes
Independent variables	
Gender	(1) Male, (2) Female
Age	(0) 44 or younger, (1) 45 and older
Religious self-identification	(0) Low or no rel. self-id., (1) Moderate or high religious self-identification
Political Orientation (GAL/TAN)	(1) Libertarian/Post-materialist, (2) Centre, (3) Traditional/Authoritarian
Country	(1) Denmark, (2) Norway, (3) Sweden

---

[2] Answers given to a five-degree scale have been reduced to the options 'Fully or partly agree', 'Neither Nor', and 'Fully or partly disagree' for all three variables.

[3] Answers given to a five-degree scale have been reduced to the two options above.

Table A.2 Critique and tolerance of religion.

	Islam is a threat to national culture		Xenophobic attitudes should be tolerated		Mockery of religion should be allowed	
	(1)	(2)	(1)	(2)	(1)	(2)
Gender	−0.401***	0.480***	−0.205	0.979***	0.504***	1.044***
	(0.141)	(0.098)	(0.133)	(0.124)	(0.133)	(0.099)
Age	0.569***	0.482***	−0.020	−0.207*	0.405***	0.655***
	(0.151)	(0.102)	(0.142)	(0.122)	(0.141)	(0.102)
Religious self-identification	−0.197	0.139	−0.076	0.299**	0.657***	0.515***
	(0.157)	(0.104)	(0.140)	(0.127)	(0.148)	(0.105)
Political orientation (GAL/TAN)						
Libertarian/Post-materialist	−0.799***	−2.914***	−1.384***	−1.826***	1.051***	0.781***
	(0.306)	(0.198)	(0.204)	(0.182)	(0.211)	(0.153)
Center	−0.391	−1.821***	−1.103***	−1.345***	0.836***	1.014***
	(0.291)	(0.181)	(0.164)	(0.141)	(0.175)	(0.135)
Traditional/Authoritarian	Ref. cat.	Ref. cat.	Ref. cat.	Ref. cat.	Ref. cat.	Ref. cat.
Country						
Denmark	0.245	0.527***	0.621***	0.567***	0.632***	0.180
	(0.182)	(0.126)	(0.171)	(0.151)	(0.168)	(0.125)
Norway	0.197	0.342***	0.378**	0.562***	0.256	0.336***
	(0.169)	(0.117)	(0.171)	(0.145)	(0.171)	(0.117)
Sweden	Ref. cat.	Ref. cat.	Ref. cat.	Ref. cat.	Ref. cat.	Ref. cat.
Intercept	−0.514	2.207***	−0.832***	0.974***	0.174	2.150***
	(0.363)	(0.236)	(0.269)	(0.229)	(0.278)	(0.206)
N	2,374		2,401		2,378	

Notes: The reference category on the dependent variable is 'Fully or partly disagree' for all of the models; (1) Neither Nor; (2) Fully or partly agree. All models are multinomial logistic regression models. Standard errors in parentheses. *** p<0.01, ** p<0.05, * p<0.1

Table A.3 Participation in discussions of news on religious extremism.

	Discussion of news on rel. extremism	Online debate on news on rel. extremism
Gender	− 0.354***	− 0.785***
	(0.090)	(0.166)
Age	0.117	− 0.489***
	(0.095)	(0.159)
Religious self-identification	0.291***	0.176
	(0.094)	(0.164)
Political orientation (GAL/TAN)		
Libertarian/Post-Materialist	− 0.383***	− 0.188
	(0.139)	(0.220)
Center	− 0.479***	− 0.596***
	(0.119)	(0.198)
Traditional/Authoritarian	Ref. cat.	Ref. cat.
Country		
Denmark	− 0.115	− 0.184
	(0.113)	(0.198)
Norway	− 0.075	− 0.126
	(0.108)	(0.183)
Sweden	Ref. cat.	Ref. cat.
Intercept	0.008	− 0.549*
	(0.181)	(0.296)
N	2,419	2,151

Notes: Both models are logistic regression models. Standard errors in parentheses. *** $p<0.01$, ** $p<0.05$.
* $p<0.1$

Author Bios

Mona Abdel-Fadil is an ethnographer and postdoctoral researcher at the Department of Media and Communication at the University of Oslo. She is Editor in Chief of the 'Religion: Going Public' blog and the coordinator of the Nordic Network on Media and Religion. Publications include 'Identity Politics in a Mediatized Religious Environment on Facebook: Yes to Wearing the Cross Whenever and Wherever I Choose' (*Journal of Religion in Europe,* 2017), 'Conflict and Affect Among Conservative Christians on Facebook' (*Online – Heidelberg Journal of Religions on the Internet*, 2016), and 'Let's Talk About Sex: Counselling Muslim Selves Online' (*CyberOrient,* 2016). Email: mona.abdel-fadil@media.uio.no

Maximilian Broberg is a PhD student at the Uppsala Religion and Society Research Centre, Uppsala University. He is currently engaged in a project on religious education and teacher professionalism in Swedish religious education (RE). His main academic interest concerns how various forms of media discourses make their way into RE classrooms and how teachers and students engage with such discourses. Email: maximilian.broberg@crs.uu.se

Lynn Schofield Clark is Professor and Chair of the Department of Media, Film and Journalism Studies and Director of the Estlow Center for Journalism and New Media at the University of Denver. She is also an affiliate Professor at the University of Copenhagen. She is the first author of *Young People and the Future of News* (Cambridge University Press, 2017) and author of *The Parent App: Understanding Families in a Digital Age* (Oxford University Press, 2013) and *From Angels to Aliens: Teenagers, the Media, and the Supernatural* (Oxford University Press, 2005). Email: lynn.clark@du.edu

Marie Gillespie is Professor of Sociology at the Open University. Her teaching and research interests revolve around media and migration, transnational and diasporic cultures, religion, and social change. Books include *Social Media, Religion and Spirituality* (De Gruyter, 2013, co-edited with David Herbert), *Diasporas and Diplomacy: Cosmopolitan Contact Zones at the BBC World Service* (Routledge, 2013), and *Drama for Development: Cultural Translation and Social Change* (Sage, 2011). Her recent research includes projects on forced and irregular displacement and digital connectivity, and artistic and cultural diplomacy in conflict societies. Email: marie.gillespie@open.ac.uk

Janna Egholm Hansen is currently Assistant Professor at VIA University College, in Holstebro, Denmark. Previously she was working as a postdoctoral fellow at the University of Agder in Kristiansand, Norway, where she did research related to the project 'Cultural Conflict 2.0: Shedding new light on the conditions of co-existence in urban spaces'. She is also the author of a number of scientific articles, including the co-authored '"You Are No Longer My Flesh and Blood": Social Media and the Negotiation of a Hostile Mediatised Environment by Danish "Reverts" to Islam' (*Nordic Journal of Religion and Society,* 2017, with David Herbert). Email: jann@via.dk

David Herbert is Professor of Sociology at Kingston University London and Professor of Religious Studies at the University of Agder. His research interests are religion, media, migration, and social change. His is the author of *Religion and Civil Society* (Ashgate 2003) and *Creating Community Cohesion* (Palgrave, 2013) and co-editor of *Social Media and Religion* (De Gruyter, 2013, with Marie Gillespie). His current projects include Cultural Conflict 2.0: Religion, Media and Locality in North European Cities (2014–18) and Searching for a New Sense of Connection: The Sociality of Millennial Unbelievers (2018–19). Email: david.herbert@kingston.ac.uk

Stig Hjarvard, PhD, is Professor of Media Studies at the University of Copenhagen. His research interests include media and religion, news media, media history, media sociology, and mediatization theory. He is the author of *The Mediatization of Culture and Society* (Routledge, 2013) and co-editor of *Mediatization and Religion: Nordic Perspectives* (Nordicom, 2012, with Mia Lövheim) and *The Dynamics of Mediatized Conflicts* (Peter Lang, 2015, with Mikkel Fugl Eskjær and Mette Mortensen). Email: stig@hum.ku.dk

Linnea Jensdotter is a PhD student at the Faculty of Theology, Uppsala University. She is currently working on her PhD project on religion and politics in hybrid media spaces in a Swedish context. Her main academic interest concerns the role of religion in the Swedish public sphere, with focus on politics and media. Email: linnea.jensdotter@teol.uu.se

Haakon H. Jernsletten is a former research assistant for the Engaging with Conflicts in Mediatized Religious Environments (CoMRel) project. He holds a Master's degree in Political Science from the University of Oslo, where he specialized in comparative politics and quantitative research methods. He is also co-author of the article 'Religion Between Politics and Media: Conflicting Attitudes Towards Islam in Scandinavia' (*Journal of Religion*, 2017). Email: haakon.jernsletten@gmail.com

Louise Lund Liebmann holds a PhD in religious studies from the University of Copenhagen, was during the CoMRel research project a postdoctoral fellow at the University of Agder and is currently a postdoctoral researcher at Roskilde University. Among her most recent publication is 'Interfaith Dialogue in Christian Norway: Enactment of Inclusive Religiosity as Civilized Behavior' (*Journal of Religion in Europe* 2017). Her research interests include governance of religion, gender in Islam, religious and ethnic minorities in Scandinavia, and postcolonial theory. Email: liebmann@ruc.dk

Liv Ingeborg Lied is Professor of Religious Studies at MF Norwegian School of Theology, Religion and Society in Oslo, Norway. Lied is co-author of *Det folk vil ha: Religion og populærkultur* [What people want: Religion and popular culture] (Universitetsforlaget, 2011) as well as a series of journal articles on religion, popular culture, media history, and pedagogy. From 2009 to 2012 she served as Director of the Teacher Training Program at MF. Email: liv.i.lied@mf.no

Knut Lundby is Professor at the Department of Media and Communication, University of Oslo. He has a background in sociology and wrote his doctoral dissertation in sociology of religion. Lundby is among the founding members of the international research community on Media, Religion, and Culture and edited *Rethinking Media, Religion, and* Culture (Sage, 1997, with Stewart M. Hoover). He is editor of the handbook on *Mediatization of Communication* (De Gruyter Mouton, 2014), of *Mediatization: Concept, Changes, Consequences* (Peter Lang, 2009) and of *Religion Across Media* (Peter Lang 2013). Email: knut.lundby@media.uio.no

Author Bios

Mia Lövheim is Professor in Sociology of Religion at the Faculty of Theology, Uppsala University, and theme leader within the Centre of Excellence research programme Impact of Religion: Challenges for Society, Law and Democracy at Uppsala University. She is President of the International Society for Media, Religion and Culture (ISMRC). Her research focus is on religion in the Swedish daily press, public service media, and social media. She is the editor of *Media, Religion and Gender: Key Issues and New Challenges* (Routledge, 2013) and *Mediatization and Religion: Nordic Perspectives* (Nordicom, 2012, with Stig Hjarvard). Email: mia.lovheim@teol.uu.se

Birgit Meyer is Professor of Religious Studies at Utrecht University. Trained as a cultural anthropologist, she studies religion from a global and post-secular perspective, seeking to synthesize grounded fieldwork and theoretical reflection in a broad multidisciplinary setting. Her most recent publications include *Sensational Movies: Video, Vision and Christianity in Ghana* (California University Press, 2015), *Creativity in Transition: Politics and Aesthetics of Cultural Production Across the Globe* (Berghahn Books, 2016, co-edited with Maruška Svašek), 'Iconic Religion in Urban Space' (a special issue of *Material Religion*, 2016, co-edited with Kim Knott and Volkhard Krech) , and *Taking Offense. Religion, Art and Visual Culture in Plural Configurations* (Fink, 2018, ed. with Christiane Kruse and Anne-Marie Korte). Email: b.meyer@uu.nl

Pål Repstad is emeritus Professor in Sociology of Religion at the University of Agder in Norway. Former editor of *Nordic Journal of Religion and Society*. He is the co-author of *An Introduction to the Sociology of Religion* (Ashgate 2006, with Inger Furseth). Contributions in *Christianity in the Modern World: Changes and Controversies* (Routledge, 2014, ed. by Giselle Vincett and Elijah Obinna), in *Sociological Theory and the Question of Religion* (Routledge, 2014, ed. by Andrew McKinnon and Marta Trzebiatowska), and in *Religion and Welfare in Europe. Gendered and Minority Perspectives* (Policy Press 2017, ed. by Lina Molokotos-Liederman). Honorary doctor at Uppsala University. Email: pal.repstad@uia.no

Mattias Pape Rosenfeldt is a PhD fellow at Uppsala University focusing on contemporary trends in theological discourse and organization of progressive Islamic activism in Scandinavia. He has earlier been affiliated to the University of Copenhagen as a research assistant and course instructor, and is the author of 'How Much Religion is There in the Public Space?' (*Religion*, 2007) and 'Giving Satirical Voice to Religious Conflict' (*Nordic Journal of Religion and Society*, 2017, with Stig Hjarvard). Email: mattias.rosenfeldt@teol.uu.se

Audun Toft is a PhD fellow at MF Norwegian School of Theology, Religion and Society. His field of research is the use of media in religious education in Upper Secondary Schools in Norway. He holds a Master's degree in religious studies and has until recently been an assistant Professor at Nord University, Norway, teaching in the fields of religion, ethics, and cultural studies. Previous research is mainly focused on religious education, and the role of religion in kindergartens. Email: audun.toft@mf.no

Index

Note: Page numbers followed by n and a number indicate footnotes. Page numbers in *italics* indicate figures and tables.

Abdel-Fadi, Mona
– biographical sketch   343
– chapters by   83–96, 97–116, 281–298
– comments on   335, 337
academic boredom   248–249, 253
Ádám, Zoltán   108n2
affective publics   101, 110
age
– and discussing religious extremism   44–46, *45*
– and religious tolerance   43–44
Aggebo, Claes-Göran   144
Akerhaug, Lars   175
Ali, Akmal   196
Allern, Sigurd   27
Allport, Gordon   182
Aly, Ramy   146
Ammerman, Nancy   182–183
amplification   55, *56*, 56–57, 61, 132, 300, 303–309, 317   see also media dynamics
Angel School   68
Asp, Kent   139
asylum seekers
– church criticism of policy concerning   172, 173–175
– local Christian attitudes toward   177–181, 182–183
– media coverage of   266
– and media influence   181–182
– policy in Norway   171–173
audiences   301–302, 309–311

banal religion   6, 71, 76, 91, 334–336
   see also mediatized religion
banal securitization   193–198, 285
Bataclan attacks (Paris)   264
Bauman, Zygmunt   181
Baumgartner, Christoph   113
BBC   84–85

Beckford, James   74
Bennett, Lance   54
Bilenberg, Line   120, 122, 124
Blach-Ørsten, Mark   27
Black, Tracey   146
boundary struggles   25–26
Bozóki, András   108n2
Breivik, Anders Behring   23, 191
Broberg, Maximilian
– biographical sketch   343
– chapter by   225–241
– comments on   230n10
Brochmann, Grete   197–198
Brubaker, Rogers   22–23, 68–69
Brune, Ylva   136–137, 139

Casanova, José   93
Castells, Manuel   215–216
Cesari, Jocelyne   285n2
Charlie Hebdo   55–59, 192, 264
Christianism   23
Christianity/Christians
– associated with national identity/culture   35–36, 68–69, 101–106, 111, 283
– and church involvement in politics   172, 173–175
– contesting meaning of   110–112
– and de-Christianization   252
– as dominant religion in Norway   188
– and local attitude toward asylum seekers   177–181, 182–183
– Lutheran church in Scandinavia   17, 21, 35–36, 66–67
– portrayed as 'good religion'   289–290
– sacred values of   112–113
– and support for religious expression   37–38, *38*, 67
citizenship   189n6, 197–198
civic settings   see local civic settings
civilizationism   23

Clark, Lynn Schofield
- biographical sketch 343
- chapter by 315–331
classrooms *see* religious education
cognitive frames 270–271
Cohen, Bernard 269
collective-connective action distinction 54
conflict
- conflict-centred media coverage 265–267
- defined 4
- emphasized in religious education 252, 255
- and globalization 319, 326–327
- mediatization of 138–139, 191, 307–309
- and perceived threat of Islam 40, 40–42, 41, 43–44, 68–69, 106
connectivity 28
contact hypothesis 182
controversy, defined 4
conversion, religious 211–215
co-structuring 55, 56, 58–59, 119, 132, 158, 159–160, 300, 301, 303–309, 317, 336 *see also* media dynamics
Cottle, Simon 138
Couldry, Nick 74n2, 207
Council for Religious and Life Stance Communities in Norway (STL) 174, 197–198, 199
counter-information 182
counter-publics 159–161, 305
cross-wearing campaign *see* YWC
cultural racism 207
cultural-religious diversity *see also* national identity/culture
- attitudes toward 37–38, *38*, 43–48, *45*, 67
- challenges in managing 283–286
- growth of, in Scandinavia 20–22
- and ideal citizens 286–290
- impact on PSM 88–90
- spatial distribution of 161–164
- state support for 195–196
- and successful social integration 166–167
'culture war' 324–325

Dansk Folkeparti 24
Davie, Grace 36, 66
debates *see also* YWC
- analysis of public 127–131
- fostered by documentaries 123–125
- minority voices in 125–127, *126*, *127*
democratic corporatist model 26–28
Denmark *see also* Rebellion from the Ghetto
- attitudes toward Muslims in 207–209
- and dual identity of Danish Muslims 210–215
- media representation of Islam in 205–206
- PSM in 85, 89
- and self-presentation of Danish Muslims 210–215
de-radicalization 195
de Souza e Silva, Adriana 157
Detlefsen, Louise 120, 121, 123
digitalization 27–28
Dijck, José van 54
diversity *see* cultural-religious diversity
Døving, Cora Alexa 265
DR 85, 89, 120–121
dual identity 210–215, 219–221
Duffy, Bobby 163
Duyvendak, Jan Willem 165
Dynewall, Johan 230n10

ECRI (European Commission Against Racism and Intolerance) 205–206
education *see* religious education
Eliade, Mircea 320
Eljammal, Donna 147–149, 288–289
Engelstad, Fredrik 24
Enjolras, Bernard 25–26
Entman, Robert M. 57, 127–128, 270–271
equality, and sameness 18–19
Eskjær, Mikkel Fugl 138–139, 160
Esping-Andersen typology 16
essentialized identities 287
ethnicity, and dual identity 210–215, 219–221
ethnification 19
ethno-religious diversity *see* cultural-religious diversity

Ettema, James S.   283
European Commission Against Racism and Intolerance (ECRI)   205–206
extremism   see religious extremism

Facebook   100, 147–149   see also YWC
Faten tar valget (*Faten makes her choice*)   288–289
Figenschou, Tine Ustad   140, 181
Fillmore, Charles J.   271
filter bubble effect   161
foreign fighters (*fremmedkrigere*)   187
framing/frames
– as concept   55, 56, 57–58, 127–128, 139, 270–271, 300, 317
– human-interest frame   140, 149
– of ideal citizen   286–290
– managing dominant frames   283–286
– news framework   265–266
– and patterns of interaction   303–309
– phone-in sessions as   142–147
– process of   282–283
– in public debate on Islam/immigration   127–131, 132
– radical Islamist (RI) frame   272–274
– and social interaction   193
– of 'the Muslim woman'   290–292
freedom of expression
– in Scandinavian law   25
– support for   37–38, 38, 67, 147–149, 288–290
freedom of speech   25, 57, 58, 59
Fremskrittspartiet   24
Frere-Smith, Tom   163
Furnes, Erik   175
Furseth, Inger   22

Geertz, Clifford   99, 120, 320
gender
– and discussing religious extremism   44–46, 45
– gendered interactions   292–294
– and religious tolerance   43–44, 47–48
– and 'the Muslim woman' trope   290–292
generic new frames   139
Gielen, Amy-Jane   164
Gijsberts, Merove   162

Gillespie, Marie
– biographical sketch   343
– chapter by   315–331
globalization   319, 326–327
Gordon, Eric   157
Greider, Göran   144
Griera, Mar   200n13
Grødem, Anne   197–198
Gullestad, Marianne   18–19, 269–270, 287, 292
Güveli, Ayşe   162

Hahn, Tithi   141
Halafoff, Anna   197
Hallin, Daniel   26–27
Hansen, Janna
– biographical sketch   343
– chapter by   205–222
– comments on   155–156, 158
Hartman, Johan   90
Hassan, Yahya   120, 122
headscarves   see hijabs
Heelas, Woodhead   111
Heidbring, Jakob   143
Heide, Mette   120–121, 122–123, 131–132
Hepp, Andreas   74n2
Herbert, David
– biographical sketch   343–344
– chapters by   33–49, 155–170, 205–222
– comments on   146, 155–156, 158, 337
hijabs
– campaign against banning   158–159
– negative projections on   291–292
– public support of   147–149, 288–290
– and self-presentation   216–217
hijacking religion   111, 113–114
Hill, Michael   72
Hjarvard, Stig
– biographical sketch   344
– chapters by   33–49, 51–64, 83–96, 117–134
– comments on   26, 69, 70–71, 138–139, 156, 158, 160, 302, 334
Hjelm, Titus   72
Hoffmann Meyer, Mette   120, 122
homogeneity   18–20, 208, 320–321
homosexuality   129–130

Hultén, Gunilla 87
human-interest frame 140, 149
Hussain, Ubaydullah 25n12
hypervisibility 292
Hyves 158–159

ideal citizen, frame of 286–290
identity see national identity/culture
identity work 197
immigration see also cultural-religious diversity; Islam/Muslims
– church criticism of policy concerning 172, 173–175
– demographic challenge of 14
– as global phenomenon 321–324
– impact in Scandinavia 22–24
– local Christian attitudes toward 177–181, 182–183
– and media influence 181–182
– policies on 171–173
– representation of, in media 139
– and spatial distribution 161–164
Inglehart-Welzel cultural map 20, 21
institutionalization 318
integrative religious education 227
interactions, with media 299–303, 309–311
interreligious dialogue
– funding initiatives for 193–195
– and Muslim belonging 192–193, 196–201
– research on 189–190
IS (Islamic State) 263, 266
Islam/Muslims see also asylum seekers
– associated with religious extremism and controversy 191–192, 194, 262, 267–270, 272–274, 324–325
– and belonging in society 192–193, 196–201
– Danish attitudes toward 207–209
– documentary portrayals of 121–123
– and dual identity 210–215, 219–221
– growth in Scandinavia 21–22
– and ideal citizens 286–290
– managing dominant frames of 283–286
– and MAV 125–127, 126, 127
– perceived as threat 40, 40–42, 41, 43–44, 68–69, 106
– public debates on 127–131
– representation of, in Danish media 205–206
– representation of, in Norwegian media 187–189, 190–195, 262–267
– representation of, in religious education 250–252, 267–268, 272–276
– representation of, in Swedish media 136–137, 139–140, 145, 147–150
– securitization of 69, 193–195, 285
– and self-presentation 215–218
– and support for religious expression 37–38, 38, 67, 147–148, 288–290
– and 'the Muslim woman' trope 290–292

Jacobsen, Sara Jul 125
Jaktlund, Carl-Henric 144
Jensdotter, Linnea
– biographical sketch 344
– chapter by 135–152
Jensen, Gudrun T. 209
Jernsletten, Haakon H.
– biographical sketch 344
– chapters by 33–49, 339–342
journalism on religion 6, 71, 76, 91, 138, 335 see also mediatized religion; public service media

Kahn, Yasri 65–66
Kierkegaard, Søren 183
Kinnvall, Catarina 194, 285
Kit, Sivin 159n2
Kraft, Siv Ellen 71, 265
Krekar, Mullah 263

Lakoff, George 275
Lalouni, Jalal 141
laptops, in classrooms 245–247, 248–249
Larsen, Anna M. Grøndahl 140, 181
Larsen, Charlotte Åsland 180–181
Leer-Helgesen, Bjarte 178
legacy media see public service media
Leurs, Koen 158–159

Liebmann, Louise Lund
- biographical sketch   344
- chapters by   187–204, 281–298
- comments on   155, 157–158, 165, 335

Lied, Liv Ingeborg
- biographical sketch   344
- chapters by   65–78, 243–258
- comments on   335–336

Listhaug, Sylvi   171–173, 175, 178, 306
lived religion   291
local civic settings
- Christian attitude toward asylum seekers in   177–181, 182–183
- governance in   164–165
- interreligious forums in   189
- media dynamics in   305–306
- media influence in   181–182
- mediatization in   156–161
- Muslim belonging and participation in   190–193, 196–201
- and spatial distribution of diversity   161–164
- and successful social integration   166–167

Löfstedt, Malin   230n10
Louise, Märtha   68
Lövheim, Mia
- biographical sketch   345
- chapters by   33–49, 65–78, 83–96, 135–152
- comments on   334, 335–336

Lubbers, Marcel   162
Lundby, Knut
- biographical sketch   344
- chapters by   3–9, 13–31, 33–49, 51–64, 83–96, 299–313
- comments on   53, 156, 158, 333, 334, 335

Lutheran Christianity   17, 21, 35–36, 66–67

Maalouf, Amin   287
Al-Mahdi Hussaini, Faten   288–290
Maliepaard, Mieke   162
Mamdani, Mahmood   286n3
Mancini, Paolo   26–27

Människor och tro (*People and Belief*)
- and audience   310–311
- Facebook page   147–149
- and media dynamics   303–304
- overview   135–136, 137–138
- phone-in sessions   142–147
- topics covered in   140–142, 150

mashallah   148
mass media   see media, the
MAV (minority actors' voices)   125–127, *126, 127*
May, Theresa   327–328
McCombs, Maxwell   269
media, the   see also public service media; social media
- and conflict-centred coverage   265–267
- coverage of asylum seekers   181–182
- coverage of religion   39, *39*, *91*, 91–93, *92*
- coverage of religious extremism   265–266, 324–325
- influence on religious education topics   233–234, 262–265, 274–275
- and 'media welfare states'   26–28

media dynamics
- amplification   55, *56*, 56–57, 61, 132, 300, 303–309, 317
- co-structuring   55, *56*, 58–59, 119, 132, 158, 159–160, 300, 301, 303–309, 317, 336
- framing and performative agency   55, *56*, 57–58   see also framing/frames
- in local civic settings   305–306
- overview   317–318
- in public service media   303–304
- in religious education   237–240, 306–307
- typology of   54–56, *56*

media literacy   238
media logic   139, 301, 311
media materials   232–233, 235–236, 247, 249–254
media-saturation   245–248
mediation   5–6
mediatization theory   5–6, 53, 226, 244, 256, 260, 299–303

mediatized religion
- approaches to studying   72, 75–76, 299–303
- banal religion   6, 71, 76, 91, 334–336
- and BBC   84–85
- as concept   6–8, 53–54, 93–94, 318–319, 334–336
- and conflict   138–140, 191, 307–309 see also religious extremism
- forms of   70–71
- journalism on religion   6, 71, 76, 91, 138, 335   see also public service media
- in local civic settings   156–161   see also local civic settings
- in public schools   see religious education
- reflections on   294–295, 309–312, 316–319, 326
- religious media   6, 53, 71, 76, 91–92, 182, 306, 335, 338
- research on   69–70, 70
- and transfer of authority   93
Merkel, Angela   177
meta-talk   131
Meyer, Birgit
- biographical sketch   345
- chapter by   333–338
- comments on   73
Michailidou, Asimina   288
Midden, Eva   158–159
migration   see immigration
Miller, Daniel   293
minority actors' voices (MAV)   125–127, 126, 127
minority-majority religious interaction   see interreligious dialogue
Mission Investigation (*Uppdrag granskning*)   52
Moors, Annelies   73
Mortensen, Mette   138–139, 160
Mosques Behind the Veil   51–52
multiculturalism   219–221, 229
multiple identity   210–215, 219–221
Muslims   see Islam/Muslims
myths, national   319–321

Nadim, Marjan   125

national identity/culture
- Christianity associated with   35–36, 68–69, 101–106, 111–112, 283
- and dual identity   210–215, 219–221
- and ideal citizens   286–290
- Islam perceived as threat to   40, 40–42, 41, 43–44, 68–69, 106
- Muslim belonging in   190–193, 196–201
- myths of   319–321
- PSM as defence of   88
nationalism   23
neo-corporatism   16, 25
neo-liberalism   164–165
Nesbitt-Larking, Paul   194, 285
networked crowd   160
neutrality policy, of NRK   98
news framework   265–266
news media logic   139, 301, 311
Nielsen, Jørgen   208
Noelle-Neumann, Elisabeth   59–60
Nordbø, Torolf   175
Nordic Model   24–26
Nordic Region   14, 16
Norway   see also YWC
- Christian attitudes toward asylum seekers in   177–181, 182–183
- and church involvement in politics   172, 173–175
- educational system in   227–229
- immigration policy in   171–173
- media influence in   181–182
- media representation of Islam in   187–189, 190–195, 262–267
- Muslim belonging in   192–193, 196–201
- and *På tro og Are*   249–252, 255–256
- PSM in   85, 88–89
- support for diversity in   195–196
NRK (Norsk rikskringkasting)   85, 88–89, 98

official fear   181
Omdal, Sven Egil   174

P4   85
Papacharissi, Zizi   101
På tro og Are   249–252, 255–256
Paus, Ole   177

pedagogical artefacts   232–233, 235–236, 247, 249–254
People and Belief   see Människor och tro
performative agency   55, 56, 57–58   see also framing/frames; media dynamics
phone-in sessions   142–147
Platt, Lucinda   162
Plus Pictures   120, 121, 122
Poell, Thomas   54
Poles   220
political orientation
– and discussing religious extremism   44–46, 45
– and religious tolerance   43–44
– in Scandinavia   36–37, 37
politicization   68
politics
– church involvement in   172, 173–175
– gendered involvement in   293
– and immigration policy   171–173
– and rise of populism   23, 24, 118
– and voting patterns   162–163
Ponzanesi, Sandra   158–159
Poole, Elizabeth   265–266
populism   23, 24, 118
post-secular turn   294
profound offences   113
project identity   215–218
prototypes   269–270, 287
public schools   see religious education
public service media (PSM)   see also Människor och tro; Rebellion from the Ghetto; YWC
– challenges to   87–90
– companies   85–86
– defined   83
– genres and user interest   90–93, 91, 92
– history and context of   84–85
– media dynamics in   303–304
– and rise of social media   326–328
– value of   86–87
public sphere, Nordic Model   24–26

racism, cultural   207
radical Islamist (RI) frame   272–274
radicalization   see religious extremism
Radio24syv   85

Radio Norge   85
Rebellion from the Ghetto (Oprør fra ghettoen)
– and audience   310–311
– downplaying 'religion' in   308
– and media dynamics   303–304
– minority voices in debate about   125–127, 126, 127
– producer intentions for   120–125
– public debate about   127–131
– research on   118–120
refugees   see asylum seekers
Reith, John   84–85
religion   see also Christianity/Christians; cultural-religious diversity; Islam/Muslims; mediatized religion
– authority of   93–94
– defined   72–75
– diversity in Scandinavia   20–22
– and 'hijacking religion' concept   111, 113–114
– and lived religion   291
– media coverage of   39, 39, 91, 91–93, 92
– phone-in sessions on   142–147
– politicization of   68–69
– as popular new topic   141–142
– and secularization   66–67, 71, 325–326
– state support of   17, 66–67
religiosity   35, 35–36
religious education
– and academic boredom   248–249, 253
– and correcting prejudice   266–267
– and educational systems in Norway and Sweden   221–229
– facts vs reality in   236–237
– lesson topics influenced by news media   233–234, 262–265, 274–275
– media dynamics in   237–240, 306–307
– and media-saturated classrooms   245–248
– relevance of   234–236
– representation of Islam in   250–252, 267–268, 272–276
– representation of religion in   255–256
– research on   230–231, 244–245, 260–261

- use of media materials in 232–233, 247, 249–254
religious expression 37–38, 38, 67, 147–149, 288–290
religious extremism
- associated with Islam 191–192, 194, 267–268, 269–270, 272–274
- discussing 44–46, 45
- media coverage of 265–266, 324–325
religious media 6, 53, 71, 76, 91–92, 182, 306, 335, 338 see also mediatized religion
Repstad, Pål
- biographical sketch 345
- chapters by 13–31, 171–185
- comments on 155, 158
reversion, as term 211n3
Rokkan, Stein 19–20
Rosenfeldt, Mattias Pape
- biographical sketch 345
- chapter by 117–134
Roy, Olivier 111, 113
Rushy's Roulette 126

Samadi, Mona 143
sameness, and equality 18–19
Sami people 19
Sandberg, Elisabeth 144
Sauer, Birgit 293
Scandinavia
- attitudes toward diversity in 37–38, 38, 43–48, 45, 67
- countries in 14–16
- homogeneity in 18–20
- impacted by immigration 22–24, 323
- map 15
- as 'media welfare states' 26–28
- perceptions of 316–317
- political orientation in 36–37, 37
- public sphere in 24–26
- religiosity in 35, 35–36
- religious diversity in 20–22
- as secular 20–21, 21, 66–67, 325–326
- state and church in 17, 35–36, 66–67
- as welfare state 16–17
Schinkel, Willem 198, 200
Scholten, Peter 166

schools see religious education
Schrøder, Kim Christian 301, 302, 311
Scuzzarello, Sarah 219–220
secularity/secularization 20–21, 21, 66–67, 71, 325–326
securitization 69, 193–198, 285
Segerberg, Alexandra 54
Selbekk, Vebjørn 175
self-presentation 215–218
Sende Osen, Are 250–252, 256
separative religious education 227n3
Shaw, Donald 269
Sherefay, Sonya 150
Silverstone, Roger 320
Sjöborg, Anders 230n10
Skam 87
Skånberg, Tuve 143–144
social constructionist approach, to religion 74–76
social interactions, with media 299–303, 309–311
social media see also YWC
- and audiences as participants 157
- in classrooms 246
- influence on communication 59–61, 61
- and mediatized civic settings 156–161
- prominence of 326–328
- self-presentation of Muslims on 217–218
- and social interaction 53–54
- and support for religious expression 147–149
Somalis 219–220
spiral of silence theory 59–60, 160–161
SR 86
state and church 17, 35–36, 66–67
The State of the Nation (Rikets tilstand) 52
stereotypes see also framing/frames
- accentuated in religious education 255–256
- and banal securitization 194–195, 285
- and contact hypothesis 182
- overcoming and subverting 197–200, 215–218
STL (Council for Religious and Life Stance Communities in Norway) 174, 197–198, 199

Sturmark, Christer   143–144
substantive approach, to religion   72–73, 75–76
Suhr, Christian   52
Sverigedemokraterna   24
SVT   86, 89
Sweden   see also *Människor och tro*
– dual identity in   219–221
– educational system in   227–228, 229–230
– media representation of Islam in   136–137, 139–140, 145, 147–150
– PSM in   85, 89, 136–137
symbols (religious)   see also hijabs; YWC
– and neutrality policies   98
– phone-in sessions on   144
– tolerance for   37–38, 67
Syrian fighters (*syriakrigere*)   187
Syvertsen, Trine   86
Sællmann, Siv Kristin   97

Tambini, Damian   86
tensions, defined   4
terrorism   see religious extremism
thick descriptions   99
Thorbjørnsrud, Kjersti   140, 181
Thornborrow, Joanna   146
Tocqueville, Alexis de   18–19
Toft, Audun
– biographical sketch   345
– chapters by   225–241, 243–258, 259–277
Trenz, Hans-Jörg   288
Trump, Donald   327
TV2   51–52, 85
TV4   86
Twana, Tara   144

Uitermark, Justus   164
The Ummah of the Prophet   263, 266

upper secondary schools   see religious education
UR (Utbildningsradion)   86

van Tubergen, Frank   162
veils (hijabs)   see hijabs
visibility
– and dual identity   210–215
– hypervisibility   292
– and self-presentation   215–218
voting patterns   162–163

Wang, Tricia   99
Welander, Louise   141
welfare state
– and citizenship   197–198
– educational system in   227–228
– and immigration   22–23, 195–196
– and 'media welfare states'   26–28
– in Scandinavia   16–17
Wilders, Geert   159
Wittgenstein, Ludwig   269
women   see also gender
– conversion to Islam   213–215
– participation in public debates   102, 109, 129
– and public support of hijabs   147–149, 288–290
– self-presentation of Muslim   216–218
– and 'the Muslim woman' trope   290–292

xenophobia   43–44   see also stereotypes

Yussuf, Abdikadir Mahamed   200
YWC (*Yes to wearing the cross whenever and wherever I choose*)
– and audience   310–311
– dynamics of conflict in   109–114
– establishment of   97–98
– media dynamics in   304
– research on   98–100
– types of conflict in   100–109

www.ingramcontent.com/pod-product-compliance
Lightning Source LLC
Chambersburg PA
CBHW071358300426
44114CB00016B/2107